Detecting Women

ISBN: 0-9644593-0-2

Printed on recycled paper and bound in the USA by BookCrafters of Chelsea, Michigan.

Cover design by Wendy L. Everett.
Electronic prepress and text design by Publitech of Ann Arbor, Michigan.

Library of Congress Cataloging-in-Publication Data

Heising, Willetta L., 1947-

      Detecting women: a reader's guide and checklist for mystery series
      written by women / Willetta L. Heising
      256 p. 28 cm.
      Includes index and bibliographic references.
      ISBN 0-9644593-0-2 (alk. paper)
      1. Detective and mystery stories, American—Women authors—Bibliography.
  2. Detective and mystery stories, English—Women authors—Bibliography.
  I. Title.   1994   016.8

The paper used in this publication meets the minimum requirements of American National Standard for Information Sciences—Permanence of Paper for Printed Library Materials. ANSI Z39.48-1984

To my senior partners

Whose love and support
has made all things possible.
I thank God every day
for the richest blessing of my life
which is you.

∾

Detecting Women

A Reader's Guide and Checklist
for Mystery Series Written by Women

Willetta L. Heising

1995 Edition

Purple Moon Press

Contents

A letter to mystery lovers 11

Acknowledgments 13

How to use this book 15

Lists, lists and more lists

1 Master list 19

2 Mystery types 155

3 Series characters 169

4 Settings 183

5 Mystery chronology 197

6 Pseudonyms 217

Where to look for more

7 Short stories 219

8 Periodicals 223

9 Awards and organizations 225

Let's get organized

10 Search logs 229

What's next?

11 Preview of the next edition.......... 237

Extras

12 Glossary 241

13 Bibliography 245

14 Index 247

15 About the author 255

Colophon 256

66 *The wonderful thing about books is that they allow us to enter imaginatively into someone else's life. And when we do that, we learn to sympathize with other people. But the real surprise is that we also learn truths about ourselves, about our own lives, that somehow we hadn't been able to see before.* **99**

—Katherine Womeldorf Paterson (1923–   )
U.S. children's writer in *The Horn Book* (1991)

A Letter to Mystery Lovers

I love mysteries. You love mysteries. We all love mysteries. And some of us are downright fanatical about reading our favorite mystery series in the proper order. But determining the correct order can sometimes be difficult. Just tracking down all the titles can be tricky. So what's a body to do? You could start keeping track for yourself—which is exactly what I did in 1992 when I resumed serious mystery reading after a long lapse.

I was thrilled to discover that while I wasn't looking, Nancy Drew grew up, hung out a shingle and got her own gun. Sharon McCone, Kinsey Millhone and V. I. Warshawski inspired me during my first summer of self-employment after 20 years of corporate soldiering. I was thankful that my work was a lot easier than theirs. And one thing I didn't have to worry about was getting beat up or shot at—not literally anyway. By comparison, my clients were pretty mild-mannered.

Initially, one of the things I did worry about was running out of detective stories. Little did I know my standard fare of four and five books each week was barely keeping pace with the release of new series titles by women mystery writers. In both 1993 and 1994, well over 200 new titles were released by women authors with series detective characters. How was I going to find time for all the new books, plus the great ones I'd missed in past years? And what about the wonderful series written by men and non-series mysteries and other fiction written by women and men? The phrase "So many books, so little time" took on a whole new meaning for me.

List-making seemed like a good way to get organized. But the real bonus came from sharing the lists with friends. From a practical point of view, sharing increased our chances of finding new and not-to-be-missed series. We had more readers on the job. And they started sharing with their friends and before long, people I'd never met were calling to ask when I was going to put these lists between two covers.

So, here it is—THE list of mystery series written by women. A great place to start your mystery reading if you're new at the game. A great way to get organized if you're a serious reader. Toss a copy of *Detecting Women* in your briefcase, your purse or the back seat of your car. And the next time you visit your favorite bookstore or library, you'll be more than just prepared, you'll be well-armed.

To those who ask (and I know you will), "Where are the men?" I say, "Just about everywhere you look." Dozens of fascinating male detectives have been created by women mystery writers. Some of them are legends of crime fiction. Certainly Hercule Poirot and Lord Peter Wimsey come immediately to mind. Also Reginald Wexford, Roderick Alleyn, Luis Mendoza and more recently, Milt Kovak, J. P. Beaumont and many others.

Curiously, or maybe not so curiously, very few men writing mysteries have chosen a woman detective as their protagonist. In fact, there's a chapter already in progress for the next edition of *Detecting Women* titled "Men Who Write Women Series Characters." Starting with Warren Adler's homicide detective, Fiona Fitzgerald, through R. D. Zimmerman's blind paraplegic psychologist and stock-trading genius, Dr. Madeline Phillips, we pose the question, "If the author's identity were unknown, could you spot a woman protagonist written by a man?" My reading experience tells me sometimes yes, sometimes no.

But this is a book about detecting women. The women who write crime fiction of all types. Police procedurals, private eye novels and traditional or cozy mysteries—with protagonists from all walks of life in every period in history, with settings around the world. Their detectives are men and women, old and young, gay, straight, black, white, married, single, widowed, divorced. With and without families, children, parents, siblings and companion animals. In short, they're all of us—the women who write and read mysteries. And we want to know who they are, where they come from, what issues concern them, how they got to where they are now and what has affected their lives.

I am no apologist for gender-specific interests. We read what we like. What interests us. What stretches our minds and captures our imagination. And yes, that often includes fiction and non-fiction written by men. But with all the wonderful stuff written by the women of this world, I intend to do my part to promote their work. To make sure that every woman who doesn't already know what great stories are out there for the reading, might renew her interest in reading after paging through this book. Reading is fundamental for all of us—not just the kids. So dust off your library card and don't wait until your next vacation to bring home a sackful of books. Ready, set, read!

— *Willetta L. Heising*
November 1994

Acknowledgments

∾ First and foremost, to the women who made this book possible with their gifts to us of thoughtful, inspired, touching and often brilliant writing. Thank you.

∾ To the unsung heroes of this project, the many librarians and book-sellers around the country who graciously shared their amazing knowledge long before there was a book on the drawing board. Thank you.

∾ To the staff of the Browsing Library who made countless phone calls to the basement in search of books long retired from the main-floor shelves of the Detroit Public Library. Thank you.

∾ To the Dearborn Department of Libraries staff, always helpful and wonderfully enthusiastic from the very beginning, especially Eve Durack, Nancy Levy and Jane Fox at Henry Ford Centennial Library and Peggy Bryant and Tara Gnau at Esper Branch. Thank you.

∾ To the staff of John King Used Books in Detroit, especially Sally Holliday, who provided material from her personal library, intro-duced me to her book friends and cheered me on. Thank you.

∾ To Linda Eddy and Joan Hollingsworth, secretaries and friends who took such good care of me when that's what I needed. Thank you.

∾ To my computer coach, Alan Foxx, who was a patient teacher in the early days when I was borderline computer-illiterate. Thank you.

∾ To long-time friend Trudis Heinecke, who introduced me to Black

Oak Books on a sunny Berkeley day in June 1992. Neither of us had even an inkling that visit would spark the concept for this book. Thank you.

∾ To my friends and former colleagues in the corporate world, Irene Fogarty, Claudia Gordon and Chris Snow, who individually and collectively provided wise counsel, expert advice and unwavering support for everything I obsessed about long after I was in their faces every day. Thank you.

∾ To WLK and VGH, who played a big part in getting me here. And not just because they encouraged me to "write that book" long before we knew what "that book" was. Thank you.

∾ To Tom Dorow and Anne Hughes of BookCrafters in Chelsea, Michigan who kept the faith at the finish line. Thank you.

∾ To my design editor Wendy Everett, who performed heroic feats to get this first edition to press nine months ahead of the original schedule and never once complained (at least not to me) about the impossibly tight deadlines. Thank you.

∾ To my mother, the Reverend Willetta B. Heising, who faithfully used my lists for two years and shared them with the staff of her local public library in Williamsburg, Virginia. Thank you.

∾ To my father, Captain Kenneth W. Heising (USN, Ret.), for being such a good sport about all those long-distance telephone hours devoted to mystery talk. Happy 75th Birthday, Dad! Thank you.

∾ And last but certainly not least, my boundless thanks and everlasting gratitude to Margaret Southworth, who was convinced of this book's success long before I was. She pushed and prodded, affirmed and magnified my efforts from the very beginning. I could not have done it without her.

Thank you all.

How to use this book

No matter what your preference for hunting new mysteries—by author, character, type, background, setting, or date—*Detecting Women* has a list for you. The Master List, presented in *Chapter 1*, contains all the information which is later re-presented in different formats in other lists. The Master List—complete with boxes to check for every series title—is designed to keep track of the books you've read or the books you own.

Master List

In the Master List, authors appear in alphabetical order by last name, although not last name first. A brief author profile is followed by that author's series character(s) and their book titles in order of appearance. The date that follows the title is generally the earliest date of publication. For books published first in Britain and later in the US, publication dates are sometimes years apart and titles may differ. The same is true for discrepancies between hardcover and paperback editions. Whenever more than one title is known, both are printed, with a notation indicating whether the second title is US, British or paperback.

When an author has more than one series detective, those characters are listed in alphabetical order by first name. An abbreviated character description, including the primary setting, follows the character's name. This may not be the setting for every book in the series, but it is typically the home base of the protagonist.

Whenever a book has been nominated or awarded recognition in the mystery field, that book title appears in boldface type followed by the name of the award or nomination and a star. If you're interested in reading award-winning authors, just scan the pages of *Chapter 1* looking for boldface titles and stars. Since these awards are a fairly recent phenomenon, don't discount earlier titles without starred entries. The length of the author profile will sometimes indicate her importance in the field. A description of the various mystery awards can be found in both the *Glossary* and *Chapter 9, Awards and Organizations*.

Mystery Types

Simply for the purpose of organization, the 469 mystery series presented in this first edition of *Detecting Women* have been slotted into three groups, using the standard definitions for police procedurals, P.I. novels and traditional mysteries with amateur detectives. Those group totals are shown below:

Police	99	(21%)
P.I.s	75	(16%)
Amateurs	295	(63%)
Total Series	**469**	**(100%)**

Traditional mystery series are further classified using the following backgrounds:

Academic

Animals (cats, dogs, horses and other)

Art & Antiques

Authors & Writers

Bed & Breakfast

Black

Books & Libraries

Botanical

Business & Finance

Criminal

Domestic

Ecclesiastical & Religious

Environment & Wilderness

Ethnic & Native American

Gourmet & Food

Historical (medieval, renaissance, 19th & 20th century)

Journalism (magazine, newspaper, photography and television)

Legal (attorney and judge)

Lesbian

Medical

Miscellaneous

Occult

Romantic

Secret Agents

Sports

Suburban

Technology

Theatre & Performing Arts

Women of a Certain Age

World Travelers

In this age of political correctness, I am more than slightly uncomfortable with special categories for black and lesbian women and those we've tagged "of a certain age." After some discussion with women who are older, black or lesbian, it was decided to include those special categories as long as they were not the only category in which the character appeared. Hence, the black cop and black P.I. first appear as cop and P.I. In fact, that's the only place they were listed until the decision was made to highlight black, lesbian and older women sleuths. Our logic was that anyone who wants to know can find the information here. Those who don't can ignore it.

If you count the entries in the "Amateurs" category, you'll find there are more than the 295 series identified earlier. This is because several series have more than one "background." For example, Lilian Jackson Braun's cat series appears under the Animal listing and again under Journalism (Qwill's line of work). Judith Van Gieson's Neil Hamel series is listed under Attorney and also under Environment & Wilderness. After finding a series that interests you, it's always recommended that you go back to the Master List and read the full entry for that author and series character.

Series Characters

This list was first requested by someone who wanted to know (just for fun, she said) if there was a detective who shared her name. She was certain there wasn't. Saying she was pleased to find one is an understatement. She was so excited by the news that I showed the list to others, wondering if I'd get a similar reaction. I'm now convinced that finding a same-name heroine is a secret desire for many. So for those who always wished that Nancy Drew had been "your-name" Drew, here's your chance to find her. This list will also prove useful for anyone who remembers a character's first name but hasn't a clue about the author. Whenever the series character is actually a pair, each of the partners is listed separately. For example, both Leslie Wetzon and Xenia Smith (from Annette Meyers' Wall Street series) appear in the character listing. The partner's name is always attached so you know the character is part of a series pair.

Settings

As mentioned earlier, the settings identified here are not necessarily the setting for each book in the series, but typically the home base of the series character(s). States of the US are listed in alphabetical order based on the state abbreviation. Within each state, named cities and towns appear in alphabetical order. Unspecified locations are grouped together at the beginning of each section. Locations outside the US are presented alphabetically by country and again alphabetically by city, province or region.

Mystery Chronology

The Mystery Chronology is another list that resulted from an enthusiastic response from one reader, later seconded by others, who ordered me to "keep that one; I need that list." Some fascinating patterns emerge from arranging the titles by decade:

1900s	1	1990	141
1910s	9	1991	157
1920s	35	1992	181
1930s	110	1993	234
1940s	142	1994	228
1950s	96	**1990–1994**	**941**
1960s	127		
1970s	180	1995 (partial)	62
1980s	642		
1900–1989	**1342**	**1st edition titles**	**2345**

Research in progress for the next edition has already identified 310 books which were not included in the current listing of 2345 series titles written by women. These 310 are not quite evenly split between those published before 1990 (176 titles) and those after (134). Whatever the exact number, two conclusions are apparent. First, the number of titles appearing in the last five years (1990-1994) is comparable to the number published during the preceding 30 years (1960-1989). And second, the number of titles appearing since 1990 has increased each year and shows no signs of diminishing.

Short Stories

If you're looking for short stories by your favorite author or curious about the style of an author whose work you're not familiar with, the ten anthologies presented in *Chapter 7* are a great place to start. Award-winning stories from these anthologies are noted on page 222 along with the short story bibliography.

Periodicals, Awards and Organizations

More information about periodicals, awards and organizations can be found in *Chapters 8 and 9* as well as the *Glossary*.

Search Logs

The forms presented in *Chapter 10* are provided for readers who make frequent use of library services, especially Inter-Library Loan and reserve requests and are in contact with a variety of bookdealers as part of their ongoing search for older titles.

Preview of Next Edition

The preview of the coming edition is provided to encourage feedback and participation from anyone who has information to share about authors, series characters, organizations, publications or other matters of interest to mystery readers. A fax-back or mail-back form is included. We'd love to hear from you.

Index

The index includes authors (last name first), series characters (first name first), awards and organizations. Index entries for the 401 authors included in the Master List are marked with little pen nibs for easy identification. The first index entry for each of these authors identifies her location in the Master List. Multiple mentions of an author on a single page are not separately identified. For example, Agatha Christie appears numerous times on each page early in the Mystery Chronology (*Chapter 5*), for which her corresponding index entry is 193-199.

One

⬥ Master List

Lydia Adamson is the pseudonym used by a noted mystery writer and cat lover for her Alice Nestleton series featuring the Off Off Broadway actress and her two cats—Bushy and Pancho. Adamson's newest animal series features rural New York veterinarian Deidre Quinn Nightingale.

Alice Nestleton . . . actress & cat lover in New York City

- ☑ 1 - A Cat in the Manger (1990)
- ❑ 2 - A Cat of a Different Color (1990)
- ☑ 3 - A Cat in Wolf's Clothing (1991)
- ☑ 4 - A Cat in the Wings (1992)
- ❑ 5 - A Cat by Any Other Name (1992)
- ❑ 6 - A Cat with a Fiddle (1993)
- ☑ 7 - A Cat in a Glass House (1993)
- ☑ 8 - A Cat with No Regrets (1994)
- ❑ 9 - A Cat on the Cutting Edge (1994)

Deidre Quinn Nightingale . . . veterinarian in rural New York

- ☑ 1 - Dr. Nightingale Comes Home (1994)
- ❑ 2 - Dr. Nightingale Rides the Elephant (1994)

M. J. Adamson is Mary Jo Adamson, author of a police series set in Puerto Rico featuring NYPD homicide detective Balthazar Marten and Puerto Rican cop Sixto Cardenas. The Spanish-speaking Marten is sent to Puerto Rico on an exchange program while recovering from the bombing which killed his young wife.

Balthazar Marten & Sixto Cardenas . . . NYPD homicide detective & Puerto Rican cop

- ❑ 1 - Not Till a Hot January (1987)
- ❑ 2 - A February Face (1987)
- ❑ 3 - Remember March (1988)
- ❑ 4 - April When They Woo (1988)
- ❑ 5 - May's Newfangled Mirth (1989)

Catherine Aird is the pseudonym used by Kinn Hamilton McIntosh, creator of Inspector C.D. Sloan, aptly nicknamed "Seedy" by his friends. This series, which begins in 1966, is set in the fictitious county of Calleshire. Aird is also the author of *A Most Contagious Game* (1967) involving a secret room, a murdered wife and a 200-year-old skeleton. She lives in Kent, England and is vice-chairman of the British Crime Writers Association.

Christopher Dennis "Seedy" Sloan . . . Berebury CID department head in West Calleshire, England

- ❏   1 - The Religious Body (1966)
- ❏   2 - Henrietta Who? (1968)
- ❏   3 - The Complete Steel (1969) [U.S.–The Stately Home Murder]
- ❏   4 - A Late Phoenix (1970)
- ❏   5 - His Burial Too (1973)
- ❏   6 - Slight Mourning (1975)
- ❏   7 - Parting Breath (1977)
- ❏   8 - Some Die Eloquent (1979)
- ❏   9 - Passing Strange (1980)
- ❏ 10 - Last Respects (1982)
- ❏ 11 - Harm's Way (1984)
- ❏ 12 - A Dead Liberty (1987)
- ❏ 13 - A Going Concern (1993)

Susan Wittig Albert is a former university professor and administrator who is now a full-time writer. In addition to the China Bayles series, she is the author of numerous books and articles about literature and writing, over 50 novels for young readers and *Work of Her Own, A Woman's Guide to Success off the Career Track*. Albert and her husband Bill have just launched a new historical series under the pseudonym Robin Paige.

China Bayles . . . herb shop owner & former attorney in Texas
- ❏   1 - **Thyme of Death** (1992) *Agatha & Anthony nominee* ☆
- ❏   2 - Witches' Bane (1993)
- ❏   3 - Hangman's Root (1994)
- ❏   4 - Rosemary Remembered (1995)

Irene Allen is the nom de plume of a Harvard- and Princeton-educated geologist and creator of a new mystery series featuring Elizabeth Elliot, widowed Pennsylvania Quaker meeting clerk. The author lives in Washington State.

Elizabeth Elliot . . . widowed Pennsylvania Quaker meeting clerk
- ❏   1 - Quaker Silence (1992)
- ❏   2 - Quaker Witness (1993)

Margery Allingham (1904-1966) published her first novel at the age of 19 and four years later married the artist and magazine editor who had designed its cover, Philip Youngman Carter (1904-1970). She was best known for her series detective Albert Campion who first appeared in 1929 and was thought by some to be an over-the-top caricature of Lord Peter Wimsey. Campion claimed family connections to the royal throne, yet his houseman was an ex-burglar. He later married a titled aviation engineer (Lady Amanda Fitton) and their son Rupert eventually enrolled in Harvard. After Allingham's death, her husband completed the title she had last worked on (*Cargo of Eagles*) and added two of his own creation before his death. In 1988 British television created a Campion series which was shown in the U.S. on the PBS *Mystery!* series. As a result of revived American interest, many of these titles have been reprinted in paperback and are widely available.

Albert Campion . . . Scotland Yard inspector

- ❏ 1 - The Crime at Black Dudley (1929) [U.S.–The Black Dudley Murder]
- ❏ 2 - Look to the Lady (1929) [U.S.–The Gryth Chalice Mystery]
- ❏ 3 - Mystery Mile (1930)
- ❏ 4 - Police at the Funeral (1931)
- ❏ 5 - Sweet Danger (1933) [U.S.–Kingdom of Death]
- ❏ 6 - The Fear Sign (1933)
- ❏ 7 - Death of a Ghost (1934)
- ❏ 8 - Flowers for the Judge (1936) [U.S.–Legacy in Blood]
- ❏ 9 - Dancers in Mourning (1937) [U.S.–Who Killed Chloe?]
- ❏ 10 - The Case of the Late Pig (1937)
- ❏ 11 - The Fashion in Shrouds (1938)
- ❏ 12 - Black Plumes (1940)
- ❏ 13 - Traitor's Purse (1941) [U.S.–The Sabotage Murder Mystery]
- ❏ 14 - Coroner's Pidgin (1945) [U.S.–Pearls Before Swine]
- ❏ 15 - More Work for the Undertaker (1949)
- ❏ 16 - The Tiger in the Smoke (1952)
- ❏ 17 - No Love Lost (1954)
- ❏ 18 - The Beckoning Lady (1955) [U.S.–The Estate of the Beckoning Lady]
- ❏ 19 - Ten Were Missing (1958)
- ❏ 20 - The China Governess (1962)
- ❏ 21 - The Mind Readers (1965)
- ❏ 22 - Cargo of Eagles (1968) [with Philip Youngman Carter]
- ❏ 23 - Mr. Campion's Farthing (1969) [Philip Youngman Carter]
- ❏ 24 - Mr. Campion's Falcon (1970) [Philip Youngman Carter] [U.S.–Mr. Campion's Quarry]

Christine Andreae, of Bentonville, Virginia, is a freelance writer and adjunct professor of English as well as the creator of a new series featuring English professor and poet Lee Squires. To escape the summer heat of Washington, DC, Squires signs on as the substitute cook for a Montana trail ride in the first installment which was nominated for the Edgar for best first novel.

Lee Squires . . . English professor & poet
- ❑   1 - **Trail of Murder** (1992) *Edgar nominee* ☆
- ❑   2 - Grizzly, A Murder (1994)

Sarah Andrews is a working geologist with a series detective who also works in the oil business. The author has traveled to remote parts of the U.S. as well as South America and Australia for a variety of assignments with the federal government, oil producers and environmental services.

Em Hansen . . . oil worker in Wyoming
- ❑   1 - Tensleep (1994)
- ❑   2 - A Fall in Denver (1995)

Charlotte Armstrong (1905-1969) was born in an iron-mining town in Michigan's Upper Peninsula and later attended the University of Wisconsin and Barnard College. She published poetry in the *New Yorker* and wrote two plays produced on Broadway before trying her hand at mystery writing in a short series featuring college professor MacDougal Duff. She later turned to psychological suspense with titles such as *A Dram of Poison* which earned her the Edgar award for best novel in 1956. From the late 1940s until 1970 she produced 20 non-series novels, several collections of short stories, a pair of novelettes and several scripts for *Alfred Hitchcock Presents.*

MacDougal Duff . . . retired history professor
- ❑   1 - Lay on, Mac Duff! (1942)
- ❑   2 - The Case of the Weird Sisters (1943)
- ❑   3 - The Innocent Flower (1945)

Margot Arnold is the pseudonym chosen by Petronelle Cook for her series featuring the 60-something academic crime-solving twosome of American anthropologist Penelope Spring and British archaeologist Tobias Glendower. Arnold brings her lifelong interest in both archaeology and anthropology to the globe-trotting adventures of Penny and Sir Toby. In addition to this series Arnold has written several novels of romantic suspense. A longtime resident of Cape Cod, she was educated at Oxford and has lived and traveled extensively abroad.

Penny Spring & Toby Glendower . . . American anthropologist & British archeologist

- ❑ 1 - Exit Actors, Dying (1979)
- ❑ 2 - Zadock's Treasure (1979)
- ❑ 3 - The Cape Cod Caper (1980)
- ❑ 4 - Death of a Voodoo Doll (1982)
- ❑ 5 - Lament for a Lady Laird (1982)
- ❑ 6 - Death on a Dragon's Tongue (1982)
- ❑ 7 - The Menehune Murders (1989)
- ❑ 8 - Toby's Folly (1990)
- ❑ 9 - The Catacomb Conspiracy (1991)
- ❑ 10 - Cape Cod Conundrum (1992)
- ❑ 11 - Dirge for a Dorset Druid (1994)

Nancy Atherton, born and raised in the Chicago area, now lives and works in Brooklyn, New York, where she is a freelance editor and science fiction fan. Her Aunt Dimity series was greeted with rave reviews when it was introduced in 1992.

Aunt Dimity . . . romantic ghost

- ☑ 1 - Aunt Dimity's Death (1992)
- ❑ 2 - Aunt Dimity and the Duke (1994)
- ❑ 3 - Aunt Dimity's Good Deed (1995)

Noreen Ayres, creator of the Smokey Brandon series, is also an experienced technical writer and editor of aircraft maintenance manuals and computer reference guides.

Samantha "Smokey" Brandon . . . Orange County, California sheriff's forensic expert

- ❑ 1 - A World the Color of Salt (1992)
- ❑ 2 - Carcass Trade (1994)

Marian Babson is an American author who lives in Britain and writes mysteries in the English style. In addition to more than 20 non-series novels she is the creator of two London-based series. The first features Doug Perkins, co-owner of a public relations firm. The second more humorous cast of characters is headed by a pair of aging Hollywood movie queens—Eve Sinclair and Trixie Dolan—who are looking to jump-start their careers on the London stage.

Douglas Perkins . . . London-based travel agent

- ❑ 1 - Cover-up Story (1971)
- ❑ 2 - Murder on Show (1972) [U.S.–Murder at the Cat Show]
- ❑ 3 - Tourists are for Trapping (1989)
- ❑ 4 - In the Teeth of Adversity (1990)

Eve Sinclair & Trixie Dolan . . . aging British ex-movie queens
- ❑ 1 - Reel Murder (1986)
- ❑ 2 - Encore Murder (1989)
- ❑ 3 - Shadows in Their Blood (1993)

Jo Bailey lives in Minneapolis where she has worked at an inner-city hospital for more than 15 years, providing authentic background for her "General Jack" hospital series featuring security officer Jan Gallagher of the Jackson County Medical Center, a major Midwestern trauma center. In the first installment Gallagher, a single mother of four daughters, sues the county for sex discrimination in its promotional practices.

Jan Gallagher . . . Minnesota hospital security supervisor
- ❑ 1 - Bagged (1991)
- ❑ 2 - Recycled (1993)

Nikki Baker is the creator of a new mystery series featuring lesbian stockbroker Virginia Kelly.

Virginia Kelly . . . lesbian stockbroker
- ❑ 1 - In the Game (1991)
- ❑ 2 - The Lavender House Murder (1992)

Mignon F. Ballard, of Fort Mill, South Carolina, is the author of several romantic suspense novels reminiscent of the Southern gothic style. She is also the creator of a new mystery series featuring former Georgia Peace Corps volunteer Eliza Figg.

Eliza Figg . . . former Peace Corps volunteer
- ❑ 1 - Minerva Cries Murder (1993)

Carolyn Banks is the creator of a new mystery series set in the Texas horse world of equestrienne sleuth Robin Vaughn.

Robin Vaughn . . . Texas equestrienne sleuth
- ❑ 1 - Death by Dressage (1993)

Jo Bannister is a writer and newspaper editor in Northern Ireland where she won the United Kingdom's Royal Society of Arts bronze medal for excellence in journalism. Her trilogy with Clio Rees and Harry Marsh involves a physician who leaves her medical practice to write mysteries and the local police inspector. The newer series features a pair of Castlemere cops, Liz Graham and Cal Donovan. In addition to her series titles, Bannister has written five other novels.

Dr. Clio Rees & Harry Marsh . . . mystery writer/MD & chief inspector

- ❑ 1 - Striving With Gods (1984)
- ❑ 2 - Gilgamesh (1989)
- ❑ 3 - The Going Down of the Sun (1990)

Liz Graham & Cal Donovan . . . pair of Castlemere, England cops

- ❑ 1 - A Bleeding of Innocents (1993)
- ❑ 2 - Charisma (1994)

Willetta Ann Barber, along with Rudolph F. Schabelitz, is the creator of Kit Storm, a New York City police artist whose sketches provide important clues. Each of the four books in this series, narrated by Kit's secretary Sherry Locke, is illustrated with Kit's drawings.

Christopher "Kit" Storm . . . police illustrator for the NYPD

- ❑ 1 - Murder Draws a Line (1940)
- ❑ 2 - Pencil Points to Murder (1941)
- ❑ 3 - Drawn Conclusion (1942)
- ❑ 4 - Murder Enters the Picture (1942)

Linda Barnes, born and raised in Detroit, is a Boston resident best known for Carlotta Carlyle, the cab-driving P.I. first introduced in the Edgar-award winning short story, "Lucky Penny" (1986). According to her creator, Carlotta is not casually named. Carlotta cares. She's compassionate, committed, cool, competent, competitive and she copes. And at 6' 1", she's a natural at volleyball, her sport of choice.

Barnes' earlier character, Michael Spraggue, is passionate about the theatre world, not unlike the author herself, who once taught high school drama and worked briefly as a playwright. Spraggue's delightful Aunt Mary is well worth the search for this series, introduced in 1982.

Carlotta Carlyle . . . 6' 1" cab-driving ex-cop P.I. in Boston

- ❑ 1 - **A Trouble of Fools** (1987) *Edgar nominee* ☆
- ❑ 2 - The Snake Tattoo (1989)
- ❑ 3 - Coyote (1990)
- ☑ 4 - Steel Guitar (1991)
- ❑ 5 - Snapshot (1993)
- ❑ 6 - Hardware (1995)

Michael Spraggue III . . . Boston, Massachusetts wealthy actor & ex-P.I.

- ❏ 1 - Blood Will Have Blood (1982)
- ❏ 2 - Bitter Finish (1983)
- ❏ 3 - Dead Heat (1984)
- ❏ 4 - Cities of the Dead (1986)

Nevada Barr is a U.S. park ranger whose *Track of the Cat* was awarded both the Agatha and Anthony for best first novel in 1993. Her second outing, set in Isle Royale National Park in northern Michigan, is a stunning tribute to the natural beauty of the Great Lakes.

Anna Pigeon . . . U.S. park ranger

- ☑ 1 - **Track of the Cat** (1993) *Agatha & Anthony winner* ★
- ☑ 2 - A Superior Death (1994)
  - ✓ Firestorm 1996
  - ✓ Ill Wind 1995

M. C. Beaton is the pseudonym chosen by Scotland native Marion Chesney for her Hamish Macbeth series featuring a village constable in the highlands of Scotland. Her newer series features Agatha Raisin, who like the author, lives in a charming cottage in the English Cotswolds. Chesney has also written novels of historical romance under her own name and the various pseudonyms of Helen Crampton, Ann Fairfax, Jennie Tremaine and Charlotte Ward.

Agatha Raisin . . . London advertising retiree in the Costwolds

- ❏ 1 - Agatha Raisin and the Quiche of Death (1992)
- ❏ 2 - Agatha Raisin and the Vicious Vet (1993)
- ❏ 3 - Agatha Raisin and the Potted Gardener (1994)

Hamish Macbeth . . . Scottish police constable

- ❏ 1 - Death of a Gossip (1985)
- ❏ 2 - Death of a Cad (1987)
- ❏ 3 - Death of an Outsider (1988)
- ❏ 4 - Death of a Perfect Wife (1989)
- ❏ 5 - Death of a Hussy (1990)
- ❏ 6 - Death of a Snob (1991)
- ❏ 7 - Death of a Prankster (1992)
- ❏ 8 - Death of a Glutton (1993)
- ❏ 9 - Death of a Travelling Man (1993)
- ❏ 10 - Death of a Charming Man (1994)

K. K. Beck is the pseudonym used by Seattle native Katherine Marris who has a background in advertising and previously edited a trade magazine. Beck's Iris Cooper series set in the 1920s, features a Stanford University coed, while her Jane da Silva series features a former lounge singer in present-day Seattle. In addition to her two series mysteries, Beck has also written several non-series mysteries.

Iris Cooper . . . roaring 20s Stanford coed at Stanford University

- ❏ 1 - Death in a Deck Chair (1984)
- ❏ 2 - Murder in a Mummy Case (1985)
- ❏ 3 - Peril Under the Palms (1989)

Jane da Silva . . . former lounge singer in Seattle

- ❏ 1 - A Hopeless Case (1992)
- ❏ 2 - Amateur Night (1993)
- ❏ 3 - Electric City (1994)

Sophie Belfort is the pseudonym of a Massachusetts historian who is the creator of the Boston mystery series featuring Molly Rafferty, professor of Renaissance and Reformation history, and Catholic cop Nick Hannibal.

Molly Rafferty . . . Boston, Massachusetts college history professor

- ❏ 1 - The Lace Curtain Murders (1986)
- ❏ 2 - The Marvell College Murders (1991)
- ❏ 3 - Eyewitness to Murder (1992)

Josephine Bell is the pseudonym of Doris Bell Collier Ball (1897-1987), English physician and author of historical, true crime and mystery novels who attended Newnham College, Cambridge and then University College Hospital in London. She married Dr. Norman Dyer Ball in 1923 and they practiced medicine together until his death in 1936. After closing her solo medical practice at the age of 57, she continued writing until she was 85. She was one of the founders of the British Crime Writers Association and chaired the organization in 1959. Many of her books feature medical mysteries and physician sleuths, like her series detective Dr. David Wintringham.

David Wintringham . . . British physician

- ❏ 1 - Murder in Hospital (1937)
- ❏ 2 - Fall Over Cliff (1938)
- ❏ 3 - Death at Half-Term (1939) [U.S.–Curtain Call for a Corpse]
- ❏ 4 - Death at the Medical Board (1944)
- ❏ 5 - Death in Clairvoyance (1949)
- ❏ 6 - The Summer School Mystery (1950)
- ❏ 7 - Bones in the Barrow (1953)
- ❏ 8 - The China Roundabout (1956) [U.S.–Murder on the Merry-Go-Round]
- ❏ 9 - The Seeing Eye (1958)

Liza Bennett is the author of two mysteries featuring Peg Goodenough, creative director at a New York advertising agency.

Peg Goodenough . . . New York City ad agency creative director
- ❑ 1 - Madison Avenue Murder (1989)
- ❑ 2 - Seventh Avenue Murder (1990)

Laurien Berenson is the creator of a new series featuring an amateur detective who is also a suburban wife and mother.

Suburban wife & mother
- ❑ 1 - Deep Cover (1994)

Carole Berry is the creator of a series featuring Bonnie Indermill, a Manhattan office temp with a love for tap dancing. Each one of Bonnie's work assignments provides a new setting and different cast of characters for murder and mayhem.

Bonnie Indermill . . . tap-dancing Manhattan office temp
- ❑ 1 - The Letter of the Law (1987)
- ❑ 2 - The Year of the Monkey (1988)
- ❑ 3 - Good Night, Sweet Prince (1990)
- ❑ 4 - Island Girl (1991)
- ❑ 5 - The Death of a Difficult Woman (1994)

Claudia Bishop is the pseudonym of Mary Stanton, creator of a new bed and breakfast series featuring sisters Sarah and Meg Quilliam. Sarah runs the Hemlock Falls Inn in a picturesque little town in upstate New York where sister Meg toils as the inn's chef.

Sarah & Meg Quilliam . . . Hemlock Falls, New York inn owner & chef (sisters)
- ❑ 1 - A Taste for Murder (1994)
- ❑ 2 - A Dash of Death (1995)

Veronica Black is the creator of a new series featuring a British investigative nun named Sister Joan.

Sister Joan . . . British investigative nun
- ❑ 1 - A Vow of Silence (1990)
- ❑ 2 - A Vow of Chastity (1992)
- ❑ 3 - A Vow of Sanctity (1993)
- ❑ 4 - A Vow of Obedience (1993)
- ❑ 5 - A Vow of Penance (1994)

L. L. Blackmur is the creator of two series titles set in New England featuring writer Galen Shaw and financier Julian Baugh.

Galen Shaw & Julian Baugh . . . New England writer & financier

- ❑ 1 - Love Lies Slain (1989)
- ❑ 2 - Love Lies Bleeding (1989)

Eleanor Taylor Bland, a cost accountant from Waukegan, Illinois, is the creator of Marti MacAlister, mystery fiction's first black woman homicide detective. MacAlister is a former Chicago cop and widowed mother of two who moves 60 miles out of the city to join the suburban Lincoln Prairie police force and start over after her husband is killed.

Marti MacAlister . . . black police detective in Illinois

- ❑ 1 - Dead Time (1992)
- ❑ 2 - Slow Burn (1993)
- ❑ 3 - Gone Quiet (1994)

Barbara Block, of Syracuse, New York, is the creator of a new mystery series featuring Robin Light, the recently widowed owner of Noah's Ark, a Syracuse pet shop.

Robin Light . . . Syracuse, New York pet store owner

- ❑ 1 - Chutes and Adders (1994)

J. S. Borthwick, from Thomaston, Maine, is the creator of series pair Sarah Deane, Boston graduate student in English literature and Alex McKenzie, bird-watching Boston physician. Their adventures begin in Texas with the death of Sarah's boyfriend but the pair returns to home ground after successfully solving their first case. Later in the series, Sarah becomes a professor.

Sarah Deane & Dr. Alex McKenzie . . . English professor & internist

- ❑ 1 - The Case of the Hook-Billed Kites (1982)
- ❑ 2 - The Down East Murders (1985)
- ❑ 3 - The Student Body (1986)
- ❑ 4 - Bodies of Water (1990)
- ❑ 5 - Dude on Arrival (1992)
- ❑ 6 - The Bridled Groom (1994)

D. B. Borton is the pseudonym of Ohio Wesleyan English professor Dr. Lynette Carpenter, creater of Cincinnati P.I. in training Cat Caliban. After 38 years of marriage, Cat buys an apartment building and starts work on her P.I. license. Along the way she manages to demolish all the stereotypes about mothers and women of a certain age.

> **Cat Caliban** . . . 60-something P.I.-in-training in Cincinnati, Ohio
>
> ❑   1   -   One for the Money (1993)
> ❑   2   -   Two Points for Murder (1993)
> ❑   3   -   Three is a Crowd (1994)
> ❑   4   -   Four Years Buried (1995)

Elisabeth Bowers is the creator of a mystery series set in Vancouver, British Columbia, featuring private investigator Meg Lacey who is the mother of a college-age son.

> **Meg Lacey** . . . Vancouver, British Columbia P.I.
>
> ❑   1   -   Ladies' Night (1988)
> ❑   2   -   No Forwarding Address (1991)

Eleanor Boylan is the creator of the Clara Gamadge series featuring a character who first appeared as the wife of Henry Gamadge, the New York bibliophile created by Boylan's aunt, Elizabeth Daly, said to be the favorite American writer of Agatha Christie. By 1989 when Boylan's series begins, Clara has become Henry's widow. The family adventures continue, but this time around, Clara's the one doing the detecting. Boylan is a New York native who lives on Anna Maria Island in Florida where she also writes short stories for mystery magazines.

> **Clara Gamadge** . . . New York City widow of Henry, the forgery expert
>
> ❑   1   -   Working Murder (1989)
> ❑   2   -   Murder Observed (1990)
> ❑   3   -   Murder Machree (1992)
> ❑   4   -   Pushing Murder (1993)

Lynn Bradley, from Sugar Land, Texas, is the creator of a new Houston P.I. series featuring P.I. Cole January.

> **Cole January** . . . Houston, Texas P.I.
>
> ❑   1   -   Stand-in for Murder (1994)

Maryalice

Maryalice

May 12, 1996

Francis mystery wins Poe Award

Onetime British champion jockey **Dick Francis'** "Come to Grief" has won the Mystery Writers of America's Edgar Allan Poe Award as best novel of 1995. He won the same award in 1980 and 1969.

"Come to Grief," a horse-racing thriller published by Putnam, was a virtuoso performance by the 75-year-old Francis. He reached back 16 years into his writing career to return to fictional life with memorable straight-arrow hero Sid Halley, whom he created in 1979's "Whip Hand." "Come to Grief" recounts Halley's solving of a series of horse mutilations.

The Mystery Writers of America, at its annual dinner in New York City, also gave Francis its Grand Master Award and presented Poe awards to the following:

First novel: "Penance," by **David Housewright** (Foul Play/Countryman); original paperback: "Tarnished Blue," by **William Heffernan** (Onyx); fact crime: "Circumstantial Evidence," by **Peter Early** (Bantam); critical biography: "Savage Art: A Biography of Jim Thompson," by **Robert Polito** (Knopf).

Short story: "The Judge's Boy," by **Jean R. Cooper** (Ellery Queen's Mystery Magazine); juvenile: "Looking for Jamey Bridger," by **Nancy Springer** (Dial); young adult: "Prophecy Rock," by **Rob MacGregor** (Simon & Schuster).

— Ed Kelly

"The ideas are easy," said Perry. "I always have tons of ideas. The trick is deciding what you want to spend a year working on."

Perry will be in Western New York on April 17 as part of a book tour. While here he will visit his parents, **Richard**, a former Tonawanda school superintendent, and **Elizabeth**; and his sister, **Ann Goltz**, all of whom still live in Tonawanda.

pseudonym of Mary Christianna Lewis (1907-1985) educated in India before being sent to a Franciscan financial problems forced her to leave school in her orked in a variety of unfulfilling jobs. While employed a strong dislike for one of her coworkers and wrote *Heels*, 1941) to murder the woman on paper. The after her marriage to surgeon Ronald S. Lewis, whose piration for Inspector Cockrill, Kent County six-book Cockrill series, Brand wrote romantic and near-fantasy.

County, England constable

se (1941)

ger (1944)

is Residence (1946) [U.S.–The Crooked Wreath]

ebel (1948)

ular (1953) [U.S.–Fog of Doubt]

(1955)

Michigan native and former writer for the *Detroit Free* as the originator of the cat craze in contemporary eries featuring newspaper columnist Jim Qwilleran d Yum Yum. The first three installments appeared 20 years passed before she revived the series in an Edgar nomination. Braun, her husband Earl and o III and Pitti Sing divide their time between Michigan

Yum Yum . . . Midwestern ex-police reporter & cats

o Could Read Backwards (1966)
o Ate Danish Modern (1967)
o Turned On and Off (1968)
ho Saw Red (1986) *Edgar nominee* ☆
ho Played Brahms (1987) *Anthony nominee* ☆
ho Played Post Office (1987)
ho Knew Shakespeare (1988)
ho Sniffed Glue (1988)
ho Went Underground (1989)
ho Talked to Ghosts (1990)
ho Lived High (1990)

- ❏ 12 - The Cat Who Knew a Cardinal (1991)
- ☑ 13 - The Cat Who Moved a Mountain (1992)
- ❏ 14 - The Cat Who Wasn't There (1993)
- ☑ 15 - The Cat Who Went into the Closet (1994)
- ❏ 16 - The Cat Who Came to Breakfast (1994)
- ☑ 17 - The Cat Who Blew the Whistle (1995)

Carol Brennan, who lives in Dutchess County, New York, is a public relations consultant who took a two-year break to sell luxury Manhattan real estate before writing the second installment in her series featuring Liz Wareham, Manhattan PR consultant.

Liz Wareham . . . Manhattan public relations consultant
- ❏   1 - Headhunt (1991)
- ❏   2 - Full Commission (1992)

Emily Brightwell is the creator of a new Victorian mystery series featuring Inspector Witherspoon and his housekeeper Mrs. Jeffries.

Inspector Witherspoon & Mrs. Jeffries . . . Victorian inspector & housekeeper
- ❏   1 - The Inspector and Mrs. Jeffries (1993)
- ❏   2 - Mrs. Jeffries Dusts for Clues (1993)
- ❏   3 - The Ghost and Mrs. Jeffries (1993)
- ❏   4 - Mrs. Jeffries Takes Stock (1994)
- ❏   5 - Mrs. Jeffries on the Ball (1994)

Toni Brill is the pseudonym used by a husband and wife writing team for their mystery series featuring Midge Cohen, a New York city children's author who is also fluent in Russian.

Midge Cohen . . . New York City children's author fluent in Russian
- ❏   1 - Date With a Dead Doctor (1991)
- ❏   2 - Date With a Plummeting Publisher (1993)

D. C. Brod is Deborah Cobban Brod, creator of the Quint McCauley series set in the western suburbs of Chicago. Described as a medium-boiled P.I., the ex-big city cop starts the series as a department store security chief and turns to private investigation in book two. Brod is currently at work on a novel of suspense set in the British Isles.

Quint McCauley . . . Chicago ex-cop turned P.I.
- ❏   1 - Murder in Store (1989)
- ❏   2 - Error in Judgment (1990)
- ❏   3 - Masquerade in Blue (1991) [paperback title–Framed in Blue]
- ❏   4 - Brothers in Blood (1993)

Rita Mae Brown, of Charlottesville, Virginia, is a best-selling author, Emmy-nominated screenwriter, poet and adopted mother of Sneaky Pie Brown, her tiger cat collaborator. Brown and Sneaky Pie are the creators of a mystery series featuring postmistress Mary Minor Haristeen (Harry to her friends) of Crozet,

Virginia, and her tiger cat Mrs. Murphy, along with their friends Tee Tucker (a Welsh corgi), Simon the possum and Harry's ex-husband, the local veterinarian. Brown was an established novelist with more than six other titles to her credit before launching this series which the *New York Times Review of Books* called "charming...with wise, disarming wit."

Mary Minor Haristeen . . . small-town postmistress & cat in Crozet, Virginia

- ☑ 1 - Wish You Were Here (1990)
- ☑ 2 - Rest in Pieces (1992)
- ☑ 3 - Murder at Monticello (1994)

Pay dirt murder she meowed

Edna Buchanan won a Pulitzer Prize for her police-beat reporting for *The Miami Herald* and is the creator of a new series featuring Miami crime reporter Britt Montero. Buchanan is also the author of true crime and autobiographical work including *Never Let Them See You Cry*, *The Corpse Had a Familiar Face* and *Nobody Lives Forever*.

Britt Montero . . . Miami, Florida newspaper crime reporter

- ❑ 1 - Contents Under Pressure (1992)
- ❑ 2 - Miami, It's Murder (1994)
- ❑ 3 - Suitable for Framing (1995)

Pat Burden is the creator of a cozy English mystery series featuring retired constable Henry Bassett who is perfectly content in his Herefordshire cottage, tending his pigs, chickens and garden. The tale of a bizarre crime which upsets his domesticity earned Burden an Agatha nomination for best first traditional mystery in 1990.

Henry Bassett . . . retired cop in Herefordshire, England

- ❑ 1 - **Screaming Bones** (1990) *Agatha nominee* ☆
- ❑ 2 - Wreath of Honesty (1990)
- ❑ 3 - Bury Him Kindly (1992)

Jan Burke and her newspaper reporter character, Irene Kelly, both live and work on the southern California coast. Burke's first manuscript was bought unagented and unsolicited by Simon & Schuster and went on to earn Agatha and Anthony nominations for best first mystery novel.

Irene Kelly . . . California newspaper reporter

- ☑ 1 - **Goodnight, Irene** (1993) *Agatha & Anthony nominee* ☆
- ❑ 2 - Sweet Dreams, Irene (1994)
- ❑ 3 - Dear Irene (1995)

Gwendoline Butler has published almost 60 novels since 1956 and is the author of a long-running series featuring London Inspector John Coffin, who is more enthusiastically received in the author's native England than the U.S. She has also written seven non-series novels, including the historical mystery that won a Silver Dagger in 1973 (*A Coffin for Pandora*)—not part of the Inspector Coffin series despite the title. Under the pseudonym Jennie Melville she writes another police series and numerous titles of romantic suspense and historical fiction.

> **John Coffin** . . . London police inspector
> - ❑ 1 - Dead in a Row (1957)
> - ❑ 2 - The Dull Dead (1958)
> - ❑ 3 - The Murdering Kind (1958)
> - ❑ 4 - Death Lives Next Door (1960)
> - ❑ 5 - Make Me a Murderer (1961)
> - ❑ 6 - Coffin in Oxford (1962)
> - ❑ 7 - A Coffin for Baby (1963)
> - ❑ 8 - Coffin Waiting (1964)
> - ❑ 9 - A Nameless Coffin (1966)
> - ❑ 10 - Coffin Following (1968)
> - ❑ 11 - Coffin's Dark Number (1969)
> - ❑ 12 - A Coffin from the Past (1970)
> - ❑ 13 - A Coffin for the Canary (1974) [U.S.–Sarsen Place]
> - ❑ 14 - Coffin on the Water (1986)
> - ❑ 15 - Coffin in Fashion (1987)
> - ❑ 16 - Coffin Underground (1988)
> - ❑ 17 - Coffin in the Black Museum (1989)
> - ❑ 18 - Coffin in the Museum of Crime (1989)
> - ❑ 19 - Coffin and the Paper Man (1991)
> - ❑ 20 - Coffin on Murder Street (1992)
> - ❑ 21 - Cracking Open a Coffin (1993)
> - ❑ 22 - A Coffin for Charley (1994)

Dorothy Cannell, a British expatriate living in Illinois, is the creator of Ellie and Ben Haskell and the dotty Tramwell sisters who pop in and out after their introduction in the second installment of this charmingly eccentric series set almost entirely in England. Ellie is an unmarried overweight interior decorator in the first outing where she hires an escort to hunt treasure and ends up marrying him and inheriting the castle. He's an aspiring chef who writes trashy novels to support his later works of literature.

> **Ben & Ellie Haskell & the Tramwells** . . . interior decorator & writer/chef with a pair of sister sleuths in London, England
> - ☑ 1 - The Thin Woman (1984)
> - ❑ 2 - Down the Garden Path: A Pastoral Mystery (1985)
> - ❑ 3 - **The Widow's Club** (1988) *Agatha & Anthony nominee* ☆
> - ❑ 4 - Mum's the Word (1990)
> - ❑ 5 - Femmes Fatal (1992)
> - ❑ 6 - How to Murder Your Mother-in-law (1994)

Taffy Cannon introduced Los Angeles series detective, Nan Robinson, an attorney-investigator for the California State Bar in 1993. Prior to launching her mystery series, Cannon had written one other novel and an Academy-Award nominated short film.

Nan Robinson . . . Los Angeles, California investigator for the State Bar

- ❑   1   -   A Pocketful of Karma   (1993)
- ❑   2   -   Tangled Roots   (1995)

P. M. Carlson taught psychology and statistics at Cornell University before introducing her statistician sleuth, New Yorker Maggie Ryan, in 1985. The series opens with Maggie as a college student and follows her through marriage and motherhood. In 1992, Carlson launched the Marti Hopkins series featuring a young woman sheriff in southern Indiana. Both series have been nominated for several mystery awards. Carlson is a past president of Sisters in Crime.

Maggie Ryan . . . statistician & mother in New York City

- ❑   1   -   Audition for Murder   (1985)
- ❑   2   -   **Murder is Academic**   (1985)   *Anthony nominee* ☆
- ❑   3   -   Murder is Pathological   (1986)
- ❑   4   -   **Murder Unrenovated**   (1987)   *Anthony & Macavity nominee* ☆
- ❑   5   -   Rehearsal for Murder   (1988)
- ❑   6   -   **Murder in the Dog Days**   (1990)   *Edgar nominee* ☆
- ❑   7   -   Murder Misread   (1990)
- ❑   8   -   Bad Blood   (1991)

Martine LaForte Hopkins . . . southern Indiana deputy sheriff

- ❑   1   -   **Gravestone**   (1992)   *Agatha, Anthony, Edgar & Macavity nominee* ☆
- ❑   2   -   Bloodstream   (1995)

Sarah Caudwell is the pseudonym used by English barrister Sarah Cockburn for her mystery series featuring Oxford professor Hilary Tamar, an expert in medieval law frequently called upon to assist five young barristers who practice together in a London firm. Many of Caudwell's fans continue to puzzle over the question—Is the wise professor a woman or a man? Thus far, the author has declined to settle the debate

Hilary Tamar . . . Oxford professor of medieval law

- ❑   1   -   Thus Was Adonis Murdered   (1981)
- ❑   2   -   The Shortest Way to Hades   (1985)
- ❑   3   -   **The Sirens Sang of Murder**   (1989)   *Anthony winner* ★

Sally Chapman spent nine years with IBM and was well acquainted with life in the Silicon Valley before launching her mystery series featuring computer investigator Juliet Blake.

Juliet Blake . . . Silicon Valley computer executive
- ❑ 1 - Raw Data (1991)
- ❑ 2 - Love Bytes (1994)

Kate Charles is an American living in England who brings personal experience as a church administrator to her ecclesiastical mystery series featuring solicitor David Middleton-Brown and artist Lucy Kingsley. David and Lucy meet in the first installment when David is hired by a priest who is being blackmailed. Anglican politics and church art and architecture play dominant roles in this series.

Lucy Kingsley & David Middleton-Brown . . . artist & solicitor
- ❑ 1 - A Deadly Drink of Wine (1991)
- ❑ 2 - The Snares of Death (1993)

Agatha Christie (1890-1976) is undoubtedly the world's best-known woman mystery writer, with two of the all-time best-loved series characters ever created, Hercule Poirot and Miss Jane Marple. In addition to being the undisputed master of the cozy mystery, she is one of the best-selling authors in the history of the world. Almost 20 years after her death she continues to sell millions of books.

It is reported that this shy, quiet woman wrote many of her novels in the bathtub and learned much about drugs and poisons while working as a hospital volunteer during the First World War. She later became a top mystery playwright and credited with writing the longest running play in London history (*The Mousetrap*, 1954). She was the first to be named Grand Master by the Mystery Writers of America and was later made a Dame Commander of the Order of the British Empire in 1971.

Hercule Poirot . . . former Belgian cop turned London-based private detective
- ❑ 1 - The Mysterious Affair at Styles (1920)
- ❑ 2 - Murder on the Links (1923)
- ❑ 3 - The Murder of Roger Ackroyd (1926)
- ❑ 4 - The Big Four (1927)
- ❑ 5 - The Mystery of the Blue Train (1928)
- ❑ 6 - Dead Man's Mirror (1931)
- ❑ 7 - Peril at End House (1931)
- ❑ 8 - Lord Edgeware Dies (1933) [U.S.–Thirteen at Dinner]
- ❑ 9 - Three-Act Tragedy (1934) [U.S.–Murder in Three Acts]
- ❑ 10 - Murder on the Orient Express (1934) [U.S.–Murder in the Calais Coach]
- ❑ 11 - Death in the Clouds (1935) [U.S.–Death in the Air]

❑ 12 - Murder in Mesopotamia (1936)
❑ 13 - Cards on the Table (1936)
❑ 14 - The ABC Murders (1936) [U.S.–The Alphabet Murders]
❑ 15 - Dumb Witness (1937) [U.S.–Poirot Loses a Client]
❑ 16 - Death on the Nile (1937)
❑ 17 - Murder in the Mews (1937) [U.S.–Dead Man's Mirror]
❑ 18 - A Holiday for Murder (1938)
❑ 19 - Appointment with Death (1938)
❑ 20 - Hercule Poirot's Christmas (1938) [U.S.–Murder for Christmas]
❑ 21 - Sad Cypress (1939)
❑ 22 - One, Two, Buckle My Shoe (1940) [U.S.–The Patriotic Murders]
❑ 23 - Evil Under the Sun (1941)
❑ 24 - Five Little Pigs (1941) [U.S.–Murder in Retrospect]
☑ 25 - The Hollow (1946) [U.S.–Murder After Hours]
❑ 26 - Taken at the Flood (1948) [U.S.–There is a Tide]
❑ 27 - Mrs. McGinty's Dead (1952) [U.S.–Blood Will Tell]
❑ 28 - After the Funeral (1953) [U.S.–Funerals are Fatal]
❑ 29 - Hickory, Dickory, Dock (1955) [U.S.–Hickory, Dickory, Death]
❑ 30 - Dead Man's Folly (1956)
❑ 31 - Cat Among the Pigeons (1959)
❑ 32 - The Clocks (1963)
❑ 33 - Third Girl (1966)
❑ 34 - Hallowe'en Party (1969)
❑ 35 - Elephants Can Remember (1972)
❑ 36 - The Last Curtain (1975)

Miss Jane Marple . . . elderly spinster living in St. Mary's Mead, England

❑   1 - The Murder at the Vicarage (1930)
❑   2 - The Moving Finger (1942)
☑   3 - The Body in the Library (1942)
❑   4 - A Murder is Announced (1950)
❑   5 - They Do It with Mirrors (1952) [U.S.–Murder With Mirrors]
❑   6 - A Pocket Full of Rye (1953)
☑   7 - 4:50 from Paddington (1957) [U.S.–What Mrs. McGillicuddy Saw]
❑   8 - The Mirror Cracked from Side to Side (1962) [U.S.–The Mirror Cracked]
❑   9 - A Caribbean Mystery (1964)
❑ 10 - At Bertram's Hotel (1965)
❑ 11 - Nemesis (1971)
❑ 12 - Sleeping Murder (1976)

Tuppence & Tommy Beresford . . . English adventurers for hire; intelligence agents

❑   1 - The Secret Adversary (1922)
❑   2 - Partners in Crime (1929) [short stories]
❑   3 - N or M? (1941)
❑   4 - By the Pricking of My Thumbs (1968)
❑   5 - Postern of Fate (1973)

Joyce Christmas is the author of non-mystery novels and children's plays in addition to her series featuring Lady Margaret Priam, an English noblewoman living in New York City. Lady Margaret's friends are socialites and royalty but she pursues a romantic relationship with a police detective. Christmas has recently introduced a new series detective retired Connecticut businesswoman Betty Trenka.

Betty Trenka . . . retired Connecticut businesswoman

- ❏ 1 - This Business is Murder (1993)

Lady Margaret Priam . . . Englishwoman in New York City

- ❏ 1 - Suddenly in Her Sorbet (1988)
- ❏ 2 - Simply to Die For (1989)
- ❏ 3 - A Fete Worse than Death (1990)
- ❏ 4 - A Stunning Way to Die (1991)
- ❏ 5 - Friend or Faux (1991)
- ❏ 6 - It's Her Funeral (1992)

Jill Churchill is the pseudonym of Janice Young Brooks who also writes historical novels. Her charming mystery series features Jane Jeffry, a young, suburban Miss Jane Marple with kids, a dog and the busy schedule of a single mother. Jane's first adventure was awarded an Agatha for best first cozy mystery.

Jane Jeffry . . . Chicago, Illinois suburban single mother

- ❏ 1 - **Grime & Punishment** (1989) *Agatha winner* ★
- ❏ 2 - A Farewell to Yarns (1991)
- ❏ 3 - A Quiche Before Dying (1993)
- ❏ 4 - A Fridge Too Many (1993)
- ❏ 5 - A Knife to Remember (1994)

Carol Higgins Clark, daughter of famed suspense writer Mary Higgins Clark, is a graduate of Mount Holyoke College. Before launching her Regan Reilly series— nominated for an Agatha as best first novel—the younger Clark worked as her mother's research assistant. She has acted professionally on stage, film and television.

Regan Reilly . . . Los Angeles P.I.

- ❏ 1 - **Decked** (1992) *Agatha nominee* ☆
- ❏ 2 - Snagged (1993)
- ❏ 3 - Iced (1994)

Carolyn Chambers Clark, of St. Petersburg, Florida, is the creator of two new series with women protagonists—St. Petersburg RN Megan Baldwin and Florida P.I. Theresa Franco.

Megan Baldwin . . . St. Petersburg, Florida registered nurse
- ❏ 1 - Deadlier Than Death (1993)

Theresa Franco . . . P.I.
- ❏ 1 - Dangerous Alibis (1994)

Anna Clarke has written numerous non-series mysteries set in the literary world, so it is no surprise that her series detective is an English professor at the University of London.

Paula Glenning . . . British professor & writer
- ❏ 1 - Last Judgment (1985)
- ❏ 2 - Cabin 3033 (1986)
- ❏ 3 - The Mystery Lady (1986)
- ❏ 4 - Murder in Writing (1988)
- ❏ 5 - The Whitelands Affair (1989)
- ❏ 6 - The Case of the Paranoid Patient (1991)
- ❏ 7 - The Case of the Ludicrous Letters (1994)

Melissa Cleary is the author of a new mystery series for dog lovers, featuring college film instructor Jackie Walsh, her ten-year-old son Peter and their Alsatian shepherd Jake—a retired police dog who is rescued by Jackie and Peter in the first installment.

Jackie Walsh & Jake . . . college film instructor with her ex-police dog in the bustling Midwestern small town of Palmer
- ❏ 1 - A Tail of Two Murders (1992)
- ❏ 2 - Dog Collar Crime (1993)
- ❏ 3 - Hounded to Death (1993)
- ❏ 4 - Skull and Dog Bones (1994)
- ❏ 5 - First Pedigree Murder (1994)
- ❏ 6 - The Maltese Puppy (1995)

Ann Cleeves is perhaps best known for her bird-watching series featuring George Palmer-Jones, an official of the Home Office, and his wife Molly. Cleeves' second series featuring Inspector Stephen Ramsey is a traditional British police mystery.

George & Molly Palmer-Jones . . . ex-Home Office official/bird-watcher & wife
- ❏ 1 - A Bird in the Hand (1986)
- ❏ 2 - Come Death and High Water (1987)
- ❏ 3 - Murder in Paradise (1989)
- ❏ 4 - A Prey to Murder (1989)
- ❏ 5 - Sea Fever (1991)
- ❏ 6 - Another Man's Poison (1993)
- ❏ 7 - The Mill on the Shore (1994)

Stephen Ramsey . . . British Inspector
- ❑   1 - A Lesson in Dying (1990)
- ❑   2 - Murder in My Backyard (1991)
- ❑   3 - A Day in the Death of Dorothea Cassidy (1992)
- ❑   4 - Killjoy (1995)

Liza Cody is probably the only mystery writer who has studied painting at the Royal Academy School of Art and worked at Madame Tussaud's Wax Museum. Cody's hard-boiled detective Anna Lee is an operative with a London security firm, while her newer detective is a female wrestler, junkyard security guard and small-time criminal. Both series have won awards.

Anna Lee . . . private investigator for small London firm
- ❑   1 - **Dupe** (1980) *Creasey winner* ★
- ❑   2 - Bad Company (1982)
- ❑   3 - Stalker (1984)
- ❑   4 - Head Case (1985)
- ❑   5 - Under Contract (1986)
- ❑   6 - **Backhand** (1991) *Edgar nominee* ☆

Eva Wylie . . . London wrestler & security guard
- ❑   1 - **Bucket Nut** (1993) *Silver Dagger winner* ★
- ❑   2 - Monkey Wrench (1994)

Carolyn Coker is the creator of a mystery series set in the art world with Andrea Perkins, restorer of paintings for a Boston Museum. Coker has extensive television experience both on camera and off as an administrator.

Andrea Perkins . . . art historian and restorer of paintings at a Boston museum
- ❑   1 - The Other David (1984)
- ❑   2 - The Hand of the Lion (1987)
- ❑   3 - The Balmoral Nude (1990)
- ❑   4 - Appearance of Evil (1993)

Anna Ashwood Collins, of Jekyll Island, Georgia, is the creator of a new series featuring New York efficiency expert Abby Doyle who specializes in crime solving for the affluent. Collins is a past executive director of the International Association of Crime Writers and a former field agent for the U.S. Department of Labor.

Abigail Doyle . . . New York City efficiency expert
- ❑   1 - Deadly Resolutions (1994)

Barbara Comfort, from Landgrove, Vermont, is the creator of a Vermont series featuring artist and painter Tish McWhinney.

Tish McWhinney . . . Vermont artist & painter
- ❑ 1 - Phoebe's Knee (1986)
- ❑ 2 - Green Mountain Murder (1987)
- ❑ 3 - The Vermont Village Murder (1988)
- ❑ 4 - Grave Consequences (1989)
- ❑ 5 - The Cashmere Kid (1993)

Susan Conant is the creator of a popular mystery series featuring Holly Winter, magazine columnist for *Dog's Life* and owner of the lovable malamute Rowdy. Set in Cambridge, Massachusetts, this series involves varied aspects of the dog world. Conant and her husband, along with their two cats and two Alaskan malamutes, live in Massachusetts where she serves as state coordinator of the Alaskan Malamute Protection League.

Holly Winter . . . 30-something dog trainer & magazine columnist in Cambridge, Massachusetts
- ❑ 1 - A New Leash on Death (1989)
- ❑ 2 - Dead and Doggone (1990)
- ❑ 3 - A Bite of Death (1991)
- ❑ 4 - Paws Before Dying (1992)
- ❑ 5 - Gone to the Dogs (1992)
- ❑ 6 - Bloodlines (1992)
- ❑ 7 - Ruffly Speaking (1993)
- ❑ 8 - Black Ribbon (1995)

Natasha Cooper is a pseudonym for the British creator of an amateur sleuth leading a double life. As Willow King she works Tuesday through Thursday as a civil servant administrator for the Department of Old Age Pensions (DOAP), with a wardrobe and flat as drab as her job. After leaving the office on Thursday evening, her first stop is for the manicure, make-up and hair which transform her into Cressida Woodruffe, writer of romance novels with a glamorous apartment and housekeeper cook.

Willow King & Cressida Woodruffe . . . British civil servant & romance novelist
- ❑ 1 - A Common Death (1990)
- ❑ 2 - Poison Flowers (1991)
- ❑ 3 - Bloody Roses (1992)
- ❑ 4 - Bitter Herbs (1993)

Susan Rogers Cooper is the creator of Milt Kovak, Oklahoma sheriff's deputy, who unexpectedly meets the woman who'll change his life in book #4 of this wonderful series. Cooper later introduced E. J. (Eloise Janine) Pugh, Texas housewife, mother and romance novelist. Cooper's most recent series features Kimmey Kruse, a young Chicago stand-up comic.

E. J. Pugh . . . Texas housewife & mother & romance writer
- ❏ 1 - One, Two, What Did Daddy Do? (1992)

Kimmey Kruse . . . stand-up comic in Chicago, Illinois
- ❏ 1 - Funny as a Dead Comic (1993)
- ❏ 2 - Funny as a Dead Relative (1994)

Milton Kovak . . . Prophesy County, Oklahoma chief deputy
- ❏ 1 - The Man in the Green Chevy (1988)
- ❏ 2 - Houston in the Rear View Mirror (1990)
- ❏ 3 - Other People's Houses (1990)
- ❏ 4 - Chasing Away the Devil (1991)
- ❏ 5 - Dead Moon on the Rise (1994)

Patricia Daniels Cornwell is a former crime reporter for the *Charlotte Observer* who, after six years in the Virginia Medical Examiner's Office, launched her best-selling series starring Dr. Kay Scarpetta, Medical Examiner. Scarpetta works closely with the Richmond police department and the Behavioral Sciences Division of the FBI. Her first case swept the mystery awards for 1990. Before creating her forensic series, Cornwell wrote the 1983 biography of Ruth Graham, wife of evangelist Billy Graham.

Kay Scarpetta . . . Richmond, Virginia chief medical examiner
- ❏ 1 - **Postmortem** (1990)
   Edgar, Creasey, Anthony & Macavity winner ★
- ❏ 2 - Body of Evidence (1991)
- ❏ 3 - All that Remains (1992)
- ☑ 4 - **Cruel and Unusual** (1993) ***Gold Dagger winner*** ★
- ❏ 5 - The Body Farm (1994)

Alisa Craig is the pseudonym chosen by Charlotte MacLeod for her two Canadian mystery series. The more traditional series features Royal Canadian Mounted Police (RCMP) officer Madoc Rhys and his wife Janet. The Grub-and-Stakers series, set in Lobelia Falls, Ontario, features without a doubt the zaniest character names in mystery fiction. This series tells the adventures of Dittany Henbit Monk and her husband Osbert, a writer of westerns, along with his aunt Arethusa, writer of romance novels.

Madoc & Janet Rhys . . . RCMP Inspector & wife
- ❏ 1 - A Pint of Murder (1980)

❏ 2 - Murder Goes Mumming (1981)
❏ 3 - The Terrible Tide (1983)
❏ 4 - A Dismal Thing to Do (1986)
❏ 5 - Trouble in the Brasses (1989)
❏ 6 - The Wrong Rite (1992)

Dittany Henbit & Osbert Monk . . . garden club member & western author husband

❏ 1 - The Grub-and-Stakers Move a Mountain (1981)
❏ 2 - The Grub-and-Stakers Quilt a Bee (1985)
❏ 3 - The Grub-and-Stakers Pinch a Poke (1988)
❏ 4 - The Grub-and-Stakers Spin a Yarn (1990)
❏ 5 - The Grub-and-Stakers House a Haunt (1993)

Frances Crane was born in Lawrenceville, Illinois, but lived in Europe for many years where she wrote articles and short stories for American publications. After her return to Lawrenceville in her early 40s, she started the long-running series featuring globe-trotting husband and wife detectives Pat and Jean Abbot. The two meet over murder on their first vacation and for 24 years and 26 books they look everywhere for a vacation without homicide.

Pat & Jean Abbot . . . husband & wife traveling detection team from San Francisco

❏ 1 - The Turquoise Shop (1941)
❏ 2 - The Golden Box (1942)
❏ 3 - The Yellow Violet (1943)
❏ 4 - The Pink Umbrella (1943)
❏ 5 - The Applegreen Cat (1943)
❏ 6 - The Amethyst Spectacles (1944)
❏ 7 - The Indigo Necklace (1945)
❏ 8 - The Cinnamon Murder (1946)
❏ 9 - The Shocking Pink Hat (1946)
❏ 10 - Murder on the Purple Water (1947)
❏ 11 - Black Cypress (1948)
❏ 12 - The Flying Red Horse (1949)
❏ 13 - The Daffodil Blonde (1950)
❏ 14 - Murder in Blue Street (1951) [Britain–Murder in Blue Hour]
❏ 15 - The Polkadot Murder (1951)
❏ 16 - Thirteen White Tulips (1953)
❏ 17 - Murder in Bright Red (1953)
❏ 18 - The Coral Princess Murders (1954)
❏ 19 - Death in Lilac Time (1955)
❏ 20 - Horror on the Ruby X (1956)
❏ 21 - The Ultraviolet Widow (1956)
❏ 22 - The Man in Gray (1958) [Britain–The Gray Stranger]
❏ 23 - The Buttercup Case (1958)
❏ 24 - Death Wish Green (1960)
❏ 25 - The Amber Eyes (1962)
❏ 26 - The Body Beneath a Mandarin Tree (1965)

Hamilton Crane is the pseudonym chosen by Sarah J. Mason for her work continuing the Miss Seeton series featuring English spinster and retired art teacher Emily Dorothea Seeton. The series was originated by Heron Carvic, who wrote the first five novels before his death in 1980. Hampton Charles wrote another three titles in this series before Mason took over and quickened the pace with her first Miss Seeton title in 1991.

Mason has another series under her own name featuring Detective Superintendent Trewley and Sergeant Stone of the Allingham police department.

Miss Emily D. Seeton . . . retired British art teacher

- ❏   1   -   Miss Seeton Sings (1980s) [Heron Carvic]
- ❏   2   -   Odds on Miss Seeton (1980s) [Heron Carvic]
- ❏   3   -   Picture Miss Seeton (1980s) [Heron Carvic]
- ❏   4   -   Witch Miss Seeton (1980s) [Heron Carvic]
- ❏   5   -   Miss Seeton Draws the Line (1980s) [Heron Carvic]
- ❏   6   -   Advantage Miss Seeton (1990) [Hampton Charles]
- ❏   7   -   Miss Seeton at the Helm (1990) [Hampton Charles]
- ❏   8   -   Miss Seeton, By Appointment (1990) [Hampton Charles]
- ❏   9   -   Miss Seeton Cracks the Case (1991)
- ❏ 10   -   Miss Seeton Paints the Town (1991)
- ❏ 11   -   Miss Seeton Rocks the Cradle (1992)
- ❏ 12   -   Hands Up, Miss Seeton (1992)
- ❏ 13   -   Miss Seeton By Moonlight (1992)
- ❏ 14   -   Miss Seeton Plants Suspicion (1993)
- ☑ 15   -   Miss Seeton Goes to Bat (1993)
- ❏ 16   -   Starring Miss Seeton (1994)
- ❏ 17   -   Miss Seeton Undercover (1994)
- ❏ 18   -   Miss Seeton Rules (1994)

Camilla T. Crespi was born in Prague to an American mother and Italian father in the diplomatic corps. She came to the U.S. as a teenager and later earned degrees from Barnard College and Columbia University. Not unlike the author, her series detective is a food-loving Italian who works as an art buyer for a New York advertising agency.

Simona Griffo . . . New York City advertising executive & gourmet cook

- ❏   1   -   The Trouble with a Small Raise (1991)
- ❏   2   -   The Trouble with Moonlighting (1991)
- ❏   3   -   The Trouble with Too Much Sun (1992)
- ❏   4   -   The Trouble with Thin Ice (1993)

Deborah Crombie, of Trophy Club, Texas, writes a British police series featuring Superintendent Duncan Kincaid and Sergeant Gemma James. Crombie worked in advertising and publishing before moving to Edinburgh after marrying a Scot. She later lived in Chester, England before returning to Texas. Her first Kincaid and James title was nominated for an Agatha for best first novel.

Duncan Kincaid & Gemma James . . . Scotland Yard superintendent & sergeant

❏ 1 - **A Share in Death** (1993) *Agatha nominee* ☆
❏ 2 - All Shall Be Well (1994)

Amanda Cross is the pseudonym of Carolyn G. Heilbrun, Phi Beta Kappa from Wellesley College with MA and PhD degrees in English from Columbia University. She has taught at Brooklyn College and Columbia, served as president of the Modern Language Association, been awarded five honorary doctorates and published numerous scholarly works in addition to her mystery series featuring English professor Kate Fansler.

Kate Fansler . . . New York City university English professor

❏ 1 - In the Last Analysis (1964)
☑ 2 - The James Joyce Murder (1967)
❏ 3 - Poetic Justice (1970)
❏ 4 - The Theban Mysteries (1972)
❏ 5 - The Question of Max (1976)
❏ 6 - Death in a Tenured Position (1981)
❏ 7 - Sweet Death, Kind Death (1984)
❏ 8 - No Word from Winifred (1986)
❏ 9 - A Trap for Fools (1989)
❏ 10 - The Players Come Again (1990)
❏ 11 - An Imperfect Spy (1995)

Ann Crowleigh is the author of a new historical mystery series set in Victorian London with twin sisters Miranda and Claire Clively.

Miranda & Clare Clively . . . Victorian London twin sisters

❏ 1 - Dead as Dead Can Be (1993)

Laura Crum is the creator of a new mystery series featuring northern California horse veterinarian Gail McCarthy.

Gail McCarthy . . . northern California horse veterinarian

❏ 1 - Cutter (1994)

Clare Curzon is the pseudonym used by Eileen-Marie Duell of Buckinghamshire for her Thames Valley mystery series featuring Detective Superintendent Mike Yeadings, director of the Serious Crimes Squad. The author has worked throughout Europe as an interpreter, translator, probation officer and social secretary. She has also written a number of other novels under the names Marie Buchanan and Rhona Petrie.

> **Mike Yeadings** . . . Thames Valley, England detective superintendent of Serious Crimes Squad
>
> - ❏   1 -   A Leaven of Malice (1979)
> - ❏   2 -   Special Occasion (1981)
> - ❏   3 -   I Give You Five Days (1983)
> - ❏   4 -   Masks and Faces (1984)
> - ❏   5 -   The Trojan Hearse (1985)
> - ❏   6 -   The Quest for K (1986)
> - ❏   7 -   Trail of Fire (1987)
> - ❏   8 -   Shot Bolt (1988)
> - ❏   9 -   Three-Core Lead (1988)
> - ❏   10 -   The Face in the Stone (1989)
> - ❏   11 -   The Blue-Eyed Boy (1991)
> - ❏   12 -   Cat's Cradle (1992)
> - ❏   13 -   First Wife, Twice Removed (1993)
> - ❏   14 -   Death Prone (1994)

Barbara D'Amato won both the Anthony and Agatha for her true crime title *The Doctor, The Murder, The Mystery* and was featured with this 20-year-old murder on TV's *Unsolved Mysteries*. She has written musical comedies, suspense and other mystery novels, including two early titles featuring Dr. Gerritt De Graaf. Her Cat Marsala series features a Chicago freelance magazine writer who investigates big stories like gambling and prostitution. D'Amato is also the author of Anthony-nominated *On My Honor* which was written under the pseudonym of Malacai Black. She is the 1994-95 president of Sisters in Crime.

> **Cat Marsala** . . . Chicago, Illinois freelance investigative journalist
>
> - ❏   1 -   Hardball (1990)
> - ❏   2 -   Hard Tack (1991)
> - ❏   3 -   Hard Luck (1992)
> - ❏   4 -   Hard Women (1993)
> - ❏   5 -   Hard Case (1994)
>
> **Gerritt De Graaf** . . . physician
>
> - ❏   1 -   The Hands of Healing Murder (1980)
> - ❏   2 -   The Eyes on Utopia Murders (1981)

Mary Daheim is a Seattle native with two mystery series and numerous historical romances to her credit.

Emma Lord . . . small-town newspaper owner & editor in Alpine, Washington

- ❏ 1 - The Alpine Advocate (1992)
- ❏ 2 - The Alpine Betrayal (1993)
- ❏ 3 - The Alpine Christmas (1993)
- ❏ 4 - The Alpine Decoy (1994)
- ❏ 5 - The Alpine Escape (1995)

Judith McMonigle . . . Washington bed & breakfast owner

- ❏ 1 - Just Desserts (1991)
- ❏ 2 - Fowl Prey (1991)
- ❏ 3 - Holy Terrors (1992)
- ❏ 4 - Bantam of the Opera (1993)
- ❏ 5 - Fit of Tempera (1994)

Catherine Dain is the pseudonym used by Judith Garwood as creator of the Freddie O'Neal series featuring a hard-boiled Reno P.I. with a love for flying and a gun in her cowboy boot. Dain, with a theatre arts degree from UCLA and a graduate degree from the University of Southern California, worked as a TV newscaster before turning to mystery writing. Like Freddie O'Neal, the author was raised in Reno and lives with two cats.

Freddie O'Neal . . . Reno, Nevada plane-flying P.I.

- ❏ 1 - **Lay It on the Line** (1992) *Shamus nominee* ☆
- ❏ 2 - Sing a Song of Death (1993)
- ❏ 3 - Walk a Crooked Mile (1994)
- ❏ 4 - Lament for a Dead Cowboy (1994)
- ❏ 5 - Bet Against the House (1995)

Elizabeth Daly (1878-1967), reported to be Agatha Christie's favorite American mystery writer, had a BA from Bryn Mawr and an MA from Columbia. She tutored English and French and for many years produced and directed amateur theatre. She was the creator of 16 novels featuring New York bibliophile and forgery expert Henry Gamadge—a series started when she was 61. At the age of 82 she was awarded a special Edgar by the Mystery Writers of America in recognition of her entire body of work. The Gamadge stories continue with Henry's widow Clara, in a series written by Daly's niece, Eleanor Boylan.

Henry Gamadge . . . New York City author & bibliophile

- ❏ 1 - Unexpected Night (1940)
- ❏ 2 - Deadly Nightshade (1940)
- ❏ 3 - Murder in Volume 2 (1941)
- ❏ 4 - The House Without the Door (1942)
- ❏ 5 - Norhing Can Rescue Me (1943)
- ❏ 6 - Evidence of Things Seen (1943)

❏ 7 - Arrow Pointing Nowhere (1944)
❏ 8 - The Book of the Dead (1944)
❏ 9 - Any Shape or Form (1945)
❏ 10 - Somewhere in the House (1946)
❏ 11 - The Wrong Way Down (1946)
❏ 12 - Night Walk (1947)
❏ 13 - The Book of the Lion (1948)
❏ 14 - And Dangerous to Know (1949)
❏ 15 - Death and Letters (1950)
❏ 16 - The Book of the Crime (1951)
❏ 17 - Shroud for a Lady (1956)

Denise Danks is the creator of a mystery series featuring London computer journalist Georgina Powers. Danks spent much of 1994 traveling and researching in the U.S., after being awarded the Raymond Chandler Fulbright Award.

Georgina Powers . . . British computer journalist in London

❏ 1 - User Deadly (1989)
❏ 2 - Frame Grabber (1992)
❏ 3 - Wink a Hopeful Eye (1994)

Diane Mott Davidson is the creator of Colorado's culinary sleuth Goldy Bear, owner of Goldilocks Catering, where everything is "just right." In addition to Goldy's catering adventures, readers enjoy her original recipes created especially for this series. The supporting cast includes her son Arch, one ex-husband and Goldy's dessert-loving best friend who happens to be another ex-wife of the same ex-husband. Before writing full time, Davidson was a prep school teacher, volunteer counselor, tutor and licensed lay preacher in the Episcopal church.

Goldy Bear . . . Colorado caterer & single mother

❏ 1 - **Catering to Nobody** (1990)
         Agatha, Anthony & Macavity nominee ☆
❏ 2 - Dying for Chocolate (1992)
❏ 3 - Cereal Murders (1993)
❏ 4 - The Last Suppers (1994)

Dorothy Salisbury Davis, author of more than 20 mystery novels, is a seven-time Edgar nominee, past president of the Mystery Writers of America and one of the founding directors of Sisters in Crime. She was named Grand Master in 1984 and later received a lifetime achievement Anthony Award in 1989. Although her first crime novel (*The Judas Cat*) was published in 1949, Davis did not create a series detective until the 1976 arrival of Julie Hayes, former New York City actress and columnist who tells fortunes in Times Square.

Julie Hayes . . . former actress & columnist in New York City

❑   1   -   A Death in the Life   (1976)
❑   2   -   Scarlet Night   (1980)
❑   3   -   Lullaby of Murder   (1984)
❑   4   -   The Habit of Fear   (1987)

Lindsey Davis

Lindsey Davis, born and raised in Birmingham, England, joined the civil service after reading English at Oxford. She currently lives in London where she writes a brilliant historical series featuring Marcus Didius Falco and the world of first century Rome. Falco is a plebeian P.I. and staunch republican who much to his own discomfort finds himself in the employ of the emperor Vespasian. Falco's love interest is the patrician Helena Justina.

Marcus Didius Falco . . . P.I. in ancient Rome

❑   1   -   Silver Pigs   (1989)
❑   2   -   Shadows in Bronze   (1990)
❑   3   -   Venus in Copper   (1991)
❑   4   -   Iron Hand of Mars   (1992)
❑   5   -   Incident at Palmyra   (1994)
❑   6   -   Poseiden's Gold   (1994)

Janet Dawson is the creator of Oakland P.I. Jeri Howard, whose first case won the St. Martin's Press/Private Eye Writer's Association contest for best first P.I. novel. It was also nominated for the Anthony, Shamus and Macavity awards. Dawson lives in Alameda, California where she has been a newspaper reporter, an enlisted journalist and an officer in the U.S. Navy.

Jeri Howard . . . Oakland, California P.I.

❑   1   -   **Kindred Crimes**   (1990)
            Anthony, Shamus, Macavity nominee ☆ & *SMP/PWA winner* ★
❑   2   -   Till the Old Men Die   (1993)
❑   3   -   Take a Number   (1993)
❑   4   -   Don't Turn Your Back on the Ocean   (1994)

Marele Day is the creator of a mystery series featuring Australian P.I. Claudia Valentine whose 1992 adventure was the Shamus winner for best paperback original that year.

Claudia Valentine . . . Australian P.I.

❑   1   -   The Life and Crimes of Harry Lavender   (1988)
❑   2   -   The Case of the Chinese Boxes   (1990)
❑   3   -   **The Last Tango of Delores Delgado**   (1992)   *Shamus winner* ★

Jane Dentinger has a BFA in acting and directing from Ithaca College and has worked professionally in regional theatre, Off Broadway and Joe Papp's Shakespeare in the Park. While writing the Jocelyn O'Roarke series featuring a working actor and director, Dentinger herself has continued to work as a director and acting coach. Getting to know theatrical statesman Frederick Revere, lover of Shakespeare and limericks, is the unexpected bonus of this wonderful series and worth twice the price of every installment, even in hard cover.

Jocelyn O'Roarke . . . Broadway actress & director in New York City
- ❑   1 -   Murder on Cue (1983)
- ❑   2 -   First Hit of the Season (1984)
- ❑   3 -   Death Mask (1988)
- ❑   4 -   Dead Pan (1992)
- ❑   5 -   The Queen is Dead (1994)

Jo Dereske, from Everett, Washington, is the creator of a new series featuring Washington librarian Helma Zukas.

Helma Zukas . . . Washington State librarian
- ❑   1 -   Miss Zukas and the Library Murders (1994)

Denise Dietz is the creator of series character Ellie Bernstein, diet group leader and dessert-maven sleuth. Dietz says her writing is inspired by her experience as a waitress, Weight Watchers lecturer, professional singer, newspaper reporter and film extra at Paramount. She is a graduate of the University of Wisconsin and currently lives in Denver where she is an over-the-top fan of the Broncos.

Ellie Bernstein . . . diet group leader
- ❑   1 -   Throw Darts at a Cheesecake (1993)
- ❑   2 -   Beat Up a Cookie (1994)

Doris Miles Disney (1907-1976) was born in rural Connecticut and worked in the insurance business in Hartford before starting her writing career in 1936 with an early series featuring small-town cop Jim O'Neill. Her best known series detective is Boston-based insurance investigator Jefferson Di Marco who falls in love with a murderer in the opening title. She also wrote a 1950s trilogy with postal inspector David Madden and 30 other non-series mysteries.

Jeff Di Marco . . . Boston, Massachusetts insurance investigator
- ❑   1 -   Dark Road (1946)
- ❑   2 -   Family Skeleton (1949)
- ❑   3 -   Straw Man (1951) [Britain–The Case of the Straw Man]
- ❑   4 -   Trick or Treat (1955) [Britain–The Halloween Murder]
- ❑   5 -   Method in Madness (1957) [Britain–Quiet Violence]
- ❑   6 -   Did She Fall or Was She Pushed? (1959)
- ❑   7 -   Find the Woman (1962)
- ❑   8 -   The Chandler Policy (1971)

Hildegarde Dolson was a New York freelance writer before her 1965 marriage to widower Richard Lockridge, who along with his first wife Frances created the immensely popular Mr. and Mrs. North mystery series. Dolson launched her own mystery series in 1971 with feisty Connecticut illustrator Lucy Ramsdale and her tenant, homicide inspector James McDougal. Lucy's witty repartee, especially in the first two installments, is well worth the trouble to locate these little gems.

Lucy Ramsdale & James McDougal . . . Connecticut illustrator & homicide inspector

- ❏ 1 - To Spite Her Face (1971)
- ❏ 2 - A Dying Fall (1973)
- ❏ 3 - Please Omit Funeral (1975)
- ❏ 4 - Beauty Sleep (1977)

R. B. Dominic is the pseudonym used by Mary Latsis and Martha Henissart to create the Ben Safford series featuring a Democratic congressman from Ohio. Although they jealously guard their personal privacy, Latsis and Henissart are known to be an economist and attorney, respectively, living in Massachusetts. They also write the John Putnam Thatcher series under another pseudonym, Emma Lathen. Ben Safford, like John Putnam Thatcher, is ably assisted in his detecting by clever colleagues.

Ben Safford . . . Ohio Democratic congressman

- ❏ 1 - Murder Sunny Side Up (1968)
- ❏ 2 - Murder in High Place (1970)
- ❏ 3 - There is No Justice (1971)
- ❏ 4 - Epitaph for a Lobbyist (1974)
- ❏ 5 - Murder out of Commission (1976)
- ❏ 6 - The Attending Physician (1980)
- ❏ 7 - Unexpected Developments (1984)

Carole Nelson Douglas is the author of 29 novels of mystery, fantasy, science fiction and romance, as well as historical and mainstream. She is the creator of the award-winning series with diva-detective Irene Adler, the only woman to outwit Sherlock Holmes. She is also the author of a series with Temple Barr, Las Vegas publicist and Midnight Louie, the big black tomcat sleuth who now has his own fan newsletter. Douglas and her artist husband live in Fort Worth, Texas with their six cats.

Irene Adler . . . Paris, France 19th century sleuth

- ❏ 1 - **Good Night, Mr. Holmes** (1990)
  American Mystery Award winner ★
- ❏ 2 - Good Morning, Irene (1990)
- ❏ 3 - Irene at Large (1992)
- ❏ 4 - Irene's Last Waltz (1994)

Temple Barr & Midnight Louie . . . Las Vegas, Nevada public relations freelancer & tomcat sleuth

- ❏ 1 - Catnap (1992)
- ❏ 2 - Pussyfoot (1993)
- ❏ 3 - Cat on a Blue Monday (1994)
- ❏ 4 - Cat in a Crimson Haze (1995)

Lauren Wright Douglas is the creator of lesbian P.I. Caitlin Reece who works on Vancouver Island, British Columbia. The detective's strong supporting cast of independent professionals includes a physician, a cop, an animal psychologist and an electronics expert.

Caitlin Reece . . . Victoria, Canada lesbian detective

- ❏ 1 - The Always Anonymous Beast (1987)
- ❏ 2 - Ninth Life (1989)
- ❏ 3 - The Daughters of Artemis (1991)
- ❏ 4 - A Tiger's Heart (1992)
- ❏ 5 - Goblin Market (1993)
- ❏ 6 - A Rage of Maidens (1994)

Alison Drake is a pseudonym for T. J. MacGregor who also writes the St. James and McCleary series featuring a pair of south Florida P.I.s. As Alison Drake, she is the creator of the Aline Scott series featuring a woman police officer on the fictional island of Tango Key—a tropical Florida paradise where her house is on stilts and she keeps a pet skunk named Wolfe.

Aline Scott . . . small resort town police detective in south Florida

- ❏ 1 - Tango Key (1988)
- ❏ 2 - Fevered (1988)
- ❏ 3 - Black Moon (1989)
- ❏ 4 - High Strangeness (1992)

Margaret Duffy, who lives in Scotland, is the creator of the action-packed series featuring British agents Ingrid Langley and Patrick Gillard. An American newspaper reviewer once said that her "wonderful sense of humor and frighteningly insightful view of male-female relationships" make these books "impossible to put down."

Ingrid Langley & Patrick Gillard . . . novelist/British agent & British army major

- ❏ 1 - A Murder of Crows (1987)
- ❏ 2 - Death of a Raven (1988)
- ❏ 3 - Brass Eagle (1989)
- ❏ 4 - Who Killed Cock Robin? (1990)
- ❏ 5 - Rook-Shoot (1991)

Sarah Dunant, British television journalist turned novelist, is the creator of Hannah Wolfe, London P.I., and Marla Masterson, British professor of Anglo Saxon literature.

Hannah Wolfe . . . London P.I.

❏ 1 - **Birth Marks** (1992) *Gold Dagger nominee* ☆
❏ 2 - **Fat Lands** (1993) *Silver Dagger winner* ★

Marla Masterson . . . young British professor of Anglo-Saxon literature in U.S.

❏ 1 - Snowstorms in a Hot Climate (1988)

Susan Dunlap says her life is boring, as a writer's should be. But she has created three California series detectives whose lives are anything but dull. Jill Smith is a Berkeley homicide detective with more than her share of unusual crimes, quirky suspects and police department politics to contend with. Kiernan O'Shaughnessy, who lives at the beach near La Jolla, is a former San Francisco medical examiner turned investigator whose ex-football player houseman just happens to be a gourmet cook. And Vejay Haskell, whose adventures were re-released in paperback in 1994, reads meters for Pacific Gas & Electric in the picturesque Russian River region of northern California. Dunlap is a past president of Sisters in Crime.

Jill Smith . . . Berkeley, California homicide detective

❏ 1 - Karma (1981)
❏ 2 - As a Favor (1984)
❏ 3 - Not Exactly a Brahmin (1985)
❏ 4 - Too Close to the Edge (1987)
❏ 5 - A Dinner to Die For (1987)
❏ 6 - Diamond in the Buff (1990)
❏ 7 - Death and Taxes (1992)
❏ 8 - Time Expired (1993)

Kiernan O'Shaughnessy . . . former San Francisco medical examiner turned P.I. in La Jolla, California

❏ 1 - Pious Deception (1989)
❏ 2 - Rogue Wave (1991)
❏ 3 - High Fall (1994)

Vejay Haskell . . . northern California meter reader for Pacific Gas & Electric

❏ 1 - An Equal Opportunity Death (1983)
❏ 2 - The Bohemian Connection (1985)
❏ 3 - The Last Annual Slugfest (1986)

*Michael Dymock
The more into understand Cats (1993)*

Mignon G. Eberhart, born in Nebraska, published her 59th novel in 1988, exactly 59 years after her first mystery featuring nurse Sarah Keate. The second title in this series was awarded the Scotland Yard Prize in 1930. She also wrote a four-book series with police detective Jacob Wait, published in the mid-1930s.

Eberhart, past president of the Mystery Writers of America, also served on the faculty of the Famous Writers School. Her books have been translated into more than a dozen languages and adapted for radio, television and film. When she was named Grand Master by the Mystery Writers of America in 1970, she was the first woman to be so honored since Agatha Christie in 1954.

Sarah Keate & Lance O'Leary . . . nurse & wealthy police detective
- ❑ 1 - The Patient in Room 18 (1929)
- ❑ 2 - While the Patient Slept (1930) **Scotland Yard Prize winner** ★
- ❑ 3 - The Mystery of Hunting's End (1930)
- ❑ 4 - From This Dark Stairway (1931)
- ❑ 5 - Murder by an Aristocrat (1932)
- ❑ 6 - Wolf in Man's Clothing (1942)
- ❑ 7 - Man Missing (1954)

Marjorie Eccles of Berkhamsted, England, is the creator of a police series featuring Detective Chief Inspector Gil Mayo, a Yorkshire man. She also wrote seven romance novels under two pseudonyms (Judith Bordill and Jennifer Hyde) before turning to mystery writing.

Gil Mayo . . . detective chief inspector in England
- ❑ 1 - Cast a Cold Eye (1988)
- ❑ 2 - Death of a Good Woman (1989)
- ❑ 3 - Requiem for a Dove (1990)
- ❑ 4 - More Deaths than One (1990)
- ❑ 5 - Late of this Parish (1994)

Rosemary Edghill is the creator of a new mystery series featuring Karen Hightower, also known as Bast the white witch, who is a Manhattan graphics designer by day.

Karen Hightower . . . Manhattan graphic designer & white witch
- ❑ 1 - Speak Daggers to Her (1994)
- ❑ 2 - Book of Moons (1995)

Janet Evanovich, of Fairfax, Virginia, is the creator of a new series featuring neophyte bounty hunter Stephanie Plum of Trenton, New Jersey.

Stephanie Plum . . . Trenton, New Jersey neophyte bounty hunter
- ❑ 1 - One for the Money (1994)

Elizabeth Eyre is one of the pseudonyms used by Jill Staynes and Margaret Storey, former teachers and lifelong friends who are writing partners for two mystery series. As Elizabeth Eyre, they are creators of the historical series set in Renaissance Italy featuring Sigismondo, the Duke of Rocca's agent. These stories are full of schemes and conspiracies with rich historical backgrounds. Staynes and Storey also write the Inspector Bone series as Susannah Stacey.

Sigismondo . . . Italian agent of a Renaissance duke

- ❏ 1 - Death of the Duchess (1992)
- ❏ 2 - Curtains for the Cardinal (1993)
- ❏ 3 - Poison for the Prince (1994)

Ann C. Fallon, of Forest Hills, New York, is the creator of a contemporary Irish series featuring Dublin solicitor James Fleming.

James Fleming . . . Dublin solicitor

- ❏ 1 - Blood is Thicker (1990)
- ❏ 2 - Where Death Lies (1991)
- ❏ 3 - Dead Ends (1992)
- ❏ 4 - Potter's Field (1993)

Gillian B. Farrell, actor and founder of the Byrdcliffe Actors' Theatre, worked as a detective before starting her Annie McGrogan series featuring a New York actress just returned from Los Angeles. Farrell once served papers on a Mafia Don during his divorce and helped Bernie Goetz with his defense. She brings her own intimate knowledge of both the theatre and P.I. world to this new series.

Annie McGrogan . . . New York City P.I. & actor just back from Los Angeles

- ❏ 1 - Alibi for an Actress (1992)
- ❏ 2 - Murder and a Muse (1994)

Quinn Fawcett is a pseudonym used by the creator of a new historical series featuring Madame Victoire Vernet, the wife of a French policeman in the time of Napoleon.

Mme. Victoire Vernet . . . French wife of Napoleonic gendarme

- ❏ 1 - Napoleon Must Die (1993)
- ❏ 2 - Death Wears a Crown (1993)

Connie Feddersen, of Union City, Oklahoma, is the creator of a new series featuring CPA Amanda Hazard and country cop Dick Thorn of Vamoose, Oklahoma.

Amanda Hazard . . . Oklahoma small-town Certified Public Accountant

- ❑ 1 - Dead in the Water (1993)
- ❑ 2 - Dead in the Cellar (1994)
- ❑ 3 - Dead in the Melons (1995)

Jean Femling is the creator of a southern California series featuring Orange County insurance claims investigator Martha Brant, who answers to the name Moz. Half-Filipino, she is often mistaken for Mexican and regularly encounters racial prejudice and discrimination.

Martha "Moz" Brant . . . southern California insurance claims investigator

- ❑ 1 - Hush, Money (1989)
- ❑ 2 - Getting Mine (1991)

E. X. Ferrars is the pseudonym of Morna Doris MacTaggart Brown, known in England as Elizabeth Ferrars. Born in what was then Burma, she earned a diploma in journalism from London's University College in 1928 and wrote her first mystery in 1940 at the age of 33. When her work crossed the Atlantic Ferrar's American publisher insisted on initials to hide the fact the author was a woman, and added the X for effect. For more than 50 years she has produced one or two books each year, including several short series. Most recently she began a new series with journalist Sara Marriott and continues the series launched in 1978 with Virginia and Felix Freer. Ferrars was a founding member of the British Crime Writers Association which she chaired in 1977-78. She received a Silver Dagger in 1981.

Sara Marriott . . . journalist

- ❑ 1 - Answer Came There None (1993)

Virginia & Felix Freer . . . physiotherapist & businessman in England

- ❑ 1 - Last Will and Testament (1978)
- ❑ 2 - In at the Kill (1978)
- ❑ 3 - Frog in the Throat (1980)
- ❑ 4 - Thinner than Water (1981)
- ❑ 5 - Death of a Minor Character (1983)
- ❑ 6 - I Met Murder (1985)
- ❑ 7 - Beware of the Dog (1992)

S.L. Florian is the creator of a new romantic mystery series featuring the Viscountess Delia Guilietta Ross-Merlani, Professor of Philosophy, Doctor of Letters and former dancer with the Monte Carlo Ballet, who is assisted in her first case by Dr. Daniel Elliot, New York's Assistant Medical Examiner.

Viscountess Delia Ross-Merlani . . . English-Italian noblewoman in New York

❏   1 - Born to the Purple (1992)

Katherine V. Forrest, of San Francisco, California, is the creator of a series featuring lesbian homicide detective Kate Delafield of the LAPD. The second installment of this Lambda award winning series has been optioned by Hollywood film director Tim Hunter.

Kate Delafield . . . LAPD lesbian homicide detective

❏   1 - Amateur City (1984)
❏   2 - Murder at the Nightwood Bar (1986)
❏   3 - The Beverly Malibu (1989)
❏   4 - Murder by Tradition (1991)

Earlene Fowler is a native Californian who says her Southern and Western heritage account for the appearance of quilts, cattle, smart-mouthed women, cowboys and a sexy Latino cop in her new mystery series starring Benni Harper, ex-rancher and folk art museum curator on the California coast.

Albenia "Benni" Harper . . . central California ex-rancher & folk art museum curator

❏   1 - Fool's Puzzle (1994)
❏   2 - Irish Chain (1995)

Valerie Frankel is an editor at *Mademoiselle* and creator of a New York series featuring Times Square P.I. and smart-mouth Wanda Mallory.

Wanda Mallory . . . New York City detective agency owner

❏   1 - A Deadline for Murder (1991)
❏   2 - Murder on Wheels (1992)
❏   3 - Prime Time for Murder (1994)

Anthea Fraser, of Hertfordshire, England, is the creator of a British police series featuring Inspector David Webb. Fraser began her writing career with short stories and then moved from romantic fiction to paranormal fiction, before settling in crime fiction with Webb as her point of view. Her work has been translated into seven languages.

David Webb . . . British police inspector

❏   1 - A Necessary End (1986)
❏   2 - A Shroud for Delilah (1986)
❏   3 - The Nine Bright Shiners (1988)
❏   4 - Six Proud Walkers (1989)

Antonia Pakenham Fraser, born in London, the daughter of Lord Longford, who was himself a writer, earned her BA and MA in history at Oxford. She is the author of a long-running mystery series featuring British television personality and investigative journalist Jemima Shore. Fraser has also written a number of critically-acclaimed historical biographies including Mary, Queen of Scots, Cromwell and The Wives of Henry VIII. She is a past chairman of the British Crime Writers Association and lives in London with her husband, dramatist Harold Pinter.

Jemima Shore . . . British TV interviewer

- ☑ 1 - Quiet as a Nun (1977)
- ❏ 2 - The Wild Island (1978)
- ☑ 3 - A Splash of Red (1981)
- ❏ 4 - Cool Repentance (1982)
- ❏ 5 - Oxford Blood (1985)
- ❏ 6 - Jemima Shore's First Case & Other Stories (1986)
- ❏ 7 - Your Royal Hostage (1987)
- ❏ 8 - The Cavalier Case (1991)
- ❏ 9 - Jemima Shore at the Sunny Grave (1993) [9 stories]

Margaret Frazer is the pseudonym used by Mary Pulver Kuhfeld of St. Louis Park, Minnesota and Gail Bacon for their medieval mystery series featuring Sister Frevisse, hosteler of the priory at St. Frideswide. Kuhfeld is probably better known as Mary Monica Pulver, creator of the series featuring Peter and Kori Price Brichter.

Sister Frevisse . . . medieval nun in England

- ❏ 1 - The Novice's Tale (1992)
- ❏ 2 - **The Servant's Tale** (1993) *Edgar nominee* ☆
- ❏ 3 - The Outlaw's Tale (1994)
- ❏ 4 - The Bishop's Tale (1994)

Mickey Friedman is the creator of a mystery series featuring American expatriate journalist Georgia Lee Maxwell who lives in Paris.

Georgia Lee Maxwell . . . Paris-based freelance writer

- ❏ 1 - Magic Mirror (1988)
- ❏ 2 - A Temporary Ghost (1989)

Margot J. Fromer, of Silver Spring, Maryland brings her medical background to the mysteries she has written with protagonist Amanda Knight, a hospital director of nursing.

Amanda Knight . . . hospital director of nursing

- ❏ 1 - Scalpel's Edge (1991)
- ❏ 2 - Night Shift (1993)

Frances Fyfield is the pseudonym of Frances Hegarty, a solicitor specializing in criminal law and creator of two British legal series. The longer series features London Crown Prosecutor Helen West and Detective Superintendent Geoffrey Bailey whose first outing was nominated for both an Edgar and Anthony. The shorter series features Sarah Fortune, solicitor with a prestigious British firm. Under her own name, Hegarty has also written several psychological novels.

Helen West . . . London Crown Prosecutor
- ❑ 1 - **A Question of Guilt** (1988) *Anthony & Edgar nominee* ☆
- ❑ 2 - Not That Kind of Place (1990)
- ❑ 3 - Deep Sleep (1991)
- ❑ 4 - Shadow Play (1993)

Sarah Fortune . . . lawyer in prestigious British firm
- ❑ 1 - Shadows on the Mirror (1989)
- ❑ 2 - Perfectly Pure and Good (1994)

Susan Geason is the creator of a new mystery series set in Sydney, Australia featuring private investigator Syd Fish.

Syd Fish . . . Sydney, Australia P.I.
- ❑ 1 - Shaved Fish (1993)
- ❑ 2 - Dogfish (1993)
- ❑ 3 - Sharkbait (1993)

Elizabeth George, born in Warren, Ohio, received degrees in English and counseling from universities in southern California where she now resides. Her best-selling series features Scotland Yard Inspector and eighth earl of Asherton Thomas Lynley and his working class partner Sergeant Barbara Havers. The supporting cast also includes forensic pathologist Simon Allcourt-St. James, his photographer wife Deborah and his laboratory assistant Lady Helen Clyde. The first installment in this intense psychological series won both the Anthony and Agatha awards for best first novel in 1988. The book also received nominations for the Edgar and Macavity awards that year.

Thomas Lynley & Barbara Havers . . . Scotland Yard inspector & detective sergeant
- ❑ 1 - **A Great Deliverance** (1988) *Agatha & Anthony winner* ★ *Edgar & Macavity nominee* ☆
- ❑ 2 - Payment in Blood (1989)
- ❑ 3 - Well-Schooled in Murder (1990)
- ❑ 4 - A Suitable Vengeance (1991)
- ❑ 5 - For the Sake of Elena (1992)
- ❑ 6 - Missing Joseph (1993)
- ❑ 7 - Playing for the Ashes (1994)

Dorothy Gilman wrote a dozen children's books under her married name of Dorothy Gilman Butters before launching her series featuring the CIA's most unlikely agent, New Jersey grandmother Emily Pollifax. Mrs. Pollifax travels the globe narrowly escaping danger, often one quick step ahead of her pursuers. In addition to the Mrs. Pollifax titles, Gilman has written five other novels of adventure and suspense along with numerous short stories. She has also been a teacher of drawing and creative writing.

Mrs. Pollifax . . . New Jersey grandmother & CIA agent

- ❏   1 - The Unexpected Mrs. Pollifax (1966)
- ❏   2 - The Amazing Mrs. Pollifax (1970)
- ❏   3 - The Elusive Mrs. Pollifax (1971)
- ❏   4 - A Palm for Mrs. Pollifax (1973)
- ❏   5 - Mrs. P   n Safari (1976)
- ❏   6 - Mrs. Pollifax on the China Station (1983)
- ❏   7 - Mrs. Pollifax and the Hong Kong Buddha (1985)
- ❏   8 - Mrs. Pollifax and the Golden Triangle (1988)
- ❏   9 - Mrs. Pollifax and the Whirling Dervish (1990)
- ❏ 10 - Mrs. Pollifax and the Second Thief (1993)
- ❏ 11 - Mrs. Pollifax Pursued (1995)

Noreen Gilpatrick is the creator of a new police series featuring Seattle police detective Kate McLean. Prior to starting her mystery writing career, Gilpatrick worked in both the print and broadcast media, including a stint on the staff of *Psychology Today*. She once owned her own advertising agency in Seattle and lived on an island in Puget Sound. Her first novel (*The Piano Man*) won the Malice Domestic award for best first traditional mystery.

Kate McLean . . . Seattle, Washington police detective

- ❏   1 - Final Design (1993)

Jaqueline Girdner lives in Marin County, California where she has been a psychiatric aide, a family law attorney and entrepreneur, before launching her mystery series featuring Kate Jasper, gag gift wholesaler.

Kate Jasper . . . Marin County, California gag gift wholesaler

- ❏   1 - Adjusted to Death (1991)
- ❏   2 - The Last Resort (1991)
- ❏   3 - Murder Most Mellow (1992)
- ❏   4 - Fat-Free and Fatal (1993)
- ❏   5 - Tea-Totally Dead (1994)
- ❏   6 - A Stiff Critique (1995)

E. X. Giroux is the pseudonym of Canadian author Doris Shannon for her English mystery series featuring barrister Robert Forsythe and his secretary Abigail Sanderson who sometimes does the larger share of detecting in their partnership. Giroux lives in British Columbia, not far from the Washington State border.

Robert Forsythe & Abigail Sanderson . . . London barrister & his secretary
- ❏ 1 - A Death for Adonis (1984)
- ❏ 2 - A Death for a Darling (1985)
- ❏ 3 - A Death for a Dancer (1986)
- ❏ 4 - A Death for a Doctor (1986)
- ❏ 5 - A Death for a Dilletante (1987)
- ❏ 6 - A Death for a Dietician (1988)
- ❏ 7 - A Death for a Dreamer (1989)
- ❏ 8 - A Death for a Double (1990)
- ❏ 9 - A Death for a Dancing Doll (1991)
- ❏ 10 - A Death for a Dodo (1993)

Leslie Glass, playwright and author of three previous non-series novels, is the creator of a new series featuring police detective April Woo of the NYPD. The opening installment has been described as a police procedural with the insights of an analyst's couch. Glass is actively involved with a number of forensic and psychologic projects as an advisor to the John Jay College of Criminal Justice. The married mother of two teenagers divides her time among New York City, Martha's Vineyard and Sarasota, Florida.

April Woo . . . New York City police detective
- ❏ 1 - Burning Time (1993)
- ❏ 2 - Hanging Time (1994)

Alison Glen is the shared pseudonym used by writing partners Cheryl Meredith Lowry and Louise Vetter of Columbus, Ohio, for their new series featuring Columbus freelance writer Charlotte Sams.

Charlotte Sams . . . Columbus, Ohio freelance writer
- ❏ 1 - Showcase (1992)
- ❏ 2 - Trunk Show (1995)

Alison Gordon was the first woman journalist to cover major league baseball when she wrote about the Toronto Blue Jays during the 1980s. It's no surprise that her woman sleuth is sportswriter Kate Henry who covers the fictional Toronto Titans. If you like to read about writers at work, you'll enjoy this series. If you're also a baseball fan, you'll be in heaven.

Kate Henry . . . Toronto, Canada baseball newswriter

- ❏ 1 - The Dead Pull Hitter (1989)
- ❏ 2 - Safe at Home (1991)
- ❏ 3 - Night Game (1993)

Paula Gosling was born and raised in Detroit where she worked in advertising before moving to England and writing *A Running Duck* (renamed *Fair Game* in the U.S.) which won the Creasey award for best first novel and was later made into the Sylvester Stallone film *Cobra*. The first title in the Jack Stryker and Kate Trevorne series, set in the American Midwest, was awarded the coveted Gold Dagger for best novel in 1985. Three years later Gosling became chairman of the British Crime Writers Association, a title previously held by Lady Antonia Fraser and Simon Brett. Gosling's 1994 title *A Few Dying Words* returns to Blackwater Bay (the setting of Jack and Kate's previous outing) but features different characters. The Great Lakes setting will likely continue as the venue for other Blackwater Bay mysteries.

Jack Stryker & Kate Trevorne . . . Ohio homicide cop & English professor

- ❏ 1 - **Monkey Puzzle** (1985) *Gold Dagger winner* ★
- ❏ 2 - Backlash (1989)
- ❏ 3 - The Body in Blackwater Bay (1992)

Blackwater Bay mystery . . . police series with a Great Lakes setting

- ❏ 1 - A Few Dying Words (1994)

Luke Abbott . . . English cop

- ❏ 1 - The Wychford Murders (1986)
- ❏ 2 - Death Penalties (1991)

Sue Grafton is the creator of the Kinsey Millhone series, often referred to as the alphabet mysteries. The series was launched in 1982 with the second title following in 1985. Grafton has added a book a year ever since, typically in early May to celebrate Kinsey's birthday. The daughter of mystery writer C.W. Grafton, she has also written a number of screenplays.

Along with Sara Paretsky and Marcia Muller, Grafton is widely recognized as one of the Big Three in contemporary P.I. fiction. Together with their characters, these three writers revolutionized crime fiction in the 1980s. Grafton has been awarded four Anthonys and a Shamus for her Kinsey novels.

Kinsey Millhone . . . Santa Teresa, California ex-cop P.I.

- ❏ 1 - **"A" is for Alibi** (1982) *Anthony winner* ★
- ❏ 2 - **"B" is for Burglar** (1985) *Anthony & Shamus winner* ★
- ❏ 3 - **"C" is for Corpse** (1986) *Anthony winner* ★
- ❏ 4 - "D" is for Deadbeat (1987)
- ❏ 5 - "E" is for Evidence (1988)

❑   6 - "F" is for Fugitive (1989)
❑   7 - **"G" is for Gumshoe** (1990) *Anthony winner* ★
❑   8 - "H" is for Homicide (1991)
❑   9 - **"I" is for Innocent** (1992) *American Mystery Award winner* ★
❑ 10 - "J" is for Judgment (1993)
❑ 11 - "K" is for Killer (1994)

☑ 12   *L is for Lawless*

Caroline Graham, of Birmingham, England, is the creator of the police series featuring Chief Inspector Tom Barnaby whose first outing was awarded a Macavity for best first mystery. Graham is also a playwright with experience in both stage and television and the author of several children's books.

Tom Barnaby . . . chief inspector

❑ 1 - **The Killings at Badger's Drift** (1987) *Macavity winner* ★
❑ 2 - Death of a Hollow Man (1989)
❑ 3 - Death in Disguise (1993)

Ann Granger lives in Bicester, England near the city of Oxford and has worked in the diplomatic service in various parts of the world, much like her series protagonist, foreign service officer Meredith Mitchell. The series cast prominently features Chief Inspector Alan Markby who would like nothing better than to see Meredith retire from the service and join him in the Cotswolds.

Meredith Mitchell . . . British Foreign Service officer

❑ 1 - Say it with Poison (1991)
❑ 2 - A Season for Murder (1992)
❑ 3 - Cold in the Earth (1993)
❑ 4 - Murder Among Us (1993)
❑ 5 - Where Old Bones Lie (1994)

Linda Grant is the creator of San Francisco P.I. Catherine Sayler, corporate crime specialist. Catherine's assistant Jesse, the young computer whiz who later becomes her partner, adds a convincing technical dimension to their cases. The third installment of this Anthony-nominated series is a not-to-be-missed case of sexual harassment that turns to murder. Grant is a past president of Sisters in Crime.

Catherine Sayler . . . San Francisco, California private investigator

❑ 1 - **Random Access Murder** (1988) *Anthony nominee* ☆
❑ 2 - Blind Trust (1990)
❑ 3 - **Love Nor Money** (1991) *Anthony nominee* ☆
❑ 4 - A Woman's Place (1994)

Lesley Grant-Adamson is the author of two mystery series set in London. One features reporter Rain Morgan; the other showcases P.I. Laura Flynn. The author has been a feature writer on the *Guardian*, one of England's leading national newspapers and a freelance writer of television documentaries and fiction.

Laura Flynn . . . London private investigator
- ❏ 1 - Too Many Questions (1991)
- ❏ 2 - The Dangerous Edge (1994)

Rain Morgan . . . newspaper reporter in London
- ❏ 1 - Death on Widow's Walk (1985)
- ❏ 2 - The Face of Death (1985)
- ❏ 3 - Guilty Knowledge (1986)
- ❏ 4 - Wild Justice (1987)
- ❏ 5 - Threatening Eye (1988)
- ❏ 6 - Curse the Darkness (1990)

Gallagher Gray is the pseudonym of Katy Munger, a North Carolina native and graduate of the University of North Carolina at Chapel Hill. She once worked in the personnel department of a private bank on Wall Street. She is now a New York-based writer and creator of the mystery series featuring 50-something T. S. Hubbert and his 80-something Aunt Lil, a former dress designer. Recently retired after 35 years in personnel with a New York City law firm, T. S. is drafted as a sleuthing partner by the feisty Lillian, who is determined that her nephew give up his new-found habit of watching TV soap operas.

T. S. Hubbert & Auntie Lil . . . New York City retired human resources manager & his dress designer aunt
- ❏ 1 - Partners in Crime (1991)
- ❏ 2 - A Cast of Killers (1992)

Christine Green is the creator of a new English mystery series featuring nurse and medical investigator Kate Kinsella and an even newer series featuring a boozy Irishman and young, new policewoman.

Kate Kinsella . . . British nurse & medical investigator
- ❏ 1 - Deadly Errand (1991)
- ❏ 2 - Deadly Admirer (1992)

Boozy Irishman & new policewoman
- ❏ 1 - Death in the Country (1994)

Kate Green teaches a graduate course in writing at Hamline University and is a published poet and the author of six children's books, including *Fossil Family Tales* and *A Number of Animals*, her collaboration with British engraver Christopher Wormell. She is the creator of professional psychic Theresa Fortunato who assists LAPD homicide detective Oliver Jardino in the Edgar-nominated *Shattered Moon*. The second installment of this series, *Black Dreams*, received the 1993 Minnesota Book Award. Green has also written two non-series mystery-suspense thrillers—*Night Angel* and *Shooting Star*. Her undergraduate degree is from the University of Minnesota and her MA is from Boston University.

> **Theresa Fortunato & Oliver Jardino** . . . professional psychic & LAPD detective
> ❑   1 - **Shattered Moon** (1986) *Edgar nominee* ☆
> ❑   2 - Black Dreams (1993)

Diane M. Greenwood, who describes herself as an ecclesiastical civil servant, is the creator of a mystery series featuring the Reverend Theodora Braithwaite, British deaconess. The author holds degrees from Oxford (classics) and London University (theology) and works for the diocese of Rochester in Greenwich, England.

> **Rev. Theodora Braithwaite** . . . British deaconess
> ❑   1 - Clerical Errors (1991)
> ❑   2 - Unholy Ghosts (1992)
> ❑   3 - Idol Bones (1993)

Kerry Greenwood is the creator of a series set in 1920s Australia featuring investigator Phryne Fisher.

> **Phryne Fisher** . . . 1920s Australian sleuth
> ❑   1 - Deathly Misadventure (1989) [aka Cocaine Blues]
> ❑   2 - Flying Too High (1991)
> ❑   3 - Murder on the Ballarat Train (1993)

Martha Grimes, a native of Garrett County Maryland, writes a popular mystery series featuring Inspector Richard Jury, an English police detective. She earned both her BA and MA degrees from the University of Maryland and teaches English at Montgomery College in Tacoma Park, Maryland. She occasionally teaches detective fiction at Johns Hopkins and makes an annual visit to England for book research. Her 1992 novel *End of the Pier* is a non-series mystery set in the U.S.

> **Inspector Richard Jury** . . . Scotland Yard investigator
> ❑   1 - The Man with a Load of Mischief (1981)
> ❑   2 - The Old Fox Deceived (1982)
> ❑   3 - The Anondyne Necklace (1983)

    ❏   4 - The Dirty Duck (1984)
    ❏   5 - Jerusalem Inn (1984)
    ❏   6 - Help the Poor Struggler (1985)
    ❏   7 - The Deer Leap (1985)
    ❏   8 - I am the Only Running Footman (1986)
    ❏   9 - The Five Bells and Bladebone (1987)
    ❏ 10 - The Old Silent (1989)
    ❏ 11 - The Old Contemptibles (1990)

Lucretia Grindle is the creator of a new English mystery series featuring Detective Superintendent Inspector H. W. Ross.

Inspector H. W. Ross . . . detective superintendent in England

    ❏   1 - The Killing of Ellis Martin (1993)
    ❏   2 - So Little to Die For (1994)

Sally Gunning, who lives and works on Cape Cod, is the creator of the Peter Bartholomew series set on Nashtoba Island, Massachusetts.

Peter Bartholomew . . . Massachusetts small business owner

    ❏   1 - Hot Water (1990)
    ❏   2 - Under Water (1992)
    ❏   3 - Ice Water (1993)
    ❏   4 - Troubled Water (1993)
    ❏   5 - Rough Water (1994)

Carolyn A. Haddad lives in the Chicago suburbs and is the creator of Becky Belski, a Chicago computer investigator. Haddad is also the author of four earlier novels.

Becky Belski . . . Chicago, Illinois computer investigator

    ❏   1 - Caught in the Shadows (1992)

Jane Haddam (rhymes with Adam) is the pseudonym used by Orania Papazoglou for her holiday series featuring retired FBI agent Gregor Demarkian. Under the Papazoglou name she is also the creator of a series featuring Patience Campbell McKenna—romance novelist turned crime writer. Before turning to mystery writing Papazoglou was editor of *Greek Accent* magazine and freelanced for *Glamour*, *Mademoiselle* and *Working Woman*. She also wrote two psychological thrillers under the Papazoglou name, but remains best known for her work as Jane Haddam which has been nominated for an Edgar and an Anthony.

Gregor Demarkian . . . Philadelphia, Pennsylvania former FBI department head

- ❑ 1 - **Not a Creature was Stirring** (1990) *Edgar & Anthony nominee* ☆
- ❑ 2 - Precious Blood (1991)
- ❑ 3 - Act of Darkness (1991)
- ❑ 4 - Quoth the Raven (1991)
- ❑ 5 - A Great Day for the Deadly (1992)
- ❑ 6 - Feast of Murder (1992)
- ❑ 7 - A Stillness in Bethlehem (1992)
- ❑ 8 - Murder Superior (1993)
- ❑ 9 - Festival of Deaths (1993)
- ❑ 10 - Bleeding Hearts (1994)

Lisa Haddock is the creator of a new mystery series featuring newspaper copy editor Carmen Ramirez.

Carmen Ramirez . . . newspaper copy editor

- ❑ 1 - Edited Out (1994)

Jean Hager is the creator of two mystery series about contemporary Cherokee life in Oklahoma. The Mitch Bushyhead series features a half-Cherokee police chief who grew up and married outside the tribe. After his wife's death he has to cope with raising his teenage daughter alone. The second Cherokee series features Molly Bearpaw, civil rights investigator for the Native American Advocacy Council.

Hager's newest series features Tess Darcy, proprietor of Iris House, an elegant bed and breakfast in Victoria Springs, Missouri.

Mitch Bushyhead . . . Buckskin, Oklahoma police chief of Cherokee descent

- ❑ 1 - The Grandfather Medicine (1989)
- ❑ 2 - Night Walker (1990)
- ❑ 3 - Ghostland (1992)

Molly Bearpaw . . . Oklahoma Cherokee civil rights investigator

- ❑ 1 - Ravenmocker (1992)
- ❑ 2 - The Redbird's Cry (1994)

Tess Darcy . . . Ozarks bed & breakfast

- ❑ 1 - Blooming Murder (1994)

Mary Bowen Hall once described her series featuring the fiercely independent part-time salvage dealer Emma Chizzit as "California cozies." Before her death in 1994, Hall made a significant contribution to the field with her ambitious survey on women protagonists in mystery fiction, jointly sponsored by Sisters in Crime and the National Women's History Project.

Emma Chizzit . . . Sacramento, California salvage dealer
- ❑ 1 - Emma Chizzit and the Queen Anne Killer (1989)
- ❑ 2 - Emma Chizzit and the Sacramento Stalker (1990)
- ❑ 3 - Emma Chizzit and the Napa Nemesis (1992)
- ❑ 4 - Emma Chizzit and the Mother Lode Marauder (1993)

Patricia Hall is the creator of a new British police series featuring Inspector Alex Sinclair and social worker Kate Weston.

Alex Sinclair & Kate Weston . . . British Inspector & social worker
- ❑ 1 - The Poison Pool (1993)

Mollie Hardwick is the creator of Doran Fairweather, owner of an antiques business and close personal friend of local vicar Rodney Chelmarsh, who has a quote from literature or Scripture for absolutely everything. Art, antiques, religion and literature figure prominently in these perfect cozies. Hardwick also writes historical novels and is best known for her *Upstairs, Downstairs* series brought to life on public television.

Doran Fairweather . . . British antiques dealer
- ❑ 1 - Malice Domestic (1986)
- ❑ 2 - Parson's Pleasure (1987)
- ❑ 3 - Uneaseful Death (1988)
- ❑ 4 - The Bandersnatch (1989)
- ❑ 5 - Perish in July (1989)
- ❑ 6 - The Dreaming Damozel (1990)

Charlaine Harris is the author of the Aurora "Roe" Teagarden series featuring a 20-something librarian whose first adventure was nominated for an Agatha. In later installments Roe joins her mother's real estate firm and tries her hand at selling houses. Harris has written several non-series mysteries which are also set in the South with strong independent women protagonists.

Aurora Teagarden . . . Georgia librarian turned real estate agent
- ❑ 1 - **Real Murders** (1990) *Agatha nominee* ☆
- ❑ 2 - A Bone to Pick (1992)
- ❑ 3 - Three Bedrooms, One Corpse (1994)
- ❑ 4 - The Julius House (1995)

Lee Harris is the pseudonymous author of the Edgar-nominated mystery series featuring New Yorker Christine Bennett, a former nun. Each title represents a holiday murder, typically one involving the church.

Christine Bennett . . . New York ex-nun

- ❏ 1 - **The Good Friday Murder** (1992) *Edgar nominee* ☆
- ❏ 2 - The Yom Kippur Murder (1992)
- ❏ 3 - The Christening Day Murder (1993)
- ❏ 4 - The St. Patrick's Day Murder (1994)
- ❏ 5 - The Christmas Night Murder (1994)

Cynthia Harrod-Eagles, well-known British historical novelist, was born in London and studied at the University of Edinburgh and University College, London, where she received her BA in English. Before launching her police series featuring Detective Inspector Bill Slider, she wrote more than 30 historical and fantasy novels. Her passions are music, gardening, history, horses, architecture and the English countryside. In addition to her writing, she finds time to play in several amateur orchestras.

Bill Slider . . . detective inspector in England

- ❏ 1 - Orchestrated Death (1991)
- ❏ 2 - Death Watch (1992)
- ❏ 3 - Death To Go (1994)

Carolyn G. Hart is perhaps best known for her Death on Demand series featuring South Carolina mystery bookstore owner Annie Laurance and her sleuthing partner Max Darling. This series often features mystery writing heroes of the past and has won a virtual trophy case of awards. Hart has also introduced a series featuring veteran Oklahoma journalist Henrietta O'Dwyer Collins, known to her friends as Henrie O. In addition to her adult mystery series, Hart has written five juvenile mysteries and numerous short stories. She is a former assistant professor of professional writing at the University of Oklahoma and a past president of Sisters in Crime.

Annie Laurance & Max Darling . . . South Carolina bookstore owner & investigator

- ❏ 1 - **Death on Demand** (1987) *Anthony & Macavity nominee* ☆
- ❏ 2 - Design for Murder (1987)
- ❏ 3 - **Something Wicked** (1988) *Agatha & Anthony winner* ★
- ☑ 4 - **Honeymoon with Murder** (1988) *Anthony winner* ★
- ☑ 5 - **A Little Class on Murder** (1989) *Agatha & Anthony nominee* ☆
  Macavity winner ★
- ❏ 6 - **Deadly Valentine** (1990) *Agatha & Macavity nominee* ☆
- ☑ 7 - **The Christie Caper** (1991) *Anthony & Macavity nominee* ☆
- ❏ 8 - **Southern Ghost** (1992) *Agatha & Anthony nominee* ☆
- ☑ 9 - The Mint Julep Murder (1995)

Henrietta O'Dwyer Collins . . . South Carolina 70-something reporter

- ☑ 1 - **Dead Man's Island** (1993) *Agatha winner* ★
- ❏ 2 - Scandal in Fair Haven (1994)

Ellen Hart claims that her twelve years as a sorority house kitchen manager at the University of Minnesota were more than sufficient inspiration to commit murder—but strictly on paper. She is the author of the Jane Lawless series featuring a lesbian Minneapolis restaurant owner and her college friend Cordelia Thorn, artistic director of a St. Paul theatre. Jane's father, prominent criminal attorney Raymond Lawless, is a continuing cast member whose influence changes along with the story. Hart recently introduced a new series featuring Sophie Greenway, magazine editor and part-time food critic for a Minneapolis newspaper, married to Bram Baldric, Minneapolis radio talk-show host.

Jane Lawless . . . Minnesota lesbian restaurateur

- ❏ 1 - Hallowed Murder (1989)
- ❏ 2 - Vital Lies (1991)
- ❏ 3 - Stage Fright (1992)
- ❏ 4 - A Killing Cure (1993)
- ❏ 5 - A Small Sacrifice (1994)

Sophie Greenway . . . magazine editor and food critic for Minneapolis newspaper

- ❏ 1 - This Little Piggy Went to Murder (1994)

Jeanne Hart is the creator of a mystery trilogy featuring homicide detective Carl Pedersen and his wife Freda of fictional Bay Cove (read Santa Cruz), California. *Fetish*, which earned a Macavity nomination for best first mystery, tells the story of three single, middle-aged women whose lives are changed after they run a local newspaper ad seeking a shared escort. Following the author's sudden death in the summer of 1990, family friend and mystery writer Lia Matera prepared Hart's last completed manuscript for publication.

Carl & Freda Pedersen . . . California police lieutenant & wife

- ❏ 1 - **Fetish** (1980s) *Macavity nominee* ☆
- ❏ 2 - Some Die Young (1980s)
- ❏ 3 - Threnody for Two (1991)

Gini Hartzmark attended the law and business schools of the University of Chicago and wrote business and economics textbooks before turning to novel writing. She also wrote articles on a variety of topics for Chicago newspapers and national magazines. Her Edgar-nominated series features Katherine Prescott Milholland, a Chicago attorney specializing in mergers and acquisitions. Hartzmark currently lives in Arizona.

> **Katherine Prescott Milholland** . . . Chicago, Illinois corporate attorney
> - ❏ 1 - **Principal Defense** (1992) *Edgar nominee* ☆
> - ❏ 2 - Final Option (1994)

S. T. Haymon was born in Norwich, England and lives in London where she writes the critically-acclaimed police series featuring Benjamin Jurnet. The *Washington Post* has said "it can only be a matter of time before the critics discover S. T. Haymon and recognize a serious novelist who just happens to write mysteries." She is often mentioned along with other British greats Dorothy Sayers, P.D. James and Martha Grimes.

> **Benjamin Jurnet** . . . detective inspector in England
> - ❏ 1 - Death and the Pregnant Virgin (1980)
> - ❏ 2 - **Ritual Murder** (1982) *Silver Dagger winner* ★
> - ❏ 3 - Stately Homicide (1984)
> - ❏ 4 - Death of a God (1987)
> - ❏ 5 - A Very Particular Murder (1989)
> - ❏ 6 - Death of a Warrior Queen (1991)
> - ❏ 7 - A Beautiful Death (1994)

Sparkle Hayter is the creator of a new mystery series featuring Robin Hudson, a New York City cable news reporter.

> **Robin Hudson** . . . New York City cable news reporter
> - ❏ 1 - What's a Girl Gotta Do (1994)

Louise Hendrickson, who worked in the medical field prior to writing full time, shares her keen interest in forensic science with her protagonist, Dr. Amy Prescott of the Western Washington Crime Laboratory in Seattle. Amy's father, who sometimes consults with her on unusual cases, is the medical examiner on one of the islands in Puget Sound. Hendrickson lives with her husband Gene in Renton, Washington. They are the parents of three grown children.

> **Amy Prescott** . . . Seattle, Washington crime lab physician
> - ❏ 1 - With Deadly Intent (1993)
> - ❏ 2 - Grave Secrets (1994)

Sue Henry lives and writes in Anchorage, Alaska, which is the setting for her mystery series featuring Alaska State Trooper Alex Jensen and his musher friend Jessie Arnold. Their first adventure was the winner of both the Anthony and Macavity for best first novel in 1991. Henry is the current editor of *Books-in-Print* for Sisters in Crime.

Jessie Arnold & Sgt. Alex Jensen . . . Anchorage, Alaska sled dog racer & trooper

❏ 1 - **Murder on the Iditarod Trail** (1991) *Anthony & Macavity winner* ★
❏ 2 - Termination Dust (1995)

Joan Hess is the creator of two popular series detectives who live and work in small Arkansas towns. Arly Hanks, police chief of Maggody, heads a cast of vintage Southern characters, including the good old boy who watches TV with his pet pig. The second series features Claire Malloy, bookstore owner in a small college town, and the mother of an annoying teenage daughter. Under the name Joan Hadley, Hess also wrote two novels featuring Theo Bloomer, a plant-loving retiree with a nose for crime detection—*Night-Blooming Cereus* (1986) and *Deadly Ackee* (1990).

Arly Hanks . . . small-town Arkansas police chief

❏ 1 - Malice in Maggody (1987)
☑ 2 - Mischief in Maggody (1988)
❏ 3 - Much Ado in Maggody (1989)
❏ 4 - Mortal Remains in Maggody (1991)
❏ 5 - Madness in Maggody (1991)
❏ 6 - Maggody in Manhattan (1992)
❏ 7 - **O Little Town of Maggody** (1993) *Agatha & Anthony nominee* ☆
❏ 8 - Martians in Maggody (1994)

Claire Malloy . . . small-town bookstore owner

❏ 1 - **Strangled Prose** (1986) *Anthony nominee* ☆
NO ❏ 2 - The Murder at the Murder at the Mimosa Inn (1986)
❏ 3 - Dear Miss Demeanor (1987)
❏ 4 - A Really Cute Corpse (1988)
❏ 5 - **A Diet to Die For** (1989) *American Mystery Award winner* ★
❏ 6 - Roll Over and Play Dead (1991)
❏ 7 - Death by the Light of the Moon (1992)
❏ 8 - Poisoned Pins (1993)
❏ 9 - Tickled to Death (1994)

Patricia Highsmith was born in Texas and educated in New York, although she has lived much of her life in Switzerland. She is the author of suspense classic *Stranger on a Train* (made famous by Alfred Hitchcock) and several highly acclaimed short story collections, including *The Animal Lover's Book of Beastly Murder*. In the early 1950s she wrote a novel about lesbian relationships (*The Price of Salt*) under the pseudonym Claire Morgan.

Her series featuring the charming and successful forger-impersonator Tom Ripley began in 1955 and continues today. Highsmith was awarded a Silver Dagger for *Two Faces of January* in 1964 and has also received the O. Henry Memorial Award and Le Grand Prix de Litterature Policiere. While the *New Yorker* called her novels "peerlessly disturbing," Gore Vidal said "she is certainly one of the most interesting writers of this dismal century."

Tom Ripley . . . charming forger & psychopath in England

- ❏   1 - The Talented Mr. Ripley (1955)
- ❏   2 - Ripley Underground (1970)
- ❏   3 - Ripley's Game (1974)
- ❏   4 - The Boy Who Followed Ripley (1980)
- ❏   5 - Ripley Under Water (1992)

Lynn S. Hightower was born in Chattanooga, Tennessee and currently lives in the South where she works full-time writing fiction. She is the author of *Alien Blues* and *Alien Eyes*, futuristic police procedurals and *Satan's Lambs*, which received a Shamus award for best first P.I. novel and was chosen by the Literary Guild as an alternate selection. Her 1995 suspense thriller *Flashpoint* will feature both a female cop and a female killer.

Lena Padget . . . Lexington, Kentucky P.I.

- ❏   1 - **Satan's Lambs** (1993) *Shamus winner* ★

Sonora Blair . . . homicide detective in Cincinnati, Ohio

- ❏   1 - Flashpoint (1995)

Isabelle Holland is the creator of a mystery series featuring the Reverend Claire Aldington, psychologist and priest at St. Anselm's Episcopal Church in Manhattan—a wealthy congregation in an inner-city neighborhood. The Rev. Aldington is also a widow with a problem teenage stepdaughter.

Rev. Claire Aldington . . . New York Episcopal priest

- ❏   1 - The Lost Madonna (1983)
- ❏   2 - A Death at St. Anselm's (1984)
- ❏   3 - Flight of the Archangel (1985)
- ❏   4 - A Lover Scorned (1986)
- ❏   5 - A Fatal Advent (1989)
- ❏   6 - The Long Search (1990)

Gerelyn Hollingsworth is the creator of a new mystery series featuring Kansas City P.I. Frances Finn.

Frances Finn . . . Kansas City P.I.

- ❏   1 - Murder at St. Adelaide's (1994)

Hazel Holt

Hazel Holt lives in Somerset, England and is the creator of the Mrs. Malory series featuring a 50-something widowed literary magazine writer from the village of Taviscombe. Her son is the writer Tom Holt.

Sheila Malory . . . British literary magazine writer in English small town

- ❑ 1 - Mrs. Malory Investigates (1989) [Britain–Gone Away]
- ❑ 2 - The Cruellest Month (1991)
- ❑ 3 - Mrs. Malory and the Festival Murders (1993)
- ❑ 4 - The Shortest Journey (1994)
- ❑ 5 - Mrs. Malory Detective in Residence (1994)

Susan Holtzer

Susan Holtzer spent most of her life in Ann Arbor, Michigan, the setting for *Something To Kill For*, which won the St. Martin's Press award for best first traditional mystery. Holtzer, who now lives in San Francisco, earned her MA degree in journalism from the University of Michigan, where she also worked on *The Michigan Daily* during her undergraduate days.

Anneke Haagen . . . Ann Arbor, Michigan computer consultant

- ❑ 1 - **Something to Kill For** (1994) *Malice Domestic & SMP winner* ★
- ❑ 2 - Curly Smoke (1995)

Kay Hooper

Kay Hooper is the creator of an Atlanta series featuring Lane Montana, a finder of lost things and Trey Fortier, homicide detective. Their supporting cast includes Lane's artist twin brother and her Siamese cat Choo. In the second outing she takes the lieutenant to meet her family and an unscheduled murder takes center stage at the reunion.

Lane Montana & Trey Fortier . . . finder of lost things & Atlanta homicide detective

- ❑ 1 - Crime of Passion (1991)
- ❑ 2 - House of Cards (1991)

Ruby Horansky

Ruby Horansky is the creator of a new mystery series featuring NYPD homicide detective Nikki Trakos.

Nikki Trakos . . . New York City homicide detective

- ❑ 1 - Dead Ahead (1990)
- ❑ 2 - Dead Center (1994)

Wendy Hornsby, a southern California native with graduate degrees in ancient and medieval history, teaches history at California State University at Long Beach. Her earlier mystery series features history professor Kate Teague and homicide detective Roger Tejeda. The more recent Maggie MacGowen series stars a documentary film maker with a teenage daughter, a stalwart neighbor and a handsome homicide detective with his teenage son.

Kate Teague & Roger Tejeda . . . southern California college professor & homicide detective

- ❏ 1 - No Harm (1987)
- ❏ 2 - Half a Mind (1990)

Maggie MacGowen . . . California investigative film maker

- ❏ 1 - Telling Lies (1992)
- ❏ 2 - Midnight Baby (1993)
- ❏ 3 - Bad Intent (1994)

Melodie Johnson Howe is a Los Angeles native who dreamed of becoming a movie star and novelist. After attending Stephens College in Columbia, Missouri and the University of Southern California, she was discovered by Universal Studios and signed her first acting contract. While working in television, movies and commercials, she studied writing at UCLA and produced her first novel, which was nominated for three mystery awards as best first novel.

Claire Conrad & Maggie Hill . . . California P.I. & secretary

- ❏ 1 - **The Mother Shadow** (1989) *Agatha, Anthony & Edgar nominee* ☆
- ❏ 2 - Beauty Dies (1994)

Marian J. A. Jackson is the creator a mystery series set in the early 1900s, featuring American heiress Abigail Patience Danforth, who wants to become the world's first female consulting detective. She asks the advice of Sir Arthur Conan Doyle who is less than enthusiastic about her plans. Much of the first installment takes place in England, but the second finds Abigail in the American West.

Abigail Patience Danforth . . . 19th century consulting detective

- ❏ 1 - The Punjat's Ruby (1990)
- ❏ 2 - The American Pearl (1990)
- ❏ 3 - Cat's Eye (1991)
- ❏ 4 - Diamond Head (1992)
- ❏ 5 - The Sunken Treasure (1994)

Muriel Resnick Jackson is the creator of a new mystery series featuring Merrie Lee Spencer, former New Yorker transplanted to North Carolina.

> **Merrie Lee Spencer** . . . ex-New Yorker in North Carolina
> ❏   1 - The Garden Club (1992)

Jonnie Jacobs was a high school English teacher and counselor, and later an attorney with a large San Francisco law firm before writing her first mystery featuring amateur sleuth and housewife Kate Austen. She has two titles scheduled for release in 1995—the second installment of Kate Austen and the first in a new series featuring attorney Kali O'Brien. Jacobs lives with her husband and two sons near San Francisco where she is an active member of Mystery Writers of America and Sisters in Crime.

> **Kate Austen** . . . Bay area single mother in Walnut Hills, California
> ❏   1 - Murder Among Neighbors (1994)

Nancy Baker Jacobs is a former working private eye and author of four suspense novels, six non-fiction books, and a mystery series featuring Minneapolis P.I. Devon MacDonald. Three of Jacob's suspense titles have been optioned for motion pictures.

> **Devon MacDonald** . . . Minnesota ex-teacher P.I.
> ❏   1 - The Turquoise Tattoo (1991)
> ❏   2 - A Slash of Scarlett (1992)
> ❏   3 - The Silver Scalpel (1993)

P. D. James is Phyllis Dorothy James White, who spent 30 years in British Civil Service, including the Police and Criminal Law Departments of the Home Office. She is the recipient of numerous prizes and honors, including the Order of the British Empire and three Silver Daggers, in addition to a Diamond Dagger for lifetime achievement. Six of her novels have been filmed and broadcast on British and American television. She has served as a magistrate and governor of the BBC.

Her well-known series characters are police commander and published poet Adam Dalgleish and Cordelia Gray, who each make appearances in the other's books. Cordelia is introduced in 1972 when she inherits a private enquiry firm from her former partner (*An Unsuitable Job for a Woman*). The book was hailed at the time as a landmark for no-nonsense women investigators.

> **Adam Dalgleish** . . . published poet of Scotland Yard
> ❏   1 - Cover Her Face (1962)
> ❏   2 - A Mind to Murder (1963)
> ❏   3 - Unnatural Causes (1967)

- ❏ 4 - Shroud for a Nightingale (1971)
- ❏ 5 - The Black Tower (1975)
- ❏ 6 - Death of an Expert Witness (1977)
- ❏ 7 - Devices and Desires (1982)
- ❏ 8 - **A Taste for Death** (1986) *Macavity & Silver Dagger winner* ★

Cordelia Gray . . . fledgling P.I. in London

- ❏ 1 - An Unsuitable Job for a Woman (1972)
- ❏ 2 - The Skull Beneath the Skin (1982)

J. A. Jance is Judith A. Jance, creator of the well-known and much-loved Seattle series featuring J. P. Beaumont, hard-drinking homicide cop with the high-rise condo and fast car. She has also written the first two installments of a new law enforcement series featuring Arizona sleuth Joanna Bradley. Jance has been a high school English teacher and a school librarian on an Arizona Indian reservation. She also sold life insurance for ten years.

J. P. Beaumont . . . Seattle, Washington homicide detective

- ❏ 1 - Until Proven Guilty (1985)
- ❏ 2 - Injustice for All (1986)
- ❏ 3 - Trial by Fury (1986)
- ❏ 4 - Taking the Fifth (1987)
- ❏ 5 - Improbable Cause (1988)
- ❏ 6 - A More Perfect Union (1988)
- ❏ 7 - Dismissed with Prejudice (1989)
- ❏ 8 - Minor in Possession (1990)
- ❏ 9 - Payment in Kind (1991)
- ❏ 10 - **Without Due Process** (1992) *American Mystery Award winner* ★
- ❏ 11 - **Failure to Appear** (1993) *American Mystery Award winner* ★
- ❏ 12 - Lying in Wait (1994)

Joanna Bradley . . . Arizona deputy sheriff's widow

- ❏ 1 - Desert Heat (1993)
- ❏ 2 - Tombstone Courage (1994)

Lucille Kallen has written for television and the theatre in addition to creating the mystery series featuring editor C. B. Greenfield and reporter Maggie Rome, who plays Archie to his Nero Wolfe. Their first adventure was an American Book Award nominee.

Maggie Rome & C. B. Greenfield . . . Connecticut reporter & editor/publisher

- ❏ 1 - Introducing C. B. Greenfield (1979)
- ❏ 2 - The Tanglewood Murder (1980)
- ❏ 3 - No Lady in the House (1982)
- ❏ 4 - The Piano Bird (1984)
- ❏ 5 - A Little Madness (1986)

Leona Karr, of Denver, Colorado is the author of several gothic and romantic suspense novels, including the best-selling *Stranger in the Mist*. She is also the creator of a new mystery series featuring Addie Devore, a newspaper owner in a small Colorado town.

Addie Devore . . . Colorado small-town newspaper owner

- ❏   1 - Murder in Bandora (1993)

Faye Kellerman is the creator of an award-winning mystery series featuring LAPD detective Peter Decker, an ethnic Jew reared as a Baptist by his adoptive parents, and Rina Lazarus, an Orthodox Jewish widow with two young sons. Born in St. Louis, Kellerman earned a BA in mathematics and her DDS degree at UCLA, where she met her husband Jonathan Kellerman, a clinical children's psychologist and mystery writer.

Peter Decker & Rina Lazarus . . . LAPD detective & wife

- ❏   1 - **The Ritual Bath** (1986) *Macavity Award winner* ★
- ❏   2 - Sacred and Profane (1987)
- ❏   3 - The Quality of Mercy (1989)
- ❏   4 - Milk and Honey (1990)
- ❏   5 - Day of Atonement (1992)
- ❏   6 - False Prophet (1992)
- ❏   7 - Grievous Sin (1993)
- ❏   8 - Sanctuary (1994)

Mary Ann Kelly, a former model and song lyricist, is the creator of a mystery series featuring photographer Claire Breslinsky, recently returned to her childhood neighborhood in Queens after ten years abroad. The series cast also includes Claire's two sisters—Zinnie the police officer and Carmela the fashion columnist. Kelly, who has lived in Europe and India, is now back in her native Queens where she lives with her husband and young son.

Claire Breslinsky . . . New York City freelance photographer

- ❏   1 - Parklane South, Queens (1990)
- ❏   2 - Foxglove (1992)

Nora Kelly is the creator of history professor Gillian Adams who during the first installment travels to Cambridge where she assists Scotland Yard in solving the murder of another professor. In the second title she returns to Vancouver, British Columbia where she chairs the history department at the University of the Pacific Northwest. Like her series protagonist, Kelly is a professor of history.

Gillian Adams . . . University of the Pacific Northwest (Canada) history chair

- ❏   1 - In the Shadow of King's (1984)
- ❏   2 - My Sister's Keeper (1992)
- ❏   3 - Body Chemistry (1993)

Susan Kelly is the creator of Liz Connors, Cambridge freelance magazine writer and former English professor. The first book in this series (*Gemini Man*) was nominated for an Anthony as best first novel of 1985. It was also voted one of the top ten books that year by the National Mystery Readers Poll. Kelly has a doctorate in medieval literature from the University of Edinburgh and has been a consultant to the Massachusetts Criminal Justice Training Council as well as a teacher of crime-report writing at the Cambridge Police Academy. Like her immensely likable series protagonist, Kelly is a former English professor who lives and works in Cambridge, Massachusetts.

Liz Connors . . . Cambridge, Massachusetts freelance crime writer
- ❏ 1 - **The Gemini Man** (1985) *Anthony nominee* ☆
- ❏ 2 - The Summertime Soldiers (1986)
- ❏ 3 - Trail of the Dragon (1988)
- ❏ 4 - Until Proven Innocent (1990)
- ❏ 5 - And Soon I'll Come to Kill You (1991)
- ❏ 6 - Out of the Darkness (1992)

Susan B. Kelly, creator of the Hop Valley series with Detective Inspector Nick Trevellyan and Alison Hope, was born in the Thames Valley region of England and worked for twelve years as a computer programmer before writing full time. When her novels crossed the Atlantic, her U.S. publisher added the B to distinguish her from the American Susan Kelly. Alison Hope is the savvy and successful owner of a London software company that relocates to the Hop Valley in the first installment where Alison is also a suspect in the death of her cousin and former business partner

Alison Hope & Nick Trevellyan . . . Hop Valley, England software designer & detective inspector
- ❏ 1 - Hope Against Hope (1990)
- ❏ 2 - Time of Hope (1990)
- ❏ 3 - Hope Will Answer (1993)
- ❏ 4 - Kid's Stuff (1994)

Toni L. P. Kelner, like her series character Laura Fleming, grew up in North Carolina and later moved to Boston where she now lives. Kelner also writes software documentation.

Laura Fleming . . . Byerly, North Carolina small-town detective
- ❏ 1 - Down Home Murder (1993)
- ❏ 2 - Dead Ringer (1994)
- ❏ 3 - Trouble Looking for a Place to Happen (1995)

Susan Kenney teaches English at Colby College in Maine where she received a creative writing grant from the National Endowment for the Arts after winning the 1982 O. Henry Prize for a short story. Her mystery series features English professor Roz Howard and British artist and painter Alan Stewart.

Roz Howard & Alan Stewart . . . American professor & British painter
- ❑ 1 - Garden of Malice (1983)
- ❑ 2 - Graves of Academe (1985)
- ❑ 3 - One Fell Sloop (1990)

Karen Kijewski, creator of the triple-award-winning Kat Colorado series, is a former high school English teacher and bartender. Like her character Kat, she lives and works in Sacramento, California.

Kat Colorado . . . Sacramento, California P.I.
- ❑ 1 - **Katwalk** (1988) *Anthony, Shamus & SMP/PWA winner* ★
- ❑ 2 - Katapult (1990)
- ❑ 3 - Kat's Cradle (1991)
- ❑ 4 - Copy Kat (1992)
- ❑ 5 - Wild Kat (1994)
- ❑ 6 - Alley Cat Blues (1995)

Laurie R. King is a third-generation native of the San Francisco area who has lived briefly in 20 countries on five continents since her marriage to an Anglo-Indian professor of religious studies. Her series opener with San Francisco homicide detectives Kate Martinelli and Alonzo Hawkin won the 1993 Edgar for best first novel. She is also the author of a recent novel featuring Mary Russell, a teenage student of Sherlock Holmes.

Kate Martinelli & Alonzo Hawkin . . . homicide detectives in San Francisco
- ❑ 1 - **A Grave Talent** (1993) *Edgar winner* ★ *Anthony nominee* ☆

Kate Kingsbury is the pseudonym of Doreen Roberts for her new Edwardian mystery series featuring the Pennyfoot Hotel and its owner and manager Cecily Sinclair.

Cecily Sinclair . . . hotel owner in Edwardian England
- ❑ 1 - Room With a Clue (1993)
- ❑ 2 - Do Not Disturb (1994)
- ❑ 3 - Service for Two (1994)
- ❑ 4 - Eat, Drink, and Be Buried (1994)
- ❑ 5 - Check-out Time (1995)

Mary Kittredge was once a respiratory therapist for a major city hospital in the state of Connecticut, which is also the setting for her two mystery series. Witty and resourceful Charlotte Kent is a freelance writer who once found a client dead at her desk. The independently wealthy Edwina Crusoe is a registered nurse and medical consultant whose rich mother is a successful romance novelist.

Charlotte Kent . . . Connecticut freelance writer

- ❏ 1 - Murder in Mendocino (1987)
- ❏ 2 - Dead and Gone (1989)
- ❏ 3 - Poison Pen (1990)

Edwina Crusoe . . . Connecticut RN & medical consultant

- ❏ 1 - Fatal Diagnosis (1990)
- ❏ 2 - Rigor Mortis (1991)
- ❏ 3 - Cadaver (1992)
- ❏ 4 - Walking Dead Man (1992)
- ❏ 5 - Desperate Remedy (1993)

Alanna Knight, a historical novelist and expert on Robert Louis Stevenson, is also the creator of a mystery series set in Victorian Edinburgh featuring police inspector Jeremy Faro. The inspector is a widower whose two young daughters live with their grandmother in Orkney, but a grown stepson, Dr. Vincent Laurie, is frequently on hand to assist unofficially.

Jeremy Faro . . . Victorian detective inspector in Edinburgh, Scotland

- ❏ 1 - Enter Second Murderer (1988)
- ❏ 2 - Bloodline (1989)
- ❏ 3 - Deadly Beloved (1989)
- ❏ 4 - Killing Cousins (1990)

Kathryn Lasky Knight is the author of numerous children's books under the name Kathryn Laksy. Her first adult novel is the opening title of her mystery series featuring Calista Jacobs, an illustrator of children's books in Cambridge, Massachusetts, who starts a sleuthing career with the hunt for her husband's killer. Other regulars in this cast are Calista's son Charley, the computer wizard, and Archie Baldwin, an archaeologist from the Smithsonian Institute.

Calista Jacobs . . . award-winning illustrator of children's books

- ❏ 1 - Trace Elements (1986)
- ❏ 2 - Mortal Words (1990)
- ❏ 3 - Mumbo Jumbo (1991)
- ❏ 4 - Dark Swain (1994)

Phyllis Knight is the creator of a new mystery series featuring Lil Ritchie, a lesbian P.I. from Portland, Maine. The author lives in Virginia.

Lil Ritchie . . . Portland, Maine lesbian P.I.
- ❑   1 -   Switching the Odds (1992)
- ❑   2 -   Shattered Rhythms (1994)

Gabrielle Kraft is a former executive story editor and story analyst at major Hollywood film studios. She is also the creator of a four-book mystery series featuring Jerry Zalman, Beverly Hills attorney and deal maker, whose first adventure was nominated for an Edgar award. This series has been described as smart and snappy and full of sarcastic commentary on the Looney Tunes of LaLa Land.

Jerry Zalman . . . Beverly Hills, California deal maker
- ❑   1 -   **Bullshot** (1987) *Edgar nominee* ☆
- ❑   2 -   Screwdriver (1988)
- ❑   3 -   Let's Rob Roy (1989)
- ❑   4 -   Bloody Mary (1990)

Rochelle Majer Krich is the creator of LAPD homicide detective Jessie Drake, nominated for an Agatha with her first installment of this new series. Krich's first mystery, the Anthony award winning *Where's Mommy Now?* is scheduled for late 1994 film release retitled *Perfect Alibi,* starring Teri Garr and Hector Elizondo. Krich chairs a high school English department and serves on the national board of Mystery Writers of America. She has also written several other non-series mysteries.

Jessie Drake . . . Los Angeles, California detective
- ❑   1 -   **Fair Game** (1993) *Agatha nominee* ☆
- ❑   2 -   Angel of Death (1994)
- ❑   3 -   Speak No Evil (1995)

Kathleen Kunz is a native of St. Louis and creator of the first professional genealogist sleuth, Terry Girard. Kunz teaches professional writing at the University of Oklahoma and has published articles and short fiction in *Ellery Queen Mystery* magazine, *Good Housekeeping* and *Parents* magazine.

Terry Girard . . . St. Louis, Missouri genealogist for hire
- ❑   1 -   Murder Once Removed (1993)
- ❑   2 -   Death in a Private Place (1995)

Sarah Lacey is the creator of a new mystery series featuring Yorkshire tax inspector Leah Hunter.

> **Leah Hunter** . . . Yorkshire tax inspector
> - ❏ 1 - File Under: Deceased (1993)
> - ❏ 2 - File Under: Missing (1994)
> - ❏ 3 - File Under: Arson (1995)

J. Dayne Lamb is the creator of amateur detective Teal Stewart, stalwart CPA from Boston's Beacon Hill. Born in San Francisco but raised in Brookline, Massachusetts, Lamb is a former CPA with a BA in philosophy from Hope College in Michigan and an MS in accounting from Northeastern University.

> **Teal Stewart** . . . Boston, Massachusetts Certified Public Accountant
> - ❏ 1 - Questionable Behavior (1993)
> - ❏ 2 - A Question of Preference (1994)
> - ❏ 3 - Inquestioned Loyalty (1995)

Mercedes Lambert is the creator of Whitney Logan, 20-something Los Angeles attorney and her street smart sometimes partner, Lupe, a Chicana prostitute. Lambert lives in Montebello, California with her two children, where she is working on her second novel.

> **Whitney Logan** . . . 20-something Los Angeles attorney
> - ❏ 1 - Dogtown (1991)

Marsha Landreth, a native of Denver with a degree in theatre arts, currently lives in Los Angeles where she writes screenplays. She is the creator of the Dr. Samantha Turner mystery series and has written a civil war biography of General Sherman. She also writes medical sagas under the name Tyler Cortland and has published at least one western novel.

> **Dr. Samantha Turner** . . . Wyoming medical examiner
> - ❏ 1 - The Holiday Murders (1992)
> - ❏ 2 - A Clinic for Murder (1993)
> - ❏ 3 - Vial Murders (1995)

Jane Langton is the creator of the Homer Kelly series featuring a Thoreau scholar and former policeman living the rich New England history of Boston and Concord. Many of Langton's devoted readers enjoy her pen and ink sketches as much as the stories themselves.

> **Homer Kelly** . . . Harvard professor & retired detective in Massachusetts
>
> ❑   1   -   The Transcendental Murder   (1964)
> ❑   2   -   Dark Nantucket Noon   (1975)
> ❑   3   -   The Memorial Hall Murder   (1978)
> ❑   4   -   Natural Enemy   (1982)
> ❑   5   -   Emily Dickinson is Dead   (1984)
> ❑   6   -   Good and Dead   (1986)
> ❑   7   -   Murder at the Gardner   (1988)
> ❑   8   -   The Dante Game   (1991)
> ❑   9   -   God in Concord   (1992)
> ❑   10   -   Divine Inspiration   (1993)

Janet LaPierre, a former high school English teacher, writes novels of mystery and suspense typically set on the northern coast of California. Her series detectives are Vince Gutierrez, police chief of Port Silva, and Meg Halloran, teacher and single mother. Later in the series another cop & single mother pair take the lead roles while Vince and Meg become supporting characters.

> **Vince Gutierrez & Meg Halloran** . . . Port Silva, Washington police chief & high school English teacher
>
> ❑   1   -   **Unquiet Grave** (1987)   *Macavity nominee*   ☆
> ❑   2   -   Children's Games   (1989)
> ❑   3   -   Cruel Mother   (1990)
> ❑   4   -   Grandmother's House   (1991)
> ❑   5   -   **Old Enemies** (1993)   *Anthony nominee*   ☆

Lynda LaPlante is the creator of a mystery series featuring London's Detective Chief Inspector Jane Tennison, star of the PBS television *Mystery!* series.

> **Jane Tennison** . . . London detective chief inspector
>
> ❑   1   -   Prime Suspect   (1993)
> ❑   2   -   Prime Suspect 2   (1993)
> ❑   3   -   Prime Suspect 3   (1994)

Emma Lathen is the pseudonym used by Mary Latsis and Martha Henissart to write more than 20 titles in the John Putnam Thatcher series since 1961. Thatcher is senior vice president of Sloan Guaranty Trust in New York City and is ably assisted in his business and financial detecting by his stalwart secretary Miss Corsa and several banking colleagues. Although they jealously guard their personal privacy, Latsis and Henissart are known to be an economist and attorney, respectively, living in Massachusetts. They also write the Ben Safford series under another pseudonym, R.B. Dominic.

John Putnam Thatcher . . . New York City Wall Street financial whiz

- ❏   1 -   Banking on Death (1961)
- ❏   2 -   A Place for Murder (1963)
- ❏   3 -   **Accounting for Murder** (1964) *Silver Dagger winner* ★
- ❏   4 -   Murder Makes the Wheels Go 'Round (1966)
- ❏   5 -   Death Shall Overcome (1966)
- ❏   6 -   **Murder Against the Grain** (1967) *Gold Dagger winner* ★
- ❏   7 -   A Stitch in Time (1968)
- ❏   8 -   Come to Dust (1968)
- ❏   9 -   When in Greece (1969)
- ❏ 10 -   Murder to Go (1969)
- ❏ 11 -   Pick Up Sticks (1970)
- ❏ 12 -   Ashes to Ashes (1971)
- ❏ 13 -   The Longer the Thread (1971)
- ❏ 14 -   Murder Without Icing (1972)
- ❏ 15 -   Sweet and Low (1974)
- ❏ 16 -   By Hook or By Crook (1975)
- ❏ 17 -   Double, Double, Oil and Trouble (1978)
- ❏ 18 -   Going for the Gold (1981)
- ❏ 19 -   **Green Grow the Dollars** (1982) *Ellery Queen winner* ★
- ❏ 20 -   Something in the Air (1988)
- ❏ 21 -   East is East (1991)
- ❏ 22 -   Right on the Money (1993)

Janet Laurence brings both cooking and writing experience to her mystery series involving Darina Lisle, daring food professional. This series offers a superabundance of glorious food descriptions, but no actual recipes. In addition to her cooking experience, Laurence has been a contributing writer for the *Daily Telegraph* and *Country Life* in England,

Darina Lisle . . . British caterer, chef & food writer

- ❏ 1 -   A Deepe Coffyn (1988)
- ❏ 2 -   A Tasty Way to Die (1991)
- ❏ 3 -   Hotel Morgue (1992)
- ❏ 4 -   Recipe for Death (1993)
- ❏ 5 -   Death and the Epicure (1994)

Janice Law is the creator of the Anna Peters series featuring a Washington, DC P.I. with a background in international oil. Golf enthusiasts will enjoy book five where Anna accompanies her illustrator husband Harry to the British Open.

Anna Peters . . . international oil company secretary turned private investigator in Washington, DC

- ❑ 1 - The Big Payoff (1976)
- ❑ 2 - Gemini Trip (1977)
- ❑ 3 - Under Orion (1978)
- ❑ 4 - The Shadow of the Palms (1980)
- ❑ 5 - Death Under Par (1981)
- ❑ 6 - Time Lapse (1992)
- ❑ 7 - A Safe Place to Die (1993)
- ❑ 8 - Backfire (1994)

Donna Leon is an American expatriate living in Venice, the setting for her mystery series involving Italian police officer Guido Brunetti and his wealthy wife. Leon teaches English at the University of Maryland extension in Venice and is familiar with the local U.S. military installation which she uses in book two. The opening title in this series won Japan's Suntory prize for best suspense novel.

Guido Brunetti . . . Venetian policeman

- ❑ 1 - Death a la Fenice (1992)
- ❑ 2 - Death in a Strange Country (1993)

Gillian Linscott, formerly a Parliamentary reporter for the BBC, is the creator of Edwardian suffragette Nell Bray who first deals with a fashionable murder in Biarritz and then moves into a World War I military hospital during book two. Linscott also wrote a historical mystery set in Africa.

Nell Bray . . . British suffragette

- ❑ 1 - Sister Beneath the Sheet (1991)
- ❑ 2 - Hanging on the Wire (1992)
- ❑ 3 - Stage Fright (1993)

Frances & Richard Lockridge are the pen names of Frances Louise Davis (1896-1963) and Richard Orsen (1899-1982), creators of the immensely popular Mr. and Mrs. North mystery series introduced in 1940 and still in print more than 50 years later. Born in St. Joseph and educated at the University of Missouri, Richard was a Kansas City newspaper reporter when he married Frances, also a reporter. After their move to New York he wrote for the *New York Sun* and the *New Yorker* before they launched the Norths with her story line and his characters. After Frances' death in 1963 Richard wrote only two more Mr. and Mrs. North titles, although he continued with non-series mysteries and several suspense novels. In 1965 he married New York freelance writer Hildegarde Dolson who created a mystery series of her own during the 1970s.

Pam & Jerry North . . . New York City husband & wife book publishers

- ❏   1   -   The Norths Meet Murder   (1940)
- ❏   2   -   Murder Out of Turn   (1941)
- ❏   3   -   A Pinch of Poison   (1941)
- ❏   4   -   Death on the Aisle   (1942)
- ❏   5   -   Hanged for a Sheep   (1942)
- ❏   6   -   Death Takes a Bow   (1943)
- ❏   7   -   Killing the Goose   (1944)
- ❏   8   -   Payoff for the Banker   (1945)
- ❏   9   -   Death of a Tall Man   (1946)
- ❏   10   -   Murder within Murder   (1946)
- ❏   11   -   Untidy Murder   (1947)
- ❏   12   -   Murder is Served   (1948)
- ❏   13   -   The Dishonest Murder   (1949)
- ❏   14   -   Murder in a Hurry   (1950)
- ❏   15   -   Murder Comes First   (1951)
- ❏   16   -   Dead as a Dinosaur   (1952)
- ❏   17   -   Death Has a Small Voice   (1953)
- ❏   18   -   Curtain for a Jester   (1953)
- ❏   19   -   A Key to Death   (1954)
- ❏   20   -   Death of an Angel   (1955)
- ❏   21   -   Voyage into Violence   (1956)
- ❏   22   -   The Long Skeleton   (1958)
- ❏   23   -   Murder is Suggested   (1959)
- ❏   24   -   The Judge is Reversed   (1960)
- ❏   25   -   Murder Has its Points   (1961)
- ❏   26   -   Murder by the Book   (1963)

Mary Logue is the creator of a new mystery series featuring Minneapolis journalist Laura Malloy.

Laura Malloy . . . Minneapolis, Minnesota journalist

- ❏   1   -   Still Explosion   (1993)

Randye Lorden, born and raised in Chicago, has lived in New York for a number of years. Her short fiction has been published in *Ellery Queen Mystery Magazine* and *New Mystery*. The first installment of Lorden's new mystery series featuring Sydney Sloane was nominated for a Shamus award for best first P.I. novel.

Sydney Sloane . . . New York City upper west side private investigator

- ❏   1   -   **Brotherly Love**   (1993)   *Shamus nominee*   ☆
- ❏   2   -   Sister's Keeper   (1994)

M. K. Lorens is Margaret Keilstrup Lorens of Fremont, Nebraska, creator of a mystery series featuring Shakespearean scholar Winston Marlowe Sherman. In addition to Sherman's college teaching, he writes mystery novels as a woman (he's the pseudonymous Henrietta Slocum) whose series sleuth just happens to be a man (Winchester Hyde). The professor's lady-love is a concert pianist (Sarah Cromwell) whose younger brother (David) the actor lives with them—along with the professor's retired colleague Edward Merriman—in the family mansion (Sarah's, that is). Think of these mysteries as an aerobics workout for the brain.

Winston Marlowe Sherman . . . Shakespeare professor and mystery writer

- ❑ 1 - Sweet Narcissus (1990)
- ❑ 2 - Dreamland (1992)
- ❑ 3 - Sorrowheart (1993)
- ❑ 4 - Ropedancer's Fall (1990)
- ❑ 5 - Deception Island (1991)

Margaret Lucke is a native of Washington, DC who currently lives near San Francisco where she works as a journalist, editor and business writer. Her first mystery featuring San Francisco P.I. Jessica Randolph was nominated for an Anthony.

Jessica Randolph . . . San Francisco, California P.I.

- ❑ 1 - **A Relative Stranger** (1991) *Anthony nominee* ☆

Nan & Ivan Lyons are authors of the comedy classic *Someone is Killing the Great Chefs of Europe*, featuring chef Natasha O'Brien. The 1978 film starred Jacqueline Bisset as chef Natasha O'Brien and Robert Morley as one of the unluckier chefs.

Natasha O'Brien & Millie Ogden . . . pair of culinary artists

- ❑ 1 - Someone is Killing the Great Chefs of Europe (1976)
- ❑ 2 - Someone is Killing the Great Chefs of America (1993)

T. J. MacGregor is Trish Janeshutz MacGregor, creator of the action-packed south Florida P.I. series starring Quin St. James and Mike McCleary, owners of the husband and wife investigations firm which they founded. As Trish Janeshutz she has published several non-series suspense thrillers. As Alison Drake she writes the Aline Scott series and an occasional horror novel.

Quin St. James & Mike McCleary . . . south Florida P.I. & cop

- ❑ 1 - **Dark Fields** (1986) *Shamus nominee* ☆
- ❑ 2 - Kill Flash (1987)
- ❑ 3 - Death Sweet (1988)
- ❑ 4 - On Ice (1989)
- ❑ 5 - Kin Dread (1990)

❏ 6 - Death Flats (1991)
❏ 7 - Spree (1992)
❏ 8 - Storm Surge (1993)
❏ 9 - Blue Pearl (1994)

Charlotte MacLeod is the creator of two series under her own name, both with charming New England settings. The Peter Shandy series features the professor and his librarian wife at an agricultural college in rural Massachusetts. The Sarah Kelling series features blue-blooded Sarah and her quirky Boston family along with Sarah's investigator husband Max. MacLeod also writes two series set in Canada under the name Alisa Craig.

Peter Shandy & Helen Marsh Shandy . . . rural Balaclava County, Massachusetts college botany professor & librarian wife

❏ 1 - Rest You Merry (1978)
❏ 2 - The Luck Runs Out (1979)
❏ 3 - Wrack and Rune (1982)
❏ 4 - Something the Cat Dragged In (1983)
❏ 5 - The Curse of the Giant Hogweed (1985)
❏ 6 - **The Corpse in Oozak's Pond** (1986) *Edgar nominee* ☆
❏ 7 - Vane Pursuit (1989)
❏ 8 - An Owl Too Many (1991)
❏ 9 - Something in the Water (1994)

Sarah Kelling & Max Bittersohn . . . Boston, Massachusetts investigative couple

❏ 1 - The Family Vault (1979)
❏ 2 - The Withdrawing Room (1980)
❏ 3 - The Palace Guard (1981)
❏ 4 - The Bilbao Looking Glass (1983)
❏ 5 - The Convivial Codfish (1984)
❏ 6 - The Plain Old Man (1985)
❏ 7 - The Silver Ghost (1987)
❏ 8 - The Recycled Citizen (1987)
❏ 9 - The Gladstone Bag (1989)
❏ 10 - The Resurrection Man (1992)
❏ 11 - The Odd Job (1995)

Valerie S. Malmont grew up on Okinawa where her father reorganized the local police force after World War II. She has degrees from the University of New Mexico and the University of Washington and has worked as a librarian in Washington, Virginia, Pennsylvania and Taiwan. She currently lives in rural Pennsylvania, much like her amateur sleuth Tori Miracle. The second title in this series will be released in 1995 and Malmont is at work on the third.

Tori Miracle . . . ex-NYC crime writer turned Pennsylvania novelist

❏ 1 - Death Pays the Rose Rent (1994)

Jessica Mann was educated at Cambridge where she studied archaeology and Anglo-Saxon. Her series detectives are both archaeologists, Professor Thea Crawford and her student Tamara Hoyland. Hoyland is later recruited to work as a Department E spy, using her archaeological work as a convenient cover. Mann, a respected critic for *British Book News* and the BBC, is also the author of the 1981 critical study of English women mystery authors, *Deadlier Than the Male*.

Tamara Hoyland . . . British secret agent & archaeologist
- ❑ 1 - Funeral Sites (1982)
- ❑ 2 - No Man's Island (1983)
- ❑ 3 - Grave Goods (1984)
- ❑ 4 - A Kind of Healthy Grave (1986)
- ❑ 5 - Death Beyond the Nile (1988)
- ❑ 6 - Faith, Hope and Homicide (1991)

Thea Crawford . . . archaeology professor
- ❑ 1 - Troublecross (1972) [aka The Only Security]
- ❑ 2 - Captive Audience (1975)

Linda French Mariz is the author of a new mystery series featuring Laura Ireland, University of Washington volleyball star and graduate student. Mariz is currently writing a trilogy featuring a pair of sister sleuths—one a historian, the other a wrestler. Born in New Orleans and raised in Atlanta, Mariz is a nationally-ranked butterfly swimmer with degrees in history from the University of Missouri at Columbia and Western Washington University. She lives in Bellingham, Washington.

Laura Ireland . . . Seattle, Washington graduate student volleyball player
- ❑ 1 - Body English (1992)
- ❑ 2 - Snake Dance (1992)

Margaret Maron is the creator of two very different series characters—New York cop Sigrid Harald and North Carolina judge Deborah Knott. After winning a 1991 Agatha for the short story, "Deborah's Judgment," Maron swept the mystery awards the following year for best novel with the series opener. Maron is a past president of Sisters in Crime and an active member of the Carolina Crime Writers Association and Mystery Writers of America. She lives on a farm outside Raleigh, North Carolina.

Deborah Knott . . . North Carolina attorney turned district judge
- ❑ 1 - **Bootlegger's Daughter** (1992)
  Agatha, Anthony, Edgar & Macavity winner ★
- ❑ 2 - **Southern Discomfort** (1993) ***Agatha & Anthony nominee*** ☆
- ❑ 3 - Shooting at Loons (1994)

Sigrid Harald . . . New York City police lieutenant

- ❑   1 - One Coffee With (1981)
- ❑   2 - Death of a Butterfly (1984)
- ❑   3 - Death in Blue Folders (1985)
- ❑   4 - The Right Jack (1987)
- ❑   5 - Baby Doll Games (1988)
- ❑   6 - **Corpus Christmas** (1989) *Agatha & American Mystery nominee* ☆
- ❑   7 - Past Imperfect (1991)

Ngaio Marsh (1895-1982), a native of New Zealand, was working as an interior decorator in London when she wrote her first of 32 mysteries featuring aristocratic police inspector, Roderick Alleyn, second son of a baronet. His social connections were especially useful in crime-solving among the upper classes during his 48-year detecting career.

As founder of the British Commonwealth Theatre Company, Marsh's interest in theatre featured prominently in her mystery plots and settings. She was named to the Order of the British Empire in 1948 and Dame Commander in 1966, both honors for her theatre activities rather than mystery writing. In 1977 she was named Grand Master by the Mystery Writers of America.

Roderick Alleyn . . . inspector son of a baronet

- ❑   1 - A Man Lay Dead (1934)
- ❑   2 - Enter a Murderer (1935)
- ❑   3 - The Nursing Home Murder (1936)
- ❑   4 - Death in Ecstasy (1936)
- ❑   5 - Vintage Murder (1937)
- ❑   6 - Artists in Crime (1938)
- ❑   7 - Death in a White Tie (1938)
- ❑   8 - Overture to Death (1939)
- ❑   9 - Death at the Bar (1940)
- ❑ 10 - Death of a Peer (1940) [Britain–Surfeit of Campreys]
- ❑ 11 - Death and the Dancing Footman (1941)
- ❑ 12 - Color Scheme (1943)
- ❑ 13 - Died in the Wool (1945)
- ❑ 14 - Final Curtain (1947)
- ❑ 15 - Swing, Brother, Swing (1949) [U.S.–A Wreath for Rivera]
- ❑ 16 - Opening Night (1951) [U.S.–Night at the Vulcan]
- ❑ 17 - Spinsters in Jeopardy (1953)
- ❑ 18 - Scales of Justice (1955)
- ❑ 19 - Death of a Fool (1956) [Britain–Off With His Head]
- ❑ 20 - Swinging in the Shrouds (1958)
- ❑ 21 - False Scent (1959)
- ☑ 22 - Hand in Glove (1962)
- ❑ 23 - Dead Water (1963)
- ❑ 24 - Killer Dolphin (1966) [Britain–Death at the Dolphin]
- ☑ 25 - Clutch of Constables (1969)
- ❑ 26 - When in Rome (1971)

    ☑ 27 - Tied up in Tinsel (1972)
    ❏ 28 - Black as He's Painted (1974)
    ❏ 29 - Last Ditch (1977)
    ❏ 30 - Grave Mistake (1978)
    ❏ 31 - Photo-Finish (1980)
    ❏ 32 - Light Thickens (1982)

Lee Martin is the pseudonym of Ft. Worth police veteran Anne Wingate who holds a PhD in English and has authored mystery novels as Lee Martin, Anne Wingate and Martha G. Webb. The author's eight years of police experience, much of it with the major crime scene unit, give the Deb Ralston series a realistic punch. Ralston also manages to juggle a trio of adopted children, each with a different ethnic heritage, and a husband who works full time while completing a graduate degree. Wingate lives in Salt Lake City, Utah.

    Deb Ralston . . . Ft. Worth, Texas police detective & mother
       ❏ 1 - Too Sane a Murder (1984)
       ❏ 2 - A Conspiracy of Strangers (1986)
       ❏ 3 - Death Warmed Over (1988)
       ❏ 4 - Murder at the Blue Owl (1988)
       ❏ 5 - Hal's Own Murder Case (1989)
       ❏ 6 - Deficit Ending (1990)
       ❏ 7 - The Mensa Murders (1990)
       ❏ 8 - Hacker (1992)
       ❏ 9 - The Day That Dusty Died (1993)
      ❏ 10 - Inherited Murder (1994)

Sarah Jill Mason is perhaps best known as Hamilton Crane, her pseudonym for continuing the Miss Seeton series originated by Heron Carvic. Mason is also the creator of another English village series featuring Detective Superintendent Trewley and his female partner Sergeant Stone, judo black belt and former medical student.

    D. S. Trewley & Sgt. Stone . . . English village detective partners
       ❏ 1 - Murder in the Maze (1993)
       ❏ 2 - Frozen Stiff (1993)
       ❏ 3 - Corpse in the Kitchen (1994)
       ❏ 4 - Dying Breath (1994)

Lia Matera, former teaching fellow at Stanford University Law School, is the author of two San Francisco attorney series. Willa Jansson, the daughter of aging-but-still-active Berkeley radicals, has been described by the *New York Times* as "among the most articulate and surely the wittiest of amateur sleuths." The Jansen series opens with Willa still a law student.

Matera's second series featuring the brilliant Laura Di Palma is dark by comparison. The dragon defense attorney with a paid-for Mercedes and a high-profile life is on a collision course with one ex-husband and two former lovers making new demands.

Laura Di Palma . . . San Francisco, California attorney
- ❏ 1 - The Smart Money (1988)
- ❏ 2 - The Good Fight (1990)
- ❏ 3 - A Hard Bargain (1992)
- ❏ 4 - Face Value (1994)

Willa Jansson . . . California attorney
- ❏ 1 - **Where Lawyers Fear to Tread** (1986) *Anthony nominee* ☆
- ❏ 2 - **A Radical Departure** (1987) *Edgar nominee* ☆
- ❏ 3 - Hidden Agenda (1989)
- ❏ 4 - Prior Convictions (1991)

Linda Mather is the creator of a new mystery series featuring professional astrologer Jo Hughes.

Jo Hughes . . . professional astrologer
- ❏ 1 - Blood of an Aries (1994)

Stephanie Matteson is the creator of a mystery series featuring Charlotte Graham Oscar-winning actress of film and stage. These novels do not provide actual theatre settings but are rich in the detail chosen for each story, starting with the chic New York spa setting for book one.

Charlotte Graham . . . New York City Oscar-winning actress
- ❏ 1 - Murder at the Spa (1990)
- ❏ 2 - Murder on the Cliff (1991)
- ❏ 3 - Murder at Teatime (1991)
- ❏ 4 - Murder on the Silk Road (1992)
- ❏ 5 - Murder at the Falls (1993)
- ❏ 6 - Murder on High (1994)

Francine Matthews is the creator of a new mystery series featuring Nantucket P.I. Meredith "Merry" Folger.

Meredith "Merry" Folger . . . Nantucket, Massachusetts P.I.
- ❏ 1 - Death in the Off Season (1994)

A. E. Maxwell is the husband and wife writing team of Ann and Evan Maxwell, creators of the Fiddler and Fiora series. Fiddler is independently wealthy, thanks to his Uncle Jake's ill-gotten gains and Fiora's investment banking genius. Fiddler's buddy Benny, the Ice Cream King of Saigon, provides electronics wizardry for many of their high action capers. In addition to the Fiddler and Fiora series, Ann has written 35 other titles—science fiction and romantic suspense as Ann Maxwell and romance as Elizabeth Lowell. Evan is a former reporter for the *Los Angeles Times*. The Maxwells currently live in the San Juan Islands of Washington state.

Fiddler & Fiora (ex-husband & wife) . . . California detective & investment banker
- ❏ 1 - Just Another Day in Paradise (1985)
- ❏ 2 - The Frog and the Scorpion (1986)
- ❏ 3 - Gatsby's Vineyard (1987)
- ❏ 4 - Just Enough Light to Kill (1988)
- ❏ 5 - The Art of Survival (1989)
- ❏ 6 - Money Burns (1991)
- ❏ 7 - The King of Nothing (1992)
- ❏ 8 - Murder Hurts (1993)

Melanie McAllester is the creator of a new police series featuring lesbian homicide detectives Elizabeth Mendoza and Ashley Johnson.

Elizabeth Mendoza & Ashley Johnson . . . lesbian homicide detectives
- ❏ 1 - The Lessons (1994)

Taylor McCafferty is an identical twin who was born and raised in Lousiville, Kentucky. She has a degree in fine art from the University of Louisiana and has worked as an art director and advertising copywriter for a Louisville ad agency. Her Haskell Blevins series features a P.I. from Pigeon Fork, Kentucky.

Haskell Blevins . . . Pigeon Fork, Kentucky P.I.
- ❏ 1 - Pet Peeves (1990)
- ❏ 2 - Ruffled Feathers (1992)
- ❏ 3 - Bed Bugs (1993)
- ❏ 4 - Thin Skins (1994)

Lise McClendon is the creator of a new mystery series featuring Montana gallery owner and art forgery expert Alix Thorssen.

Alix Thorssen . . . Montana gallery owner & art forgery expert
- ❏ 1 - The Bluejay Shaman (1994)

Helen McCloy (1904-1994), creator of the Dr. Basil Willing series, was the first woman president of the Mystery Writers of America when elected in 1950. After studying at the Sorbonne in the early 1920s, she later served as foreign art critic for several American publications in Europe, before returning to the U.S. in 1932. She wrote at least 15 non-series novels, in addition to the mystery criticism which earned her an Edgar in 1953. She was named Grand Master by the Mystery Writers of America in 1989, one of only eight women to be so honored since Agatha Christie in 1954.

Dr. Basil Willing . . . medical advisor to New York City district attorney

- ❑ 1 - Dance of Death (1938) [Britain–Design for Dying]
- ❑ 2 - The Man in the Moonlight (1940)
- ❑ 3 - The Deadly Truth (1941)
- ❑ 4 - Who's Calling (1942)
- ❑ 5 - Cue for Murder (1942)
- ❑ 6 - The Goblin Market (1943)
- ❑ 7 - The One That Got Away (1945)
- ❑ 8 - Through a Glass Darkly (1950)
- ❑ 9 - Alias Basil Willing (1951)
- ❑ 10 - The Long Body (1955)
- ❑ 11 - Two-thirds of a Ghost (1956)
- ❑ 12 - Mr. Splitfoot (1968)
- ❑ 13 - Burn This (1980)

Sharyn McCrumb has created popular characters in mystery, science fiction and folklore and is a recognized voice of Appalachian culture and mythology. Her primary mystery character is Elizabeth MacPherson, forensic anthropologist and cousin of the disappearing bride in McCrumb's first series opener.

Her award-winning science fiction satire has college professor James Owen Mega exploring the zany world of sci-fi fandom as author Jay Omega. Her latest series features Appalachian sheriff Spencer Arrowood opening with the charmed title, *If Ever I Return, Pretty Peggy-O*.

Elizabeth MacPherson . . . forensic anthropologist

- ❑ 1 - Sick of Shadows (1984)
- ❑ 2 - Lovely in her Bones (1985)
- ❑ 3 - Highland Laddie Gone (1986)
- ❑ 4 - Paying the Piper (1988)
- ❑ 5 - The Windsor Knot (1990)
- ❑ 6 - Missing Susan (1991)
- ❑ 7 - MacPherson's Lament (1992)

Ballad series w/Spencer Arrowood . . . Appalachian sheriff

- ❑ 1 - If Ever I Return, Pretty Peggy-O (1990)
- ❑ 2 - The Hangman's Beautiful Daughter (1992)
- ❑ 3 - She Walks These Hills (1994)

James Owen Mega . . . science-fiction author & college professor
- ❏   1   -   **Bimbos of the Death Sun** (1988) *Edgar winner* ★
- ❏   2   -   Zombies of the Gene Pool (1992)

Val McDermid is the creator of two mystery series—Manchester P.I. Kate Brannigan and journalist Lindsay Gordon. Kate lives next door to rock music journalist Richard Barclay who is also her lover. Lindsay is a self-described cynical socialist lesbian feminist. During much of 1994, McDermid traveled throughout the United States interviewing working women P.I.s for her forthcoming book *Woman Eyes* expected in 1995.

Kate Brannigan . . . Manchester, England P.I.
- ❏   1   -   Dead Beat (1992)
- ❏   2   -   Kickback (1993)
- ❏   3   -   Crack Down (1994)

Lindsay Gordon . . . lesbian journalist in Glasgow, Scotland
- ❏   1   -   Report for Murder (1990)
- ❏   2   -   Open and Shut (1991)

Patricia McFall, of Orange County, California, is a university writing instructor and active member of several mystery organizations. She's traveled extensively in Europe and Asia and lived for a year in Sapporo and Kyoto, Japan, the setting for her first novel *Night Butterfly*, named one of the ten best mysteries of 1992 by the *Los Angeles Times*.

Nora James . . . American graduate student of linguistics working in Japan
- ❏   1   -   Night Butterfly (1992)

Patricia McGerr (1917-1985), a native of Nebraska, earned a BA from the University of Nebraska and an MA in journalism from Columbia by the age of 20. She spent six years in Washington, DC as public relations director for the American Road Builders Association and later edited a construction industry magazine before going freelance in 1948. Her first novel *Pick Your Victim* (1946) was called a masterpiece by critic Jacques Barzun. Her only series detective, Selena Mead, widowed Washington magazine writer and counterspy, appears in numerous short stories, several novelettes and two novels. McGerr wrote 11 other non-series novels between 1947 and 1975.

Selena Mead . . . British government agent
- ❏   1   -   Is There a Traitor in the House (1964)
- ❏   2   -   Legacy of Danger (1970)

Janet McGiffin is the creator of a new medical mystery series featuring Dr. Maxene St. Clair, emergency room physician at an inner city hospital in Milwaukee, Wisconsin, a city the author knows well. McGiffin is currently living in Tel Aviv, Israel.

Dr. Maxene St. Clair . . . Milwaukee, Wisconsin emergency room physician

❑   1 - Emergency Murder (1992)
❑   2 - Prescription for Death (1993)

Jill McGown is the creator of a well-received police series featuring Chief Inspector Lloyd (whose first name is a series mystery) and his partner and lover Judy Hill. McGown also writes non-series puzzle and suspense novels under her own name and as Elizabeth Chaplin.

Chief Inspector Lloyd & Judy Hill . . . Welsh Detective Inspectors

❑   1 - A Perfect Match (1983)
❑   2 - Murder at the Old Vicarage (1988)
❑   3 - Gone to Her Death (1989)
❑   4 - The Murders of Mrs. Austin & Mrs. Beale (1991)
❑   5 - The Other Woman (1992)
❑   6 - Murder Now and Then (1993)

Christine McGuire is a prosecutor in a northern California district attorney's office where she heads the Special Prosecutions Unit. She also teaches at the FBI academy in Quantico, Virginia. Her first book, *Perfect Victim*, was a non-fiction account of a sexual enslavement case and a #1 *New York Times* bestseller which sold over one million copies. McGuire's new mystery series features Kathryn Mackay, a northern California prosecuting attorney.

Kathryn Mackay . . . northern California prosecuting attorney

❑   1 - Until Proven Guilty (1993)

Bridget McKenna is the author of the Caley Burke P.I. series set in northern California. She also writes science fiction and fantasy and was nominated for awards (Nebula and Hugo) in both genres in 1994. She is currently collaborating on a San Francisco mystery with Marti McKenna.

Caley Burke . . . 30-something northern California P.I.

❑   1 - Murder Beach (1993)
❑   2 - Dead Ahead (1994)
❑   3 - Caught Dead (1995)

Karin McQuillan was a Peace Corps volunteer in east Africa where she was often the first white woman ever seen in remote villages accessible only by canoe. She and her series detective Jazz Jasper, independent safari leader in Kenya, are passionate about conservation issues and the land, the animals and the people of Africa.

Jazz Jasper . . . American safari guide in Kenya

- ❑   1 - Deadly Safari (1990)
- ❑   2 - Elephants' Graveyard (1993)
- ❑   3 - The Cheetah Chase (1994)

M. R. D. Meek is Margaret Reid Duncan Meek of Cornwall, England, who began writing detective fiction in 1980 after a varied life as a wife, mother and solicitor. Her Honours Law Degree is from London University where she enrolled after the death of her first husband. Her legal background provides authentic detail for her series detective solicitor Lennox Kemp.

Lennox Kemp . . . London solicitor detective

- ❑   1 - With Flowers that Fell (1983) [#1 in Britain]
- ❑   2 - Hang the Consequences (1984) [#1 in U.S.]
- ❑   3 - The Split Second (1985)
- ❑   4 - In Remembrance of Rose (1986)
- ❑   5 - A Worm of Doubt (1987)
- ❑   6 - A Mouthful of Sand (1988)
- ❑   7 - A Loose Connection (1989)
- ❑   8 - This Blessed Plot (1990)
- ❑   9 - Touch & Go (1993)

Leslie Meier is the creator of a new series featuring amateur sleuth Lucy Stone who lives in a small New England town.

Lucy Stone . . . small-town amateur sleuth in Maine

- ❑   1 - Mail-Order Murder (1993)
- ❑   2 - Tippy-Toe Murder (1994)

Jennie Melville is the pseudonym used by Gwendoline Butler for her English mystery series featuring constable Charmian Daniels of the suburban Deerham Hills police department. Under the Melville name, the author has also written 15 non-series novels including historical and romantic suspense.

Charmian Daniels . . . Deerham Hills police detective

- ❏   1   -   Come Home and Be Killed   (1962)
- ❏   2   -   Burning is a Substitute for Loving   (1963)
- ❏   3   -   Murderer's Houses   (1964)
- ❏   4   -   There Lies Your Love   (1965)
- ❏   5   -   Nell Alone   (1966)
- ❏   6   -   A Different Kind of Summer   (1967)
- ❏   7   -   A New Kind of Killer   (1970)
- ❏   8   -   Murder Has a Pretty Face   (1981)
- ❏   9   -   Windsor Red   (1988)
- ❏   10   -   Murder in the Garden   (1989)
- ❏   11   -   Making Good Blood   (1989)
- ❏   12   -   Witching Murder   (1990)
- ❏   13   -   Dead Set   (1993)
- ❏   14   -   Footsteps in the Blood   (1993)

D. R. Meredith is Doris Meredith, former librarian and bookseller, Amarillo resident and creator of two continuing series set in the Texas Panhandle. The first features honest and courageous Sheriff Charles Matthews of fictional Crawford County, Texas. The second is set in the real Texas town of Canadian with its lovely Victorian homes, brick streets and giant cottonwood trees. This is the venue of John Lloyd Branson, wise and good defense attorney, and his smart and lovely assistant, Lydia Fairchild, a law student from Southern Methodist University in Dallas. She calls him John Lloyd and he calls her Miss Fairchild as they struggle to keep their personal attraction under wraps.

Charles Matthews . . . west Texas sheriff

- ❏   1   -   The Sheriff & the Panhandle Murders   (1984)
- ❏   2   -   The Sheriff & the Branding Iron Murders   (1985)
- ❏   3   -   The Sheriff & the Folsom Man Murders   (1987)
- ❏   4   -   The Sheriff & the Pheasant Hunt Murders   (1993)

John Lloyd Branson & Lydia Fairchild . . . Texas defense attorney & assistant

- ❏   1   -   Murder by Impulse   (1987)
- ❏   2   -   Murder by Deception   (1989)
- ❏   3   -   Murder by Masquerade   (1990)
- ❏   4   -   Murder by Reference   (1991)
- ❏   5   -   Murder by Sacrilege   (1993)

Annette Meyers is currently senior vice president of an executive search firm specializing in the brokerage industry. She was previously assistant to theatre producer and director Hal Prince. So it's only natural that her Smith & Wetzon series has one foot on Wall Street and the other on Broadway. She is working on a psychological novel and serves as national secretary of Sisters in Crime. She and her husband Martin also write a 17th century historical series as Maan Meyers.

Xenia Smith & Leslie Wetzon . . . pair of Wall Street headhunters
- ❏ 1 - The Big Killing (1989)
- ❏ 2 - Tender Death (1990)
- ❏ 3 - The Deadliest Option (1991)
- ❏ 4 - Blood on the Street (1992)
- ❏ 5 - Murder: The Musical (1993)
- ❏ 6 - These Bones Were Made for Dancing (1994)

Margaret Millar (1915-1994) might have been better known in her own right had she not been married to Kenneth Millar, who as Ross Macdonald was critically acclaimed for his Lew Archer series. Born in Kitchener, Ontario, she wrote her first mystery while confined to bed with a heart ailment at the age of 26, while her husband was a graduate student at the University of Michigan.

Her earliest series detective was psychiatrist Paul Prye, whose police contact, Inspector Sands of the Toronto Police Department, was given his own series beginning in 1943. After her daughter's death in 1970, Millar stopped writing for six years, until introducing attorney Tom Aragon in 1976. One of her non-series works, *A Beast in View*, won the Edgar for best novel in 1955. President of the Mystery Writers of America in 1957 and 1958, she was later named Grand Master in 1982, one of only eight women to be so honored since Agatha Christie in 1954.

Inspector Sands . . . police detective in Toronto, Canada
- ❏ 1 - Wall of Eyes (1943)
- ❏ 2 - The Iron Gates (1945)

Paul Prye . . . psychiatrist in Toronto, Canada
- ❏ 1 - The Invisible Worm (1941)
- ❏ 2 - The Weak-Eyed Bat (1942)
- ❏ 3 - The Devil Loves Me (1942)

Tom Aragon . . . California attorney
- ❏ 1 - Ask Me for Tomorrow (1976)
- ❏ 2 - The Murder of Miranda (1979)
- ❏ 3 - Mermaid (1982)

Marlys Millhiser, a resident of Boulder, Colorado, is the creator of Charlie Greene, Hollywood literary agent and single mother. The author's short stories and feature articles appear in numerous mystery publications. She has also written non-series novels, including *The Mirror* and *Willing Hostage*.

Charlie Greene . . . Hollywood literary agent

- ❏ 1 - Murder at Moot Point (1992)
- ❏ 2 - Death of the Office Witch (1993)
- ❏ 3 - Murder in a Hot Flash (1995)

Gladys Mitchell (1901-1983) was born in Oxfordshire and earned a diploma in history at University College, London in 1926 after starting a teaching career that was to last 40 years. Her series featuring Dame Beatrice Bradley is chock full of Mitchell's two favorite subjects—Freudian psychology and witchcraft. Only a few of these titles were published in the U.S. She also wrote mystery and non-mystery novels under two male pseudonyms. As Stephen Hockaby she wrote five non-mystery novels. As Malcolm Torrie she produced a series featuring Timothy Herring, director of the Society for the Preservation of Buildings of Historic Interest.

Beatrice Lestrange Bradley . . . London psychiatrist & consultant to Home Office

- ❏ 1 - Speedy Death (1929)
- ❏ 2 - The Saltmarsh Murders (1932)
- ❏ 3 - Death at the Opera (1934) [U.S.–Death in the Wet]
- ❏ 4 - St. Peter's Finger (1938)
- ❏ 5 - When Last I Died (1941)
- ❏ 6 - Laurels are Poison (1942)
- ❏ 7 - The Rising of the Moon (1945)
- ❏ 8 - The Dancing Druids (1948)
- ❏ 9 - Tom Brown's Body (1949)
- ❏ 10 - Faintly Speaking (1954)
- ❏ 11 - Watson's Choice (1955)
- ❏ 12 - Spotted Hemlock (1958)
- ❏ 13 - Say It with Flowers (1960)
- ❏ 14 - Death of a Delft Blue (1964)
- ❏ 15 - The Death-Cap Dancers (1981)
- ❏ 16 - The Crozier Pharaohs (1984)

Timothy Herring . . . preservation society director

- ❏ 1 - Heavy as Lead (1966)
- ❏ 2 - Late and Cold (1967)
- ❏ 3 - Your Secret Friend (1968)
- ❏ 4 - Churchyard Salad (1969)
- ❏ 5 - Shades of Darkness (1970)
- ❏ 6 - Bismarck Herrings (1971)

Gwen Moffat is an experienced climber, youth hostel director, journalist, novelist and professional climbing guide. In addition to her series featuring Miss Pink, she has authored several non-fiction titles, including *Hard Road West*, the account of her journey across America alone on the California Trail. She also wrote a historical novel based on that same adventure (*The Buckskin Girl*). Moffat lives in Wales.

Melinda Pink . . . Utah writer & mountain climber

- ❏ 1 - Lady With a Cool Eye (1973)
- ❏ 2 - Miss Pink at the Edge of the World (1975)
- ❏ 3 - Over the Sea to Death (1976)
- ❏ 4 - Persons Unknown (1978)
- ❏ 5 - Miss Pink's Mistake (1982)
- ❏ 6 - Die Like a Dog (1982)
- ❏ 7 - Last Chance Country (1983)
- ❏ 8 - Grizzly Trail (1984)
- ❏ 9 - Snare (1987)
- ❏ 10 - The Stone Hawk (1989)
- ❏ 11 - Rage (1990)

Miriam Grace Monfredo is the creator of Glynis Tryon, fictional librarian and suffragette from Seneca Falls, New York, who meets Elizabeth Cady Stanton at a historic meeting on women's rights in 1848. By 1854 (in the second book), Tryon is involved with the Underground Railway and the town constable who wants to marry her. Monfredo, a former director of a legal and historical research firm, has also been a newspaper columnist and feature writer with a specialty in women's history. Her mysteries are part of a thoughtfully planned body of work to tell the story of women's rights issues, the first of which was nominated for both the Agatha and Macavity awards.

Glynis Tryon . . . mid 19th century Seneca Falls, New York librarian & suffragette

- ☑ 1 - **Seneca Falls Inheritance** (1992) ***Agatha & Macavity nominee*** ☆
- ❏ 2 - North Star Conspiracy (1993)
- ❏ 3 - Blackwater Spirits (1995)

Yvonne E. Montgomery is the creator of Denver stockbroker Finny Aletter whose boss is murdered in the first installment. *Publisher's Weekly* called this series "Nancy Drew with an MBA and a sex life."

Finny Aletter . . . Denver, Colorado stockbroker turned carpenter

- ❏ 1 - Scavengers (1987)
- ❏ 2 - Obstacle Course (1990)

Susan Moody, a native of Oxford, England, is the creator of two mystery series with unusual women protagonists. The first features Penelope Wanawake, beautiful, black, six-foot daughter of Englishwoman Lady Helena Hurley and Dr. Benjamin Wanawake, African ambassador to the United Nations. Educated in England, France, Switzerland and the United States, Penny travels the globe as a freelance photographer. Her love interest is antiques dealer and jewel thief Barnaby Midas, who steals from the rich to aid her fundraising efforts for world famine relief.

Moody's newer series features British biology teacher turned bridge professional Cassandra Swann. Moody, who spent 10 years living in Tennessee during the 1960s, also writes fiction under the name of Susannah James.

Cassandra Swann . . . British biology teacher turned bridge professional
- ❏ 1 - Death Takes a Hand (1993) [Britain–Takeout Double]
- ❏ 2 - Grand Slam (1994)

Penny Wanawake . . . 6-ft. photographer daughter of black UN diplomat in England
- ❏ 1 - Penny Black (1984)
- ❏ 2 - Penny Dreadful (1984)
- ❏ 3 - Penny Post (1985)
- ❏ 4 - Penny Royal (1986)
- ❏ 5 - Penny Wise (1988)
- ❏ 6 - Penny Pinching (1989)
- ❏ 7 - Penny Saving (1993)

Kate Morgan is the pseudonym used by Ann Hamilton Whitman for her Dewey James series featuring a 60-something small-town librarian who is also the widow of a police chief. Her hometown knows her as slightly eccentric and given to quoting often from the literary classics.

Dewey James . . . 60-something small-town librarian
- ❏ 1 - A Slay at the Races (1990)
- ❏ 2 - Murder Most Fowl (1991)
- ❏ 3 - Home Sweet Homicide (1992)
- ❏ 4 - Mystery Loves Company (1992)
- ❏ 5 - Days of Crime and Roses (1992)
- ❏ 6 - Wanted Dude or Alive (1994)

Ann Morice is the pseudonym used by Felicity Shaw for her 23-book series which debuted in 1970 with English actress Theresa "Tessa" Crichton. Married to a film director, this author has also written several plays and four non-series novels. Her series regulars include Tessa's cousin, playwright Toby Crichton, Toby's daughter Ellen and detective inspector Robin Price who becomes Tessa's husband in book two. Owing in part to her husband's work with UNESCO and the World Bank, Morice has lived in Egypt, Kenya, Cyprus, Sudan, Tunisia, Uganda, India, France, Taiwan and the United States.

Tessa Crichton . . . English actress sleuth

- ❏ 1 - Death in the Grand Manor (1970)
- ❏ 2 - Murder in Married Life (1971)
- ❏ 3 - Death in the Round (1972)
- ❏ 4 - Death of a Dog (1973)
- ❏ 5 - Murder on French Leave (1973)
- ❏ 6 - Death of a Dutiful Daughter (1974)
- ❏ 7 - Death of a Heavenly Twin (1974)
- ❏ 8 - Killing with Kindness (1975)
- ❏ 9 - Nursery Tea and Poison (1975)
- ❏ 10 - Death of a Wedding Guest (1976)
- ❏ 11 - Murder in Mimicry (1977)
- ❏ 12 - Scared to Death (1977)
- ❏ 13 - Murder by Proxy (1978)
- ❏ 14 - Murder in Outline (1979)
- ❏ 15 - Men in Her Death (1981)
- ❏ 16 - Sleep of Death (1982)
- ❏ 17 - Hollow Vengeance (1982)
- ❏ 18 - Murder Post-Dated (1983)
- ❏ 19 - Getting Away with Murder (1984)
- ❏ 20 - Dead on Cue (1985)
- ❏ 21 - Publish and Be Killed (1986)
- ❏ 22 - Treble Exposure (1987)
- ❏ 23 - Fatal Charm (1988)

Patricia Moyes is the author of a long-running series featuring globe-trotting Scotland Yard Chief Superintendent Henry Tibbett and his wife Emmy. Their travels reflect the author's varied residences—Switzerland, The Netherlands, Washington, DC and the British Virgin Islands as well as her favorite sports—skiing and sailing. Born in Ireland and educated in England, Moyes launched her writing career with a World War II documentary script on radar. She has written screenplays, served as assistant editor for *Vogue* magazine and company secretary for Peter Ustinov Productions and served in the Women's Auxiliary Air Force.

Henry & Emmy Tibbett . . . Scotland Yard Inspector & wife

- ❏ 1 - Dead Men Don't Ski (1959)
- ❏ 2 - Down Among the Dead Men (1961)
- ❏ 3 - Death on the Agenda (1962)

❏   4   -   Murder a la Mode   (1963)
❏   5   -   Falling Star   (1964)
❏   6   -   Johnny Underground   (1965)
❏   7   -   Murder Fantastical   (1967)
❏   8   -   Death and the Dutch Uncle   (1968)
❏   9   -   Many Deadly Returns   (1970)
❏   10   -   **Season of Snows and Sins**   (1971)   *Edgar winner* ★
❏   11   -   The Curious Affair of the Third Dog   (1973)
❏   12   -   Black Widower   (1975)
❏   13   -   The Coconut Killings   (1977)
❏   14   -   Who is Simon Warwick?   (1979)
❏   15   -   Angel Death   (1980)
❏   16   -   A Six-Letter Word for Death   (1983)
❏   17   -   Night Ferry to Death   (1985)
❏   18   -   Black Girl, White Girl   (1989)
❏   19   -   Twice in a Blue Moon   (1993)

Marcia Muller is widely credited as the first American author to write a detective series starring a woman private eye. In 1977 *Edwin of the Iron Shoes* launched the career of Sharon McCone, investigator for All Souls Legal Cooperative in San Francisco. Muller, a Detroit native and University of Michigan graduate, moved to the Bay area after college, where she has lived and worked since. In 1993 she was honored with a life achievement award by the Private Eye Writers of America.

Don't miss #6 in the McCone series where the Nameless Detective and Sharon McCone put their heads together at a San Diego convention of investigators. McCone narrates the odd-numbered chapters and Nameless the even ones, in a she-said-he-said routine that will make you grin. Muller and Pronzini have also collaborated on numerous short story anthologies in addition to their 1986 reference work, *1001 Midnights: The Aficionado's Guide to Mystery and Detective Fiction.*

Muller has created three California detectives:

Elena Oliverez . . . Mexican arts museum curator in Santa Barbara

     ❏   1   -   The Tree of Death   (1983)
     ❏   2   -   The Legend of the Slain Soldiers   (1985)
     ❏   3   -   Beyond the Grave   (1986)   [with Bill Pronzini]

Joanna Stark . . . Napa Valley international art investigator

     ❏   1   -   The Cavalier in White   (1986)
     ❏   2   -   There Hangs the Knife   (1988)
     ❏   3   -   Dark Star   (1989)

Sharon McCone . . . San Francisco legal co-op investigator

     ❏   1   -   Edwin of the Iron Shoes   (1977)
     ❏   2   -   Ask the Cards a Question   (1982)
     ❏   3   -   The Cheshire Cat's Eye   (1983)
     ❏   4   -   Games to Keep the Dark Away   (1984)

☑ 5 - Leave a Message for Willie (1984)
❑ 6 - Double (1984) [with Bill Pronzini]
❑ 7 - There's Nothing to be Afraid Of (1985)
❑ 8 - Eye of the Storm (1988)
❑ 9 - There's Something in a Sunday (1989)
❑ 10 - **The Shape of Dread** (1989) *American Mystery Award winner* ★
❑ 11 - Trophies and Dead Things (1990)
❑ 12 - Where Echoes Live (1991)
❑ 13 - Pennies on a Dead Woman's Eyes (1992)
❑ 14 - **Wolf in the Shadows** (1993) *Anthony winner* ★
    Edgar & Shamus nominee ☆
❑ 15 - Till the Butchers Cut Him Down (1994)

Amy Myers is the creator of a Victorian mystery series featuring master chef Auguste Didier who is both British and French.

Auguste Didier . . . British-French master chef in late Victorian England
❑ 1 - Murder in Pug's Parlour (1982)
❑ 2 - Murder in the Limelight (1987)

Tamar Myers is the creator of a new mystery series featuring Magdalena Yoder who owns and operates a Mennonite inn in Pennsylvania.

Magdalena Yoder . . . Pennsylvania Mennonite inn owner & operator
❑ 1 - Too Many Crooks Spoil the Broth (1994)

Magdalen Nabb is an Englishwoman who has lived in Florence since 1975, the setting for her mystery series featuring the very appealing Marshal Salvatore Guarnaccia. Nabb was originally a potter, but now paints exquisite portraits of the city of Florence and the people who live there. In addition to her Guarnaccia series she has also written a novel, one play and three novels for juveniles featuring a young girl named Josie Smith.

Salvatore Guarnaccia . . . Italian police marshal in Florence
❑ 1 - Death of an Englishman (1981)
❑ 2 - Death of a Dutchman (1982)
❑ 3 - Death in Springtime (1983)
❑ 4 - Death in Autumn (1984)
❑ 5 - The Marshal and the Murderer (1987)
❑ 6 - The Marshal and the Madwoman (1988)
❑ 7 - The Marshal's Own Case (1990)
❑ 8 - The Marshal Makes His Report (1991)
❑ 9 - The Marshal at the Villa Torrini (1994)

Janet Neel is the creator of John McLeish of Scotland Yard and civil servant Francesca Wilson whose first adventure won the John Creasey first novel prize from the British Crime Writers Association. This series has lots of wonderful music background thanks to Francesca's four brothers, one of whom is a rock star. The author, like her female protagonist, was once an administrator in Britain's Department of Trade and Industry, but now works in London's financial district

John McLeish & Francesca Wilson . . . detective inspector & civil servant in England

- ❏ 1 - **Death's Bright Angel** (1988) *Creasey Award winner* ★
- ❏ 2 - Death on Site (1989)
- ❏ 3 - **Death of a Partner** (1994) *Gold Dagger nominee* ☆
- ❏ 4 - Death Among the Dons (1994)

Barbara Neely is the creator of Blanche White, whose first outing was awarded both the Agatha and Anthony for best first novel. Neely's short fiction has been published in various anthologies. She lives in Jamaica Plain, Massachusetts.

Blanche White . . . middle-aged black domestic

- ❏ 1 - **Blanche on the Lamb** (1992)
  Agatha, Anthony and Macavity winner ★
- ❏ 2 - Blanche Among the Talented Tenth (1994)

Sharan Newman is the creator of a historical series featuring novice and scholar Catherine LeVendeur in 12th century France. Herself a medievalist, Newman is completing a PhD in history. She has also written an Arthurian trilogy, science fiction short stories and numerous academic papers.

Catherine LeVendeur . . . novice & scholar in 12th century France

- ❏ 1 - **Death Comes as Epiphany** (1993)
  Agatha, Anthony & Macavity nominee ☆
- ❏ 2 - The Devil's Door (1994)

Suzanne North is the creator of a new series featuring Phoebe Fairfax Calgary TV video photographer.

Phoebe Fairfax . . . TV video photographer from Calgary, Canada

- ❏ 1 - Healthy, Wealthy & Dead (1994)

Meg O'Brien is the creator of series detective Jessica James, investigative reporter, smart-mouthed investigator and recovering alcoholic from Rochester, New York. Her sometimes lover is mobster Marcus Andrelli from the elite branch of the New York mob where everybody went to Harvard and drugs and prostitution are out. O'Brien once lived in Rochester, but is now a resident of Redondo Beach, California.

Jessica James . . . Rochester, New York newspaper reporter
- ❏ 1 - The Daphne Decisions (1990)
- ❏ 2 - Salmon in the Soup (1990)
- ❏ 3 - Hare Today, Gone Tomorrow (1991)
- ❏ 4 - Eagles Die Too (1992)
- ❏ 5 - Thin Ice (1993)

Maxine O'Callaghan, a native of Tennessee, has written horror and dark suspense, in addition to romance and mystery. Her five titles in the Delilah West series feature an Orange County P.I. whose husband and business partner is murdered in the first book. Delilah is sometimes cited as the first contemporary American woman P.I., based on her 1974 introduction in an *Alfred Hitchcock Mystery Magazine* short story.

O'Callaghan will introduce a new series detective in 1995—child psychologist Dr. Anne Menlo.

Delilah West . . . Orange County, California P.I.
- ❏ 1 - Death is Forever (1980)
- ❏ 2 - Run from Nightmare (1981)
- ❏ 3 - Hit and Run (1989)
- ❏ 4 - Set-Up (1991)
- ❏ 5 - Trade-Off (1994)

Carol O'Connell is the creator of a new series featuring Kathleen Mallory, NYPD cop raised by a police inspector and his wife after a youth of crime on the streets of New York.

Kathleen Mallory . . . NYPD cop
- ❏ 1 - Mallory's Oracle (1994)

Catherine O'Donnell is the creator of a new series featuring NYPD homicide detective Karen Levinson.

Karen Levinson . . . New York City homicide detective
- ❏ 1 - Skins (1993)

Lillian O'Donnell is best known for Norah Mulcahaney, NYPD star of crime fiction's longest-running police series, featuring a woman officer who starts as a rookie in 1960. O'Donnell, who originally trained as an actor, director and stage manager, has also written two other series with women protagonists.

The Mici (pronounced Mitzi) Anhalt series features a Hungarian-American (like O'Donnell herself) caseworker with the Crime Victim's Compensation Board. The Gwenn Ramadge series, O'Donnell's newest, debuted in 1990, featuring a young woman P.I. some think reminiscent of Cordelia Gray.

Gwenn Ramadge . . . New York City P.I. for corporate investigations
- ❏ 1 - A Wreath for the Bride (1990)
- ❏ 2 - Used to Kill (1993)

Mici Anhalt . . . New York City criminal justice investigator
- ❏ 1 - Aftershock (1977)
- ❏ 2 - Falling Star (1979)
- ❏ 3 - Wicked Designs (1980)

Norah Mulcahaney . . . NYPD detective
- ❏ 1 - The Phone Calls (1972)
- ❏ 2 - Don't Wear Your Wedding Ring (1973)
- ❏ 3 - Dial 557 R-A-P-E (1974)
- ❏ 4 - The Baby Merchants (1975)
- ❏ 5 - Leisure Dying (1976)
- ❏ 6 - No Business Being a Cop (1979)
- ❏ 7 - The Children's Zoo (1981)
- ❏ 8 - Cop Without a Shield (1983)
- ❏ 9 - Ladykiller (1984)
- ❏ 10 - Casual Affairs (1985)
- ❏ 11 - The Other Side of the Door (1987)
- ❏ 12 - **A Good Night to Kill** (1989) *American Mystery Award winner* ★
- ❏ 13 - A Private Crime (1991)
- ❏ 14 - Pushover (1992)
- ❏ 15 - Lockout (1994)

Sister Carol Anne O'Marie, CSJ, taught Catholic school in Arizona and California for 20 years before becoming director of a shelter for homeless women. Her series character, Sister Mary Helen, is a 70-something San Francisco nun with a talent for running into murder.

Sister Mary Helen . . . San Francisco, California 70-something nun
- ❏ 1 - A Novena for Murder (1984)
- ❏ 2 - Advent of Dying (1986)
- ❏ 3 - The Missing Madonna (1988)
- ☑ 4 - Murder in Ordinary Time (1991)
- ❏ 5 - Murder Makes a Pilgrimmage (1993)

Shannon OCork of New York City is the author of a three-book series featuring Theresa Tracy Baldwin, sports photographer for a New York daily newspaper.

Theresa Tracy Baldwin . . . sports photographer for New York daily

- ❏ 1 - Sports Freak (1980)
- ❏ 2 - End of the Line (1981)
- ❏ 3 - Hell Bent for Heaven (1983)

Susan Oleksiw is the creator of police chief Joe Silva and editor of the 1988 *Reader's Guide to the Classic British Mystery*, which provides short synopses of the works of 121 authors up to 1985. Within the almost 600 pages of this ambitious work, Oleksiw provides helpful information about the British class system and structure of the metropolitan and local police forces.

Joe Silva . . . chief of police in Washington State

- ❏ 1 - Murder in Mellingham (1993)
- ❏ 2 - Double Take (1994)

B. J. Oliphant is a pseudonym used by Sheri S. Tepper, best-selling author of science fiction, who writes mysteries under two different names. As B. J. Oliphant, Tepper writes the Shirley McClintock series about a 50-something Washington, DC career woman who returns to manage the family ranch in Colorado after the death of her parents.

As A. J. Orde, she is the creator of Jason Lynx, Denver antiques dealer and compulsive puzzle-solver. His romantic interest, Grace Willis, just happens to be a Denver cop, making this series a delightful reversal of the female amateur detective with a male-cop-as-love-interest.

Shirley McClintock . . . 50-something 6' 2" ex-Washington DC insider turned Colorado rancher

- ❏ 1 - **Dead in the Scrub** (1990) *Edgar nominee* ☆
- ❏ 2 - The Unexpected Corpse (1990)
- ❏ 3 - Deservedly Dead (1992)
- ❏ 4 - Death and the Delinquent (1992)
- ❏ 5 - Death Served Up Cold (1994)

Maria Antonia Oliver, born in Manacor, Majorca, Spain, is a leading Catalan writer who is also well known as a translator of English and American classics into her native language. Her first mystery featuring Catalan investigator Lonia Guiu was well received in Europe and North America.

Lonia Guiu . . . Catalan private investigator

- ❏ 1 - A Study in Lilac (1987)
- ❏ 2 - Antipodes (1989)

A. J. Orde is a pseudonym used by Sheri S. Tepper, best-selling author of science fiction, who writes mysteries under two different names. As A. J. Orde she's the creator of Jason Lynx, Denver antiques dealer and compulsive puzzle solver. His romantic interest, Grace Willis, just happens to be a Denver cop, making this series a delightful reversal of the female amateur detective with a male-cop-as-love-interest.

As B. J. Oliphant, Tepper writes the Shirley McClintock series about a 50-something Washington, DC career woman who returns to manage the family ranch in Colorado after the death of her parents.

> **Jason Lynx** . . . Denver, Colorado antiques dealer
> - ❏   1   -   A Little Neighborhood Murder (1989)
> - ❏   2   -   Death and the Dogwalker (1990)
> - ❏   3   -   Death For Old Times' Sake (1992)
> - ❏   4   -   Looking for the Aardvark [paperback–Dead on Sunday] (1993)

Denise Osborne, of Capitola, California, has won awards for her screenplays and short films. Her new mystery series features Queenie Davilow, struggling screenwriter, who moonlights doing security checks on the Hollywood film community.

> **Queenie Davilow** . . . Hollywood screenwriter
> - ❏   1   -   Murder Offscreen (1994)
> - ❏   2   -   Cut to: Murder (1995)

Abigail Padgett is a former court investigator in San Diego who works as an advocate for the mentally ill. She has an avid interest in desert preservation and Native American cultures. Her critically acclaimed debut novel was the first to showcase an investigator living with manic depression. A powerful and informative story.

> **Barbara Joan "Bo" Bradley** . . . San Diego, California child abuse investigator
> - ❏   1   -   **Child of Silence** (1993) *Agatha & Anthony nominee* ☆
> - ❏   2   -   Strawgirl (1994)
> - ❏   3   -   Turtle Baby (1995)

Katherine Hall Page won the Agatha for best first novel with her opening title in the Faith Sibley Fairchild series in 1990. Daughter of a minister and wife of a minister, this catering detective paints her church characters and small-town New England with just the right brushes.

Faith Sibley Fairchild . . . Massachusetts minister's wife & culinary artist
- ❏ 1 - **The Body in the Belfry** (1990) *Agatha winner* ★
- ❏ 2 - The Body in the Kelp (1991)
- ❏ 3 - The Body in the Bouillon (1991)
- ❏ 4 - The Body in the Vestibule (1992)
- ❏ 5 - The Body in the Cast (1993)
- ❏ 6 - The Body in the Basement (1994)

Robin Paige is the pseudonym used by Susan Wittig Albert and her husband Bill for their charming new Victorian series set in England with an American detective. She is Kathryn Ardleigh, 25-year-old self-supporting writer of penny dreadfuls who gets called to England to act as secretary to an aunt she didn't know she had.

Kathryn Ardleigh . . . 25-year-old American author who travels to Victorian England
- ❏ 1 - Death at Bishop's Keep (1994)
- ❏ 2 - Death at Gallows Green (1995)

Orania Papazoglou is the creator of the Patience Campbell McKenna series featuring a romance novelist turned crime writer. A never-published magazine exposé on the romance publishing business became fodder for this humorous series. Before turning to mystery writing, Papazoglou was editor of *Greek Accent* magazine and freelanced for *Glamour, Mademoiselle* and *Working Woman*. She also wrote two psychological thrillers as Papazoglou, but remains best known for her Gregor Demarkian series written as Jane Haddam (rhymes with Adam).

Patience Campbell McKenna . . . 6-ft. New York ex-romance & true crime writer
- ❏ 1 - Sweet, Savage Death (1984)
- ❏ 2 - Wicked, Loving Murder (1985)
- ❏ 3 - Death's Savage Passion (1986)
- ❏ 4 - Rich, Radiant Slaughter (1988)
- ❏ 5 - Once and Always Murder (1990)

Sara Paretsky grew up in Kansas where she earned her BA in political science summa cum laude at the University of Kansas. Before turning to mystery writing full time, she was a freelance business writer and later a marketing manager for a major insurance company. She has a PhD in history and an MBA from the University of Chicago. One of the founding members of Sisters in Crime, she served as its first president in 1986.

Paretsky's series detective is V. I. Warshawski, one of the toughest and best-selling private eyes in contemporary fiction. V. I. (Victoria Iphegenia) is the daughter of a Polish cop and an Italian-Jewish opera singer. A former public defender, this P.I. has a nose for white collar crime. In addition to a Silver Dagger in 1988, Paretsky won a 1991 Anthony for *A Woman's Eye*, a collection of 21 short stories by well-known women crime writers.

> **V. I. Warshawski** . . . Chicago, Illinois attorney turned P.I.
>
> - ❏   1 - Indemnity Only (1982)
> - ❏   2 - Deadlock (1984)
> - ❏   3 - Killing Orders (1985)
> - ❏   4 - Bitter Medicine (1987)
> - ❏   5 - **Blood Shot** (1988) [Britain–Toxic Shock]
>   ***Silver Dagger winner*** ★ ***Anthony nominee*** ☆
> - ☑   6 - Burn Marks (1990)
> - ☑   7 - Guardian Angel (1991)
> - ☑   8 - Tunnel Vision (1994)

Edith Pargeter, better known for her work under the Ellis Peters pseudonym, is the creator of a mystery series featuring the Felse family of detectives who solve cases together and individually, including 13-year-old Dominic who finds a body in the opening book. Later titles spotlight Dominic's policeman father George and his mother Bunty. The second novel in this series won an Edgar award as best mystery novel of 1962. The author was awarded a Diamond Dagger for lifetime achievement in 1993.

> **Felse Family of detectives** . . . Inspector George, wife Bunty & son Dominic in Shropshire, England
>
> - ❏   1 - Fallen into the Pit (1951)
> - ❏   2 - **Death and the Joyful Woman** (1962) *Edgar winner* ★
> - ❏   3 - Flight of a Witch (1964)
> - ❏   4 - A Nice Derangement of Epitaphs (1965) [U.S.–Who Lies Here]
> - ❏   5 - The Piper on the Mountain (1966)
> - ❏   6 - Black is the Colour of My True Love's Heart (1967)
> - ❏   7 - The Grass Widow's Tale (1968)
> - ❏   8 - The House of Green Turf (1969)
> - ❏   9 - Morning Raga (1969)
> - ❏   10 - The Knocker on Death's Door (1970)
> - ❏   11 - Death to the Landlords! (1972)
> - ❏   12 - City of Gold and Shadows (1973)
> - ❏   13 - Rainbow's End (1978)

Barbara Parker is the creator of a new legal mystery series featuring corporate attorney Gail Connor.

> **Gail Connor** . . . corporate attorney
> ❏ 1 - Suspicion of Innocence (1994)

Barbara Paul is a former English and drama teacher with a working theatre background. Her historical mystery series features opera stars Enrico Caruso and Geraldine Farrar as amateur sleuths. Paul also has a police series featuring NYPD officer Marian Larch and her friend Kelly Ingram, television actress.

> **Enrico Caruso & Geraldine Farrar** . . . Italian tenor & American soprano
> ❏ 1 - A Cadenza for Caruso (1984)
> ❏ 2 - Prima Donna at Large (1985)
> ❏ 3 - A Chorus of Detectives (1987)
>
> **Marian Larch** . . . NYPD officer
> ❏ 1 - The Renewable Virgin (1984)
> ❏ 2 - You Have the Right to Remain Silent (1992)
> ❏ 3 - The Apostrophe Thief (1993)
> ❏ 4 - Fare Play (1995)

Joanne Pence is a San Francisco native and manager with the Social Security Administration. In her romantic mystery series, freelance cooking writer Angelina Amalfi gets involved with San Francisco homicide detective Paavo Smith, much to the dissatisfaction of Angelina's wealthy father and Paavo's colleagues. The first series title was nominated for "Best Romantic Suspense of 1993" by the Romance Writers of America.

> **Angelina Amalfi** . . . food columnist
> ❏ 1 - Something's Cooking (1993)
> ❏ 2 - Too Many Cooks (1994)

Anne Perry, born in London, is the creator of two historical mystery series set in Victorian England. The longer-running series (set in the late 1880s) features Inspector Thomas Pitt and his wife Charlotte who leaves her upper-middle-class home to marry the policeman after assisting him with the case featured in their first installment. Meanwhile her sister Emily marries "up" the social ladder and she and Charlotte work together "assisting" Thomas with future investigations.

The second series features Inspector William Monk who wakes up in a hospital during the mid-1850s with no recall of his identity. Lucky for Monk, capable nurse Hester Latterly is on the job. Prior to launching her mystery-writing career, Perry worked as a flight attendant, store buyer and property underwriter in Los Angeles where she lived from 1967 to 1972. She now lives in Scotland.

Inspector William Monk . . . amnesiac Victorian policeman

- ❑   1   -   **The Face of a Stranger** (1990) *Agatha nominee* ☆
- ❑   2   -   A Dangerous Mourning (1991)
- ❑   3   -   **Defend and Betray** (1992) *American Mystery Award winner* ★
- ❑   4   -   A Sudden, Fearful Death (1993)
- ❑   5   -   Sins of the Wolf (1994)

Thomas & Charlotte Pitt . . . Victorian police inspector & wife

- ❑   1   -   The Cater Street Hangman (1979)
- ❑   2   -   Callander Square (1980)
- ❑   3   -   Paragon Walk (1981)
- ❑   4   -   Resurrection Row (1981)
- ❑   5   -   Rutland Place (1983)
- ❑   6   -   Bluegate Fields (1984)
- ❑   7   -   Death in Devil's Acre (1985)
- ❑   8   -   Cardington Crescent (1987)
- ❑   9   -   Silence in Hanover Close (1988)
- ❑   10   -   Bethlehem Road (1990)
- ❑   11   -   Highgate Rise (1991)
- ❑   12   -   Belgrave Square (1992)
- ❑   13   -   Farrier's Lane (1993)
- ❑   14   -   The Hyde Park Headsman (1994)

Elizabeth Peters is only one of the pseudonyms of the talented and prolific Barbara Mertz who holds a PhD in Egyptology from the University of Chicago. As Elizabeth Peters she is the creator of three mystery series, the best-known featuring Amelia Peabody, brilliant Victorian archaeologist. Amelia's adventures include her Egyptologist husband Radcliffe Emerson and their precocious son Ramses. Peters' other series stars are Jacqueline Kirby, middle-aged librarian romance novelist and Vicky Bliss, tall, voluptuous and clever art historian.

As Barbara Micheals, she is the author of six consecutive *New York Times* best sellers and in 1987 was awarded the Anthony Grand Master for her suspense thrillers. As Barbara Mertz, she is also the author of non-fiction books on Egyptology. The author lives in a historic farmhouse in Frederick, Maryland with two dogs and six cats.

Amelia Peabody . . . Victorian feminist archaeologist

- ❑   1   -   Crocodile on the Sandbank (1975)
- ❑   2   -   The Curse of the Pharaohs (1981)
- ❑   3   -   The Mummy Case (1985)
- ❑   4   -   Lion in the Valley (1986)
- ❑   5   -   The Deeds of the Disturber (1988)
- ❑   6   -   The Last Camel Died at Noon (1991)
- ❑   7   -   The Snake, The Crocodile and the Dog (1992)

Jacqueline Kirby . . . librarian turned romance novelist

- ❑   1 - The Seventh Sinner (1972)
- ❑   2 - The Murders of Richard III (1974)
- ❑   3 - Die for Love (1984)
- ❑   4 - **Naked Once More** (1989)
     Agatha & American Mystery Award winner ★

Vicky Bliss . . . art historian in Bavaria

- ❑   1 - Borrower of the Night (1973)
- ❑   2 - Street of the Five Moons (1978)
- ❑   3 - Silhouette in Scarlet (1983)
- ❑   4 - Trojan Gold (1987)
- ❑   5 - Night Train to Memphis (1994)

Ellis Peters is the pseudonym of Edith Mary Pargeter, English novelist and mystery writer widely known as the creator of Brother Cadfael, a 12th century Welshman and herbalist at the Benedictine monastery of St. Peter and St. Paul in Shrewsbury, England. The author once worked as a chemist's assistant and served in the Royal Navy where she received the British Empire Medal in 1944. She began her publishing career with historical and straight novels written as Edith Pargeter, before launching her mystery career with the Felse Family series, also under her own name. To avoid confusing her readers, she adopted the Ellis Peters pseudonym when she initiated the Brother Cadfael series in 1977.

In addition to her work as Peters and Pargeter, she published two mysteries as Joylon Carr—*Murder in the Dispensary* (1938) and *Death Comes by Post* (1940). She has also translated numerous English works of fiction and non-fiction into Czech. She has won an Edgar and a Silver Dagger in addition to the Diamond Dagger she was awarded in 1993 by the British Crime Writers Association.

Brother Cadfael . . . Shrewsbury, England medieval monk & herbalist

- ❑   1 - A Morbid Taste for Bones (1977)
- ❑   2 - One Corpse Too Many (1979)
- ❑   3 - Monk's Hood (1980)
- ❑   4 - St. Peter's Fair (1981)
- ❑   5 - The Leper of St. Giles (1981)
- ❑   6 - The Virgin in the Ice (1982)
- ❑   7 - The Sanctuary Sparrow (1983)
- ☑   8 - The Devil's Novice (1983)
- ❑   9 - The Dead Man's Ransom (1984)
- ❑ 10 - The Pilgrim of Hate (1984)
- ❑ 11 - An Excellent Mystery (1985)
- ❑ 12 - The Raven in the Foregate (1986)
- ☑ 13 - The Rose Rent (1986)
- ❑ 14 - The Hermit of Eyton Forest (1987)
- ❑ 15 - The Confession of Brother Haluin (1988)
- ❑ 16 - The Heretic's Apprentice (1989)
- ❑ 17 - The Potter's Field (1989)

❏ 18 - Summer of the Danes (1991)
❏ 19 - The Holy Thief (1992)
☑ 20 - Brother Cadfael's Penance (1994)

Audrey Peterson

Audrey Peterson, like her series character Claire Camden, is an English professor who travels to England for academic research. Peterson is a California native who now makes her home in the Pacific Northwest. Her earlier mysteries were also set in England, with music professor Andrew Quentin and his former graduate student Jane Winfield.

Claire Camden . . . California English professor in Britain
❏ 1 - Dartmoor Burial (1992)
❏ 2 - Death Too Soon (1994)

Jane Winfield . . . British journalist & music writer
❏ 1 - The Nocturne Murder (1988)
❏ 2 - Death in Wessex (1989)
❏ 3 - Murder in Burgundy (1989)
❏ 4 - Deadly Rehearsal (1990)
❏ 5 - Elegy in a Country Graveyard (1990)
❏ 6 - Lament for Christabel (1991)

Nancy Pickard

Nancy Pickard, of Fairway, Kansas, is a ten-time nominee and five-time winner of Agatha, Anthony, Edgar and Macavity awards for her Jenny Cain mystery series featuring the director of a charitable foundation in the seaport town of Port Frederick, Massachusetts, where the bankrupt Cain Clams was once the town's largest employer. Pickard is a past president of Sisters in Crime and author of *The 27-Ingredient Chili Con Carne Murders* which is based on an unfinished manuscript left by Virginia Rich at the time of her death. Pickard has also won numerous awards for her short stories.

Jenny Cain . . . Port Frederick, Massachusetts foundation director
❏ 1 - Generous Death (1984)
❏ 2 - **Say No to Murder** (1985) *Anthony winner* ★
❏ 3 - **No Body** (1986) *Anthony nominee* ☆
❏ 4 - **Marriage is Murder** (1987) *Macavity winner* ★ *Anthony nominee* ☆
❏ 5 - **Dead Crazy** (1988) *Anthony & Agatha nominee* ☆
❏ 6 - **Bum Steer** (1989) *Agatha winner* ★
❏ 7 - **I. O. U.** (1991) *Agatha & Macavity winner* ★ *Edgar nominee* ☆
❏ 8 - But I Wouldn't Want to Die There (1993)
❏ 9 - Confession (1994)

Marissa Piesman is a prosecuting attorney in Manhattan who launched her writing career as coauthor of *The Yuppie Handbook*. Piesman is the creator of series detective Nina Fischman, neurotic New York attorney for the Legal Services Project for Seniors. Nina and her energetic mother Ida obsess in style about money, men, fashion, crime, religion and more.

Nina Fischman . . . New York City legal services attorney
- ❑ 1 - Unorthodox Practices (1989)
- ❑ 2 - Personal Effects (1991)
- ❑ 3 - Heading Uptown (1993)
- ❑ 4 - Close Quarters (1994)

Elizabeth Pincus is a San Francisco film editor, freelance writer and former private eye. Her Lambda award-winning series features Nell Fury, a lesbian P.I. working in San Francisco.

Nell Fury . . . San Francisco, California lesbian P.I.
- ❑ 1 - The Two-Bit Tango (1992)
- ❑ 2 - The Solitary Twist (1993)
- ❑ 3 - The Hangdog Hustle (1995)

Zelda Popkin is the creator of a five-book series from the early 1940s which feature former department store detective Mary Carner.

Mary Carner . . . former department store detective
- ❑ 1 - Death Wears a White Gardenia (1938)
- ❑ 2 - Murder in the Mist (1940)
- ❑ 3 - Time Off for Murder (1940)
- ❑ 4 - Dead Man's Gift (1941)
- ❑ 5 - No Crime for a Lady (1942)

Anna Porter has had a highly successful career in Canadian publishing, as editor-in-chief of McClelland and Stewart, president of Seal Books, publisher of Key Porter Books, chairman of Doubleday Canada and author of mystery thrillers. Porter's first-hand experience with the international publishing world adds a special dimension to her character Judith Hayes, freelance journalist and mother of two teenagers.

Judith Hayes . . . journalist
- ❑ 1 - Hidden Agenda (1985)
- ❑ 2 - Mortal Sins (1987)

Sandra West Prowell is a fourth-generation Montanan, cofounder of the Montana Authors Coalition and coproducer of the literary heritage map of Montana. She is the creator of the Shamus-nominated series featuring a Montana P.I. Phoebe Siegel. When Prowell isn't writing, she enjoys fishing, beading and researching herbal and medicinal plants native to Montana.

> **Phoebe Siegel** . . . Billings, Montana ex-cop P.I.
> - ❏   1 -   **By Evil Means** (1993) ***Shamus nominee*** ☆
> - ❏   2 -   The Killing of Monday Brown (1994)

Dianne G. Pugh, a Los Angeles native and UCLA graduate, currently works as a marketing director for a California computer company. She has a BA in philosophy and an MBA in marketing and finance. Her series detective Iris Thorne is a 30-something Los Angeles investment counselor

> **Iris Thorne** . . . Los Angeles investment counselor
> - ❏   1 -   Cold Call (1993)
> - ❏   2 -   Slow Squeeze (1994)

Mary Monica Pulver is the author name used by Mary Pulver Kuhfeld of St. Louis Park, Minnesota for her series featuring Illinois police detective Peter Brichter and his horse breeder wife Kori Price. Horse loving fans of police procedurals will enjoy this series where the second installment actually begins the story. Kuhfeld also writes a medieval mystery series with Gail Bacon under the shared pseudonym of Margaret Frazer.

> **Peter & Kori Price Brichter** . . . Illinois police detective & horse breeder
> - ❏   1 -   Murder at the War (1987) [aka Knight Fall]
> - ❏   2 -   The Unforgiving Minutes (1988) [prequel to #1]
> - ❏   3 -   Ashes to Ashes (1988)
> - ❏   4 -   Original Sin (1991)
> - ❏   5 -   Show Stopper (1992)

Elizabeth Quinn is the creator of a new series featuring Lauren Maxwell, a widowed mother of two and Anchorage-based naturalist-investigator for the Wild American Society.

> **Lauren Maxwell** . . . Alaska wildlife investigator PhD
> - ❏   1 -   Murder Most Grizzly (1993)

Sheila Radley is the creator of Inspector Douglas Quantrill, English village police detective, who is joined by a woman partner, Sergeant Hilary Lloyd, in the fourth book in this series.

Douglas Quantrill & Hilary Lloyd . . . Suffolk, England detective chief inspector & sergeant partner

❑   1 - Death and the Maiden (1978) [U.S.–Death in the Morning]
❑   2 - The Chief Inspector's Daughter (1980)
❑   3 - A Talent for Destruction (1982)
❑   4 - Blood on the Happy Highway (1983) [U.S.–The Quiet Road to Death]
❑   5 - Fate Worse Than Death (1985)
❑   6 - Who Saw Him Die? (1987)
❑   7 - This Way Out (1989)
❑   8 - Cross My Heart and Hope to Die (1992)

Helen Reilly (1891-1962) is the creator of NYPD homicide detective Christopher McKee, known as the Scotchman among his colleagues, in a 31-book series that ran from 1930 until 1962. During the 1930s she also wrote four non-series mysteries under her own name and three more during the 1940s under the name Kiernan Abbey. She was born in New York City where her father Dr. James Kiernan was president of Columbia University. She was married to artist Paul Reilly and two of their four daughters grew up to write prize-winning mysteries— Ursula Curtiss and Mary McMullen, fashion designer and advertising executive.

Christopher McKee . . . Manhattan homicide squad detective

❑   1 - The Diamond Feather (1930)
❑   2 - Murder in the Mews (1931)
❑   3 - McKee of Centre Street (1934)
❑   4 - The Line-up (1934)
❑   5 - Mr. Smith's Hat (1936)
❑   6 - Dead Man's Control (1936)
❑   7 - Dead for a Ducat (1939)
❑   8 - All Concerned Notified (1939)
❑   9 - Murder in Shinbone Alley (1940)
❑ 10 - Death Demands an Audience (1940)
❑ 11 - The Dead Can Tell (1940)
❑ 12 - Mourned on Sunday (1941)
❑ 13 - Three Women in Black (1941)
❑ 14 - Name Your Poison (1942)
❑ 15 - The Opening Door (1944)
❑ 16 - Murder on Angler's Island (1945)
❑ 17 - The Silver Leopard (1946)
❑ 18 - The Farmhouse (1947)
❑ 19 - Staircase 4 (1949)
❑ 20 - Murder at Arroways (1950)
❑ 21 - Lament for the Bride (1951)
❑ 22 - The Double Man (1952)
❑ 23 - The Velvet Hand (1953)

❑ 24 - Tell Her It's Murder (1954)
❑ 25 - Compartment K (1955) [Britain–Murder Rides the Express]
❑ 26 - The Canvas Dagger (1956)
❑ 27 - Ding Dong Bell (1958)
❑ 28 - Not Me, Inspector (1959)
❑ 29 - Follow Me (1960)
❑ 30 - Certain Sleep (1961)
❑ 31 - The Day She Died (1962)

Ruth Rendell, the author of more than 30 mysteries, has been called the best mystery writer anywhere in the English-speaking world. She has won three Edgars, three Gold Daggers, a Silver Dagger and a special National Book Award from the Arts Council of Great Britain. From the beginning of her career she has alternated traditional detective stories featuring Inspector Reginald Wexford with her more psychological crime novels, most of which appear under the Rendell name but some appear under the pseudonym Barbara Vine, including the critically acclaimed *Anna's Book* in 1994. Her first Barbara Vine title (*A Dark-Adapted Eye*) won the Edgar for best novel in 1986.

Rendell's Chief Inspector Wexford is described as corpulent and heavy with flint-colored eyes set in a snub-nosed ugly face. But he's a witty detective with a keen understanding of people. The author was born in London and worked for several years as a reporter and editor for newspapers in West Essex.

Reginald Wexford . . . Sussex, England chief inspector

❑ 1 - From Doon With Death (1964)
❑ 2 - A Wolf to Slaughter (1967)
❑ 3 - A New Lease on Death (1967)
❑ 4 - The Best Man to Die (1969)
❑ 5 - A Guilty Thing Surprised (1970)
❑ 6 - No More Dying Then (1971)
❑ 7 - Murder Being Once Done (1972)
❑ 8 - Some Lie and Some Die (1973)
❑ 9 - Shake Hands Forever (1975)
❑ 10 - A Sleeping Life (1978)
❑ 11 - Put on by Cunning (1981) [U.S.–Death Notes]
❑ 12 - The Speaker of Mandarin (1983)
❑ 13 - An Unkindness of Ravens (1985)
❑ 14 - The Veiled One (1988)
❑ 15 - Kissing the Grocer's Daughter (1993)
❑ 16 - Simisola (1994)

Virginia Rich is the creator of Eugenia Potter, congenial widow and good cook who divides her time between New England and Arizona, hosting lively dinner parties and delivering plenty of cooking wisdom. After Rich's death, Nancy Pickard was commissioned to complete the unfinished manuscript left by Rich, and *The 27-Ingredient Chili Con Carne Murders* is the delightful result.

Eugenia Potter . . . widowed chef in Maine and Arizona

- ❏ 1 - The Cooking School Murders (1982)
- ❏ 2 - The Baked Bean Supper Murders (1983)
- ❏ 3 - The Nantucket Diet Murders (1985)
- ❏ 4 - The 27-Ingredient Chili Con Carne Murders (1993) [Nancy Pickard]

Mary Roberts Rinehart (1876-1958) was once the highest paid writer in America and the first mystery writer with a novel on the year's best seller list (1909). She covered criminal trials and the American war effort for magazines during World War I and began her mystery writing with serials that were later published in book length. Originally trained as a nurse, she used her medical experience to write her only mystery series—featuring nurse Hilda Adams, also known as Miss Pinkerton. She wrote more than 15 non-series novels, in addition to several novelettes, numerous collections of short stories and her 1931 autobiography *My Story* which was revised in 1948. Early in her career she invested in the publishing company that was to become Farrar and Rinehart which published all her books after 1930. In 1953 she was awarded a special honor by the Mystery Writers of America.

Hilda Adams aka Miss Pinkerton . . . nurse & police agent in England

- ❏ 1 - Miss Pinkerton (1932)
- ❏ 2 - Haunted Lady (1942)
- ❏ 3 - The Wandering Knife (1952)

Candace M. Robb is the creator of Owen Archer, a Welsh archer and spy for the Archbishop, blind in one eye after a longbow incident. Robb has an MA in English literature and has completed her coursework for a PhD in medieval and Anglo-Saxon literature.

Owen Archer . . . medieval Welsh spy for the Archbishop

- ❏ 1 - The Apothecary Rose (1993)
- ❏ 2 - The Lady Chapel (1994)
- ❏ 3 - The Nun's Tale (1995)

Carey Roberts is the creator of a new police series featuring Washington, DC homicide detective Anne Fitzhugh. The author is a former individual and family therapist who lives in the Washington, DC area.

> **Anne Fitzhugh** . . . Washington, DC police detective
>
> ❏   1 -   Pray God to Die (1993)

Gillian Roberts is the pseudonym used by Judith Greber for her award-winning series featuring Amanda Pepper, 30-something high school English teacher at a Philadelphia prep school. Greber is a native Philadelphian, graduate of the University of Pennsylvania and a former high school English teacher. She presently lives in the San Francisco Bay area.

> **Amanda Pepper** . . . Philadelphia, Pennsylvania high school teacher
>
> ❏   1 -   **Caught Dead in Philadelphia** (1987) *Anthony winner* ★
> ❏   2 -   **Philly Stakes** (1989) *Agatha nominee* ☆
> ❏   3 -   I'd Rather Be in Philadelphia (1991)
> ❏   4 -   With Friends Like These (1993)
> ❏   5 -   How I Spent My Summer Vacation (1994)

Lora Roberts, born and raised in Missouri, now living in California, opened her Palo Alto series with *Revolting Development*, written as Lora Roberts Smith. Liz Sullivan, vagabond writer, is introduced in *Murder in a Nice Neighborhood* and is expected to return in 1995 in *Murder in the Marketplace*.

> **Liz Sullivan** . . . Palo Alto, California freelance writer
>
> ❏   1 -   Murder in a Nice Neighborhood (1994)
> ❏   2 -   Murder in the Marketplace (1995)

Julie Robitaille is the creator of a new mystery series featuring television sports reporter and amateur sleuth Kit Powell of San Diego, California.

> **Kit Powell** . . . San Diego, California TV sports reporter
>
> ❏   1 -   Jinx (1992)
> ❏   2 -   Iced (1994)

Nina Romberg, of Richardson, Texas, is the creator of a new series featuring Texas Caddo-Commanche medicine woman Marian Winchester.

> **Marian Winchester** . . . Texas Caddo-Commanche medicine woman
>
> ❏   1 -   The Spirit Stalker (1989)
> ❏   2 -   Shadow Walkers (1993)

Annette Roome, of Guilford, England, won the Creasey award for best first crime novel with her 1989 series opener *A Real Shot in the Arm* featuring 40-something cub reporter Christine Martin.

Christine Martin . . . 40-something cub reporter in England
- ❏ 1 - **A Real Shot in the Arm** (1989) *Creasey winner* ★
- ❏ 2 - A Second Shot in the Dark (1990)

Kate Ross is a trial attorney for a large Boston law firm. During her study of legal history at Yale Law School, she was fascinated by the lack of professional police in early 19th century England, a perfect setting for a clever amateur sleuth. Her series detective is the charming and elegant Julian Kestrel whose manservant Dipper is a former pickpocket.

Julian Kestrel . . . early 19th century Londoner
- ❏ 1 - Cut to the Quick (1993)
- ❏ 2 - A Broken Vessel (1994)

Rebecca Rothenberg of Los Angeles is the creator of a new series featuring MIT microbiologist Claire Sharples who leaves her Boston research post for a new job in the agricultural heartland of California. The first installment was nominated for both an Anthony and Agatha award.

Claire Sharples . . . California former MIT scholar & microbiologist
- ❏ 1 - **The Bulrush Murders** (1991) *Agatha & Anthony nominee* ☆
- ❏ 2 - The Dandelion Murders (1994)

Jennifer Rowe is an award-winning Australian writer and creator of a mystery series featuring Australian television researcher Birdie Birdwood. Rowe is also editor of *The Australian Women's Weekly*.

Verity "Birdie" Birdwood . . . Australian TV researcher
- ❏ 1 - Murder by the Book (1989)
- ❏ 2 - Grim Pickings (1991)
- ❏ 3 - Death in Store (1992) [short stories with Birdie]
- ❏ 4 - The Makeover Murders (1993)
- ❏ 5 - Stranglehold (1994)

Betty Rowlands, of Gloucester, England, is the creator of a mystery series featuring Melissa Craig, successful British crime novelist who leaves London to write from a quiet cottage in the Cotswolds.

> **Melissa Craig** . . . British mystery writer
> - ❏ 1 - Murder in the Cotswolds (1989)
> - ❏ 2 - A Little Gentle Sleuthing (1990)
> - ❏ 3 - Finishing Touch (1993)
> - ❏ 4 - Over the Edge (1993)
> - ❏ 5 - Exhaustive Inquiries (1994)

Medora Sale was born in Windsor, Ontario where her father was an attorney and official in the court system. With a BA in modern languages and a PhD in medieval studies, she has worked as a teacher, welfare case worker, advertising freelancer and translator while living in England, Switzerland, France and the United States. Her series detectives are John Sanders, Toronto homicide detective, and Harriet Jeffries, freelance architectural photographer. The first book in this series received the Ellis Award for best first mystery.

> **John Sanders & Harriet Jeffries** . . . Toronto, Canada police detective & architectural photographer
> - ❏ 1 - **Murder on the Run** (1986) *Ellis winner* ★
> - ❏ 2 - Murder in Focus (1989)
> - ❏ 3 - Murder in a Good Cause (1990)
> - ❏ 4 - Sleep of the Innocent (1991)
> - ❏ 5 - Pursued by Shadows (1992)
> - ❏ 6 - Short Cut to Santa Fe (1994)

Eve K. Sandstrom is a former award-winning reporter and columnist for the *Lawton Constitution* in Oklahoma, the home state for her series characters Sam and Nicky Titus after they are abruptly relocated from Germany soon after their marriage. Sam is an army criminal investigations officer and Nicky a working photojournalist and daughter of a general.

> **Sam & Nicky Titus** . . . ex-Army CID sheriff/rancher & his photojournalist wife in Oklahoma
> - ❏ 1 - Death Down Home (1990)
> - ❏ 2 - The Devil Down Home (1991)
> - ❏ 3 - The Down Home Heifer Heist (1993)

Corinne Holt Sawyer, former actor and TV writer, is a former director of academic special projects at Clemson University in South Carolina. She is also the creator of Angela Benbow and Caledonia Wingate, widows of Navy admirals and residents of a posh retirement community in southern California. They are physical and temperamental opposites—an engaging pair in the little old lady amateur tradition. Their first adventure was nominated for an Agatha.

Angela Benbow & Caledonia Wingate . . . 70-something admirals' widows in California

- ❏ 1 - **The J. Alfred Prufrock Murders** (1988) *Agatha nominee* ☆
- ❏ 2 - Murder in Gray & White (1989)
- ❏ 3 - Murder by Owl Light (1992)
- ❏ 4 - The Peanut Butter Murders (1993)
- ❏ 5 - Murder Has No Calories (1994)

Dorothy L. Sayers (1893-1957) was born in Oxford where her father was director of the Christchurch Cathedral Choir School. She learned Latin by the age of seven, picked up French from her governess, and later earned both BA and MA degrees from Oxford while teaching and working as a reader for a publishing company. During the 1920s she worked at a London advertising agency for seven years where she sold Coleman's mustard using the cartoon figures of a British colonel—which later inspired the creation of Colonel Mustard for the board game *Clue*. Sayers' renowned series detective is Lord Peter Wimsey, second son of the fifteenth Duke of Denver, pianist, book collector and criminologist. His love interest and future detecting partner Harriet Vane first appears in *Strong Poison*.

Lord Peter Wimsey . . . pianist, book collector & criminologist

- ❏ 1 - Whose Body? (1923)
- ☑ 2 - Clouds of Witness (1926)
- ☑ 3 - Unnatural Death (1927) [U.S.–The Dawson Pedigree]
- ☑ 4 - The Unpleasantness at the Bellona Club (1928)
- ☑ 5 - Lord Peter Views the Body (1929)
- ☑ 6 - Strong Poison (1930)
- ☑ 7 - Five Red Herrings (1931) [U.S.–Suspicious Characters]
- ☑ 8 - Have His Carcase (1932)
- ☑ 9 - Murder Must Advertise (1933)
- ❏ 10 - Hangman's Holiday (1933) [short story collection]
- ☑ 11 - The Nine Tailors (1934)
- ☑ 12 - Gaudy Night (1935)
- ☑ 13 - Busman's Honeymoon (1937)
- ❏ 14 - In the Teeth of the Evidence (1939)

S. E. Schenkel, of Farmington, Michigan, is the creator of a new series featuring Kate Frederick and her husband of 30 years, chief of detectives Ray.

Ray & Kate Frederick . . . Michigan chief of detectives & his wife of 30 years
- ❏ 1 - In Blacker Moments (1994)
- ❏ 2 - Death Days (1995)

Margaret Scherf created several series detectives for mysteries she wrote starting in the late 1940s, including a retired women pathologist, Dr. Grace Severance, whose first outing was set in Arizona. New York City was the backdrop for interior decorators Henry and Emily Bryce who first appear in 1949 and not again until 1963. Scherf also wrote some earlier stories featuring Martin Buell, an Episcopal rector from Montana who does some lively sleuthing despite his bishop's disapproval.

Dr. Grace Severance . . . retired pathologist
- ❏ 1 - The Banker's Bones (1968)
- ❏ 2 - To Cache a Millionaire (1972)
- ❏ 3 - The Beaded Banana (1978)

Emily & Henry Bryce . . . Manhattan interior decorators
- ❏ 1 - The Gun in Daniel Webster's Bust (1949)
- ❏ 2 - The Diplomat and the Gold Piano (1963)

Norma Schier is the author of a four-book series featuring Colorado district attorney Kay Barth.

Kay Barth . . . Colorado district attorney
- ❏ 1 - Death on the Slopes (1978)
- ❏ 2 - Murder by the Book (1979)
- ❏ 3 - Death Goes Skiing (1979)
- ❏ 4 - Demon at the Opera (1980)

Sandra Scoppettone, of Southold, New York, is the creator of the lesbian P.I. series featuring Lauren Laurano of Greenwich Village and her psychotherapist lover Kip. Scoppettone's first mysteries were published under the name Jack Early, including *A Creative Kind of Killer,* a non-series title which won the Shamus for best first P.I. novel in 1984. Scoppettone did not reveal her identity as Jack Early until recently.

Lauren Laurano . . . Greenwich Village lesbian P.I.
- ❏ 1 - **Everything You Have is Mine** (1991) [writing as Jack Early] ***Shamus winner*** ★
- ❏ 2 - I'll Be Leaving You Always (1993)
- ❏ 3 - My Sweet Untraceable You (1994)

Rosie Scott is the creator of amateur detective Glory Day, a New Zealand artist and singer.

> **Glory Day** . . . New Zealand artist & singer
> ❏ 1 - Glory Days (1989)

Lisa Scottoline is a Philadelphia lawyer, and like her protagonist, a good Italian girl who went to the University of Pennsylvania and started her legal career in a large corporate law firm. Scottoline now works part time for the chief judge of a federal appeals court, the background for her latest mystery.

> **Mary DiNunzio** . . . Philadelphia attorney
> ❏ 1 - **Everywhere That Mary Went** (1993) *Edgar nominee* ☆
> ❏ 2 - Final Appeal (1994)

Kate Sedley has chosen 15th century England as her mystery venue, with Roger the Chapman (a peddler) as her series detective. His mother originally sent him to a Benedictine monastery, but Roger answers the call of the outside world where he becomes acquainted with the Duke of Gloucester and future king Richard III.

> **Roger the Chapman** . . . medieval chapman (peddler) in England
> ❏ 1 - Death and the Chapman (1992)
> ❏ 2 - The Plymouth Cloak (1993)
> ❏ 3 - The Weaver's Tale (1993)

Diane K. Shah is an experienced journalist and mystery author who has recreated Hollywood in the late 1940s for her series with Paris Chandler, assistant to the gossip columnist on the *Los Angeles Examiner*. Shah is also coauthor of LAPD chief Daryl Gates' autobiography, *Chief*.

> **Paris Chandler** . . . 1940s Hollywood P.I.
> ❏ 1 - As Crime Goes By (1990)
> ❏ 2 - Dying Cheek to Cheek (1992)

Sarah Shankman is the creator of Georgia journalist Samantha Adams, whose first two titles originally appeared under the name of Alice Storey. Shankman returned to the use of her own name for the third installment and continues perfecting her unique blend of wit and humor. She is currently working on a new series set in Nashville with the first title, *I Still Miss My Man But My Aim is Getting Better*.

Samantha Adams . . . Atlanta, Georgia investigative reporter

- ❏ 1 - First Kill All the Lawyers (1988) [writing as Alice Story]
- ❏ 2 - Then Hang All the Liars (1989) [writing as Alice Story]
- ❏ 3 - Now Let's Talk of Graves (1990)
- ❏ 4 - She Walks in Beauty (1991)
- ❏ 5 - The King is Dead (1992)
- ❏ 6 - He Was Her Man (1993)

Dell Shannon (1921-1988) is one of several pseudonyms used by Elizabeth Linnington during a prolific writing career which produced mysteries, historical novels and romantic suspense. For more than 20 years she completed an average of three books a year for a lifetime total of 88 novels. Although she was single and lived alone most of her life, her series mysteries reverberate with family life. Shannon's first and perhaps favorite detective was Lieutenant Luis Rodolfo Vicente Mendoza, head of LAPD Homicide. Inheriting millions allowed him to drive fancy cars, dress like a prince and comfortably enjoy a wife, three kids, an adopted grandmother, cats, dogs and a flock of sheep on his refurbished country estate. An unusual detective indeed.

Luis Mendoza . . . Los Angeles, California dapper & wealthy homicide lieutenant

- ❏ 1 - Case Pending (1960)
- ❏ 2 - The Ace of Spades (1960)
- ❏ 3 - Extra Kill (1961)
- ❏ 4 - Knave of Hearts (1962)
- ❏ 5 - Death of a Busybody (1963)
- ❏ 6 - Double Bluff (1963)
- ❏ 7 - Root of All Evil (1964)
- ❏ 8 - Mark of Murder (1964)
- ❏ 9 - The Death Bringers (1965)
- ❏ 10 - Death by Inches (1965)
- ❏ 11 - Coffin Corner (1966)
- ❏ 12 - With a Vengeance (1966)
- ❏ 13 - Chance to Kill (1966)
- ❏ 14 - Rain with Violence (1967)
- ❏ 15 - Kill with Kindness (1968)
- ❏ 16 - Schooled to Kill (1969)
- ❏ 17 - Crime on Their Hands (1969)
- ❏ 18 - Unexpected Death (1970)
- ❏ 19 - Whim to Kill (1971)
- ❏ 20 - The Ringer (1971)
- ❏ 21 - Murder with Love (1972)
- ❏ 22 - With Intent to Kill (1972)
- ❏ 23 - No Holiday for Crime (1973)
- ❏ 24 - Spring of Violence (1973)
- ❏ 25 - Crime File (1974)
- ❏ 26 - Deuces Wild (1975)
- ❏ 27 - Streets of Death (1976)
- ❏ 28 - Appearances of Death (1977)

❑ 29 - Cold Trail (1978)
❑ 30 - Felony at Random (1979)
❑ 31 - Felony File (1980)
❑ 32 - Murder Most Strange (1981)
❑ 33 - The Motive on Record (1982)
❑ 34 - Exploit of Death (1983)
❑ 35 - Destiny of Death (1984)
❑ 36 - Chaos of Crime (1985)
❑ 37 - Blood Count (1986)
❑ 38 - Murder by the Tale (1987) [short stories]

Stella Shepherd, who practiced medicine before she turned to writing, has special knowledge about the use of drugs and poisons to commit murder. Her Richard Montgomery titles are police procedurals with a diabolical medical twist.

Inspector Richard Montgomery . . . Nottingham CID Inspector in England

❑ 1 - Black Justice (1989)
❑ 2 - Murderous Remedy (1990)
❑ 3 - Thinner Than Blood (1992)

Sharon Gwyn Short is an experienced technical and business writer in the computer industry, with her own computer whiz detective, P.I. Patricia Delaney. Short has a BA in English and an MA in Technical Communication from Bowling Green State University. She is an Ohio native.

Patricia Delaney . . . Cincinnati, Ohio computer whiz P.I.

❑ 1 - Angel's Bidding (1994)
❑ 2 - Past Pretense (1994)

Celestine Sibley first introduced her series detective Kathryn Kincaid in *The Malignant Heart* in 1958. The second installment was 33 years in the making and the once young Katy Kincaid is now a widow, but still a reporter. Like Kincaid, Sibley is also a veteran Atlanta newswriter.

Kate Kincaid Mulcay . . . veteran newspaperwoman in Atlanta, Georgia

❑ 1 - The Malignant Heart (1958)
❑ 2 - Ah, Sweet Mystery (1991)
❑ 3 - Straight as an Arrow (1992)
❑ 4 - Dire Happenings at Scratch Ankle (1993)

Sheila Simonson teaches history and English at Clark College in Vancouver, Washington and is the creator of the Lark Dodge series featuring a West coast book dealer and her homicide detective husband.

> **Lark Dailey Dodge** . . . 6-ft. bookdealer in northern California
>
> ❏   1 - Larkspur (1990)
> ❏   2 - Skylark (1992)
> ❏   3 - Mudlark (1993)

Dorothy Simpson began her Luke Thanet series about the family man police inspector in 1981. She was awarded the Silver Dagger by the British Crime Writers Association for the fifth book in the series and continues to charm her fans with contemporary tales of English urban family life.

> **Inspector Luke Thanet** . . . British police inspector
>
> ❏   1 - The Night She Died (1981)
> ❏   2 - Six Feet Under (1982)
> ❏   3 - Puppet for a Corpse (1983)
> ❏   4 - Close Her Eyes (1984)
> ❏   5 - **Last Seen Alive** (1985) *Silver Dagger winner* ★
> ❏   6 - Dead on Arrival (1986)
> ❏   7 - Element of Doubt (1987)
> ❏   8 - Suspicious Death (1988)
> ❏   9 - Dead by Morning (1989)
> ❏ 10 - Doomed to Die (1991)
> ❏ 11 - Wake Her Dead (1992)
> ❏ 12 - No Laughing Matter (1993)

L. V. Sims is the creator of the Dixie Struthers series featuring one of the first women to join the San Jose, California police department. As the daughter and granddaughter of Irish cops she is prepared for the challenges of sexism and discrimination. The high-tech crimes of the computer world provide an intriguing backdrop for these police procedurals.

> **Dixie T. Struthers** . . . San Jose, California police detective
>
> ❏   1 - Murder is Only Skin Deep (1987)
> ❏   2 - To Sleep, Perchance to Kill (1988)

Shelley Singer grew up in Minneapolis and began her career as a UPI reporter in Chicago. She currently lives in the San Francisco Bay area which is also the setting for her two series. Jake Samson is an ex-Chicago cop who lands in Oakland after leaving the Midwest. Using press credentials provided by his friend the magazine editor, Jake solves a series of crimes with the assistance of Rosie the carpenter who rents a small cottage on his property. Singer's newer series features Barrett Lake, the high school history teacher who'd rather be a P.I. Singer also teaches mystery writing and does book reviews for Pacifica Public Radio.

Barrett Lake . . . Berkeley, California high school history teacher
- ❏ 1 - Following Jane (1993)
- ❏ 2 - Picture of David (1993)
- ❏ 3 - Searching for Sara (1994)
- ❏ 4 - Interview with Mattie (1995)

Jake Samson & Rosie Vicente . . . Berkeley, California ex-cop & carpenter tenant
- ❏ 1 - Samson's Deal (1983)
- ❏ 2 - Free Draw (1984)
- ❏ 3 - Full House (1986)
- ❏ 4 - Spit in the Ocean (1987)
- ❏ 5 - Suicide King (1988)

Edith Skom, of Winnetka, Illinois, is the creator of college English professor Elizabeth Austin whose first adventure was nominated for three awards for best first mystery.

Elizabeth Austin . . . midwestern English professor
- ❏ 1 - **The Mark Twain Murders** (1989)
  Agatha, Anthony & Macavity nominee ☆

Gillian Slovo grew up in South Africa where her father is a senior official with the African National Congress and her mother was an anti-apartheid activist killed by a letter bomb. Slovo's character, Kate Baeier, is a left-wing Portuguese, saxophone-playing, freelance journalist-investigator whose milieu is a London of racial diversity, street politics and activist ferment.

Kate Baeier . . . London freelance journalist turned detective
- ❏ 1 - Morbid Symptoms (1984)
- ❏ 2 - Death Comes Staccato (1987)
- ❏ 3 - Death by Analysis (1988)

Barbara Burnett Smith is the creator of a new series featuring Jolie Wyatt, aspiring novelist. Smith, who writes and directs mystery dinner theatre and weekend plays, is also a training consultant in Austin, Texas.

Jolie Wyatt . . . aspiring novelist & writer's group member in Texas
- ❏   1 - Writers of the Purple Sage (1994)

Evelyn E. Smith is the creator of a zany series featuring art teacher and painter down-on-her-luck Susan Melville who inadvertently sets herself up as a freelance assassin when she shoots the speaker at a charity function. Miss Melville has high standards and will not take a contract unless the victim deserves to die. She is scrupulous about paying her income tax and always produces a painting to match a contract payment.

Susan Melville . . . New York City freelance assassin & painter
- ❏   1 - Miss Melville Regrets (1986)
- ❏   2 - Miss Melville Returns (1987)
- ❏   3 - Miss Melville's Revenge (1989)
- ❏   4 - Miss Melville Rides a Tiger (1991)
- ❏   5 - Miss Melville Runs for Cover (1994)

Janet L. Smith is a Seattle attorney whose series character Annie MacPherson is similarly employed. If you enjoy law firm politics, this series delivers with latte.

Annie MacPherson . . . Seattle, Washington attorney
- ❏   1 - Sea of Troubles (1990)
- ❏   2 - Practice to Deceive (1992)
- ❏   3 - A Vintage Murder (1994)

Joan Smith is the creator of Loretta Lawson, professor of English and active feminist scholar at the University of London. This is a thoughtful academic series with an added twist.

Loretta Lawson . . . British feminist professor
- ❏   1 - A Masculine Ending (1987)
- ❏   2 - Why Aren't They Screaming (1988)
- ❏   3 - Don't Leave Me This Way (1990)
- ❏   4 - What Men Say (1994)

Julie Smith, born in Annapolis, raised in Savannah and educated at the University of Mississippi, is a former reporter for the *New Orleans Times-Picayune* and *San Francisco Chronicle*. She has three series detectives to her credit. Freelance writer Paul MacDonald solves real crimes so that he can afford to write the fictional ones. Attorney Rebecca Schwartz, a nice Jewish girl from Marin County, opens her first adventure playing the piano in a feminist bordello. Smith's newest series features Skip Langdon, a daughter of New Orleans high society who becomes a police officer.

    Paul MacDonald . . . ex-reporter & mystery writer in San Francisco
- ❑   1 -   True-Life Adventure (1985)
- ❑   2 -   Huckleberry Fiend (1987)

    Rebecca Schwartz . . . San Francisco defense attorney
- ❑   1 -   Death Turns a Trick (1982)
- ❑   2 -   The Sourdough Wars (1984)
- ❑   3 -   Tourist Trap (1986)
- ❑   4 -   Dead in the Water (1991)
- ❑   5 -   Other People's Skeletons (1993)

    Skip Langdon . . . 6-ft. police detective in New Orleans
- ❑   1 -   **New Orleans Mourning** (1990) *Edgar winner* ★
- ❑   2 -   The Axeman's Jazz (1991)
- ❑   3 -   Jazz Funeral (1993)
- ❑   4 -   New Orleans Beat (1994)

Michelle Spring, of Cambridge, England, is the creator of private investigator Laura Principal.

    Laura Principal . . . British academic turned P.I.
- ❑   1 -   Every Breath You Take (1994)

Patricia Houck Sprinkle, of Miami, Florida, is the creator of the series featuring widowed public relations executive Sheila Travers who spent a number of years in Japan with her husband, the abusive diplomat. But Sheila's foreign service experience lands her a job in Chicago training students for the diplomatic corps, and she soon returns to her native South where she joins a Japanese firm in Atlanta.

    Sheila Travers . . . Atlanta, Georgia public relations executive
- ❑   1 -   Murder at Markham (1988)
- ❑   2 -   Murder in the Charleston Manner (1990)
- ❑   3 -   Murder on Peachtree Street (1991)
- ❑   4 -   Somebody's Dead in Snellville (1992)
- ❑   5 -   Death of a Dunwoody Matron (1993)
- ❑   6 -   A Mystery Bred in Buckhead (1994)

Elizabeth Daniels Squire wrote two non-fiction books and another mystery before launching her series about the forgetful Peaches Dann. Squire was born into a newspaper publishing family and has worked as a columnist in Beirut and as a police reporter in Connecticut. She currently lives in North Carolina where she writes a nationally syndicated column.

Peaches Dann . . . 50-something North Carolina widow
- ❏ 1 - Who Killed What's-Her-Name? (1994)
- ❏ 2 - Remember the Alibi (1994)
- ❏ 3 - Memory Can Be Murder (1995)

Dana Stabenow, born in Alaska and raised on a fish tender, is the creator of award-winning series detective Aleut Kate Shugak, a former investigator for the district attorney's office in Anchorage, and her half-dog, half-wolf Mutt. This series resonates with the exotic landscape of the Alaskan bush and the fiercely independent people who live there.

Kate Shugak . . . native Alaskan ex-D. A. investigator
- ❏ 1 - **A Cold Day for Murder** (1992) *Edgar winner* ★
- ❏ 2 - A Fatal Thaw (1993)
- ❏ 3 - Dead in the Water (1993)
- ❏ 4 - A Cold-Blooded Business (1994)
- ❏ 5 - Play With Fire (1995)

Susannah Stacey is one of the pseudonyms used by Jill Staynes and Margaret Storey, former teachers and longtime friends who are writing partners for two mystery series. As Susannah Stacey, they are the creators of the Inspector Bone series featuring the wise and quiet Englishman who is raising his daughter alone after the death of his wife. As Elizabeth Eyre, they write a historical series set in Renaissance Italy.

Inspector Robert Bone . . . widowed British police inspector
- ❏ 1 - Goodbye Nanny Gray (1987)
- ❏ 2 - A Knife at the Opera (1988)
- ❏ 3 - Body of Opinion (1988)
- ❏ 4 - Grave Responsibility (1990)
- ❏ 5 - The Late Lady (1992)

Veronica Stallwood is the creator of a new series featuring Oxford novelist Kate Ivory.

Kate Ivory . . . Oxford novelist in England
- ❏ 1 - Death and the Oxford Box (1993)
- ❏ 2 - Oxford Exit (1995)

Triss Stein is the creator of Kay Engles, a nationally-known reporter who finds murder at her class reunion in the opening installment.

    Kay Engles . . . nationally-known reporter

❏   1 - Murder at the Class Reunion (1993)

Susan Steiner, of Forest Knolls, California, is the creator of Alex Winter, P.I. with the California firm of Abromowitz & Stewart and owner of a one-eyed black cat named Ms. Watson.

    Alex Winter . . . California P.I.

❏   1 - Murder on Her Mind (1989)

❏   2 - Library: No Murder Aloud (1993)

Serita Stevens, born and raised in Chicago, is a registered nurse and graduate of the University of Illinois Medical Center in Chicago where she grew up. She specializes in psychiatric nursing and has authored *Deadly Doses: A Writer's Guide to Poisons* which was nominated for an Anthony and a Macavity award. She is also the creator of the Fanny Zindel series featuring a Jewish grandmother sleuth.

    Fanny Zindel . . . Jewish grandmother

❏   1 - Read Sea, Dead Sea (1991)

❏   2 - Bagels for Tea (1993)

Dorothy Sucher, an experienced psychotherapist, mother and editor of a small-town weekly newspaper, is the creator of Sabina Swift, Washington, DC, P.I. and her young sidekick Vic Newman. *Dead Men Don't Give Seminars* was nominated for an Agatha as best first traditional mystery.

    Sabina Swift . . . Georgetown detective agency owner

❏   1 - **Dead Men Don't Give Seminars** (1988) *Agatha nominee* ☆

❏   2 - Dead Men Don't Marry (1989)

Winona Sullivan's first mystery was named best first P.I. novel of 1991 in a contest sponsored by St. Martin's Press, Macmillan London and the Private Eye Writers of America. Her unusual protagonist is Sister Cecile Buddenbrooks, an heiress and a nun whose father disapproved of her vocation. He left her his fortune on the condition that it not be spent for religious purposes, so she finances her P.I. work with her inheritance and later donates the fees to her Boston convent. A former teacher and CIA analyst, Sullivan is the mother of seven and lives with her husband and their four youngest in an ancient farmhouse in Carver, Massachusetts.

Sister Cecile Buddenbrooks . . . nun & licensed P.I. in Boston
- ❑   1 - **A Sudden Death at the Norfolk Cafe** (1993) *SMP/PWA winner* ★

Elizabeth Atwood Taylor, of San Francisco, is a native of San Antonio, Texas, educated at Vassar (art history) and Bryn Mawr (social work). She worked as a film editor, TV news reporter, social worker and art therapist before starting her mystery series featuring Maggie Elliott, a former film maker turned P.I. in San Francisco. A young widow and recently reformed alcoholic, Maggie teams up with much older ex-cop Richard Patrick O'Reagan to solve the mystery of her half-sister's death in a cable car accident.

Maggie Elliott . . . ex-film maker turned P.I. in San Francisco
- ❑   1 - The Cable Car Murder (1981)
- ❑   2 - Murder at Vassar (1987)
- ❑   3 - The Northwest Murders (1992)

L. A. Taylor, of Minneapolis, has been writing virtually all her life. Her published work includes a prize-winning volume of poetry titled *Changing the Past* and *Footnote to Murder*, a mystery featuring Minneapolis library researcher Marge Brock. Taylor is also the creator of the J. J. Jamison series featuring a Minneapolis computer engineer who is also an investigator for CATCH—the Committee for Analysis of Tropospheric and Celestial Happenings.

J.J. Jamison . . . Minneapolis computer engineer and CATCH investigator
- ❑   1 - Only Half a Hoax (1984)
- ❑   2 - Deadly Objectives (1985)
- ❑   3 - Shed Light on Death (1985)

Phoebe Atwood Taylor (1909-1976) was born in Boston, descended from Mayflower pilgrims and published her first novel (*The Cape Cod Mystery*) the year after she graduated from Barnard College. Her series detective is Asey Mayo, "The Codfish Sherlock," a man who never tells his age despite the number of characters who try to figure it out. Although Taylor published nothing in the mystery field after 1951, her Cape Cod mysteries remain popular and in print more than 40 years later. As Alice Tilton she also wrote a Boston series featuring Leonidas Witherall, retired professor, Shakespeare look-alike and secret author of pulp thrillers.

Asey Mayo . . . former sailor & auto racer in Cape Cod, Massachusetts
- ❑   1 - The Cape Cod Mystery (1931)
- ❑   2 - Death Lights a Candle (1932)
- ❑   3 - The Mystery of the Cape Cod Players (1933)
- ❑   4 - The Mystery of the Cape Cod Tavern (1934)
- ❑   5 - Sandbar Sinister (1934)
- ❑   6 - The Tinkling Symbol (1935)

❑   7 - Deathblow Hill (1935)
❑   8 - The Crimson Patch (1936)
❑   9 - Out of Order (1936)
❑ 10 - Figure Away (1937)
❑ 11 - Octagon House (1937)
❑ 12 - The Annulet of Gilt (1938)
❑ 13 - Banbury Bog (1938)
❑ 14 - Spring Harrowing (1939)
❑ 15 - The Deadly Sunshade (1940)
❑ 16 - The Criminal C.O.D. (1940)
❑ 17 - The Perennial Border (1941)
❑ 18 - 3 Plots for Asey Mayo (1942)
❑ 19 - Six Iron Spiders (1942)
❑ 20 - Going, Going, Gone (1943)
❑ 21 - Proof of the Pudding (1945)
❑ 22 - Punch with Care (1946)
❑ 23 - The Asey Mayo Trio (1946)
❑ 24 - Diplomatic Corpse (1951)

Josephine Tey (1896-1952) is the pseudonym used by playwright and mystery writer Elizabeth Mackintosh, often called "the mystery writer for people who hate mysteries," owing to her fondness for focusing on the characters rather than the hunt for the guilty. Her series detective, Alan Grant of Scotland Yard, is a gentleman of independent means who works because he enjoys it. The first Grant book was originally published under the pseudonym Gordon Daviot but later reissued under Josephine Tey.

Before starting a writing career, Tey studied and taught physical education and at the age of 50 produced her only novel with a woman protagonist—*Miss Pym Disposes* (1946). Miss Lucy Pym, retired physical education teacher and writer of pop psychology, tries to use her knowledge to solve a murder at a girls physical education college.

Inspector Alan Grant . . . Scotland Yard detective

☑ 1 - The Man in the Queue (1929) [writing as Gordon Daviot]
☑ 2 - A Shilling for Candles (1936)
☑ 3 - The Franchise Affair (1949)
❑ 4 - To Love and Be Wise (1950)
☑ 5 - The Daughter of Time (1951)
☑ 6 - The Singing Sands (1952)

Joyce Thompson is the creator of Seattle forensic artist Freddy Bascomb, featured in the mystery thriller *Bones*. The author of four earlier novels and two collections of short fiction, Thompson has taught fiction workshops at universities and writing conferences throughout the West. She lives with her two children in a beachfront cabin on an island in Puget Sound.

Frederika Bascomb . . . Seattle, Washington forensic artist

   ❏   1 - Bones (1991)

June Thomson earned her BA with honors from Bedford College, University of London and taught English for 20 years before turning to mystery writing. She is the creator of Inspector Finch, the simple Essex cop who lives with his unmarried sister. When this series was reprinted in the U.S., Inspector Finch mysteriously became Inspector Rudd. Thomson is also the author of two recent short story collections—*The Secret Files of Sherlock Holmes* (1990) and *The Secret Chronicles of Sherlock Holmes* (1992).

     Inspector Finch (Insp. Rudd in the U.S.) . . . Essex, England police inspector

      ❏   1 - Not One of Us (1971)
      ❏   2 - Death Cap (1973) [comes to the U.S. with Insp. renamed Rudd]
      ❏   3 - The Long Revenge (1974)
      ❏   4 - Case Closed (1977)
      ❏   5 - A Question of Identity (1977)
      ❏   6 - Deadly Relations (1979) [U.S.–The Habit of Loving]
      ❏   7 - Alibi in Time (1980)
      ❏   8 - Shadow of a Doubt (1981)
      ❏   9 - To Make a Killing (1982) [U.S.–Portrait of Lilith]
      ❏ 10 - Sound Evidence (1984)
      ❏ 11 - A Dying Fall (1985)
      ❏ 12 - The Dark Stream (1986)
      ❏ 13 - No Flowers by Request (1987)
      ❏ 14 - Rosemary for Remembrance (1988)
      ❏ 15 - The Spoils of Time (1989)
      ❏ 16 - Past Reckoning (1990)
      ❏ 17 - Foul Play (1991)

Alice Tilton is the pseudonym used by Phoebe Atwood Taylor for her Boston series featuring Leonidas Witherall, retired professor, Shakespeare look-alike, hunter of rare books and secret author of pulp fiction. Witherall is financially well-to-do thanks to the commercial success of his fictional character, Lieutenant Haseltine, hero of thrillers and radio.

     Leonidas Witherall . . . retired Boston academic and secret author of pulp fiction

      ❏   1 - Beginning with a Bash (1937)
      ❏   2 - The Cut Direct (1938)
      ❏   3 - Cold Steal (1939)
      ❏   4 - The Left Leg (1940)
      ❏   5 - The Hollow Chest (1941)
      ❏   6 - File for Record (1943)
      ❏   7 - Dead Earnest (1944)
      ❏   8 - The Iron Clew (1947) [Britain–The Iron Hand]

Kathy Hogan Trocheck is a Florida native with a journalism degree from the University of Georgia who spent 14 years as a newspaper reporter, primarily with *The Atlanta Journal-Constitution*. Her series detective, Julia Callahan Garrity, is a burned-out ex-cop and part-time P.I. who owns and operates the House Mouse cleaning service with her mother Edna Mae.

Julia Callahan Garrity . . . Atlanta, Georgia ex-cop cleaning lady
- ❏ 1 - **Every Crooked Nanny** (1992) *Macavity nominee* ☆
- ❏ 2 - **To Live and Die in Dixie** (1993) *Agatha & Anthony nominee* ☆
- ❏ 3 - Homemade Sin (1994)
- ❏ 4 - Happy Never After (1995)

Margaret Truman writes Washington, DC mysteries with titles featuring national landmarks. Several of these classic puzzle cases involve the recurring characters of Mac Smith and Annabel Reed, law professor and his attorney wife turned gallery owner. As the daughter of a former president, the author is definitely in-the-know when it comes to power politics and political intrigue in our nation's capital.

Mackenzie Smith & Annabel Reed . . . Washington, DC law professor & attorney wife turned gallery owner
- ☑ 1 - Murder at the Kennedy Center (1989)
- ☑ 2 - Murder at the National Cathedral (1990)
- ☑ 3 - Murder on the Potomac (1994)

Margit Falk . . . ex-combat pilot & government attorney in Washington, DC
- ☑ 1 - Murder at the Pentagon (1992)

Kerry Tucker, of Guilford, Connecticut, is the creator of Libby Kincaid, New York City photojournalist. Tucker is also the author of *Greetings from New York—A Visit to Manhattan in Postcards*.

Libby Kincaid . . . New York City magazine photographer
- ❏ 1 - Still Waters (1991)
- ❏ 2 - Cold Feet (1992)
- ❏ 3 - Death Echo (1993)
- ❏ 4 - Drift Away (1994)

Peg Tyre is a Pulitzer Prize-winning crime reporter for *New York Newsday* and a former magazine writer for *New York* magazine. She is also the creator of a new series featuring a woman crime reporter in search of a front page story who meets a detective in search of love in the midst of murder in Brooklyn. Tyre is a graduate of Brown University and lives in New York with her husband, novelist Peter Blauner, and their son.

> **Kate Murray** . . . newspaper reporter for New York's *Daily Herald*
> - ❏ 1 - Strangers in the Night (1994)

Dorothy Uhnak was a New York transit cop for 14 years before quitting the force to write *Policewoman: A Young Woman's Initiation into the Realities of Justice* in 1964. Her award-winning series with Christie Opara recounts the discrimination that Uhnak herself experienced on the job.

Uhnak is best known for her big, best-selling police novels such as *Law and Order,* which became a three-hour TV-movie starring Darren McGavin and Suzanne Pleshette.

> **Christine Opara** . . . 20-something New York City police detective
> - ❏ 1 - **The Bait** (1968) *Edgar winner* ★
> - ❏ 2 - The Witness (1969)
> - ❏ 3 - **The Ledger** (1970) *Grand Prix de Litteratue Policiere winner* ★

Deborah Valentine is the creator of detective Kevin Bryce and artist Katharine Craig who first meet when she is suspected of using a piece of sculpture as a murder weapon. The idyllic setting is an upscale community near Lake Tahoe.

> **Katharine Craig & Kevin Bryce** . . . California sculptor & ex-sheriff's detective
> - ❏ 1 - Unorthodox Methods (1989)
> - ❏ 2 - A Collector of Photographs (1989)
> - ❏ 3 - **Fine Distinctions** (1991) *Edgar nominee* ☆

Judith Van Gieson, a Northwestern University graduate, writes a hard-boiled attorney-investigator series featuring Neil Hamel of Albuquerque, New Mexico. Neil is passionate about the environment and tequila. Her accordion-playing auto mechanic (who is also her lover) calls her Chiquita. She calls him The Kid.

> **Neil Hamel** . . . Albuquerque, New Mexico attorney
> - ❏ 1 - North of the Border (1988)
> - ❏ 2 - Raptor (1990)
> - ❏ 3 - The Other Side of Death (1991)
> - ❏ 4 - The Wolf Path (1992)
> - ❏ 5 - **The Lies that Bind** (1993) *Shamus nominee* ☆
> - ❏ 6 - Parrot Blues (1995)

Anca Vlasopolos has written crime fiction's only female detective in Detroit with police lieutenant Sharon Dair of the sex crimes division. Her first investigation in print (*Missing Members*) concerns a Bobbitt crime before its time.

> **Sharon Dair** . . . sex crimes police detective in Detroit
>> ❏   1   -   Missing Members (1990)

Hannah Wakefield is the shared pseudonym for two American-born women who were raised in the U.S. but moved to London in the early 1970s. One is a former editor who divides her time between writing and teaching, while the other is a practicing lawyer who collaborates on the story and characters. Their novels feature Dee Street, an American attorney and partner in a women-owned London law firm.

> **Dee Street** . . . American attorney in London
>> ❏   1   -   The Price You Pay (1987)
>> ❏   2   -   A Woman's Own Mystery (1990)

Mary Willis Walker, of Austin, Texas, is the creator of two new female detectives—dog trainer Kate Driscoll, introduced in the award-winning opener *Zero at the Bone*, and Texas crime writer and reporter Mollie Cates.

> **Kate Driscoll** . . . Texas dog trainer
>> ❏   1   -   **Zero at the Bone** (1991)
>>   ***Agatha & Macavity winner*** ★ ***Edgar nominee*** ☆

> **Mollie Cates** . . . Texas true crime writer & reporter
>> ❏   1   -   The Red Scream (1994)

Marilyn Wallace, the daughter of a New York City police officer, has written novels of suspense (the Taconic Hills series), and won awards for her mystery series and the five-volume *Sisters In Crime* short story anthologies which she edited.

> **Jay Goldstein & Carlos Cruz** . . . Oakland, California homicide detectives
>> ❏   1   -   **A Case of Loyalties** (1986) *Macavity winner* ★
>> ❏   2   -   **Primary Target** (1988) *Anthony nominee* ☆
>> ❏   3   -   **A Single Stone** (1991) *Anthony nominee* ☆

Patricia Wallace is Patricia Wallace Estrada, author of 17 books, including the Sydney Bryant P.I. series and 11 horror novels, in addition to her first suspense novel due out in 1995. She has degrees in both film and police science and has worked for NBC as a freelance story analyst.

> **Sydney Bryant** . . . San Diego, California private investigator
> - ❏ 1 - Small Favors (1988)
> - ❏ 2 - Deadly Grounds (1989)
> - ❏ 3 - Blood Lies (1991)
> - ❏ 4 - Deadly Devotion (1994)
> - ❏ 5 - August Nights (1995)

Lee Wallingford is a former teacher and librarian who lives in Oregon where she writes a series featuring two officers of the U.S. Forest Service—Frank Carver and Ginny Trask.

> **Ginny Trask & Frank Carver** . . . Oregon forest fire dispatcher & ex-cop
> - ❏ 1 - Cold Tracks (1991)
> - ❏ 2 - Clear Cut Murder (1993)

Jill Paton Walsh is the creator of a new series featuring nurse Imogen Quy.

> **Imogen Quy** . . . nurse
> - ❏ 1 - The Wyndham Case (1993)

Mignon Warner was born in Australia, but currently lives in England where she works with her husband in the design and manufacture of apparatus for magic. She spends much of her free time doing research on the occult and other psychic phenomena. Her series character is the clairvoyante Edwina Charles.

> **Edwina Charles** . . . British clairvoyante
> - ❏ 1 - A Medium for Murder (1976)
> - ❏ 2 - The Tarot Murders (1978)
> - ❏ 3 - Death in Time (1980)
> - ❏ 4 - The Girl Who Was Clairvoyant (1982)
> - ❏ 5 - Devil's Knell (1983)
> - ❏ 6 - Illusion (1984)
> - ❏ 7 - Speak No Evil (1985)

Clarissa Watson is co-owner and director of a New York art gallery which she helped to found. Her series detective, Persis Willum, is an art curator whose adventures involve the art world and Long Island high society. For non-mystery fun, Watson served as editor of *The Sensuous Carrot*, a collection of gourmet recipes from artists around the world.

Persis Willum . . . New York City art curator
- ❑ 1 - The Fourth Stage of Gainsborough Brown (1977)
- ❑ 2 - The Bishop in the Back Seat (1980)
- ❑ 3 - Runaway (1985)
- ❑ 4 - Last Plane from Nice (1988)
- ❑ 5 - Somebody Killed the Messenger (1988)

Charlene Weir is a native of Kansas who studied and worked in the public health field in Oklahoma before moving to northern California. Her physician series detective moves from California to Kansas where she is unexpectedly widowed in the opening title which was nominated for an Anthony and won the Agatha for best first traditional mystery.

Susan Wren . . . ex-San Francisco cop now Kansas police chief
- ❑ 1 - **The Winter Widow** (1992)
  Malice Domestic winner ★ *Anthony nominee* ☆
- ❑ 2 - **Consider the Crows** (1993) *Anthony nominee* ☆
- ❑ 3 - Family Medicine (1995)

Pat Welch is the creator of Helen Black, a lesbian P.I. and ex-cop in San Francisco.

Helen Black . . . San Francisco, California ex-cop lesbian P.I.
- ❑ 1 - Murder by the Book (1990)

Carolyn Wells (1869-1942) first became known as a writer of books for girls and editor of anthologies and later as the originator of master sleuth Fleming Stone. Her first mystery was the Stone opener in 1909 and she is well remembered for another early contribution—the first how-to book about detective stories—*The Technique of the Mystery Story* (1913). Between 1918 and 1923, she also wrote a series about a psychic detective named Pennington Wise, and non-series mysteries under the name Rowland Wright.

Fleming Stone . . . New York City intellectual private investigator
- ❑ 1 - The Clue (1909)
- ❑ 2 - The Gold Bag (1911)
- ❑ 3 - A Chain of Evidence (1912)
- ❑ 4 - The Maxwell Mystery (1913)
- ❑ 5 - Anybody but Anne (1914)

❏   6   -   The Whit Alley   (1915)
❏   7   -   The Curved Blades   (1916)
❏   8   -   The Mark of Cain   (1917)
❏   9   -   Vicky Van   (1918)
❏   10   -   The Diamond Pin   (1919)
❏   11   -   Raspberry Jam   (1920)
❏   12   -   The Mystery of the Sycamore   (1921)
❏   13   -   The Mystery Girl   (1922)
❏   14   -   Feathers Left Around   (1923)
❏   15   -   Spooky Hollow   (1923)
❏   16   -   The Furthest Fury   (1924)
❏   17   -   Prilligirl   (1924)
❏   18   -   Anything but the Truth   (1925)
❏   19   -   The Daughter of the House   (1925)
❏   20   -   The Bronze Hand   (1926)
❏   21   -   The Red-Haired Girl   (1926)
❏   22   -   All at Sea   (1927)
❏   23   -   Where's Emily   (1927)
❏   24   -   The Crime in the Crypt   (1928)
❏   25   -   The Tannahill Tangle   (1928)
❏   26   -   The Tapestry Room Murder   (1929)
❏   27   -   Triple Murder   (1929)
❏   28   -   The Doomed Five   (1930)
❏   29   -   The Ghosts' High Noon   (1930)
❏   30   -   Horror House   (1931)
❏   31   -   The Umbrella Murder   (1931)
❏   32   -   Fuller's Earth   (1932)
❏   33   -   The Roll-Top Desk Mystery   (1932)
❏   34   -   The Broken O   (1933)
❏   35   -   The Clue of the Eyelash   (1933)
❏   36   -   The Master Murderer   (1933)
❏   37   -   Eyes in the Wall   (1934)
❏   38   -   In the Tiger's Case   (1934)
❏   39   -   The Visiting Villian   (1934)
❏   40   -   The Beautiful Derelict   (1935)
❏   41   -   For Goodness Sake   (1935)
❏   42   -   The Wooden Indian   (1935)
❏   43   -   The Huddle   (1936)
❏   44   -   Money Musk   (1936)
❏   45   -   Murder in the Bookshop   (1936)
❏   46   -   The Mystery of the Tarn   (1937)
❏   47   -   The Radio Studio Murder   (1937)
❏   48   -   Gilt-Edged Guilt   (1938)
❏   49   -   The Killer   (1938)
❏   50   -   The Missing Link   (1938)
❏   51   -   Calling All Suspects   (1939)
❏   52   -   Crime Tears On   (1939)
❏   53   -   The Importance of Being Murdered   (1939)
❏   54   -   Crime Incarnate   (1940)
❏   55   -   Devil's Work   (1940)

❑ 56 - Murder on Parade (1940)
❑ 57 - Murder Plus (1940)
❑ 58 - The Black Night Murders (1941)
❑ 59 - Murder at the Casino (1941)
❑ 60 - Who Killed Caldwell (1942)

Patricia Wentworth is the pseudonym of Dora Amy Elles (1878-1961) who wrote nine mysteries before introducing in 1928 the character who would make her famous—retired governess and spinster private eye Miss Maud Silver. Wentworth then wrote 16 non-series novels before returning Miss Silver to center stage and 30 more adventures. Miss Silver became so popular in the U.S. during the 1940s that Lippincott's of Philadelphia became her primary publisher and British editions were released later.

Miss Maud Silver . . . London, England retired governess & spinster P.I.

❑ 1 - Grey Mask (1928)
❑ 2 - The Case is Closed (1937)
❑ 3 - Lonesome Road (1939)
❑ 4 - In the Balance (1941) [Britain–Danger Point]
❑ 5 - The Chinese Shawl (1943)
❑ 6 - The Clock Strikes Twelve (1944)
❑ 7 - Miss Silver Deals with Death (1944) [Britain–Miss Silver Intervenes]
❑ 8 - The Key (1944)
❑ 9 - She Came Back (1945) [Britain–The Traveller Returns]
❑ 10 - Pilgrim's Rest (1946)
❑ 11 - The Latter End (1947)
❑ 12 - Wicked Uncle (1947) [Britain–The Spotlight]
❑ 13 - The Eternity Ring (1948)
❑ 14 - The Case of William Smith (1948)
❑ 15 - Miss Silver Comes to Stay (1949)
❑ 16 - The Catharine Wheel (1949)
❑ 17 - Through the Wall (1950)
❑ 18 - The Ivory Dagger (1950)
❑ 19 - Anna, Where Are You? (1951)
❑ 20 - Watersplash (1951)
❑ 21 - Ladies' Bane (1952)
❑ 22 - Out of the Past (1953)
❑ 23 - The Vanishing Point (1953)
❑ 24 - The Silent Pool (1953)
❑ 25 - The Benevent Treasure (1954)
❑ 26 - The Gazebo (1955)
❑ 27 - The Listening Eye (1955)
❑ 28 - The Fingerprint (1956)
❑ 29 - Poison in the Pen (1957)
❑ 30 - The Alington Inheritance (1958)
❑ 31 - The Girl in the Cellar (1961)

Valerie Wilson Wesley is the executive editor of *Essence* magazine and creator of black P.I. Tamara Hayle, single parent and ex-cop from the mean streets of Newark, New Jersey. A graduate of Howard University and the Columbia Graduate School of Journalism, Wesley says she was inspired to write a black woman P.I. by Walter Mosley, Edgar-nominated creator of Los Angeles P.I. Easy Rawlins.

    Tamara Hayle . . . Newark, New Jersey black P.I. ex-cop
- ❏   1 -   When Death Comes Stealing (1994)

Carolyn Wheat was once a Brooklyn defense attorney with the Legal Aid Society (like her Cass Jameson character) and has taught mystery writing at the New School in New York City. After a nine-year absence, Wheat is reviving her Edgar-nominated series with the third installment in hardcover and the simultaneous re-release of the earlier two titles in paperback.

    Cass Jameson . . . Brooklyn, New York criminal lawyer
- ❏   1 -   **Dead Man's Thoughts** (1983)   *Edgar nominee* ☆
- ❏   2 -   Where Nobody Dies (1986)
- ❏   3 -   Fresh Kills (1995)

Gloria White is the creator of the Ronnie (Veronica) Ventana series featuring a San Francisco P.I. whose now-deceased parents were cat burglars. The first title in the series was nominated for an Edgar and named audio best of the year by *Publishers Weekly*. The entire series is available on audio book and has been translated to German, Japanese and Italian.

    Ronnie Ventana . . . San Francisco, California burglars' daughter P.I.
- ❏   1 -   **Murder on the Run** (1991)   *Anthony nominee* ☆
- ❏   2 -   Money to Burn (1993)
- ❏   3 -   Charged with Guilt (1995)

Teri White won an Edgar in 1982 with her first novel about two Vietnam vets who hire out as hit men (*Triangle*). Her later work continues in the buddy-book tradition featuring both cop and criminal pairs.

    Spaceman Kowalski & Blue Maguire . . . Los Angeles cop pair with a prickly partnership
- ❏   1 -   Bleeding Hearts (1984)
- ❏   2 -   Tightrope (1986)

Kate Wilhelm published her first short story in 1956 and her first novel in 1963. For more than 30 years she has been producing prize-winning science fiction, as well as horror, mystery, mainstream fiction, psychological novels, suspense and comic novels. She has won the two most prestigious prizes in science fiction—the Hugo and Nebula awards—for which she is best known.

Wilhelm has also created several series detectives, including Charlie Meiklejohn and Constance Leidl. He is a former New York City arson investigator turned P.I., while she is a PhD practicing psychologist. Wilhelm's legal mystery protagonists are Oregon defense attorney Barbara Holloway and Oregon judge Sarah Drexler.

Barbara Holloway . . . Oregon defense attorney
- ❏ 1 - Death Qualified (1991)
- ❏ 2 - The Best Defense (1994)

Charlie Meiklejohn & Constance Leidl . . . ex-arson investigator P.I. & psychologist
- ❏ 1 - The Hamlet Trap (1987)
- ❏ 2 - The Dark Door (1988)
- ❏ 3 - Smart House (1989)
- ❏ 4 - Sweet, Sweet Poison (1990)
- ❏ 5 - Seven Kinds of Death (1992)

Sarah Drexler . . . Oregon judge
- ❏ 1 - Justice for Some (1993)

Barbara Wilson, co-founder of Seattle's Seal Press, writes two lesbian feminist mystery series. Wilson's first title featuring Cassandra Reilly, globe-trotting Spanish translator, won an award for best crime novel with a European setting from the British Crime Writers Association. Her Pam Nilsen series features Pam and her twin sister Penny and their family printing business which they turn into a collective.

Cassandra Reilly . . . London-based Spanish translator
- ❏ 1 - **Gaudi Afternoon** (1990) *BCWA winner* ★
- ❏ 2 - Trouble in Transylvania (1993)

Pam Nilsen . . . Seattle, Washington lesbian printing company owner
- ❏ 1 - Murder in the Collective (1984)
- ❏ 2 - Sisters of the Road (1986)
- ❏ 3 - The Dog Collar Murders (1989)

Ann Wingate is a former Texas police officer with a PhD in English who writes both fiction and non-fiction under three names. As Wingate she publishes the Mark Shigata series about a Japanese-American ex-FBI agent turned chief of police in Bayport, Texas and for Writer's Digest Books in 1992 she authored *Scene of the Crime: A Writer's Guide to Crime Scene Investigations.*

Under the Lee Martin pseudonym she writes the Deb Ralston series and early in her writing career she produced several non-series novels under the name of Martha G. Webb.

Mark Shigata . . . Japanese-American former-FBI agent turned chief of police in Bayport, Texas

- ❏ 1 - Death by Deception (1988)
- ❏ 2 - The Eye of Anna (1989)
- ❏ 3 - The Buzzards Must Also Be Fed (1991)
- ❏ 4 - Exception to Murder (1992)
- ❏ 5 - Yakuza, Go Home! (1993)

Mary Wings, a Chicago native, lived in the Netherlands for eight years where she wrote the first two titles of her hard-boiled lesbian series featuring investigator Emma Victor. She has also written a gothic thriller and been nominated for the Raymond Chandler Fulbright award.

Emma Victor . . . lesbian activist & former publicist who moved to California from Massachusetts

- ❏ 1 - She Came Too Late (1987)
- ❏ 2 - She Came in a Flash (1990)

Susan Wolfe is a practicing attorney in Palo Alto, California who won an Edgar for best first novel of 1989. The Dean of Stanford Law School described her book as "a diverting tale of legal skullduggery" in the high-tech practice of law in Silicon Valley.

Sarah Nelson . . . Silicon Valley, California police inspector

- ❏ 1 - **The Last Billable Hour** (1989) *Edgar winner* ★

Valerie Wolzien is the creator of Susan Henshaw, suburban Connecticut housewife whose neighborhood seems to have a crime for every holiday and social occasion. Susan's friend police detective Kathleen Gordon is also a private security consultant. Their combined professional and domestic expertise stand them in good stead to solve the local murders.

Susan Henshaw . . . Connecticut suburban sleuth

- ❏ 1 - Murder at the PTA Luncheon (1988)
- ❏ 2 - The Fortieth Birthday Body (1989)
- ❏ 3 - We Wish You a Merry Murder (1991)
- ❏ 4 - All Hallow's Evil (1992)
- ❏ 5 - An Old Faithful Murder (1992)
- ❏ 6 - A Star-Spangled Murder (1993)
- ❏ 7 - A Good Year for a Corpse (1994)
- ❏ 8 - Tis the Season to be Murdered (1994)

Sara Woods is the pseudonym of Sara Bowen-Judd (1922-1935) who used her own experience working in a solicitor's office to produce 48 titles in the Anthony Maitland series, often called the British Perry Mason. She was born and educated in England, but didn't start writing seriously until she moved to Canada. Although her setting and character are distinctly British, she is considered Canada's most successful writer of mystery fiction. She also wrote as Anne Burton, Mary Challis and Margaret Leek.

Anthony Maitland . . . English barrister drawn to murder cases

- ❏ 1 - Bloody Instructions (1962)
- ❏ 2 - Malice Domestic (1962)
- ❏ 3 - The Taste of Fears (1963) [U.S.–The Third Encounter]
- ❏ 4 - Error of the Moon (1963)
- ❏ 5 - Trusted Like the Fox (1964)
- ❏ 6 - This Little Measure (1964)
- ❏ 7 - The Windy Side of the Law (1965)
- ❏ 8 - Though I Know She Lies (1965)
- ❏ 9 - Enter Certain Murderers (1966)
- ❏ 10 - Let's Choose Executors (1966)
- ❏ 11 - The Case is Altered (1967)
- ❏ 12 - And Shame the Devil (1967)
- ❏ 13 - Knives Have Edges (1968)
- ❏ 14 - Past Praying For (1968)
- ❏ 15 - Tarry and Be Hanged (1969)
- ❏ 16 - An Improbable Fiction (1970)
- ❏ 17 - Serpent's Tooth (1971)
- ❏ 18 - The Knavish Crows (1971)
- ❏ 19 - They Love Not Poison (1972) [prequel to the entire series]
- ❏ 20 - Yet She Must Die (1973)
- ❏ 21 - Enter the Corpse (1973)
- ❏ 22 - Done to Death (1974)
- ❏ 23 - A Show of Violence (1975)
- ❏ 24 - My Life is Done (1976)
- ❏ 25 - The Law's Delay (1977)
- ❏ 26 - A Thief or Two (1977)
- ❏ 27 - Exit Murderer (1978)
- ❏ 28 - This Fatal Writ (1979)
- ❏ 29 - Proceed to Judgement (1979)
- ❏ 30 - They Stay for Death (1980)
- ❏ 31 - Weep for Her (1980)
- ❏ 32 - Dearest Enemy (1981)
- ❏ 33 - Cry Guilty (1981)
- ❏ 34 - Villains by Necessity (1982)
- ❏ 35 - Enter a Gentlewoman (1982)
- ❏ 36 - Most Grievous Murder (1982)
- ❏ 37 - The Lie Direct (1983)
- ❏ 38 - Call Back Yesterday (1983)
- ❏ 39 - Where Should He Die? (1983)
- ❏ 40 - The Bloody Book of Law (1984)
- ❏ 41 - Defy the Devil (1984)

❑ 42 - Murder's Out of Tune (1984)
❑ 43 - An Obscure Grave (1985)
❑ 44 - Away With Them to Prison (1985)
❑ 45 - Put Out the Light (1985)
❑ 46 - Nor Live So Long (1986)
❑ 47 - Most Deadly Hate (1986)
❑ 48 - Naked Villainy (1987)

Sherryl Woods is the award-winning author of over 50 novels, many of which are best-selling romances. She writes the Amanda Roberts series featuring a Georgia investigative reporter transplanted from New York and the Molly DeWitt series featuring a Miami film promoter and single mother. Woods divides her time between Key Biscayne and Los Angeles where several of her books have been optioned for television.

Amanda Roberts . . . ex-New York investigative reporter in Georgia

❑ 1 - Reckless (1989)
❑ 2 - Body and Soul (1989)
❑ 3 - Stolen Moments (1990)
❑ 4 - Ties That Bind (1991)
❑ 5 - Bank on It (1993)
❑ 6 - Hide and Seek (1993)
❑ 7 - Wages of Sin (1994)
❑ 8 - Deadly Obsession (1995)

Molly DeWitt . . . Miami, Florida film office PR staffer

❑ 1 - Hot Property (1991)
❑ 2 - Hot Secret (1992)
❑ 3 - Hot Money (1993)
❑ 4 - Hot Schemes (1994)
❑ 5 - Hot Ticket (1995)

M. K. Wren is the pseudonym of Martha Kay Renfroe, creator of Oregon bookshop owner Conan Flagg, former intelligence agent and reluctant P.I. He is also half Nez Perce Indian, art collector and Jaguar owner. In addition to her Flagg series, Wren has written a science fiction trilogy and another science fiction title.

Conan Flagg . . . Oregon bookstore owner & former intelligence agent

- ❑ 1 - Curiosity Didn't Kill the Cat (1973)
- ❑ 2 - A Multitude of Sins (1975)
- ❑ 3 - Oh Bury Me Not (1977)
- ❑ 4 - Nothing's Certain But Death (1978)
- ❑ 5 - Seasons of Death (1981)
- ❑ 6 - Wake Up, Darlin' Corey (1984)
- ❑ 7 - Dead Matter (1993)
- ❑ 8 - King of the Mountain (1995)

L. R. Wright is Laurali Wright, a Canadian author who gave up journalism to write novels. She published three works of fiction before her first mystery—the opening title in the Karl Alberg series—which was awarded the Edgar for best novel of 1985. This series is set on the coast of British Columbia where Karl is a Royal Canadian Mounted Police (RCMP) officer in his late 40s, divorced, in a developing relationship with Cassandra Mitchell, the town librarian.

Martin Karl Alberg . . . RCMP staff sergeant on the coast of British Columbia

- ❑ 1 - **The Suspect** (1985) *Edgar winner* ★
- ❑ 2 - Sleep While I Sing (1986)
- ❑ 3 - **A Chill Rain in January** (1990) *Ellis winner* ★
- ❑ 4 - Fall From Grace (1991)
- ❑ 5 - Prized Possessions (1993)
- ❑ 6 - A Touch of Panic (1994)

Chelsea Quinn Yarbro, past president of Horror Writers of America (1988-1990), is best known for her historical horror novels, including the trilogy about a female vampire named Olivia Clemens. Yarbro has also written science fiction, fantasy, westerns, other historicals, books for children, non-fiction and a mystery series—more than 40 titles in all. Her mystery series protagonist is Charles Spotted Moon, a San Francisco attorney who is also an Ojibway tribal shaman. Two-time Edgar nominee and former vice president of Mystery Writers of America, Yarbro describes herself as a composer, fortune teller and lifetime student of history.

Charles Spotted Moon . . . San Francisco attorney & Ojibway tribal shaman

- ❑ 1 - Ogilvie, Tallant & Moon (1976) [re-released as Bad Medicine in 1990]
- ❑ 2 - False Notes (1990)
- ❑ 3 - Poison Fruit (1991)
- ❑ 4 - Cat's Claw (1992)

Dorian Yeager is a native of New Hampshire and a working actor, director and freelance magazine humor writer in New York City. She is also the creator of Victoria Bowering, New York City actor, director and playwright.

> **Victoria Bowering** . . . New York City actor, writer, playwright
>
> ❏ 1 - Cancellation by Death (1992)
> ❏ 2 - Eviction by Death (1993)

Margaret Yorke is the pseudonym of Margaret Beda Larminie Nicholson, Oxford college librarian and mystery author. She launched her mystery writing career with a five-book series featuring Oxford don Patrick Grant, after turning out eleven of what she called "family problem novels." She chaired the British Crime Writers Association in 1979 and received an award from the Swedish Academy of Detection in 1982.

> **Dr. Patrick Grant** . . . Oxford don teaching English literature
>
> ❏ 1 - Dead in the Morning (1970)
> ❏ 2 - Silent Witness (1972)
> ❏ 3 - Grave Matters (1973)
> ❏ 4 - Mortal Remains (1974)
> ❏ 5 - Cast for Death (1976)

Sharon Zukowski is a Manhattan executive by day and a mystery writer by night from her home in Hackensack, New Jersey. She is also the creator of P.I. Blaine Stewart who's in partnership with her attorney sister Eileen. Their clients are often Fortune 500 and Wall Street firms with concerns too sensitive for in-house legal staffs. Before starting their very profitable investigations business, Blaine did a cop tour with the NYPD and Eileen worked for the Manhattan District Attorney.

> **Blaine Stewart** . . . ex-NYPD cop turned P.I. in Manhattan
>
> ❏ 1 - The Hour of the Knife (1991)
> ❏ 2 - Dancing in the Dark (1992)
> ❏ 3 - Leap of Faith (1994)

Two.

 **Mystery Types**

Police Procedurals

Author	Series Character	Occupation	Setting
Adamson, M. J.	Balthazar Marten & Sixto Cardenas	NYPD homicide detective & Puerto Rican cop	Puerto Rico
Aird, Catherine	Christopher Dennis "Seedy" Sloan	Berebury CID department head	West Calleshire, England
Allingham, Margery	Albert Campion	Scotland Yard inspector	London, England
Ayres, Noreen	Samantha "Smokey" Brandon	sheriff's forensic expert	Orange County, CA
Bannister, Jo	Liz Graham & Cal Donovan	pair of Castlemere cops	Castlemere, England
Barber, Willetta A.	Christopher "Kit" Storm	police illustrator for the NYPD	New York, NY
Beaton, M. C.	Hamish Macbeth	Scottish police constable	Scotland
Bland, Eleanor Taylor	Marti MacAlister	black police detective	Lincoln Prairie, IL
Brand, Christianna	Inspector Cockrill	constable	Kent County, England
Burden, Pat	Henry Bassett	retired cop	Herefordshire, England
Butler, Gwendoline	John Coffin	London police inspector	London, England
Carlson, P. M.	Martine LaForte Hopkins	southern Indiana deputy sheriff	Indiana
Cleeves, Ann	Stephen Ramsey	British Inspector	England
Cooper, Susan Rogers	Milton Kovak	chief deputy	Prophesy County, OK
Craig, Alisa	Madoc & Janet Rhys	RCMP Inspector & wife	Fredericton, NB, Canada
Crombie, Deborah	Duncan Kincaid & Gemma James	Scotland Yard Superintendent & Sgt. partner	London, England
Curzon, Clare	Mike Yeadings	Det. Superintendent Serious Crimes Squad	Thames Valley, England
Drake, Alison	Aline Scott	small resort town police detective	south Florida
Dunlap, Susan	Jill Smith	homicide detective	Berkeley, CA
Eberhart, Mignon Good	Sarah Keate & Lance O'Leary	nurse & wealthy police detective	New York, NY
Eccles, Marjorie	Gil Mayo	Detective Chief Inspector	England
Forrest, Katherine V.	Kate Delafield	LAPD lesbian homicide detective	Los Angeles, CA
Fraser, Anthea	David Webb	British police inspector	England
George, Elizabeth	Thomas Lynley & Barbara Havers	Scotland Yard Inspector & Detective Sgt.	London, England
Gilpatrick, Noreen	Kate McLean	police detective	Seattle, WA
Glass, Leslie	April Woo	police detective	New York, NY
Gosling, Paula	Jack Stryker & Kate Trevorne	homicide cop & English professor	Grantham, OH
Gosling, Paula	Luke Abbott	English cop	England
Gosling, Paula	Blackwater Bay Mystery	police series with a Great Lakes setting	Great Lakes, USA
Graham, Caroline	Tom Barnaby	Chief Inspector	England

Police Procedurals . . . continued

Author	Series Character	Occupation	Setting
Granger, Ann	Meredith Mitchell	British Foreign Service officer	England
Green, Christine	new characters	boozy Irishman & new policewoman	England
Green, Kate	Theresa Fortunato & Oliver Jardino	professional psychic & LAPD detective	Los Angeles, CA
Grimes, Martha	Richard Jury	Scotland Yard investigator	London, England
Grindle, Lucretia	H. W. Ross	Detective Superintendent	England
Hager, Jean	Mitch Bushyhead	police chief of Cherokee descent	Buckskin, OK
Hall, Patricia	Alex Sinclair & Kate Weston	British Inspector & social worker	England
Harrod-Eagles, Cynthia	Bill Slider	Detective Inspector	England
Hart, Jeanne	Carl & Freda Pedersen	police lieutenant & wife	Bay Cove, CA
Haymon, S. T.	Benjamin Jurnet	Detective Inspector	England
Hess, Joan	Arly Hanks	small-town Arkansas police chief	Maggody, AR
Hightower, Lynn	Sonora Blair	homicide detective	Cincinnati, OH
Horansky, Ruby	Nikki Trakos	homicide detective	New York, NY
Hornsby, Wendy	Kate Teague & Roger Tejeda	college professor & homicide detective	California
James, P. D.	Adam Dalgleish	published poet of Scotland Yard	London, England
Jance, J. A.	J. P. Beaumont	homicide detective	Seattle, WA
Jance, J. A.	Joanna Bradley	deputy sheriff's widow	Arizona
Kellerman, Faye	Peter Decker & Rina Lazarus	LAPD detective & wife	Los Angeles, CA
King, Laurie R.	Kate Martinelli & Alonzo Hawkin	SFPD homicide detectives	San Francisco, CA
Knight, Alanna	Jeremy Faro	Victorian detective inspector	Edinburgh, Scotland
Krich, Rochelle Majer	Jessie Drake	Los Angeles police detective	Los Angeles, CA
Langton, Jane	Homer Kelly	Harvard professor & retired detective	Cambridge, MA
LaPierre, Janet	Vince Gutierrez & Meg Halloran	police chief & school teacher	Port Silva, WA
LaPlante, Lynda	Jane Tennison	London Detective Chief Inspector	London, England
Leon, Donna	Guido Brunetti	Venetian policeman	Venice, Italy
Maron, Margaret	Sigrid Harald	police lieutenant	New York, NY
Marsh, Ngaio	Roderick Alleyn	Inspector son of a baronet	New Zealand
Martin, Lee	Deb Ralston	police detective & mother	Ft. Worth, TX
Mason, Sarah Jill	D. S. Trewley & Sgt. Stone	English village detective partners	England
McAllester, Melanie	Elizabeth Mendoza & Ashley Johnson	lesbian homicide detectives	USA
McCrumb, Sharyn	Spencer Arrowood	Appalachian sheriff	Appalachia, NC
McGown, Jill	Chief Inspector Lloyd & Judy Hill	detective inspectors	Wales
Melville, Jennie	Charmian Daniels	police detective	Deerham Hills, England
Millar, Margaret	Inspector Sands	police detective	Toronto, Ontario, Canada
Moyes, Patricia	Henry & Emmy Tibbett	Scotland Yard Inspector & wife	London, England
Nabb, Magdalen	Salvatore Guarnaccia	Italian police marshal	Florence, Italy
Neel, Janet	John McLeish & Francesca Wilson	Det. Inspector & civil servant	England
O'Connell, Carol	Kathleen Mallory	NYPD cop	New York, NY
O'Donnell, Catherine	Karen Levinson	NYPD homicide detective	New York, NY
O'Donnell, Lillian	Mici Anhalt	criminal justice investigator	New York, NY
O'Donnell, Lillian	Norah Mulcahaney	NYPD detective	New York, NY
Oleksiw, Susan	Joe Silva	chief of police	Washington
Pargeter, Edith	George, Bunty & Dominic Felse	family of detectives	Shropshire, England
Paul, Barbara	Marian Larch	NYPD officer	New York, NY
Perry, Anne	Thomas & Charlotte Pitt	Victorian police inspector & wife	England
Perry, Anne	William Monk	amnesiac Victorian policeman	England
Pulver, Mary Monica	Peter & Kori Price Brichter	police detective & horse breeder	Illinios
Radley, Sheila	Douglas Quantrill & Hilary Lloyd	Det. Chief Inspector & Sgt. partner	Suffolk, England
Reilly, Helen	Christopher McKee	Manhattan homicide squad detective	New York, NY
Rendell, Ruth	Reginald Wexford	Chief Inspector	Sussex, England

Police Procedurals . . . continued

Author	Series Character	Occupation	Setting
Roberts, Carey	Anne Fitzhugh	police detective	Washington, DC
Sale, Medora	John Sanders & Harriet Jeffries	police detective & architectural photographer	Toronto, Ontario, Canada
Sandstrom, Eve K.	Sam & Nicky Titus	ex-army CID sheriff & his wife	Holton, OK
Schenkel, S. E.	Ray & Kate Frederick	chief of detectives & his wife of 30 years	Michigan
Shannon, Dell	Luis Mendoza	dapper & wealthy homicide lieutenant	Los Angeles, CA
Shepherd, Stella	Richard Montgomery	Nottingham CID Inspector	Nottingham, England
Simpson, Dorothy	Luke Thanet	British police inspector	England
Sims, L. V.	Dixie T. Struthers	police detective	San Jose, CA
Smith, Julie	Skip Langdon	6-ft. police detective	New Orleans, LA
Stacey, Susannah	Robert Bone	widowed British police inspector	England
Tey, Josephine	Alan Grant	Scotland Yard detective	London, England
Thomson, June	Inspector Finch	police inspector	Essex, England
Uhnak, Dorothy	Christine Opara	20-something police detective	New York, NY
Vlasopolos, Anca	Sharon Dair	sex crimes police detective	Detroit, MI
Wallace, Marilyn	Jay Goldstein & Carlos Cruz	homicide detectives	Oakland, CA
Weir, Charlene	Susan Wren	ex-cop turned Kansas police chief	Kansas
White, Teri	Spaceman Kowalski & Blue Maguire	cop pair w/prickly partnership	Los Angeles, CA
Wingate, Ann	Mark Shigata	ex-FBI agent turned sheriff	Bayport, TX
Wolfe, Susan	Sarah Nelson	police inspector	Silicon Valley, CA
Wright, L. R.	Martin Karl Alberg	RCMP Staff Sgt.	British Columbia, Canada

Private Investigators

Author	Series Character	Occupation	Setting
Barnes, Linda	Carlotta Carlyle	6'1" cab-driving ex-cop P.I.	Boston , MA
Barnes, Linda	Michael Spraggue III	wealthy actor & ex-P.I.	Boston, MA
Borton, D. B.	Cat Caliban	60-something P.I.-in-training	Cincinnati, OH
Bowers, Elisabeth	Meg Lacey	P.I.	Vancouver, BC, Canada
Bradley, Lynn	Cole January	P.I.	Houston, TX
Brod, D. C.	Quint McCauley	ex-cop turned P.I.	Chicago suburb, IL
Chapman, Sally	Juliet Blake	Silicon Valley fraud investigator	Silicon Valley, CA
Christie, Agatha	Hercule Poirot	Belgian cop turned private detective	London, England
Clark, Carol Higgins	Regan Reilly	private investigator	Los Angeles, CA
Clark, Carolyn Chambers	Theresa Franco	P.I.	Florida
Cody, Liza	Anna Lee	P.I.	London, England
Dain, Catherine	Freddie O'Neal	plane-flying P.I.	Reno, NV
Davis, Lindsey	Marcus Didius Falco	P.I. in ancient Rome	Rome, Italy
Dawson, Janet	Jeri Howard	P.I.	Oakland, CA
Day, Marele	Claudia Valentine	Australian P.I.	Australia
Disney, Doris Miles	Jeff Di Marco	insurance investigator	Boston, MA
Douglas, Lauren Wright	Caitlin Reece	lesbian detective	Victoria, BC, Canada
Dunant, Sarah	Hannah Wolfe	P.I.	London, England
Dunlap, Susan	Kiernan O'Shaughnessy	former San Francisco M.E. turned P.I.	La Jolla, CA
Evanovich, Janet	Stephanie Plum	neophyte bounty hunter	Trenton, NJ
Farrell, Gillian B.	Annie McGrogan	NYC P.I. & actor just back from LA	New York, NY
Femling, Jean	Martha "Moz" Brant	insurance claims investigator	southern California
Frankel, Valerie	Wanda Mallory	detective agency owner	New York, NY
Geason, Susan	Syd Fish	Sydney P.I.	Sydney, Australia
Grafton, Sue	Kinsey Millhone	ex-cop P.I.	Santa Teresa, CA

Private Investigators ... continued

Author	Series Character	Occupation	Setting
Grant, Linda	Catherine Sayler	P.I.	San Francisco, CA
Grant-Adamson, Lesley	Laura Flynn	P.I.	London, England
Haddam, Jane	Gregor Demarkian	former FBI department head	Philadelphia, PA
Hightower, Lynn	Lena Padget	P.I.	Lexington, KY
Hollingsworth, Gerelyn	Frances Finn	P.I.	Kansas City, KS
Hooper, Kay	Lane Montana & Trey Fortier	finder of lost things & homicide detective	Atlanta, GA
Howe, Melodie Johnson	Claire Conrad & Maggie Hill	P.I. & secretary	California
Jackson, Marian J. A.	Abigail Patience Danforth	19th century consulting detective	USA
Jacobs, Nancy Baker	Devon MacDonald	ex-teacher private eye	Minneapolis, MN
James, P. D.	Cordelia Gray	fledgling P.I.	London, England
Kelner, Toni L. P.	Laura Fleming	small-town detective	Byerly, NC
Kijewski, Karen	Kat Colorado	P.I.	Sacramento, CA
Knight, Phyllis	Lil Ritchie	lesbian P.I.	Portland, ME
Lorden, Randye	Sydney Sloane	upper west side P.I.	New York, NY
Lucke, Margaret	Jessica Randolph	P.I.	San Francisco, CA
MacGregor, T. J.	Quin St. James & Mike McCleary	wife & husband P.I. team	Florida
MacLeod, Charlotte	Sarah Kelling & Max Bittersohn	investigative couple	Boston, MA
Matthews, Francine	Meredith "Merry" Folger	Nantucket P.I.	Nantucket, MA
McCafferty, Taylor	Haskell Blevins	P.I.	Pigeon Fork, KY
McDermid, Val	Kate Brannigan	P.I.	Manchester, England
McKenna, Bridget	Caley Burke	30-something northern CA P.I.	northern California
Muller, Marcia	Joanna Stark	international art investigator	Napa Valley, CA
Muller, Marcia	Sharon McCone	San Francisco legal co-op investigator	San Francisco, CA
O'Callaghan, Maxine	Delilah West	P.I.	Orange County, CA
O'Donnell, Lillian	Gwenn Ramadge	P.I. for corporate investigations	New York, NY
Oliver, Maria Antonia	Lonia Guiu	Catalan private investigator	Spain
Padgett, Abigail	Barbara Joan "Bo" Bradley	child abuse investigator	San Diego, CA
Paretsky, Sara	V. I. Warshawski	attorney turned P.I.	Chicago, IL
Pincus, Elizabeth	Nell Fury	lesbian P.I.	San Francisco, CA
Popkin, Zelda	Mary Carner	former department store detective	USA
Prowell, Sandra West	Phoebe Siegel	ex-cop P.I.	Billings, MT
Scoppettone, Sandra	Lauren Laurano	Greenwich Village lesbian P.I.	New York, NY
Shah, Diane K.	Paris Chandler	1940s Hollywood P.I.	Hollywood, CA
Short, Sharon Gwyn	Patricia Delaney	computer whiz P.I.	Cincinnati, OH
Singer, Shelley	Jake Samson & Rosie Vicente	ex-cop & carpenter tenant	Berkeley, CA
Slovo, Gillian	Kate Baeier	freelance journalist turned detective	London, England
Spring, Michelle	Laura Principal	British academic turned P.I.	England
Stabenow, Dana	Kate Shugak	native Alaskan ex-D. A. investigator	Alaska
Steiner, Susan	Alex Winter	P.I.	California
Sucher, Dorothy	Sabina Swift	Georgetown detective agency owner	Washington, DC
Sullivan, Winona	Cecile Buddenbrooks, Sister	licensed P.I. nun	Boston, MA
Taylor, Elizabeth Atwood	Maggie Elliott	ex-film maker turned P.I.	San Francisco, CA
Wallace, Patricia	Sydney Bryant	private investigator	San Diego, CA
Welch, Pat	Helen Black	ex-cop lesbian P.I.	San Francisco, CA
Wells, Carolyn	Fleming Stone	intellectual private investigator	New York, NY
Wentworth, Patricia	Maud Silver	retired governess & spinster P.I.	London, England
Wesley, Valerie Wilson	Tamara Hayle	black P.I. ex-cop	Newark, NJ
White, Gloria	Ronnie Ventana	burglar's daughter P.I.	San Francisco, CA
Wilhelm, Kate	Charlie Meiklejohn & Constance Leidl	ex-arson investigator P.I. & psychologist	New York, NY
Zukowski, Sharon	Blaine Stewart	ex-NYPD cop turned P.I. in Manhattan	New York, NY

Amateurs

Author	Series Character	Occupation	Setting

Academic

Author	Series Character	Occupation	Setting
Armstrong, Charlotte	MacDougal Duff	retired history professor	USA
Arnold, Margot	Penny Spring & Toby Glendower, Sir	Amer. anthropologist & British archeologist	World Travelers
Belfort, Sophie	Molly Rafferty	college history professor	Boston, MA
Borthwick, J. S.	Sarah Deane & Alex McKenzie, Dr.	English professor & internist	Boston, MA
Carlson, P. M.	Maggie Ryan	statistician & mother	New York, NY
Caudwell, Sarah	Hilary Tamar	Oxford professor of medieval law	Oxford, England
Clarke, Anna	Paula Glenning	British professor & writer	London, England
Crane, Hamilton	Emily D. Seeton	retired British art teacher	England
Cross, Amanda	Kate Fansler	university English professor	New York, NY
Dunant, Sarah	Marla Masterson	young professor of Anglo-Saxon literature	England
Kelly, Nora	Gillian Adams	Univ. of the Pacific Northwest history chair	British Columbia, Canada
Kenney, Susan	Roz Howard & Alan Stewart	American professor & British painter	Maine
Lorens, M. K.	Winston Marlowe Sherman	Shakespeare professor & mystery writer	USA
MacLeod, Charlotte	Peter Shandy & Helen Marsh Shandy	botany professor & librarian wife	rural Balaclava County, MA
Mann, Jessica	Tamara Hoyland	British secret agent archaeologist	England
Mann, Jessica	Thea Crawford	archaeology professor	England
Mariz, Linda French	Laura Ireland	grad student volleyball player	Seattle, WA
McCrumb, Sharyn	Elizabeth MacPherson	forensic anthropologist	USA
McCrumb, Sharyn	James Owen Mega	science fiction author & college professor	USA
McFall, Patricia	Nora James	American linguistics graduate student	Japan
Peters, Elizabeth	Amelia Peabody	Victorian feminist archaeologist	England
Peterson, Audrey	Claire Camden	California English professor in Britain	England
Roberts, Gillian	Amanda Pepper	high school teacher	Philadelphia, PA
Singer, Shelley	Barrett Lake	high school history teacher	Berkeley, CA
Skom, Edith	Elizabeth Austin	English professor	Midwest, USA
Smith, Joan	Loretta Lawson	British feminist professor	England
Tilton, Alice	Leonidas Witherall	retired academic & secret pulp fiction author	Boston, MA
Yorke, Margaret	Patrick Grant, Dr.	Oxford don teaching English literature	Oxford, England

Animals, cats

Author	Series Character	Occupation	Setting
Adamson, Lydia	Alice Nestleton	actress and cat lover	New York, NY
Braun, Lilian Jackson	Jim Qwilleran, Koko & Yum Yum	ex-police reporter & cats	Midwest, USA
Brown, Rita Mae	Mary Minor Haristeen	small-town postmistress & cat	Crozet, VA
Douglas, Carole Nelson	Temple Barr & Midnight Louie	public relations freelancer & tomcat sleuth	Las Vegas, NV

Animals, dogs

Author	Series Character	Occupation	Setting
Cleary, Melissa	Jackie Walsh & Jake	college film instructor with her ex-police dog	Midwest, USA
Conant, Susan	Holly Winter	30-something dog trainer & columnist	Cambridge, MA
Henry, Sue	Jessie Arnold & Alex Jensen	sled dog racer & Alaska State trooper	Alaska
Walker, Mary Willis	Kate Driscoll	dog trainer	Texas

Animals, horses

Author	Series Character	Occupation	Setting
Banks, Carolyn	Robin Vaughn	equestrienne sleuth	Texas
Crum, Laura	Gail McCarthy	horse veterinarian	northern California

Amateurs . . . continued

Author	Series Character	Occupation	Setting
Animals, other			
Adamson, Lydia	Deidre Quinn Nightingale	rural veterinarian	New York
Block, Barbara	Robin Light	pet store owner	Syracuse, NY
Art & Antiques			
Coker, Carolyn	Andrea Perkins	art historian & restorer of paintings	Boston, MA
Comfort, Barbara	Tish McWhinney	artist & painter	Vermont
Fowler, Earlene	Albenia "Benni" Harper	ex-rancher & folk art museum curator	central coast, California
Hardwick, Mollie	Doran Fairweather	British antiques dealer	England
Kenney, Susan	Roz Howard & Alan Stewart	American professor & British painter	Maine
McClendon, Lise	Alix Thorssen	gallery owner & art forgery expert	Montana
Mitchell, Gladys	Timothy Herring	preservation society director	England
Muller, Marcia	Elena Oliverez	Mexican arts museum curator	Santa Barbara, CA
Orde, A. J.	Jason Lynx	antiques dealer	Denver, CO
Peters, Elizabeth	Vicky Bliss	art historian	Germany
Scherf, Margaret	Emily & Henry Bryce	Manhattan interior decorators	New York, NY
Smith, Evelyn E.	Susan Melville	freelance assassin & painter	New York, NY
Valentine, Deborah	Katharine Craig & Kevin Bryce	sculptor & ex-sheriff's detective	California
Watson, Clarissa	Persis Willum	New York art curator	Long Island, NY
Authors & Writers			
Bannister, Jo	Clio Rees, Dr. & Harry Marsh	physician/mystery writer & chief inspector	England
Blackmur, L. L.	Galen Shaw & Julian Baugh	writer & financier	New England
Brill, Toni	Midge Cohen	children's author fluent in Russian	New York, NY
Cooper, Natasha	Willow King & Cressida Woodruffe	British civil servant & romance novelist	London, England
Cooper, Susan Rogers	E. J. Pugh	housewife, mother & romance writer	Texas
Daly, Elizabeth	Henry Gamadge	author & bibliophile	New York, NY
Duffy, Margaret	Ingrid Langley & Patrick Gillard	novelist/British agent & British army major	England
Friedman, Mickey	Georgia Lee Maxwell	Paris-based freelance writer	Paris, France
Glen, Alison	Charlotte Sams	freelance writer	Columbus, OH
Kittredge, Mary	Charlotte Kent	freelance writer	Connecticut
Lorens, M. K.	Winston Marlowe Sherman	Shakespeare professor & mystery writer	USA
Malmont, Valerie S.	Tori Miracle	ex-NYC crime writer turned novelist	Pennsylvania
Moffat, Gwen	Melinda Pink	writer & mountain climber	Utah
Osborne, Denise	Queenie Davilow	Hollywood screenwriter	Hollywood, CA
Paige, Robin	Kathryn Ardleigh	25-yr. old American author	Dedham, England
Papazoglou, Orania	Patience Campbell McKenna	6-ft. romance novelist turned crime writer	New York, NY
Peters, Elizabeth	Jacqueline Kirby	librarian turned romance novelist	New York, NY
Roberts, Lora	Liz Sullivan	freelance writer	Palo Alto, CA
Rowlands, Betty	Melissa Craig	British mystery writer	England
Smith, Barbara Burnett	Jolie Wyatt	aspiring novelist & writer's group member	Purple Sage, TX
Smith, Julie	Paul MacDonald	ex-reporter & mystery writer	San Francisco, CA
Stallwood, Veronica	Kate Ivory	Oxford novelist	Oxford, England
Yeager, Dorian	Victoria Bowering	NYC actor, writer & playwright	New York, NY

Amateurs . . . continued

Author	Series Character	Occupation	Setting

Bed & Breakfast

Author	Series Character	Occupation	Setting
Bishop, Claudia	Sarah & Meg Quilliam	inn owner & chef (sisters)	Hemlock Falls, NY
Daheim, Mary	Judith McMonigle	bed & breakfast owner	Washington
Hager, Jean	Tess Darcy	Ozarks bed & breakfast owner	Victoria Springs, MO
Myers, Tamar	Magdalena Yoder	Mennonite inn owner & operator	Pennsylvania

Black

Author	Series Character	Occupation	Setting
Bland, Eleanor Taylor	Marti MacAlister	black police detective	Lincoln Prairie, IL
Neely, Barbara	Blanche White	middle-aged black domestic	USA
Wesley, Valerie Wilson	Tamara Hayle	black P.I. ex-cop	Newark, NJ

Books & Libraries

Author	Series Character	Occupation	Setting
Daly, Elizabeth	Henry Gamadge	author & bibliophile	New York, NY
Dereske, Jo	Helma Zukas	Washington State librarian	Washington
Harris, Charlaine	Aurora Teagarden	20-something librarian	Georgia
Hart, Carolyn G.	Annie Laurance & Max Darling	bookstore owner & investigator	South Carolina
Hess, Joan	Claire Malloy	small-town bookstore owner	Arkansas
Knight, Kathryn Lasky	Calista Jacobs	award-winning illustrator of children's books	Cambridge, MA
Lockridge, Frances & R.	Pam & Jerry North	husband & wife book publishers	New York, NY
Morgan, Kate	Dewey James	60-something small-town librarian	New York
Simonson, Sheila	Lark Dailey Dodge	6-ft. bookdealer	northern California
Tilton, Alice	Leonidas Witherall	retired academic & secret pulp fiction author	Boston, MA
Wren, M. K.	Conan Flagg	bookstore owner & former intelligence agent	Oregon

Botanical

Author	Series Character	Occupation	Setting
Albert, Susan Wittig	China Bayles	herb shop owner & former attorney	Pecan Springs, TX
Craig, Alisa	Dittany Henbit Monk & Osbert Monk	garden club member & author of westerns	Lobelia Falls, Ontario, Canada
Peters, Ellis	Brother Cadfael	medieval monk & herbalist	Shrewsbury, England
Rothenberg, Rebecca	Claire Sharples	former MIT scholar & microbiologist	California

Business & Finance

Author	Series Character	Occupation	Setting
Babson, Marian	Douglas Perkins	London-based public relations agent	London, England
Baker, Nikki	Virginia Kelly	lesbian stockbroker	USA
Beaton, M. C.	Agatha Raisin	London advertising retiree in the Cotswolds	Cotswolds, England
Bennett, Liza	Peg Goodenough	ad agency creative director	New York, NY
Berry, Carole	Bonnie Indermill	tap-dancing Manhattan office temp	New York, NY
Brennan, Carol	Liz Wareham	Manhattan public relations consultant	New York, NY
Christmas, Joyce	Betty Trenka	retired businesswoman	Connecticut
Collins, Anna Ashwood	Abigail Doyle	New York efficiency expert	New York, NY
Douglas, Carole Nelson	Temple Barr & Midnight Louie	public relations freelancer & tomcat sleuth	Las Vegas, NV
Feddersen, Connie	Amanda Hazard	small-town Certified Public Accountant	Vamoose, OK
Ferrars, E. X.	Virginia & Felix Freer	physiotherapist & businessman	England
Girdner, Jaqueline	Kate Jasper	gag gift wholesaler	Marin County, CA
Gray, Gallagher	Theodore S. Hubbert & Auntie Lil	ret'd human resources mgr & dress designer	New York, NY
Gunning, Sally	Peter Bartholomew	small business owner	Cape Cod, MA
Haddad, Carolyn A.	Becky Belski	computer investigator	Chicago, IL

Amateurs . . . continued

Author	Series Character	Occupation	Setting
Business & Finance . . . continued			
Holtzer, Susan	Anneke Haagen	computer consultant	Ann Arbor , MI
Kelly, Susan B.	Alison Hope & Nick Trevellyan	software designer & detective inspector	Hop Valley, England
Kraft, Gabrielle	Jerry Zalman	Beverly Hills dealmaker	Los Angeles, CA
Kunz, Kathleen	Terry Girard	genealogist for hire	St. Louis, MO
Lacey, Sarah	Leah Hunter	Yorkshire tax inspector	Yorkshire, England
Lamb, J. Dayne	Teal Stewart	Certified Public Accountant	Boston, MA
Lathen, Emma	John Putnam Thatcher	Wall Street financial whiz	New York, NY
Law, Janice	Anna Peters	international oil company exec turned P.I.	Washington, DC
Maxwell, A. E.	Fiddler & Fiora Flynn	investment banker	California
Meyers, Annette	Xenia Smith & Leslie Wetzon	pair of Wall Street headhunters	New York, NY
Montgomery, Yvonne E.	Finny Aletter	stockbroker turned carpenter	Denver, CO
Pickard, Nancy	Jenny Cain	New England foundation director	Port Frederick, MA
Pugh, Dianne G.	Iris Thorne	investment counselor	Los Angeles, CA
Sprinkle, Patricia Houck	Sheila Travers	public relations executive	Atlanta, GA
Taylor, L. A.	J. J. Jamison	computer engineer & CATCH investigator	Minneapolis, MN
Wilson, Barbara	Cassandra Reilly	London-based Spanish translator	London, England
Criminal			
Highsmith, Patricia	Tom Ripley	charming forger & psychopath	England
Domestic			
Neely, Barbara	Blanche White	middle-aged black domestic	USA
Trocheck, Kathy Hogan	Julia Callahan Garrity	ex-cop cleaning lady	Atlanta, GA
Ecclesiastical & Religious			
Black, Veronica	Joan, Sister	British investigative nun	England
Charles, Kate	Lucy Kingsley & D. Middleton-Brown	artist & solicitor	England
Frazer, Margaret	Sister Frevisse	Medieval nun	England
Greenwood, Diane M.	Theodora Braithwaite, Rev.	British deaconess	England
Harris, Lee	Christine Bennett	ex-nun	New York, NY
Holland, Isabelle	Claire Aldington, Rev.	Episcopal priest	New York, NY
O'Marie, Sister Carol A.	Mary Helen, Sister	70-something nun	San Francisco, CA
Page, Katherine Hall	Faith Sibley Fairchild	minister's wife & culinary artist	Massachusetts
Peters, Ellis	Brother Cadfael	medieval monk & herbalist	Shrewsbury, England
Robb, Candace M.	Owen Archer	medieval Welsh spy for the Archbishop	England
Environment & Wilderness			
Andrews, Sarah	Em Hansen	oil worker	Wyoming
Barr, Nevada	Anna Pigeon	U.S. park ranger	USA
Cleeves, Ann	George & Molly Palmer-Jones	ex-Home Office official/bird-watcher & wife	London, England
Dunlap, Susan	Vejay Haskell	utility meter reader	northern California
Henry, Sue	Jessie Arnold & Alex Jensen	sled dog racer & Alaska State trooper	Alaska
McQuillan, Karin	Jazz Jasper	American safari guide in Africa	Kenya
Moffat, Gwen	Melinda Pink	writer & mountain climber	Utah
Oliphant, B. J.	Shirley McClintock	50-something rancher	Colorado
Quinn, Elizabeth	Lauren Maxwell	Alaska wildlife investigator PhD	Alaska
Van Gieson, Judith	Neil Hamel	attorney & investigator	Albuquerque, NM
Wallingford, Lee	Ginny Trask & Frank Carver	forest fire dispatcher & ex-cop	Oregon

Amateurs . . . continued

Author	Series Character	Occupation	Setting

Ethnic & Native American

Author	Series Character	Occupation	Setting
Hager, Jean	Molly Bearpaw	Cherokee civil rights investigator	Oklahoma
Romberg, Nina	Marian Winchester	Caddo-Commanche medicine woman	Texas
Yarbro, Chelsea Quinn	Charles Spotted Moon	attorney & Ojibway tribal shaman	San Francisco, CA

Gourmet & Food

Author	Series Character	Occupation	Setting
Crespi, Trella	Simona Griffo	advertising executive & gourmet cook	New York, NY
Davidson, Diane Mott	Goldy Bear	caterer & single mother	Colorado
Dietz, Denise	Ellie Bernstein	diet group leader	USA
Hart, Ellen	Sophie Greenway	magazine editor & newspaper food critic	Minneapolis, MN
Hart, Ellen	Jane Lawless	lesbian restaurateur	Minneapolis, MN
Laurence, Janet	Darina Lisle	British caterer, chef & food writer	England
Lyons, Nan & Ivan	Natasha O'Brien & Millie Ogden	pair of culinary artists	USA
Myers, Amy	Auguste Didier	British-French Victorian master chef	England
Page, Katherine Hall	Faith Sibley Fairchild	minister's wife & culinary artist	Massachusetts
Pence, Joanne	Angelina Amalfi	food columnist & restaurant reviewer	San Francisco, CA
Rich, Virginia	Eugenia Potter	widowed chef	Maine

Historical, Medieval

Author	Series Character	Occupation	Setting
Frazer, Margaret	Sister Frevisse	medieval nun	England
Newman, Sharan	Catherine LeVendeur	novice & scholar	France
Peters, Ellis	Brother Cadfael	medieval monk & herbalist	Shrewsbury, England
Robb, Candace M.	Owen Archer	medieval Welsh spy for the Archbishop	England
Sedley, Kate	Roger the Chapman	medieval chapman (peddler)	England

Historical, Renaissance

Author	Series Character	Occupation	Setting
Eyre, Elizabeth	Sigismondo	agent of a Renaissance duke	Italy

Historical, 19th century

Author	Series Character	Occupation	Setting
Brightwell, Emily	Inspector Witherspoon & Mrs. Jeffries	Victorian inspector & housekeeper	London, England
Crowleigh, Ann	Miranda & Clare Clively	Victorian London twin sisters	London, England
Douglas, Carole Nelson	Irene Adler	19th century French sleuth	Paris, France
Fawcett, Quinn	Victoire Vernet	wife of Napoleonic gendarme	France
Jackson, Marian J. A.	Abigail Patience Danforth	19th century consulting detective	USA
Kingsbury, Kate	Cecily Sinclair	hotel owner in Edwardian England	England
Linscott, Gillian	Nell Bray	British suffragette	England
Monfredo, Miriam Grace	Glynis Tryon	librarian & suffragette	Seneca Falls, NY
Paige, Robin	Kathryn Ardleigh	25-yr. old American author	Dedham, England
Peters, Elizabeth	Amelia Peabody	Victorian feminist archaeologist	England
Ross, Kate	Julian Kestrel	early 19th century Londoner	London, England

Historical, 1920s

Author	Series Character	Occupation	Setting
Beck, K. K.	Iris Cooper	Roaring 20s coed at Stanford University	Palo Alto, CA
Greenwood, Kerry	Phryne Fisher	1920s Australian sleuth	Australia

Amateurs . . . continued

Author	Series Character	Occupation	Setting
Journalism, magazine			
D'Amato, Barbara	Cat Marsala	freelance investigative journalist	Chicago, IL
Hart, Ellen	Sophie Greenway	magazine editor & newspaper food critic	Minneapolis, MN
Holt, Hazel	Sheila Malory	British literary magazine writer	England
Kelly, Susan	Liz Connors	freelance crime writer	Cambridge, MA
Woods, Sherryl	Amanda Roberts	ex-New York investigative reporter	Atlanta, GA
Journalism, newspaper			
Braun, Lilian Jackson	Jim Qwilleran, Koko & Yum Yum	ex-police reporter & cat	Midwest USA
Buchanan, Edna	Britt Montero	newspaper crime reporter	Miami, FL
Burke, Jan	Irene Kelly	newspaper reporter	California
Daheim, Mary	Emma Lord	small-town newspaper owner & editor	Alpine, WA
Danks, Denise	Georgina Powers	British computer journalist	London, England
Davis, Dorothy Salisbury	Julie Hayes	former actress & columnist	New York, NY
Ferrars, E. X.	Sara Marriott	journalist	England
Gordon, Alison	Kate Henry	baseball newswriter	Toronto, Ontario, Canada
Grant-Adamson, Lesley	Rain Morgan	newspaper reporter	London, England
Haddock, Lisa	Carmen Ramirez	newspaper copy editor	USA
Hart, Carolyn G.	Henrietta O'Dwyer Collins	70-something reporter	South Carolina
Kallen, Lucille	Maggie Rome & C. B. Greenfield	reporter & editor/publisher	Connecticut
Karr, Leona	Addie Devore	small-town newspaper owner	Colorado
Logue, Mary	Laura Malloy	journalist	Minneapolis, MN
McDermid, Val	Lindsay Gordon	lesbian journalist	England
O'Brien, Meg	Jessica James	newspaper reporter	Rochester, NY
Peterson, Audrey	Jane Winfield	British journalist & music writer	England
Porter, Anna	Judith Hayes	journalist	USA
Roome, Annette	Christine Martin	40-something cub reporter	England
Shankman, Sarah	Samantha Adams	investigative reporter	Atlanta, GA
Sibley, Celestine	Kate Kincaid Mulcay	veteran newspaperwoman	Atlanta, GA
Stein, Triss	Kay Engles	nationally-known reporter	USA
Tyre, Peg	Kate Murray	newspaper reporter for Daily Herald	Brooklyn, NY
Walker, Mary Willis	Mollie Cates	true crime writer & reporter	Texas
Journalism, photography			
Hornsby, Wendy	Maggie MacGowen	investigative filmmaker	California
Kelly, Mary Ann	Claire Breslinsky	freelance photographer	New York, NY
Moody, Susan	Penny Wanawake	6-ft. photographer daughter of UN diplomat	England
North, Suzanne	Phoebe Fairfax	Calgary TV video photographer	Calgary, Alberta, Canada
OCork, Shannon	Theresa Tracy Baldwin	sports photographer for New York daily	New York, NY
Tucker, Kerry	Libby Kincaid	magazine photographer	New York, NY
Journalism, television			
Fraser, Antonia P.	Jemima Shore	British TV interviewer	London, England
Hayter, Sparkle	Robin Hudson	cable news reporter	New York, NY
Robitaille, Julie	Kit Powell	TV sports reporter	San Diego, CA
Rowe, Jennifer	Verity "Birdie" Birdwood	Australian TV researcher	Australia

Amateurs . . . continued

Author	Series Character	Occupation	Setting
Legal, attorney			
Cannon, Taffy	Nan Robinson	investigator for the California State Bar	Los Angeles, CA
Caudwell, Sarah	Hilary Tamar	Oxford professor of medieval law	Oxford, England
Charles, Kate	Lucy Kingsley & D. Middleton-Brown	artist & solicitor	England
Dominic, R. B.	Ben Safford	Democratic congressman from Ohio	Washington, DC
Fallon, Ann	James Fleming	Dublin solicitor	Dublin, Ireland
Fyfield, Frances	Helen West	London Crown Prosecutor	London, England
Fyfield, Frances	Sarah Fortune	lawyer in prestigious British firm	England
Giroux, E. X.	Robert Forsythe & Abigail Sanderson	London barrister & his secretary	London, England
Hartzmark, Gini	Katherine Prescott Milholland	corporate attorney	Chicago, IL
Lambert, Mercedes	Whitney Logan	20-something Los Angeles attorney	Los Angeles, CA
Matera, Lia	Laura Di Palma	attorney	San Francisco, CA
Matera, Lia	Willa Jansson	California attorney	San Francisco, CA
McGuire, Christine	Kathryn Mackay	prosecuting attorney	northern California
Meek, M. R. D.	Lennox Kemp	London solicitor detective	Londond, England
Meredith, D. R.	John Lloyd Branson & Lydia Fairchild	defense attorney & legal assistant	Canadian, TX
Millar, Margaret	Tom Aragon	attorney	California
Parker, Barbara	Gail Connor	corporate attorney	USA
Piesman, Marissa	Nina Fischman	legal services attorney	New York, NY
Schier, Norma	Kay Barth	district attorney	Colorado
Scottoline, Lisa	Mary DiNunzio	attorney	Philadelphia, PA
Smith, Janet L.	Annie MacPherson	attorney	Seattle, WA
Smith, Julie	Rebecca Schwartz	defense attorney	San Francisco, CA
Truman, Margaret	Mackenzie Smith & Annabel Reed	law professor & attorney wife	Washington, DC
Truman, Margaret	Margit Falk	ex-combat pilot & government attorney	Washington, DC
Van Gieson, Judith	Neil Hamel	attorney & investigator	Albuquerque, NM
Wakefield, Hannah	Dee Street	American attorney	London, England
Wheat, Carolyn	Cass Jameson	Brooklyn criminal lawyer	New York, NY
Wilhelm, Kate	Barbara Holloway	defense attorney	Oregon
Woods, Sara	Anthony Maitland	English barrister drawn to murder cases	England
Yarbro, Chelsea Quinn	Charles Spotted Moon	attorney & Ojibway tribal shaman	San Francisco, CA
Legal, judge			
Maron, Margaret	Deborah Knott	district judge	North Carolina
Wilhelm, Kate	Sarah Drexler	judge	Oregon
Lesbian			
Baker, Nikki	Virginia Kelly	lesbian stockbroker	USA
Douglas, Lauren Wright	Caitlin Reece	lesbian detective	Victoria, BC, Canada
Forrest, Katherine V.	Kate Delafield	LAPD lesbian homicide detective	Los Angeles, CA
Hart, Ellen	Jane Lawless	lesbian restaurateur	Minneapolis, MN
Knight, Phyllis	Lil Ritchie	lesbian P.I.	Portland, ME
McDermid, Val	Lindsay Gordon	lesbian journalist	England
Pincus, Elizabeth	Nell Fury	lesbian P.I.	San Francisco, CA
Scoppettone, Sandra	Lauren Laurano	Greenwich Village lesbian P.I.	New York, NY
Welch, Pat	Helen Black	ex-cop lesbian P.I.	San Francisco, CA
Wilson, Barbara	Pam Nilsen	lesbian printing company owner	Seattle, WA
Wings, Mary	Emma Victor	lesbian activist & former publicist	Boston, MA

Amateurs . . . continued

Author	Series Character	Occupation	Setting
Medical			
Bailey, Jo	Jan Gallagher	hospital security supervisor	Minneapolis, MN
Bell, Josephine	David Wintringham	British physician	London, England
Clark, Carolyn Chambers	Megan Baldwin	registered nurse	St. Petersburg, FL
Cornwell, Patricia Daniels	Kay Scarpetta	Chief Medical Examiner	Richmond, VA
D'Amato, Barbara	Gerritt De Graaf	physician	USA
Ferrars, E. X.	Virginia & Felix Freer	physiotherapist & businessman	England
Fromer, Margot J.	Amanda Knight	hospital director of nursing	Washington, DC
Green, Christine	Kate Kinsella	British nurse & medical investigator	England
Hendrickson, Louise	Amy Prescott	crime lab physician	Seattle, WA
Kittredge, Mary	Edwina Crusoe	RN & medical consultant	New Haven, CT
Landreth, Marsha	Samantha Turner, Dr.	medical examiner	Wyoming
McCloy, Helen	Basil Willing, Dr.	medical advisor to NYC district attorney	New York, NY
McGiffin, Janet	Maxene St. Clair, Dr.	emergency room physician	Milwaukee, WI
Millar, Margaret	Paul Prye	psychiatrist	Toronto, Ontario, Canada
Mitchell, Gladys	Beatrice Lestrange Bradley	psychiatrist & consultant to Home Office	London, England
Rinehart, Mary Roberts	Hilda Adams	nurse	England
Scherf, Margaret	Grace Severance, Dr.	retired pathologist	Arizona
Thompson, Joyce	Frederika Bascomb	forensic artist	Seattle, WA
Walsh, Jill Paton	Imogen Quy	nurse	England
Miscellaneous			
Andreae, Christine	Lee Squires	English professor & poet	Washington, DC
Ballard, Mignon	Eliza Figg	former Peace Corps volunteer	USA
Christmas, Joyce	Margaret Priam, Lady	Englishwoman in New York City	New York, NY
Jackson, Muriel Resnick	Merrie Lee Spencer	Manhattan transplants	North Carolina
Moody, Susan	Cassandra Swann	British biology teacher turned bridge pro	England
Sayers, Dorothy L.	Peter Wimsey, Lord	pianist, book collector & criminologist	London, England
Taylor, Phoebe Atwood	Asey Mayo	former sailor & auto racer	Cape Cod, MA
Occult			
Edghill, Rosemary	Karen Hightower	Manhattan graphic designer & white witch	New York, NY
Mather, Linda	Jo Hughes	professional astrologer	USA
Warner, Mignon	Edwina Charles	British clairvoyante	England
Romantic			
Atherton, Nancy	Aunt Dimity	romantic ghost	Boston, MA
Cannell, Dorothy	Ellie & Ben Haskell & Tramwell sisters	interior decorator	London, England
Florian, S.L.	Delia Ross-Merlani, Viscountess	English-Italian noblewoman	New York, NY
Secret Agents			
Christie, Agatha	Tuppence & Tommy Beresford	adventurers for hire & intelligence agents	England
Duffy, Margaret	Ingrid Langley & Patrick Gillard	novelist/British agent & British army major	England
Gilman, Dorothy	Emily Pollifax	grandmother CIA agent	New Jersey
Mann, Jessica	Tamara Hoyland	British secret agent archaeologist	England
McGerr, Patricia	Selena Mead	British government agent	England

Amateurs . . . continued

Author	Series Character	Occupation	Setting
Sports			
Cody, Liza	Eva Wylie	wrestler & security guard	London, England
Gordon, Alison	Kate Henry	baseball newswriter	Toronto, Ontario, Canada
Mariz, Linda French	Laura Ireland	grad student volleyball player	Seattle, WA
OCork, Shannon	Theresa Tracy Baldwin	sports photographer for New York daily	New York, NY
Robitaille, Julie	Kit Powell	TV sports reporter	San Diego, CA
Suburban			
Berenson, Laurien	new character	suburban wife & mother	USA
Churchill, Jill	Jane Jeffry	suburban Chicago single mother	Chicago, IL
Jacobs, Jonnie	Kate Austen	Bay area single mother	Walnut Hills, CA
Meier, Leslie	Lucy Stone	small-town New England sleuth	Maine
Wolzien, Valerie	Susan Henshaw	suburban sleuth	Connecticut
Technology			
Danks, Denise	Georgina Powers	British computer journalist	London, England
Haddad, Carolyn A.	Becky Belski	computer investigator	Chicago, IL
Holtzer, Susan	Anneke Haagen	computer consultant	Ann Arbor, MI
Kelly, Susan B.	Alison Hope & Nick Trevellyan	software designer & detective inspector	Hop Valley, England
Taylor, L. A.	J. J. Jamison	computer engineer & CATCH investigator	Minneapolis, MN
Theatre & Performing Arts			
Adamson, Lydia	Alice Nestleton	actress & cat lover	New York, NY
Babson, Marian	Eve Sinclair & Trixie Dolan	aging British ex-movie queens	London, England
Beck, K. K.	Jane da Silva	former lounge singer	Seattle, WA
Cooper, Susan Rogers	Kimmey Kruse	stand-up comic	Chicago, IL
Davis, Dorothy Salisbury	Julie Hayes	former actress & columnist	New York, NY
Dentinger, Jane	Jocelyn O'Roarke	Broadway actress & director	New York, NY
Matteson, Stephanie	Charlotte Graham	Oscar-winning actress	New York, NY
Millhiser, Marlys	Charlie Greene	Hollywood literary agent	Hollywood, CA
Morice, Ann	Tessa Crichton	English actress sleuth	England
Paul, Barbara	Enrico Caruso & Geraldine Farrar	Italian tenor & American soprano	New York, NY
Scott, Rosie	Glory Day	artist & singer	New Zealand
Woods, Sherryl	Molly DeWitt	film office public relations staffer	Miami, FL
Yeager, Dorian	Victoria Bowering	NYC actor, writer & playwright	New York, NY
Women of a Certain Age			
Allen, Irene	Elizabeth Elliot	widowed Quaker meeting clerk	Pennsylvania
Borton, D. B.	Cat Caliban	60-something P.I.-in-training	Cincinnati, OH
Boylan, Eleanor	Clara Gamadge	widow of Henry the forgery expert	New York, NY
Christie, Agatha	Jane Marple	elderly spinster	St. Mary's Mead, England
Dolson, Hildegarde	Lucy Ramsdale & James McDougal	illustrator & homicide inspector	Connecticut
Gilman, Dorothy	Emily Pollifax	grandmother CIA agent	New Jersey
Hall, Mary Bowen	Emma Chizzit	salvage dealer	Sacramento, CA
Hart, Carolyn G.	Henrietta O'Dwyer Collins	70-something reporter	South Carolina
O'Marie, Sister Carol A.	Mary Helen, Sister	70-something nun	San Francisco, CA
Oliphant, B. J.	Shirley McClintock	50-something rancher	Colorado

Amateurs . . . continued

Author	Series Character	Occupation	Setting

Women of a Certain Age . . . continued

Author	Series Character	Occupation	Setting
Sawyer, Corinne Holt	Angela Benbow & Caledonia Wingate	70-something admirals' widows	California
Squire, Elizabeth Daniels	Peaches Dann	50-something widow	North Carolina
Stevens, Serita	Fanny Zindel	Jewish grandmother	USA

World Travelers

Author	Series Character	Occupation	Setting
Arnold, Margot	Penny Spring & Toby Glendower, Sir	Amer. anthropologist & British archeologist	World Travelers
Crane, Frances	Pat & Jean Abbot	husband & wife detection team	World Travelers
Mann, Jessica	Thea Crawford	archaeology professor	England

Three

Series Characters

3

A			
Series Character	**Occupation**	**Setting**	**Author**

A			
Abigail Doyle	New York efficiency expert	New York, NY	Collins, Anna Ashwood
Abigail Patience Danforth	19th century consulting detective	USA	Jackson, Marian J. A.
Abigail Sanderson & Robert Forsythe	secretary & London barrister	London, England	Giroux, E. X.
Adam Dalgleish	published poet of Scotland Yard	London, England	James, P. D.
Addie Devore	small-town newspaper owner	Colorado	Karr, Leona
Agatha Raisin	London advertising retiree in the Cotswolds	Cotswolds, England	Beaton, M. C.
Alan Grant	Scotland Yard detective	London, England	Tey, Josephine
Alan Stewart & Roz Howard	British painter & American professor	Maine	Kenney, Susan
Albenia "Benni" Harper	ex-rancher & folk art museum curator	central coast California	Fowler, Earlene
Albert Campion	Scotland Yard inspector	London, England	Allingham, Margery
Alex Jensen & Jessie Arnold	Alaska State trooper & sled dog racer	Alaska	Henry, Sue
Alex McKenzie, Dr. & Sarah Deane	internist & English professor	Boston, MA	Borthwick, J. S.
Alex Sinclair & Kate Weston	British Inspector & social worker	England	Hall, Patricia
Alex Winter	P.I.	California	Steiner, Susan
Alice Nestleton	actress and cat lover	New York, NY	Adamson, Lydia
Aline Scott	small resort town police detective	south Florida	Drake, Alison
Alison Hope & Nick Trevellyan	software designer & detective inspector	Hop Valley, England	Kelly, Susan B.
Alix Thorssen	gallery owner & art forgery expert	Montana	McClendon, Lise
Alonzo Hawkin & Kate Martinelli	SFPD homicide detectives	San Francisco, CA	King, Laurie R.
Amanda Hazard	small-town Certified Public Accountant	Vamoose, OK	Feddersen, Connie
Amanda Knight	hospital director of nursing	Washington, DC	Fromer, Margot J.
Amanda Pepper	high school teacher	Philadelphia, PA	Roberts, Gillian
Amanda Roberts	ex-New York investigative reporter	Atlanta, GA	Woods, Sherryl
Amelia Peabody	Victorian feminist archaeologist	England	Peters, Elizabeth
Amy Prescott	crime lab physician	Seattle, WA	Hendrickson, Louise

A . . . B . . . C

Series Character(s)	Occupation	Setting	Author

A . . . continued

Series Character(s)	Occupation	Setting	Author
Andrea Perkins	art historian & restorer of paintings	Boston, MA	Coker, Carolyn
Angela Benbow & Caledonia Wingate	70-something admirals' widows	California	Sawyer, Corinne Holt
Angelina Amalfi	food columnist & restaurant reviewer	San Francisco, CA	Pence, Joanne
Anna Lee	private investigator	London, England	Cody, Liza
Anna Peters	international oil company exec turned P.I.	Washington, DC	Law, Janice
Anna Pigeon	U.S. park ranger	USA	Barr, Nevada
Annabel Reed & Mackenzie Smith	atty. wife turned gallery owner & law professor	Washington, DC	Truman, Margaret
Anne Fitzhugh	police detective	Washington, DC	Roberts, Carey
Anneke Haagen	computer consultant	Ann Arbor, MI	Holtzer, Susan
Annie Laurance & Max Darling	bookstore owner & investigator	South Carolina	Hart, Carolyn G.
Annie MacPherson	attorney	Seattle, WA	Smith, Janet L.
Annie McGrogan	NYC P.I. & actor just back from LA	New York, NY	Farrell, Gillian B.
Anthony Maitland	English barrister drawn to murder cases	England	Woods, Sara
April Woo	police detective	New York, NY	Glass, Leslie
Arly Hanks	small-town Arkansas police chief	Maggody, AR	Hess, Joan
Asey Mayo	former sailor & auto racer	Cape Cod, MA	Taylor, Phoebe Atwood
Ashley Johnson & Elizabeth Mendoza	lesbian homicide detectives	USA	McAllester, Melanie
Auguste Didier	British-French Victorian master chef	England	Myers, Amy
Aunt Dimity	romantic ghost	Boston, MA	Atherton, Nancy
Auntie Lil & Theodore S. Hubbert	dress designer & retired human resources mgr.	New York, NY	Gray, Gallagher
Aurora Teagarden	20-something librarian	Georgia	Harris, Charlaine

B

Series Character(s)	Occupation	Setting	Author
Balthazar Marten & Sixto Cardenas	NYPD homicide detective & Puerto Rican cop	Puerto Rico	Adamson, M. J.
Barbara Havers & Thomas Lynley	Detective Sgt. & Scotland Yard Inspector	London, England	George, Elizabeth
Barbara Holloway	defense attorney	Oregon	Wilhelm, Kate
Barbara Joan "Bo" Bradley	child abuse investigator	San Diego, CA	Padgett, Abigail
Barrett Lake	high school history teacher	Berkeley, CA	Singer, Shelley
Basil Willing, Dr.	medical advisor to NYC district attorney	New York, NY	McCloy, Helen
Beatrice Lestrange Bradley	psychiatrist & consultant to Home Office	London, England	Mitchell, Gladys
Becky Belski	computer investigator	Chicago, IL	Haddad, Carolyn A.
Ben & Ellie Haskell w/ Tramwell sisters	writer/chef & interior decorator w/sister sleuths	London, England	Cannell, Dorothy
Ben Safford	Democratic congressman from Ohio	Washington, DC	Dominic, R. B.
Benjamin Jurnet	Detective Inspector	England	Haymon, S. T.
Betty Trenka	retired CT businesswoman	Connecticut	Christmas, Joyce
Bill Slider	Detective Inspector	England	Harrod-Eagles, Cynthia
Blaine Stewart	ex-NYPD cop turned P.I. in Manhattan	New York, NY	Zukowski, Sharon
Blanche White	middle-aged black domestic	USA	Neely, Barbara
Blue Maguire & Spaceman Kowalski	cop pair w/prickly partnership	Los Angeles, CA	White, Teri
Bonnie Indermill	tap-dancing Manhattan office temp	New York, NY	Berry, Carole
Britt Montero	newspaper crime reporter	Miami, FL	Buchanan, Edna
Bunty, George & Dominic Felse	family of detectives	Shropshire, England	Pargeter, Edith

C

Series Character(s)	Occupation	Setting	Author
C. B. Greenfield & Maggie Rome	editor/publisher & reporter	Connecticut	Kallen, Lucille
Cadfael, Brother	medieval monk & herbalist	Shrewsbury, England	Peters, Ellis
Caitlin Reece	lesbian detective	Victoria, BC, Canada	Douglas, Lauren Wright
Cal Donovan & Liz Graham	pair of Castlemere cops	Castlemere, England	Bannister, Jo
Caledonia Wingate & Angela Benbow	70-something admirals' widows	California	Sawyer, Corinne Holt

C

Series Character(s)	Occupation	Setting	Author

C . . . continued

Series Character(s)	Occupation	Setting	Author
Caley Burke	30-something northern CA P.I.	northern California	McKenna, Bridget
Calista Jacobs	award-winning illustrator of children's books	Cambridge, MA	Knight, Kathryn Lasky
Carl & Freda Pedersen	police lieutenant & wife	Bay Cove, CA	Hart, Jeanne
Carlos Cruz & Jay Goldstein	homicide detectives	Oakland, CA	Wallace, Marilyn
Carlotta Carlyle	6'1" cab-driving ex-cop P.I.	Boston, MA	Barnes, Linda
Carmen Ramirez	newspaper copy editor	USA	Haddock, Lisa
Cass Jameson	Brooklyn criminal lawyer	New York, NY	Wheat, Carolyn
Cassandra Reilly	London-based Spanish translator	London, England	Wilson, Barbara
Cassandra Swann	British biology teacher turned bridge pro	England	Moody, Susan
Cat Caliban	60-something P.I.-in-training	Cincinnati, OH	Borton, D. B.
Cat Marsala	freelance investigative journalist	Chicago, IL	D'Amato, Barbara
Catherine LeVendeur	novice & scholar	France	Newman, Sharan
Catherine Sayler	P.I.	San Francisco, CA	Grant, Linda
Cecile Buddenbrooks, Sister	licensed P.I. nun	Boston, MA	Sullivan, Winona
Cecily Sinclair	hotel owner in Edwardian England	England	Kingsbury, Kate
Charles Spotted Moon	attorney & Ojibway tribal shaman	San Francisco, CA	Yarbro, Chelsea Quinn
Charlie Greene	Hollywood literary agent	Hollywood, CA	Millhiser, Marlys
Charlie Meiklejohn & Constance Leidl	ex-arson investigator P.I. & psychologist	New York, NY	Wilhelm, Kate
Charlotte & Thomas Pitt	wife & Victorian police inspector	England	Perry, Anne
Charlotte Graham	Oscar-winning actress	New York, NY	Matteson, Stephanie
Charlotte Kent	freelance writer	Connecticut	Kittredge, Mary
Charlotte Sams	freelance writer	Columbus, OH	Glen, Alison
Charmian Daniels	police detective	Deerham Hills, England	Melville, Jennie
China Bayles	herb shop owner & former attorney	Pecan Springs, TX	Albert, Susan Wittig
Christine Bennett	ex-nun	New York, NY	Harris, Lee
Christine Martin	40-something cub reporter	England	Roome, Annette
Christine Opara	20-something police detective	New York, NY	Uhnak, Dorothy
Christopher "Kit" Storm	police illustrator for the NYPD	New York, NY	Barber, Willetta A.
Christopher Dennis "Seedy" Sloan	Berebury CID department head	West Calleshire, England	Aird, Catherine
Christopher McKee	Manhattan homicide squad detective	New York, NY	Reilly, Helen
Claire Aldington, Rev.	Episcopal priest	New York, NY	Holland, Isabelle
Claire Breslinsky	freelance photographer	New York, NY	Kelly, Mary Ann
Claire Camden	California English professor in Britain	England	Peterson, Audrey
Claire Conrad & Maggie Hill	P.I. & secretary	California	Howe, Melodie Johnson
Claire Malloy	small-town bookstore owner	Arkansas	Hess, Joan
Claire Sharples	former MIT scholar & microbiologist	California	Rothenberg, Rebecca
Clara Gamadge	widow of Henry the forgery expert	New York, NY	Boylan, Eleanor
Clare & Miranda Clively	Victorian London twin sisters	England	Crowleigh, Ann
Claudia Valentine	Australian P.I.	Australia	Day, Marele
Clio Rees, Dr. & Harry Marsh	physician/mystery writer & chief inspector	England	Bannister, Jo
Cockrill, Inspector	constable	Kent County, England	Brand, Christianna
Cole January	P.I.	Houston, TX	Bradley, Lynn
Conan Flagg	bookstore owner & former intelligence agent	Oregon	Wren, M. K.
Constance Leidl & Charlie Meiklejohn	psychologist & ex-arson investigator P.I.	New York, NY	Wilhelm, Kate
Cordelia Gray	fledgling P.I.	London, England	James, P. D.
Cressida Woodruffe & Willow King	romance novelist & British civil servant	London, England	Cooper, Natasha

D . . . E

Series Character(s)	Occupation	Setting	Author
D			
D. S. Trewley & Stone, Sgt.	English village detective partners	England	Mason, Sarah Jill
Darina Lisle	British caterer, chef & food writer	England	Laurence, Janet
David Middleton-Brown & L. Kingsley	solicitor & artist	England	Charles, Kate
David Webb	British police inspector	England	Fraser, Anthea
David Wintringham	British physician	London, England	Bell, Josephine
Deb Ralston	police detective & mother	Ft. Worth, TX	Martin, Lee
Deborah Knott	district judge	North Carolina	Maron, Margaret
Dee Street	American attorney	London, England	Wakefield, Hannah
Deidre Quinn Nightingale	rural veterinarian	New York	Adamson, Lydia
Delia Ross-Merlani, Viscountess	English-Italian noblewoman	New York, NY	Florian, S.L.
Delilah West	P.I.	Orange County, CA	O'Callaghan, Maxine
Devon MacDonald	ex-teacher private eye	Minneapolis, MN	Jacobs, Nancy Baker
Dewey James	60-something small-town librarian	New York	Morgan, Kate
Dittany Henbit Monk & Osbert Monk	garden club member & author of westerns	Lobelia Falls, Ont., Canada	Craig, Alisa
Dixie T. Struthers	police detective	San Jose, CA	Sims, L. V.
Dominic, George & Bunty Felse	family of detectives	Shropshire, England	Pargeter, Edith
Doran Fairweather	British antiques dealer	England	Hardwick, Mollie
Douglas Perkins	London-based public relations agent	London, England	Babson, Marian
Douglas Quantrill & Hilary Lloyd	Det. Chief Inspector & Sgt. partner	Suffolk, England	Radley, Sheila
Duncan Kincaid & Gemma James	Scotland Yard Superintendent & Sgt. partner	London, England	Crombie, Deborah
E			
E. J. Pugh	housewife, mother & romance writer	Texas	Cooper, Susan Rogers
Edwina Charles	British clairvoyante	England	Warner, Mignon
Edwina Crusoe	RN & medical consultant	New Haven, CT	Kittredge, Mary
Elena Oliverez	Mexican arts museum curator	Santa Barbara, CA	Muller, Marcia
Eliza Figg	former Peace Corps volunteer	USA	Ballard, Mignon
Elizabeth Austin	English professor	Midwest, USA	Skom, Edith
Elizabeth Elliot	widowed Quaker meeting clerk	Pennsylvania	Allen, Irene
Elizabeth MacPherson	forensic anthropologist	USA	McCrumb, Sharyn
Elizabeth Mendoza & Ashley Johnson	lesbian homicide detectives	USA	McAllester, Melanie
Ellie & Ben Haskell	interior decorator & writer/chef	London, England	Cannell, Dorothy
Ellie Bernstein	diet group leader	USA	Dietz, Denise
Em Hansen	oil worker	Wyoming	Andrews, Sarah
Emily & Henry Bryce	Manhattan interior decorators	New York, NY	Scherf, Margaret
Emily D. Seeton	retired British art teacher	England	Crane, Hamilton
Emily Pollifax	grandmother CIA agent	New Jersey	Gilman, Dorothy
Emma Chizzit	salvage dealer	Sacramento, CA	Hall, Mary Bowen
Emma Lord	small-town newspaper owner & editor	Alpine, WA	Daheim, Mary
Emma Victor	lesbian activist & former publicist	Boston, MA	Wings, Mary
Emmy & Henry Tibbett	wife & Scotland Yard Inspector	London, England	Moyes, Patricia
Enrico Caruso & Geraldine Farrar	Italian tenor & American soprano	New York, NY	Paul, Barbara
Eugenia Potter	widowed chef	Maine	Rich, Virginia
Eva Wylie	wrestler & security guard	London, England	Cody, Liza
Eve Sinclair & Trixie Dolan	aging British ex-movie queens	London, England	Babson, Marian

F...G...H

Series Character(s)	Occupation	Setting	Author

F

Series Character(s)	Occupation	Setting	Author
Faith Sibley Fairchild	minister's wife & culinary artist	Massachusetts	Page, Katherine Hall
Fanny Zindel	Jewish grandmother	USA	Stevens, Serita
Felix & Virginia Freer	businessman & physiotherapist	England	Ferrars, E. X.
Fiddler & Fiora Flynn	investment banker	California	Maxwell, A. E.
Finch, Inspector	police inspector	Essex, England	Thomson, June
Finny Aletter	stockbroker turned carpenter	Denver, CO	Montgomery, Yvonne E.
Fiora & Fiddler Flynn	investment banker	California	Maxwell, A. E.
Fleming Stone	intellectual private investigator	New York, NY	Wells, Carolyn
Frances Finn	P.I.	Kansas City, KS	Hollingsworth, Gerelyn
Francesca Wilson & John McLeish	civil servant & Det. Inspector	England	Neel, Janet
Frank Carver & Ginny Trask	ex-cop & forest fire dispatcher	Oregon	Wallingford, Lee
Freda & Carl Pedersen	wife & police lieutenant	Bay Cove, CA	Hart, Jeanne
Freddie O'Neal	plane-flying P.I.	Reno, NV	Dain, Catherine
Frederika Bascomb	forensic artist	Seattle, WA	Thompson, Joyce
Frevisse, Sister	medieval nun	England	Frazer, Margaret

G

Series Character(s)	Occupation	Setting	Author
Gail Connor	corporate attorney	USA	Parker, Barbara
Gail McCarthy	horse veterinarian	northern California	Crum, Laura
Galen Shaw & Julian Baugh	writer & financier	New England	Blackmur, L. L.
Gemma James & Duncan Kincaid	Sgt. partner & Scotland Yard Superintendent	London, England	Crombie, Deborah
George & Molly Palmer-Jones	ex-Home Office official/bird-watcher & wife	London, England	Cleeves, Ann
George, Bunty & Dominic Felse	family of detectives	Shropshire, England	Pargeter, Edith
Georgia Lee Maxwell	Paris-based freelance writer	Paris, France	Friedman, Mickey
Georgina Powers	British computer journalist	London, England	Danks, Denise
Geraldine Farrar & Enrico Caruso	American soprano & Italian tenor	New York, NY	Paul, Barbara
Gerritt De Graaf	physician	USA	D'Amato, Barbara
Gil Mayo	Detective Chief Inspector	England	Eccles, Marjorie
Gillian Adams	University of the Pacific Northwest history chair	British Columbia, Canada	Kelly, Nora
Ginny Trask & Frank Carver	forest fire dispatcher & ex-cop	Oregon	Wallingford, Lee
Glory Day	artist & singer	New Zealand	Scott, Rosie
Glynis Tryon	librarian & suffragette	Seneca Falls, NY	Monfredo, Miriam Grace
Goldy Bear	caterer & single mother	Colorado	Davidson, Diane Mott
Grace Severance, Dr.	retired pathologist	Arizona	Scherf, Margaret
Gregor Demarkian	former FBI department head	Philadelphia, PA	Haddam, Jane
Guido Brunetti	Venetian policeman	Venice, Italy	Leon, Donna
Gwenn Ramadge	P.I. for corporate investigations	New York, NY	O'Donnell, Lillian

H

Series Character(s)	Occupation	Setting	Author
H. W. Ross	Detective Superintendent	England	Grindle, Lucretia
Hamish Macbeth	Scottish police constable	Scotland	Beaton, M. C.
Hannah Wolfe	P.I.	London, England	Dunant, Sarah
Harriet Jeffries & John Sanders	architectural photographer & police detective	Toronto, Ontario, Canada	Sale, Medora
Harry Marsh & Clio Rees, Dr.	chief inspector & physician/mystery writer	England	Bannister, Jo
Haskell Blevins	P.I.	Pigeon Fork, KY	McCafferty, Taylor
Helen Black	ex-cop lesbian P.I.	San Francisco, CA	Welch, Pat
Helen Marsh Shandy & Peter Shandy	botany professor & librarian wife	rural Balaclava County, MA	MacLeod, Charlotte
Helen West	London Crown Prosecutor	London, England	Fyfield, Frances
Helma Zukas	Washington State librarian	Washington	Dereske, Jo

H . . . I . . . J

Series Character(s)	Occupation	Setting	Author

H . . . continued

Series Character(s)	Occupation	Setting	Author
Henrietta O'Dwyer Collins	70-something reporter	South Carolina	Hart, Carolyn G.
Henry & Emily Bryce	Manhattan interior decorators	New York, NY	Scherf, Margaret
Henry & Emmy Tibbett	Scotland Yard Inspector & wife	London, England	Moyes, Patricia
Henry Bassett	retired cop	Herefordshire, England	Burden, Pat
Henry Gamadge	author & bibliophile	New York, NY	Daly, Elizabeth
Hercule Poirot	former Belgian cop turned private detective	London, England	Christie, Agatha
Hilary Lloyd & Douglas Quantrill	Sgt. partner & Det. Chief Inspector	Suffolk, England	Radley, Sheila
Hilary Tamar	Oxford professor of medieval law	London, England	Caudwell, Sarah
Hilda Adams	nurse	England	Rinehart, Mary Roberts
Holly Winter	30-something dog trainer & mag. columnist	Cambridge, MA	Conant, Susan
Homer Kelly	Harvard professor & retired detective	Cambridge, MA	Langton, Jane

I

Series Character(s)	Occupation	Setting	Author
Imogen Quy	nurse	England	Walsh, Jill Paton
Ingrid Langley & Patrick Gillard	novelist/British agent & British army major	England	Duffy, Margaret
Irene Adler	19th century French sleuth	Paris, France	Douglas, Carole Nelson
Irene Kelly	newspaper reporter	California	Burke, Jan
Iris Cooper	Roaring 20s coed at Stanford University	Palo Alto, CA	Beck, K. K.
Iris Thorne	investment counselor	Los Angeles, CA	Pugh, Dianne G.

J

Series Character(s)	Occupation	Setting	Author
J. J. Jamison	computer engineer & CATCH investigator	Minneapolis, MN	Taylor, L. A.
J. P. Beaumont	homicide detective	Seattle, WA	Jance, J. A.
Jack Stryker & Kate Trevorne	homicide cop & English professor	Grantham, OH	Gosling, Paula
Jackie Walsh & Jake	college film instructor with her ex-police dog	Midwest, USA	Cleary, Melissa
Jacqueline Kirby	librarian turned romance novelist	New York, NY	Peters, Elizabeth
Jake & Jackie Walsh	ex-police dog & college film instructor	Midwest, USA	Cleary, Melissa
Jake Samson & Rosie Vicente	ex-cop & carpenter tenant	Berkeley, CA	Singer, Shelley
James Fleming	Dublin solicitor	Dublin, Ireland	Fallon, Ann
James McDougal & Lucy Ramsdale	homicide inspector & illustrator	Connecticut	Dolson, Hildegarde
James Owen Mega	science fiction author & college professor	USA	McCrumb, Sharyn
Jan Gallagher	hospital security supervisor	Minneapolis, MN	Bailey, Jo
Jane da Silva	former lounge singer	Seattle, WA	Beck, K. K.
Jane Jeffry	suburban Chicago single mother	Chicago, IL	Churchill, Jill
Jane Lawless	lesbian restaurateur	Minneapolis, MN	Hart, Ellen
Jane Marple	elderly spinster	St. Mary's Mead, England	Christie, Agatha
Jane Tennison	London Detective Chief Inspector	London, England	LaPlante, Lynda
Jane Winfield	British journalist & music writer	England	Peterson, Audrey
Janet & Madoc Rhys	wife & RCMP Inspector	Fredericton, NB, Canada	Craig, Alisa
Jason Lynx	antiques dealer	Denver, CO	Orde, A. J.
Jay Goldstein & Carlos Cruz	homicide detectives	Oakland, CA	Wallace, Marilyn
Jazz Jasper	American safari guide in Africa	Kenya	McQuillan, Karin
Jean & Pat Abbot	wife & husband detection team	World Travelers	Crane, Frances
Jeff Di Marco	insurance investigator	Boston, MA	Disney, Doris Miles
Jeffries, Mrs. & Witherspoon, Insp.	housekeeper & Victorian inspector	London, England	Brightwell, Emily
Jemima Shore	British TV interviewer	London, England	Fraser, Antonia P.
Jenny Cain	New England foundation director	Port Frederick, MA	Pickard, Nancy
Jeremy Faro	Victorian detective inspector	Edinburgh, Scotland	Knight, Alanna
Jeri Howard	P.I.	Oakland, CA	Dawson, Janet

J . . . K

Series Character(s)	Occupation	Setting	Author

J . . . continued

Series Character(s)	Occupation	Setting	Author
Jerry & Pam North	wife & husband book publishers	New York, NY	Lockridge, Frances & R.
Jerry Zalman	Beverly Hills dealmaker	Los Angeles, CA	Kraft, Gabrielle
Jessica James	newspaper reporter	Rochester, NY	O'Brien, Meg
Jessica Randolph	P.I.	San Francisco, CA	Lucke, Margaret
Jessie Arnold & Alex Jensen	sled dog racer & Alaska State trooper	Alaska	Henry, Sue
Jessie Drake	Los Angeles police detective	Los Angeles, CA	Krich, Rochelle Majer
Jill Smith	homicide detective	Berkeley, CA	Dunlap, Susan
Jim Qwilleran, Koko & Yum Yum	ex-police reporter & cats	Midwest, USA	Braun, Lilian Jackson
Jo Hughes	professional astrologer	USA	Mather, Linda
Joan, Sister	British investigative nun	England	Black, Veronica
Joanna Bradley	deputy sheriff's widow	Arizona	Jance, J. A.
Joanna Stark	international art investigator	Napa Valley, CA	Muller, Marcia
Jocelyn O'Roarke	Broadway actress & director	New York, NY	Dentinger, Jane
Joe Silva	chief of police	Washington	Oleksiw, Susan
John Coffin	London police inspector	London, England	Butler, Gwendoline
John Lloyd Branson & Lydia Fairchild	defense attorney & legal assistant	Canadian, TX	Meredith, D. R.
John McLeish & Francesca Wilson	Det. Inspector & civil servant	England	Neel, Janet
John Putnam Thatcher	Wall Street financial whiz	New York, NY	Lathen, Emma
John Sanders & Harriet Jeffries	police detective & architectural photographer	Toronto, Ontario, Canada	Sale, Medora
Jolie Wyatt	aspiring novelist & writer's group member	Purple Sage, TX	Smith, Barbara Burnett
Judith Hayes	journalist	USA	Porter, Anna
Judith McMonigle	bed & breakfast owner	Washington	Daheim, Mary
Judy Hill & Lloyd, Chief Inspector	detective inspectors	Wales	McGown, Jill
Julia Callahan Garrity	ex-cop cleaning lady	Atlanta, GA	Trocheck, Kathy Hogan
Julian Baugh & Galen Shaw	financier & writer	New England	Blackmur, L. L.
Julian Kestrel	early 19th century Londoner	London, England	Ross, Kate
Julie Hayes	former actress & columnist	New York, NY	Davis, Dorothy Salisbury
Juliet Blake	Silicon Valley fraud investigator	Silicon Valley, CA	Chapman, Sally

K

Series Character(s)	Occupation	Setting	Author
Karen Hightower	Manhattan graphic designer & white witch	New York, NY	Edghill, Rosemary
Karen Levinson	NYPD homicide detective	New York, NY	O'Donnell, Catherine
Kat Colorado	P.I.	Sacramento, CA	Kijewski, Karen
Kate & Ray Frederick	wife of 30 years & chief of detectives	Michigan	Schenkel, S. E.
Kate Austen	Bay area single mother	Walnut Hills, CA	Jacobs, Jonnie
Kate Baeier	freelance journalist turned detective	London, England	Slovo, Gillian
Kate Brannigan	P.I.	Manchester, England	McDermid, Val
Kate Delafield	LAPD lesbian homicide detective	Los Angeles, CA	Forrest, Katherine V.
Kate Driscoll	dog trainer	Texas	Walker, Mary Willis
Kate Fansler	university English professor	New York, NY	Cross, Amanda
Kate Henry	baseball newswriter	Toronto, Ontario, Canada	Gordon, Alison
Kate Ivory	Oxford novelist	England	Stallwood, Veronica
Kate Jasper	gag gift wholesaler	Marin County, CA	Girdner, Jaqueline
Kate Kincaid Mulcay	veteran newspaperwoman	Atlanta, GA	Sibley, Celestine
Kate Kinsella	British nurse & medical investigator	England	Green, Christine
Kate Martinelli & Alonzo Hawkin	SFPD homicide detectives	San Francisco, CA	King, Laurie R.
Kate McLean	police detective	Seattle, WA	Gilpatrick, Noreen
Kate Murray	newspaper reporter for Daily Herald	Brooklyn, NY	Tyre, Peg
Kate Shugak	native Alaskan ex-D. A. investigator	Alaska	Stabenow, Dana

K . . . L

Series Character(s)	Occupation	Setting	Author

K . . . continued

Series Character(s)	Occupation	Setting	Author
Kate Teague & Roger Tejeda	college professor & homicide detective	California	Hornsby, Wendy
Kate Trevorne & Jack Stryker	English professor & homicide cop	Grantham, OH	Gosling, Paula
Kate Weston & Alex Sinclair	social worker & British Inspector	England	Hall, Patricia
Katharine Craig & Kevin Bryce	sculptor & ex-sheriff's detective	California	Valentine, Deborah
Katherine Prescott Milholland	corporate attorney	Chicago, IL	Hartzmark, Gini
Kathleen Mallory	NYPD cop	New York, NY	O'Connell, Carol
Kathryn Ardleigh	25-yr. old American author	Dedham, England	Paige, Robin
Kathryn Mackay	prosecuting attorney	northern California	McGuire, Christine
Kay Barth	district attorney	Colorado	Schier, Norma
Kay Engles	nationally-known reporter	USA	Stein, Triss
Kay Scarpetta	Chief Medical Examiner	Richmond, VA	Cornwell, Patricia D.
Kevin Bryce & Katharine Craig	ex-sheriff's detective & sculptor	California	Valentine, Deborah
Kiernan O'Shaughnessy	former San Francisco M.E. turned P.I.	La Jolla, CA	Dunlap, Susan
Kimmey Kruse	stand-up comic	Chicago, IL	Cooper, Susan Rogers
Kinsey Millhone	ex-cop P.I.	Santa Teresa, CA	Grafton, Sue
Kit Powell	TV sports reporter	San Diego, CA	Robitaille, Julie
Koko, Yum Yum & Jim Qwilleran	cats & ex-police reporter	Midwest, USA	Braun, Lilian Jackson
Kori Price & Peter Brichter	horse breeder & police detective	Illinois	Pulver, Mary Monica

L

Series Character(s)	Occupation	Setting	Author
Lance O'Leary & Sarah Keate	wealthy police detective & nurse	New York, NY	Eberhart, Mignon Good
Lane Montana & Trey Fortier	finder of lost things & homicide detective	Atlanta, GA	Hooper, Kay
Lark Dailey Dodge	6-ft. bookdealer	northern California	Simonson, Sheila
Laura Di Palma	attorney	San Francisco, CA	Matera, Lia
Laura Fleming	small-town detective	Byerly, NC	Kelner, Toni L. P.
Laura Flynn	P.I.	London, England	Grant-Adamson, Lesley
Laura Ireland	grad student volleyball player	Seattle, WA	Mariz, Linda French
Laura Malloy	journalist	Minneapolis, MN	Logue, Mary
Laura Principal	British academic turned P.I.	England	Spring, Michelle
Lauren Laurano	Greenwich Village lesbian P.I.	New York, NY	Scoppettone, Sandra
Lauren Maxwell	Alaska wildlife investigator PhD	Alaska	Quinn, Elizabeth
Leah Hunter	Yorkshire tax inspector	Yorkshire, England	Lacey, Sarah
Lee Squires	English professor & poet	Washington, DC	Andreae, Christine
Lena Padget	P.I.	Lexington, KY	Hightower, Lynn
Lennox Kemp	London solicitor detective	England	Meek, M. R. D.
Leonidas Witherall	retired academic & secret author of pulp fiction	Boston, MA	Tilton, Alice
Leslie Wetzon & Xenia Smith	pair of Wall Street headhunters	New York, NY	Meyers, Annette
Libby Kincaid	magazine photographer	New York, NY	Tucker, Kerry
Lil Ritchie	lesbian P.I.	Portland, ME	Knight, Phyllis
Lindsay Gordon	lesbian journalist	England	McDermid, Val
Liz Connors	freelance crime writer	Cambridge, MA	Kelly, Susan
Liz Graham & Cal Donovan	pair of Castlemere cops	Castlemere, England	Bannister, Jo
Liz Sullivan	freelance writer	Palo Alto, CA	Roberts, Lora
Liz Wareham	Manhattan public relations consultant	New York, NY	Brennan, Carol
Lloyd, Chief Inspector & Judy Hill	detective inspectors	Wales	McGown, Jill
Lonia Guiu	Catalan private investigator	Spain	Oliver, Maria Antonia
Loretta Lawson	British feminist professor	England	Smith, Joan
Lucy Kingsley & D. Middleton-Brown	artist & solicitor	England	Charles, Kate

L . . . M

Series Character(s)	Occupation	Setting	Author

L . . . continued

Series Character(s)	Occupation	Setting	Author
Lucy Ramsdale & James McDougal	illustrator & homicide inspector	Connecticut	Dolson, Hildegarde
Lucy Stone	small-town New England sleuth	Maine	Meier, Leslie
Luis Mendoza	dapper & wealthy homicide lieutenant	Los Angeles, CA	Shannon, Dell
Luke Abbott	English cop	England	Gosling, Paula
Luke Thanet	British police inspector	England	Simpson, Dorothy
Lydia Fairchild & John Lloyd Branson	legal assistant & defense attorney	Canadian, TX	Meredith, D. R.

M

Series Character(s)	Occupation	Setting	Author
MacDougal Duff	retired history professor	USA	Armstrong, Charlotte
Mackenzie Smith & Annabel Reed	law professor & atty. wife turned gallery owner	Washington, DC	Truman, Margaret
Madoc & Janet Rhys	RCMP Inspector & wife	Fredericton, NB, Canada	Craig, Alisa
Magdalena Yoder	Mennonite inn owner & operator	Pennsylvania	Myers, Tamar
Maggie Elliott	ex-film maker turned P.I.	San Francisco, CA	Taylor, Elizabeth Atwood
Maggie Hill & Claire Conrad	secretary & P.I.	California	Howe, Melodie Johnson
Maggie MacGowen	investigative filmmaker	California	Hornsby, Wendy
Maggie Rome & C. B. Greenfield	reporter & editor/publisher	Connecticut	Kallen, Lucille
Maggie Ryan	statistician & mother	New York, NY	Carlson, P. M.
Marcus Didius Falco	P.I. in ancient Rome	Rome, Italy	Davis, Lindsey
Margaret Priam, Lady	Englishwoman in New York City	New York, NY	Christmas, Joyce
Margit Falk	ex-combat pilot & government attorney	Washington, DC	Truman, Margaret
Marian Larch	NYPD officer	New York, NY	Paul, Barbara
Marian Winchester	Caddo-Commanche medicine woman	Texas	Romberg, Nina
Mark Shigata	ex-FBI agent turned sheriff	Bayport, TX	Wingate, Ann
Marla Masterson	young professor of Anglo-Saxon literature	England	Dunant, Sarah
Martha "Moz" Brant	insurance claims investigator	southern California	Femling, Jean
Marti MacAlister	black police detective	Lincoln Prairie, IL	Bland, Eleanor Taylor
Martin Karl Alberg	RCMP Staff Sgt.	British Columbia, Canada	Wright, L. R.
Martine LaForte Hopkins	southern Indiana deputy sheriff	Indiana	Carlson, P. M.
Mary Carner	former department store detective	USA	Popkin, Zelda
Mary DiNunzio	attorney	Philadelphia, PA	Scottoline, Lisa
Mary Helen, Sister	70-something nun	San Francisco, CA	O'Marie, Sis. Carol Anne
Mary Minor Haristeen	small-town postmistress & cat	Crozet, VA	Brown, Rita Mae
Maud Silver	retired governess & spinster P.I.	London, England	Wentworth, Patricia
Max Bittersohn & Sarah Kelling	investigative couple	Boston, MA	MacLeod, Charlotte
Max Darling & Annie Laurance	investigator & bookstore owner	South Carolina	Hart, Carolyn G.
Maxene St. Clair, Dr.	emergency room physician	Milwaukee, WI	McGiffin, Janet
Meg & Sarah Quilliam	inn owner & chef (sisters)	Hemlock Falls, NY	Bishop, Claudia
Meg Halloran & Vince Gutierrez	school teacher & police chief	Port Silva, WA	LaPierre, Janet
Meg Lacey	P.I.	Vancouver, BC, Canada	Bowers, Elisabeth
Megan Baldwin	registered nurse	St. Petersburg, FL	Clark, Carolyn Chambers
Melinda Pink	writer & mountain climber	Utah	Moffat, Gwen
Melissa Craig	British mystery writer	England	Rowlands, Betty
Meredith "Merry" Folger	Nantucket P.I.	Nantucket, MA	Matthews, Francine
Meredith Mitchell	British Foreign Service officer	England	Granger, Ann
Merrie Lee Spencer	Manhattan transplants in North Carolina	North Carolina	Jackson, Muriel Resnick
Michael Spraggue III	wealthy actor & ex-P.I.	Boston, MA	Barnes, Linda
Mici Anhalt	criminal justice investigator	New York, NY	O'Donnell, Lillian
Midge Cohen	children's author fluent in Russian	New York, NY	Brill, Toni

M...N...O...P

Series Character(s)	Occupation	Setting	Author
M . . . continued			
Midnight Louie & Temple Barr	tomcat sleuth & public relations freelancer	Las Vegas, NV	Douglas, Carole Nelson
Mike McCleary & Quin St. James	husband & wife P.I. team	Florida	MacGregor, T. J.
Mike Yeadings	Det. Superintendent Serious Crimes Squad	Thames Valley, England	Curzon, Clare
Millie Ogden & Natasha O'Brien	pair of culinary artists	USA	Lyons, Nan & Ivan
Milton Kovak	chief deputy	Prophesy County, OK	Cooper, Susan Rogers
Miranda & Clare Clively	Victorian London twin sisters	London, England	Crowleigh, Ann
Mitch Bushyhead	police chief of Cherokee descent	Buckskin, OK	Hager, Jean
Mollie Cates	true crime writer & reporter	Texas	Walker, Mary Willis
Molly & George Palmer-Jones	wife & ex-Home Office official/bird-watcher	London, England	Cleeves, Ann
Molly Bearpaw	Cherokee civil rights investigator	Oklahoma	Hager, Jean
Molly DeWitt	film office public relations staffer	Miami, FL	Woods, Sherryl
Molly Rafferty	college history professor	Boston, MA	Belfort, Sophie
N			
Nan Robinson	investigator for the California State Bar	Los Angeles, CA	Cannon, Taffy
Natasha O'Brien & Millie Ogden	pair of culinary artists	USA	Lyons, Nan & Ivan
Neil Hamel	attorney & investigator	Albuquerque, NM	Van Gieson, Judith
Nell Bray	British suffragette	England	Linscott, Gillian
Nell Fury	lesbian P.I.	San Francisco, CA	Pincus, Elizabeth
Nick Trevellyan & Alison Hope	detective inspector & software designer	Hop Valley, England	Kelly, Susan B.
Nicky & Sam Titus	wife & ex-army CID sheriff	Holton, OK	Sandstrom, Eve K.
Nikki Trakos	homicide detective	New York, NY	Horansky, Ruby
Nina Fischman	legal services attorney	New York, NY	Piesman, Marissa
Nora James	American linguistics grad student	Japan	McFall, Patricia
Norah Mulcahaney	NYPD detective	New York, NY	O'Donnell, Lillian
O			
Oliver Jardino & Theresa Fortunato	LAPD detective & professional psychic	California	Green, Kate
Osbert Monk & Dittany Henbit Monk	author of westerns & garden club member	Lobelia Falls, Ont., Canada	Craig, Alisa
Owen Archer	medieval Welsh spy for the Archbishop	England	Robb, Candace M.
P			
Pam & Jerry North	husband & wife book publishers	New York, NY	Lockridge, Frances & R.
Pam Nilsen	lesbian printing company owner	Seattle, WA	Wilson, Barbara
Paris Chandler	1940s Hollywood P.I.	Hollywood, CA	Shah, Diane K.
Pat & Jean Abbot	husband & wife detection team	World Travelers	Crane, Frances
Patience Campbell McKenna	6-ft. romance novelist turned crime writer	New York, NY	Papazoglou, Orania
Patricia Delaney	computer whiz P.I.	Cincinnati, OH	Short, Sharon Gwyn
Patrick Gillard & Ingrid Langley	British army major & novelist/British agent	England	Duffy, Margaret
Patrick Grant, Dr.	Oxford don teaching English literature	Oxford, England	Yorke, Margaret
Paul MacDonald	ex-reporter & mystery writer	San Francisco, CA	Smith, Julie
Paul Prye	psychiatrist	Toronto, Ontario, Canada	Millar, Margaret
Paula Glenning	British professor & writer	London, England	Clarke, Anna
Peaches Dann	50-something widow	North Carolina	Squire, Elizabeth Daniels
Peg Goodenough	ad agency creative director	New York, NY	Bennett, Liza
Penny Spring & Toby Glendower, Sir	Amer. anthropologist & British archeologist	World Travelers	Arnold, Margot
Penny Wanawake	6-ft. photographer daughter of UN diplomat	England	Moody, Susan

P...Q...R...S

Series Character(s)	Occupation	Setting	Author

P . . . continued

Series Character(s)	Occupation	Setting	Author
Persis Willum	New York art curator	Long Island, NY	Watson, Clarissa
Peter & Kori Price Brichter	police detective & horse breeder	Illinois	Pulver, Mary Monica
Peter Bartholomew	small business owner	Cape Cod, MA	Gunning, Sally
Peter Decker & Rina Lazarus	LAPD detective & wife	Los Angeles, CA	Kellerman, Faye
Peter Shandy & Helen Marsh Shandy	botany professor & librarian wife	rural Balaclava County, MA	MacLeod, Charlotte
Peter Wimsey, Lord	pianist, book collector & criminologist	London, England	Sayers, Dorothy L.
Phoebe Fairfax	Calgary TV video photographer	Calgary, Alberta, Canada	North, Suzanne
Phoebe Siegel	ex-cop P.I.	Billings, MT	Prowell, Sandra West
Phryne Fisher	1920s Australian sleuth	Australia	Greenwood, Kerry

Q

Series Character(s)	Occupation	Setting	Author
Queenie Davilow	Hollywood screenwriter	Hollywood, CA	Osborne, Denise
Quin St. James & Mike McCleary	wife & husband P.I. team	Florida	MacGregor, T. J.
Quint McCauley	ex-cop turned P.I.	Chicago suburb, IL	Brod, D. C.

R

Series Character(s)	Occupation	Setting	Author
Rain Morgan	newspaper reporter	London, England	Grant-Adamson, Lesley
Ray & Kate Frederick	chief of detectives & his wife of 30 years	Michigan	Schenkel, S. E.
Rebecca Schwartz	defense attorney	San Francisco, CA	Smith, Julie
Regan Reilly	private investigator	Los Angeles, CA	Clark, Carol Higgins
Reginald Wexford	Chief Inspector	Sussex, England	Rendell, Ruth
Richard Jury	Scotland Yard investigator	England	Grimes, Martha
Richard Montgomery	Nottingham CID Inspector	England	Shepherd, Stella
Rina Lazarus & Peter Decker	wife & LAPD detective	Los Angeles, CA	Kellerman, Faye
Robert Bone	widowed British police inspector	England	Stacey, Susannah
Robert Forsythe & Abigail Sanderson	London barrister & his secretary	London, England	Giroux, E. X.
Robin Hudson	cable news reporter	New York, NY	Hayter, Sparkle
Robin Light	pet store owner	Syracuse, NY	Block, Barbara
Robin Vaughn	equestrienne sleuth	Texas	Banks, Carolyn
Roderick Alleyn	Inspector son of a baronet	New Zealand	Marsh, Ngaio
Roger Tejeda & Kate Teague	homicide detective & college professor	California	Hornsby, Wendy
Roger the Chapman	medieval chapman (peddler)	England	Sedley, Kate
Ronnie Ventana	burglar's daughter P.I.	San Francisco, CA	White, Gloria
Rosie Vicente & Jake Samson	carpenter tenant & ex-cop	Berkeley, CA	Singer, Shelley
Roz Howard & Alan Stewart	American professor & British painter	Maine	Kenney, Susan

S

Series Character(s)	Occupation	Setting	Author
Sabina Swift	Georgetown detective agency owner	Washington, DC	Sucher, Dorothy
Salvatore Guarnaccia	Italian police marshal	Florence, Italy	Nabb, Magdalen
Sam & Nicky Titus	ex-army CID sheriff & his wife	Holton, OK	Sandstrom, Eve K.
Samantha "Smokey" Brandon	sheriff's forensic expert	Orange County, CA	Ayres, Noreen
Samantha Adams	investigative reporter	Atlanta, GA	Shankman, Sarah
Samantha Turner, Dr.	medical examiner	Wyoming	Landreth, Marsha
Sands, Inspector	police detective	Toronto, Ontario, Canada	Millar, Margaret
Sara Marriott	journalist	England	Ferrars, E. X.
Sarah & Meg Quilliam	inn owner & chef (sisters)	Hemlock Falls, NY	Bishop, Claudia
Sarah Deane & Alex McKenzie, Dr.	English professor & internist	Boston, MA	Borthwick, J. S.

S . . . T

Series Character(s)	Occupation	Setting	Author

S . . . continued

Series Character(s)	Occupation	Setting	Author
Sarah Drexler	judge	Oregon	Wilhelm, Kate
Sarah Fortune	lawyer in prestigious British firm	England	Fyfield, Frances
Sarah Keate & Lance O'Leary	nurse & wealthy police detective	New York, NY	Eberhart, Mignon Good
Sarah Kelling & Max Bittersohn	investigative couple	Boston, MA	MacLeod, Charlotte
Sarah Nelson	police inspector	Silicon Valley, CA	Wolfe, Susan
Selena Mead	British government agent	England	McGerr, Patricia
Sharon Dair	sex crimes police detective	Detroit, MI	Vlasopolos, Anca
Sharon McCone	San Fran legal co-op investigator	San Francisco, CA	Muller, Marcia
Sheila Malory	British literary magazine writer	England	Holt, Hazel
Sheila Travers	public relations executive	Atlanta, GA	Sprinkle, Patricia Houck
Shirley McClintock	50-something rancher	Colorado	Oliphant, B. J.
Sigismondo	agent of a Renaissance duke	Italy	Eyre, Elizabeth
Sigrid Harald	police lieutenant	New York, NY	Maron, Margaret
Simona Griffo	advertising executive & gourmet cook	New York, NY	Crespi, Trella
Sixto Cardenas & Balthazar Marten	Puerto Rican cop & NYPD homicide detective	Puerto Rico	Adamson, M. J.
Skip Langdon	6-ft. police detective	New Orleans, LA	Smith, Julie
Sonora Blair	homicide detective	Cincinnati, OH	Hightower, Lynn
Sophie Greenway	magazine editor & newspaper food critic	Minneapolis, MN	Hart, Ellen
Spaceman Kowalski & Blue Maguire	cop pair w/prickly partnership	Los Angeles, CA	White, Teri
Spencer Arrowood	Appalachian sheriff	Appalachia, NC	McCrumb, Sharyn
Stephanie Plum	neophyte bounty hunter	Trenton, NJ	Evanovich, Janet
Stephen Ramsey	British Inspector	England	Cleeves, Ann
Stone, Sgt. & D. S. Trewley	English village detective partners	England	Mason, Sarah Jill
Susan Henshaw	suburban sleuth	Connecticut	Wolzien, Valerie
Susan Melville	freelance assassin & painter	New York, NY	Smith, Evelyn E.
Susan Wren	ex-cop turned Kansas police chief	Kansas	Weir, Charlene
Syd Fish	Sydney P.I.	Sydney, Australia	Geason, Susan
Sydney Bryant	private investigator	San Diego, CA	Wallace, Patricia
Sydney Sloane	upper west side private investigator	New York, NY	Lorden, Randye

T

Series Character(s)	Occupation	Setting	Author
Tamara Hayle	black P.I. ex-cop	Newark, NJ	Wesley, Valerie Wilson
Tamara Hoyland	British secret agent archaeologist	England	Mann, Jessica
Teal Stewart	Certified Public Accountant	Boston, MA	Lamb, J. Dayne
Temple Barr & Midnight Louie	public relations freelancer & tomcat sleuth	Las Vegas, NV	Douglas, Carole Nelson
Terry Girard	genealogist for hire	St. Louis, MO	Kunz, Kathleen
Tess Darcy	Ozarks bed & breakfast owner	Victoria Springs, MO	Hager, Jean
Tessa Crichton	English actress sleuth	England	Morice, Ann
Thea Crawford	archaeology professor	England	Mann, Jessica
Theodora Braithwaite, Rev.	British deaconess	England	Greenwood, Diane M.
Theodore S. Hubbert & Auntie Lil	retired human resources mgr. & dress designer	New York, NY	Gray, Gallagher
Theresa Fortunato & Oliver Jardino	professional psychic & LAPD detective	Los Angeles, CA	Green, Kate
Theresa Franco	P.I.	Florida	Clark, Carolyn Chambers
Theresa Tracy Baldwin	sports photographer for New York daily	New York, NY	OCork, Shannon
Thomas & Charlotte Pitt	Victorian police inspector & wife	England	Perry, Anne
Thomas Lynley & Barbara Havers	Scotland Yard Inspector & Detective Sgt.	London, England	George, Elizabeth

T...W...X...Y

Series Character(s)	Occupation	Setting	Author

T . . . continued

Series Character(s)	Occupation	Setting	Author
Timothy Herring	preservation society director	England	Mitchell, Gladys
Tish McWhinney	artist & painter	Vermont	Comfort, Barbara
Toby Glendower, Sir & Penny Spring	British archeologist & Amer. anthropologist	World Travelers	Arnold, Margot
Tom Aragon	attorney	California	Millar, Margaret
Tom Barnaby	Chief Inspector	England	Graham, Caroline
Tom Ripley	charming forger & psychopath	England	Highsmith, Patricia
Tommy & Tuppence Beresford	adventurers for hire & intelligence agents	England	Christie, Agatha
Tori Miracle	ex-NYC crime writer turned novelist	Pennsylvania	Malmont, Valerie S.
Trey Fortier & Lane Montana	homicide detective & finder of lost things	Atlanta, GA	Hooper, Kay
Trixie Dolan & Eve Sinclair	aging British ex-movie queens	England	Babson, Marian
Tuppence & Tommy Beresford	adventurers for hire & intelligence agents	England	Christie, Agatha

V

Series Character(s)	Occupation	Setting	Author
V. I. Warshawski	attorney turned P.I.	Chicago, IL	Paretsky, Sara
Vejay Haskell	utility meter reader	northern California	Dunlap, Susan
Verity "Birdie" Birdwood	Australian TV researcher	Australia	Rowe, Jennifer
Vicky Bliss	art historian	Germany	Peters, Elizabeth
Victoire Vernet	wife of Napoleonic gendarme	France	Fawcett, Quinn
Victoria Bowering	NYC actor, writer & playwright	New York, NY	Yeager, Dorian
Vince Gutierrez & Meg Halloran	police chief & school teacher	Port Silva, WA	LaPierre, Janet
Virginia & Felix Freer	physiotherapist & businessman	England	Ferrars, E. X.
Virginia Kelly	lesbian stockbroker	USA	Baker, Nikki

W

Series Character(s)	Occupation	Setting	Author
Wanda Mallory	detective agency owner	New York, NY	Frankel, Valerie
Whitney Logan	20-something Los Angeles attorney	Los Angeles, CA	Lambert, Mercedes
Willa Jansson	California attorney	San Francisco, CA	Matera, Lia
William Monk	amnesiac Victorian policeman	England	Perry, Anne
Willow King & Cressida Woodruffe	British civil servant & romance novelist	London, England	Cooper, Natasha
Winston Marlowe Sherman	Shakespeare professor & mystery writer	USA	Lorens, M. K.
Witherspoon, Insp. & Jeffries, Mrs.	Victorian inspector & housekeeper	London, England	Brightwell, Emily

X

Series Character(s)	Occupation	Setting	Author
Xenia Smith & Leslie Wetzon	pair of Wall Street headhunters	New York, NY	Meyers, Annette

Y

Series Character(s)	Occupation	Setting	Author
Yum Yum, Koko & Jim Qwilleran	cats & ex-police reporter	Midwest, USA	Braun, Lilian Jackson

Four

 **Settings**

Setting	Author	Series Character(s)	Occupation
Alaska (AK)			
	Henry, Sue	Jessie Arnold & Alex Jensen	sled dog racer & Alaska State trooper
	Stabenow, Dana	Kate Shugak	native Alaskan ex-D. A. investigator
	Quinn, Elizabeth	Lauren Maxwell	Alaska wildlife investigator PhD
Arkansas (AR)			
	Hess, Joan	Claire Malloy	small-town bookstore owner
Maggody	Hess, Joan	Arly Hanks	small-town Arkansas police chief
Arizona (AZ)			
	Jance, J. A.	Joanna Bradley	deputy sheriff's widow
	Scherf, Margaret	Grace Severance, Dr.	retired pathologist
California (CA)			
	Burke, Jan	Irene Kelly	newspaper reporter
	Hornsby, Wendy	Maggie MacGowen	investigative filmmaker
	Hornsby, Wendy	Kate Teague & Roger Tejeda	college professor & homicide detective
	Howe, Melodie Johnson	Claire Conrad & Maggie Hill	P.I. & secretary
	Maxwell, A. E.	Fiddler & Fiora Flynn	investment banker
	Millar, Margaret	Tom Aragon	attorney
	Rothenberg, Rebecca	Claire Sharples	former MIT scholar & microbiologist
	Sawyer, Corinne Holt	Angela Benbow & Caledonia Wingate	70-something admirals' widows
	Steiner, Susan	Alex Winter	P.I.
	Valentine, Deborah	Katharine Craig & Kevin Bryce	sculptor & ex-sheriff's detective
Bay Cove	Hart, Jeanne	Carl & Freda Pedersen	police lieutenant & wife
Berkeley	Dunlap, Susan	Jill Smith	homicide detective
Berkeley	Singer, Shelley	Barrett Lake	high school history teacher
Berkeley	Singer, Shelley	Jake Samson & Rosie Vicente	ex-cop & carpenter tenant

United States . . . continued

Setting	Author	Series Character(s)	Occupation

California (CA) . . . continued

Setting	Author	Series Character(s)	Occupation
central coast	Fowler, Earlene	Albenia "Benni" Harper	ex-rancher & folk art museum curator
Hollywood	Millhiser, Marlys	Charlie Greene	Hollywood literary agent
Hollywood	Osborne, Denise	Queenie Davilow	Hollywood screenwriter
Hollywood	Shah, Diane K.	Paris Chandler	1940s Hollywood P.I.
La Jolla	Dunlap, Susan	Kiernan O'Shaughnessy	former San Francisco M.E. turned P.I.
Los Angeles	Cannon, Taffy	Nan Robinson	investigator for the California State Bar
Los Angeles	Clark, Carol Higgins	Regan Reilly	P.I.
Los Angeles	Forrest, Katherine V.	Kate Delafield	LAPD lesbian homicide detective
Los Angeles	Green, Kate	Theresa Fortunato & Oliver Jardino	professional psychic & LAPD detective
Los Angeles	Kellerman, Faye	Peter Decker & Rina Lazarus	LAPD detective & wife
Los Angeles	Kraft, Gabrielle	Jerry Zalman	Beverly Hills dealmaker
Los Angeles	Krich, Rochelle Majer	Jessie Drake	Los Angeles police detective
Los Angeles	Lambert, Mercedes	Whitney Logan	20-something Los Angeles attorney
Los Angeles	Pugh, Dianne G.	Iris Thorne	investment counselor
Los Angeles	Shannon, Dell	Luis Mendoza	dapper & wealthy homicide lieutenant
Los Angeles	White, Teri	Spaceman Kowalski & Blue Maguire	cop pair w/prickly partnership
Marin County	Girdner, Jaqueline	Kate Jasper	gag gift wholesaler
Napa Valley	Muller, Marcia	Joanna Stark	international art investigator
northern	Crum, Laura	Gail McCarthy	horse veterinarian
northern	Dunlap, Susan	Vejay Haskell	utility meter reader
northern	McGuire, Christine	Kathryn Mackay	prosecuting attorney
northern	McKenna, Bridget	Caley Burke	30-something northern CA P.I.
northern	Simonson, Sheila	Lark Dailey Dodge	6-ft. bookdealer
Oakland	Dawson, Janet	Jeri Howard	P.I.
Oakland	Wallace, Marilyn	Jay Goldstein & Carlos Cruz	homicide detectives
Orange County	Ayres, Noreen	Samantha "Smokey" Brandon	sheriff's forensic expert
Orange County	O'Callaghan, Maxine	Delilah West	P.I.
Palo Alto	Beck, K. K.	Iris Cooper	Roaring 20s coed at Stanford University
Palo Alto	Roberts, Lora	Liz Sullivan	freelance writer
Sacramento	Hall, Mary Bowen	Emma Chizzit	salvage dealer
Sacramento	Kijewski, Karen	Kat Colorado	P.I.
San Diego	Padgett, Abigail	Barbara Joan "Bo" Bradley	child abuse investigator
San Diego	Robitaille, Julie	Kit Powell	TV sports reporter
San Diego	Wallace, Patricia	Sydney Bryant	P.I.
San Francisco	Grant, Linda	Catherine Sayler	P.I.
San Francisco	King, Laurie R.	Kate Martinelli & Alonzo Hawkin	SFPD homicide detectives
San Francisco	Lucke, Margaret	Jessica Randolph	P.I.
San Francisco	Matera, Lia	Laura Di Palma	attorney
San Francisco	Matera, Lia	Willa Jansson	California attorney
San Francisco	Muller, Marcia	Sharon McCone	San Fran legal co-op investigator
San Francisco	O'Marie, Sister Carol Anne	Mary Helen, Sister	70-something nun
San Francisco	Pence, Joanne	Angelina Amalfi	food columnist & restaurant reviewer
San Francisco	Pincus, Elizabeth	Nell Fury	lesbian P.I.
San Francisco	Smith, Julie	Paul MacDonald	ex-reporter & mystery writer
San Francisco	Smith, Julie	Rebecca Schwartz	defense attorney

United States . . . continued

Setting	Author	Series Character(s)	Occupation

California (CA) . . . continued

Setting	Author	Series Character(s)	Occupation
San Francisco	Taylor, Elizabeth Atwood	Maggie Elliott	ex-film maker turned P.I.
San Francisco	Welch, Pat	Helen Black	ex-cop lesbian P.I.
San Francisco	White, Gloria	Ronnie Ventana	burglar's daughter P.I.
San Francisco	Yarbro, Chelsea Quinn	Charles Spotted Moon	attorney & Ojibway tribal shaman
San Jose	Sims, L. V.	Dixie T. Struthers	police detective
Santa Barbara	Muller, Marcia	Elena Oliverez	Mexican arts museum curator
Santa Teresa	Grafton, Sue	Kinsey Millhone	ex-cop P.I.
Silicon Valley	Chapman, Sally	Juliet Blake	Silicon Valley fraud investigator
Silicon Valley	Wolfe, Susan	Sarah Nelson	police inspector
southern	Femling, Jean	Martha "Moz" Brant	insurance claims investigator
Walnut Hills	Jacobs, Jonnie	Kate Austen	Bay area single mother

Colorado (CO)

Setting	Author	Series Character(s)	Occupation
	Davidson, Diane Mott	Goldy Bear	caterer & single mother
	Karr, Leona	Addie Devore	small-town newspaper owner
	Oliphant, B. J.	Shirley McClintock	50-something rancher
	Schier, Norma	Kay Barth	district attorney
Denver	Montgomery, Yvonne E.	Finny Aletter	stockbroker turned carpenter
Denver	Orde, A. J.	Jason Lynx	antiques dealer

Connecticut (CT)

Setting	Author	Series Character(s)	Occupation
	Christmas, Joyce	Betty Trenka	retired businesswoman
	Dolson, Hildegarde	Lucy Ramsdale & James McDougal	illustrator & homicide inspector
	Kallen, Lucille	Maggie Rome & C. B. Greenfield	reporter & editor/publisher
	Kittredge, Mary	Charlotte Kent	freelance writer
	Wolzien, Valerie	Susan Henshaw	suburban sleuth
New Haven	Kittredge, Mary	Edwina Crusoe	RN & medical consultant

Florida (FL)

Setting	Author	Series Character(s)	Occupation
	Clark, Carolyn Chambers	Theresa Franco	P.I.
	MacGregor, T. J.	Quin St. James & Mike McCleary	wife & husband P.I. team
Miami	Buchanan, Edna	Britt Montero	newspaper crime reporter
Miami	Woods, Sherryl	Molly DeWitt	film office public relations staffer
south	Drake, Alison	Aline Scott	small resort town police detective
St. Petersburg	Clark, Carolyn Chambers	Megan Baldwin	registered nurse

Georgia (GA)

Setting	Author	Series Character(s)	Occupation
	Harris, Charlaine	Aurora Teagarden	20-something librarian
Atlanta	Hooper, Kay	Lane Montana & Trey Fortier	finder of lost things & homicide detective
Atlanta	Shankman, Sarah	Samantha Adams	investigative reporter
Atlanta	Sibley, Celestine	Kate Kincaid Mulcay	veteran newspaperwoman
Atlanta	Sprinkle, Patricia Houck	Sheila Travers	public relations executive
Atlanta	Trocheck, Kathy Hogan	Julia Callahan Garrity	ex-cop cleaning lady
Atlanta	Woods, Sherryl	Amanda Roberts	ex-New York investigative reporter

United States . . . continued

Setting	Author	Series Character(s)	Occupation

Illinois (IL)

Setting	Author	Series Character(s)	Occupation
	Pulver, Mary Monica	Peter & Kori Price Brichter	police detective & horse breeder
Chicago	Churchill, Jill	Jane Jeffry	suburban Chicago single mother
Chicago	Cooper, Susan Rogers	Kimmey Kruse	stand-up comic
Chicago	D'Amato, Barbara	Cat Marsala	freelance investigative journalist
Chicago	Haddad, Carolyn A.	Becky Belski	computer investigator
Chicago	Hartzmark, Gini	Katherine Prescott Milholland	corporate attorney
Chicago	Paretsky, Sara	V. I. Warshawski	attorney turned P.I.
Chicago suburb	Brod, D. C.	Quint McCauley	ex-cop turned P.I.
Lincoln Prairie	Bland, Eleanor Taylor	Marti MacAlister	black police detective

Indiana (IN)

Setting	Author	Series Character(s)	Occupation
	Carlson, P. M.	Martine LaForte Hopkins	southern Indiana deputy sheriff

Kansas (KS)

Setting	Author	Series Character(s)	Occupation
	Weir, Charlene	Susan Wren	ex-cop turned Kansas police chief
Kansas City	Hollingsworth, Gerelyn	Frances Finn	P.I.

Kentucky (KY)

Setting	Author	Series Character(s)	Occupation
Lexington	Hightower, Lynn	Lena Padget	P.I.
Pigeon Fork	McCafferty, Taylor	Haskell Blevins	P.I.

Louisiana (LA)

Setting	Author	Series Character(s)	Occupation
New Orleans	Smith, Julie	Skip Langdon	6-ft. police detective

Massachusetts (MA)

Setting	Author	Series Character(s)	Occupation
	Page, Katherine Hall	Faith Sibley Fairchild	minister's wife & culinary artist
Boston	Atherton, Nancy	Aunt Dimity	romantic ghost
Boston	Barnes, Linda	Carlotta Carlyle	6'1" cab-driving ex-cop P.I.
Boston	Barnes, Linda	Michael Spraggue III	wealthy actor & ex-P.I.
Boston	Belfort, Sophie	Molly Rafferty	college history professor
Boston	Borthwick, J. S.	Sarah Deane & Alex McKenzie, Dr.	English professor & internist
Boston	Coker, Carolyn	Andrea Perkins	art historian & restorer of paintings at a museum
Boston	Disney, Doris Miles	Jeff Di Marco	insurance investigator
Boston	Lamb, J. Dayne	Teal Stewart	Certified Public Accountant
Boston	MacLeod, Charlotte	Sarah Kelling & Max Bittersohn	investigative couple
Boston	Sullivan, Winona	Cecile Buddenbrooks, Sister	licensed P.I. nun
Boston	Tilton, Alice	Leonidas Witherall	retired academic & secret author of pulp fiction
Boston	Wings, Mary	Emma Victor	lesbian activist & former publicist
Cambridge	Conant, Susan	Holly Winter	30-something dog trainer & magazine columnist
Cambridge	Kelly, Susan	Liz Connors	freelance crime writer
Cambridge	Knight, Kathryn Lasky	Calista Jacobs	award-winning illustrator of children's books
Cambridge	Langton, Jane	Homer Kelly	Harvard professor & retired detective
Cape Cod	Gunning, Sally	Peter Bartholomew	small business owner
Cape Cod	Taylor, Phoebe Atwood	Asey Mayo	former sailor & auto racer
Nantucket	Matthews, Francine	Meredith "Merry" Folger	Nantucket P.I.

United States . . . continued

Setting	Author	Series Character(s)	Occupation

Massachusetts (MA) . . . continued

Setting	Author	Series Character(s)	Occupation
Port Frederick	Pickard, Nancy	Jenny Cain	New England foundation director
Balaclava County	MacLeod, Charlotte	Peter Shandy & Helen Marsh Shandy	botany professor & librarian wife

Maine (ME)

Setting	Author	Series Character(s)	Occupation
	Kenney, Susan	Roz Howard & Alan Stewart	American professor & British painter
	Meier, Leslie	Lucy Stone	small-town New England sleuth
	Rich, Virginia	Eugenia Potter	widowed chef
Portland	Knight, Phyllis	Lil Ritchie	lesbian P.I.

Michigan (MI)

Setting	Author	Series Character(s)	Occupation
	Schenkel, S. E.	Ray & Kate Frederick	chief of detectives & his wife of 30 years
Ann Arbor	Holtzer, Susan	Anneke Haagen	computer consultant
Detroit	Vlasopolos, Anca	Sharon Dair	sex crimes police detective

Minnesota (MN)

Setting	Author	Series Character(s)	Occupation
Minneapolis	Bailey, Jo	Jan Gallagher	hospital security supervisor
Minneapolis	Hart, Ellen	Jane Lawless	lesbian restaurateur
Minneapolis	Hart, Ellen	Sophie Greenway	magazine editor & newspaper food critic
Minneapolis	Jacobs, Nancy Baker	Devon MacDonald	ex-teacher private eye
Minneapolis	Logue, Mary	Laura Malloy	journalist
Minneapolis	Taylor, L. A.	J. J. Jamison	computer engineer & CATCH investigator

Missouri (MO)

Setting	Author	Series Character(s)	Occupation
St. Louis	Kunz, Kathleen	Terry Girard	genealogist for hire
Victoria Springs	Hager, Jean	Tess Darcy	Ozarks bed & breakfast owner

Montana (MT)

Setting	Author	Series Character(s)	Occupation
	McClendon, Lise	Alix Thorssen	gallery owner & art forgery expert
Billings	Prowell, Sandra West	Phoebe Siegel	ex-cop P.I.

North Carolina (NC)

Setting	Author	Series Character(s)	Occupation
	Jackson, Muriel Resnick	Merrie Lee Spencer	Manhattan transplants in North Carolina
	Maron, Margaret	Deborah Knott	district judge
	Squire, Elizabeth Daniels	Peaches Dann	50-something widow
Appalachia	McCrumb, Sharyn	Spencer Arrowood	Appalachian sheriff
Byerly	Kelner, Toni L. P.	Laura Fleming	small-town detective

New Jersey (NJ)

Setting	Author	Series Character(s)	Occupation
	Gilman, Dorothy	Emily Pollifax	grandmother & CIA agent
Newark	Wesley, Valerie Wilson	Tamara Hayle	black P.I. ex-cop
Trenton	Evanovich, Janet	Stephanie Plum	neophyte bounty hunter

New Mexico (NM)

Setting	Author	Series Character(s)	Occupation
Albuquerque	Van Gieson, Judith	Neil Hamel	attorney & investigator

United States . . . continued

Setting	Author	Series Character(s)	Occupation
Nevada (NV)			
Las Vegas	Douglas, Carole Nelson	Temple Barr & Midnight Louie	public relations freelancer & tomcat sleuth
Reno	Dain, Catherine	Freddie O'Neal	plane-flying P.I.
New York (NY)			
	Adamson, Lydia	Deidre Quinn Nightingale	rural veterinarian
	Morgan, Kate	Dewey James	60-something small-town librarian
Brooklyn	Tyre, Peg	Kate Murray	newspaper reporter for Daily Herald
Hemlock Falls	Bishop, Claudia	Sarah & Meg Quilliam	inn owner & chef (sisters)
Long Island	Watson, Clarissa	Persis Willum	New York art curator
New York	Adamson, Lydia	Alice Nestleton	actress & cat lover
New York	Barber, Willetta A.	Christopher "Kit" Storm	police illustrator for the NYPD
New York	Bennett, Liza	Peg Goodenough	ad agency creative director
New York	Berry, Carole	Bonnie Indermill	tap-dancing Manhattan office temp
New York	Boylan, Eleanor	Clara Gamadge	widow of Henry the forgery expert
New York	Brennan, Carol	Liz Wareham	Manhattan public relations consultant
New York	Brill, Toni	Midge Cohen	children's author fluent in Russian
New York	Carlson, P. M.	Maggie Ryan	statistician & mother
New York	Christmas, Joyce	Margaret Priam, Lady	Englishwoman in New York City
New York	Collins, Anna Ashwood	Abigail Doyle	New York efficiency expert
New York	Crespi, Trella	Simona Griffo	advertising executive & gourmet cook
New York	Cross, Amanda	Kate Fansler	university English professor
New York	Daly, Elizabeth	Henry Gamadge	author & bibliophile
New York	Davis, Dorothy Salisbury	Julie Hayes	former actress & columnist
New York	Dentinger, Jane	Jocelyn O'Roarke	Broadway actress & director
New York	Eberhart, Mignon Good	Sarah Keate & Lance O'Leary	nurse & wealthy police detective
New York	Edghill, Rosemary	Karen Hightower	Manhattan graphic designer & white witch
New York	Farrell, Gillian B.	Annie McGrogan	NYC P.I. & actor just back from LA
New York	Florian, S.L.	Delia Ross-Merlani, Viscountess	English-Italian noblewoman
New York	Frankel, Valerie	Wanda Mallory	detective agency owner
New York	Glass, Leslie	April Woo	police detective
New York	Gray, Gallagher	Theodore S. Hubbert & Auntie Lil	ret'd human resources manager & dress designer
New York	Harris, Lee	Christine Bennett	ex-nun
New York	Hayter, Sparkle	Robin Hudson	cable news reporter
New York	Holland, Isabelle	Claire Aldington, Rev.	Episcopal priest
New York	Horansky, Ruby	Nikki Trakos	homicide detective
New York	Kelly, Mary Ann	Claire Breslinsky	freelance photographer
New York	Lathen, Emma	John Putnam Thatcher	Wall Street financial whiz
New York	Lockridge, Frances & R.	Pam & Jerry North	husband & wife book publishers
New York	Lorden, Randye	Sydney Sloane	upper west side private investigator
New York	Maron, Margaret	Sigrid Harald	police lieutenant
New York	Matteson, Stephanie	Charlotte Graham	Oscar-winning actress
New York	McCloy, Helen	Basil Willing, Dr.	medical advisor to NYC district attorney
New York	Meyers, Annette	Xenia Smith & Leslie Wetzon	pair of Wall Street headhunters
New York	O'Connell, Carol	Kathleen Mallory	NYPD cop
New York	O'Donnell, Catherine	Karen Levinson	NYPD homicide detective
New York	O'Donnell, Lillian	Mici Anhalt	criminal justice investigator
New York	O'Donnell, Lillian	Norah Mulcahaney	NYPD detective
New York	O'Donnell, Lillian	Gwenn Ramadge	P.I. for corporate investigations
New York	OCork, Shannon	Theresa Tracy Baldwin	sports photographer for New York daily

United States . . . continued

Setting	Author	Series Character(s)	Occupation

New York (NY) . . . continued

Setting	Author	Series Character(s)	Occupation
New York	Papazoglou, Orania	Patience Campbell McKenna	6-ft. romance novelist turned crime writer
New York	Paul, Barbara	Enrico Caruso & Geraldine Farrar	Italian tenor & American soprano
New York	Paul, Barbara	Marian Larch	NYPD officer
New York	Peters, Elizabeth	Jacqueline Kirby	librarian turned romance novelist
New York	Piesman, Marissa	Nina Fischman	legal services attorney
New York	Reilly, Helen	Christopher McKee	Manhattan homicide squad detective
New York	Scherf, Margaret	Emily & Henry Bryce	Manhattan interior decorators
New York	Scoppettone, Sandra	Lauren Laurano	Greenwich Village lesbian P.I.
New York	Smith, Evelyn E.	Susan Melville	freelance assassin & painter
New York	Tucker, Kerry	Libby Kincaid	magazine photographer
New York	Uhnak, Dorothy	Christine Opara	20-something police detective
New York	Wells, Carolyn	Fleming Stone	intellectual private investigator
New York	Wheat, Carolyn	Cass Jameson	Brooklyn criminal lawyer
New York	Wilhelm, Kate	Charlie Meiklejohn & Constance Leidl	ex-arson investigator P.I. & psychologist
New York	Yeager, Dorian	Victoria Bowering	NYC actor, writer & playwright
New York	Zukowski, Sharon	Blaine Stewart	ex-NYPD cop turned P.I. in Manhattan
Rochester	O'Brien, Meg	Jessica James	newspaper reporter
Seneca Falls	Monfredo, Miriam Grace	Glynis Tryon	librarian & suffragette
Syracuse	Block, Barbara	Robin Light	pet store owner

Ohio (OH)

Setting	Author	Series Character(s)	Occupation
Cincinnati	Borton, D. B.	Cat Caliban	60-something P.I-in-training
Cincinnati	Hightower, Lynn	Sonora Blair	homicide detective
Cincinnati	Short, Sharon Gwyn	Patricia Delaney	computer whiz P.I.
Columbus	Glen, Alison	Charlotte Sams	freelance writer
Grantham	Gosling, Paula	Jack Stryker & Kate Trevorne	homicide cop & English professor

Oklahoma (OK)

Setting	Author	Series Character(s)	Occupation
	Hager, Jean	Molly Bearpaw	Cherokee civil rights investigator
Buckskin	Hager, Jean	Mitch Bushyhead	police chief of Cherokee descent
Holton	Sandstrom, Eve K.	Sam & Nicky Titus	ex-army CID sheriff & his wife
Prophesy County	Cooper, Susan Rogers	Milton Kovak	chief deputy
Vamoose	Feddersen, Connie	Amanda Hazard	small-town Certified Public Accountant

Oregon (OR)

Setting	Author	Series Character(s)	Occupation
	Wallingford, Lee	Ginny Trask & Frank Carver	forest fire dispatcher & ex-cop
	Wilhelm, Kate	Barbara Holloway	defense attorney
	Wilhelm, Kate	Sarah Drexler	judge
	Wren, M. K.	Conan Flagg	bookstore owner & former intelligence agent

Pennsylvania (PA)

Setting	Author	Series Character(s)	Occupation
	Allen, Irene	Elizabeth Elliot	widowed Quaker meeting clerk
	Malmont, Valerie S.	Tori Miracle	ex-NYC crime writer turned novelist
	Myers, Tamar	Magdalena Yoder	Mennonite inn owner & operator
Philadelphia	Haddam, Jane	Gregor Demarkian	former FBI department head
Philadelphia	Roberts, Gillian	Amanda Pepper	high school teacher
Philadelphia	Scottoline, Lisa	Mary DiNunzio	attorney

United States . . . continued

Setting	Author	Series Character(s)	Occupation
South Carolina (SC)			
	Hart, Carolyn G.	Annie Laurance & Max Darling	bookstore owner & investigator
	Hart, Carolyn G.	Henrietta O'Dwyer Collins	70-something reporter
Texas (TX)			
	Banks, Carolyn	Robin Vaughn	equestrienne sleuth
	Cooper, Susan Rogers	E. J. Pugh	housewife, mother & romance writer
	Romberg, Nina	Marian Winchester	Caddo-Commanche medicine woman
	Walker, Mary Willis	Kate Driscoll	dog trainer
	Walker, Mary Willis	Mollie Cates	true crime writer & reporter
Bayport	Wingate, Ann	Mark Shigata	ex-FBI agent turned sheriff
Canadian	Meredith, D. R.	John Lloyd Branson & Lydia Fairchild	defense attorney & legal assistant
Ft. Worth	Martin, Lee	Deb Ralston	police detective & mother
Houston	Bradley, Lynn	Cole January	P.I.
Pecan Springs	Albert, Susan Wittig	China Bayles	herb shop owner & former attorney
Purple Sage	Smith, Barbara Burnett	Jolie Wyatt	aspiring novelist & writer's group member
Utah (UT)			
	Moffat, Gwen	Melinda Pink	writer & mountain climber
Virginia (VA)			
Crozet	Brown, Rita Mae	Mary Minor Haristeen	small-town postmistress & cat
Richmond	Cornwell, Patricia Daniels	Kay Scarpetta	Chief Medical Examiner
Vermont (VT)			
	Comfort, Barbara	Tish McWhinney	artist & painter
Washington (WA)			
	Daheim, Mary	Judith McMonigle	bed & breakfast owner
	Dereske, Jo	Helma Zukas	Washington State librarian
	Oleksiw, Susan	Joe Silva	chief of police
Alpine	Daheim, Mary	Emma Lord	small-town newspaper owner & editor
Port Silva	LaPierre, Janet	Vince Gutierrez & Meg Halloran	police chief & school teacher
Seattle	Beck, K. K.	Jane da Silva	former lounge singer
Seattle	Gilpatrick, Noreen	Kate McLean	police detective
Seattle	Hendrickson, Louise	Amy Prescott	crime lab physician
Seattle	Jance, J. A.	J. P. Beaumont	homicide detective
Seattle	Mariz, Linda French	Laura Ireland	grad student volleyball player
Seattle	Smith, Janet L.	Annie MacPherson	attorney
Seattle	Thompson, Joyce	Frederika Bascomb	forensic artist
Seattle	Wilson, Barbara	Pam Nilsen	lesbian printing company owner

United States . . . continued

Setting	Author	Series Character(s)	Occupation
Washington DC			
	Andreae, Christine	Lee Squires	English professor & poet
	Dominic, R. B.	Ben Safford	Democratic congressman from Ohio
	Fromer, Margot J.	Amanda Knight	hospital director of nursing
	Law, Janice	Anna Peters	international oil company exec turned P.I.
	Roberts, Carey	Anne Fitzhugh	police detective
	Sucher, Dorothy	Sabina Swift	Georgetown detective agency owner
	Truman, Margaret	Mackenzie Smith & Annabel Reed	law professor & attorney wife turned gallery owner
	Truman, Margaret	Margit Falk	ex-combat pilot & government attorney
Wisconsin (WI)			
Milwaukee	McGiffin, Janet	Maxene St. Clair, Dr.	emergency room physician
Wyoming (WY)			
	Andrews, Sarah	Em Hansen	oil worker
	Landreth, Marsha	Samantha Turner, Dr.	medical examiner
Miscellaneous			
	Armstrong, Charlotte	MacDougal Duff	retired history professor
	Baker, Nikki	Virginia Kelly	lesbian stockbroker
	Ballard, Mignon	Eliza Figg	former Peace Corps volunteer
	Barr, Nevada	Anna Pigeon	U. S. park ranger
	Berenson, Laurien	new character	suburban wife & mother
	D'Amato, Barbara	Gerritt De Graaf	physician
	Dietz, Denise	Ellie Bernstein	diet group leader
	Haddock, Lisa	Carmen Ramirez	newspaper copy editor
	Jackson, Marian J. A.	Abigail Patience Danforth	19th century consulting detective
	Lorens, M. K.	Winston Marlowe Sherman	Shakespeare professor & mystery writer
	Lyons, Nan & Ivan	Natasha O'Brien & Millie Ogden	pair of culinary artists
	Mather, Linda	Jo Hughes	professional astrologer
	McAllester, Melanie	Elizabeth Mendoza & Ashley Johnson	lesbian homicide detectives
	McCrumb, Sharyn	Elizabeth MacPherson	forensic anthropologist
	McCrumb, Sharyn	James Owen Mega	science fiction author & college professor
	Neely, Barbara	Blanche White	middle-aged black domestic
	Parker, Barbara	Gail Connor	corporate attorney
	Popkin, Zelda	Mary Carner	former department store detective
	Porter, Anna	Judith Hayes	journalist
	Stein, Triss	Kay Engles	nationally-known reporter
	Stevens, Serita	Fanny Zindel	Jewish grandmother
Great Lakes	Gosling, Paula	Blackwater Bay Mystery	police series with a Great Lakes setting
Midwest	Braun, Lilian Jackson	Jim Qwilleran, Koko & Yum Yum	ex-police reporter & cats
Midwest	Cleary, Melissa	Jackie Walsh & Jake	college film instructor with her ex-police dog
Midwest	Skom, Edith	Elizabeth Austin	English professor
New England	Blackmur, L. L.	Galen Shaw & Julian Baugh	writer & financier
Puerto Rico	Adamson, M. J.	Balthazar Marten & Sixto Cardenas	NYPD homicide detective & Puerto Rican cop

United Kingdom

Setting	Author	Series Character(s)	Occupation
England			
	Bannister, Jo	Clio Rees, Dr. & Harry Marsh	physician/mystery writer & chief inspector
	Black, Veronica	Joan, Sister	British investigative nun
	Charles, Kate	Lucy Kingsley & David Middleton-Brown	artist & solicitor
	Christie, Agatha	Tuppence & Tommy Beresford	adventurers for hire & intelligence agents
	Cleeves, Ann	Stephen Ramsey	British Inspector
	Crane, Hamilton	Emily D. Seeton	retired British art teacher
	Duffy, Margaret	Ingrid Langley & Patrick Gillard	novelist/British agent & British army major
	Dunant, Sarah	Marla Masterson	young professor of Anglo-Saxon literature
	Eccles, Marjorie	Gil Mayo	Detective Chief Inspector
	Ferrars, E. X.	Sara Marriott	journalist
	Ferrars, E. X.	Virginia & Felix Freer	physiotherapist & businessman
	Fraser, Anthea	David Webb	British police inspector
	Frazer, Margaret	Sister Frevisse	Medieval nun
	Fyfield, Frances	Sarah Fortune	lawyer in prestigious British firm
	Gosling, Paula	Luke Abbott	English cop
	Graham, Caroline	Tom Barnaby	Chief Inspector
	Granger, Ann	Meredith Mitchell	British Foreign Service officer
	Green, Christine	Kate Kinsella	British nurse & medical investigator
	Green, Christine	new character	boozy Irishman & new policewoman
	Greenwood, Diane M.	Theodora Braithwaite, Rev.	British deaconess
	Grindle, Lucretia	H. W. Ross	Detective Superintendent
	Hall, Patricia	Alex Sinclair & Kate Weston	British Inspector & social worker
	Hardwick, Mollie	Doran Fairweather	British antiques dealer
	Harrod-Eagles, Cynthia	Bill Slider	Detective Inspector
	Haymon, S. T.	Benjamin Jurnet	Detective Inspector
	Highsmith, Patricia	Tom Ripley	charming forger & psychopath
	Holt, Hazel	Sheila Malory	British literary magazine writer
	Kingsbury, Kate	Cecily Sinclair	hotel owner in Edwardian England
	Laurence, Janet	Darina Lisle	British caterer, chef & food writer
	Linscott, Gillian	Nell Bray	British suffragette
	Mann, Jessica	Tamara Hoyland	British secret agent archaeologist
	Mann, Jessica	Thea Crawford	archaeology professor
	Mason, Sarah Jill	D. S. Trewley & Sgt. Stone	English village detective partners
	McDermid, Val	Lindsay Gordon	lesbian journalist
	McGerr, Patricia	Selena Mead	British government agent
	Mitchell, Gladys	Timothy Herring	preservation society director
	Moody, Susan	Penny Wanawake	6-ft. photographer daughter of black UN diplomat
	Moody, Susan	Cassandra Swann	British biology teacher turned bridge pro
	Morice, Ann	Tessa Crichton	English actress sleuth
	Myers, Amy	Auguste Didier	British-French Victorian master chef
	Neel, Janet	John McLeish & Francesca Wilson	Det. Inspector & civil servant
	Perry, Anne	Thomas & Charlotte Pitt	Victorian police inspector & wife
	Perry, Anne	William Monk	amnesiac Victorian policeman
	Peters, Elizabeth	Amelia Peabody	Victorian feminist archaeologist
	Peterson, Audrey	Claire Camden	California English professor in Britain

United Kingdom . . . continued

Setting	Author	Series Character(s)	Occupation

England . . . continued

Setting	Author	Series Character(s)	Occupation
	Peterson, Audrey	Jane Winfield	British journalist & music writer
	Rinehart, Mary Roberts	Hilda Adams	nurse
	Robb, Candace M.	Owen Archer	Medieval Welsh spy for the Archbishop
	Roome, Annette	Christine Martin	40-something cub reporter
	Rowlands, Betty	Melissa Craig	British mystery writer
	Sedley, Kate	Roger the Chapman	medieval chapman (peddler)
	Simpson, Dorothy	Luke Thanet	British police inspector
	Smith, Joan	Loretta Lawson	British feminist professor
	Spring, Michelle	Laura Principal	British academic turned P.I.
	Stacey, Susannah	Robert Bone	widowed British police inspector
	Walsh, Jill Paton	Imogen Quy	nurse
	Warner, Mignon	Edwina Charles	British clairvoyante
	Woods, Sara	Anthony Maitland	English barrister drawn to murder cases
Castlemere	Bannister, Jo	Liz Graham & Cal Donovan	pair of Castlemere cops
Cotswolds	Beaton, M. C.	Agatha Raisin	London advertising retiree in the Cotswolds
Dedham	Paige, Robin	Kathryn Ardleigh	25-yr. old American author
Deerham Hills	Melville, Jennie	Charmian Daniels	police detective
Essex	Thomson, June	Inspector Finch	police inspector
Herefordshire	Burden, Pat	Henry Bassett	retired cop
Hop Valley	Kelly, Susan B.	Alison Hope & Nick Trevellyan	software designer & detective inspector
Kent County	Brand, Christianna	Inspector Cockrill	constable
London	Allingham, Margery	Albert Campion	Scotland Yard inspector
London	Babson, Marian	Douglas Perkins	London-based public relations agent
London	Babson, Marian	Eve Sinclair & Trixie Dolan	aging British ex-movie queens
London	Bell, Josephine	David Wintringham	British physician
London	Brightwell, Emily	Inspector Witherspoon & Mrs. Jeffries	Victorian inspector & housekeeper
London	Butler, Gwendoline	John Coffin	London police inspector
London	Cannell, Dorothy	Ellie & Ben Haskell w/ the Tramwell sisters	interior decorator & writer/chef w/sister sleuths
London	Christie, Agatha	Hercule Poirot	former Belgian cop turned private detective
London	Clarke, Anna	Paula Glenning	British professor & writer
London	Cleeves, Ann	George & Molly Palmer-Jones	ex-Home Office official/bird-watcher & wife
London	Cody, Liza	Eva Wylie	wrestler & security guard
London	Cody, Liza	Anna Lee	private investigator
London	Cooper, Natasha	Willow King & Cressida Woodruffe	British civil servant & romance novelist
London	Crombie, Deborah	Duncan Kincaid & Gemma James	Scotland Yard Superintendent & Sgt. partner
London	Crowleigh, Ann	Miranda & Clare Clively	Victorian London twin sisters
London	Danks, Denise	Georgina Powers	British computer journalist
London	Dunant, Sarah	Hannah Wolfe	P.I.
London	Fraser, Antonia Pakenham	Jemima Shore	British TV interviewer
London	Fyfield, Frances	Helen West	London Crown Prosecutor
London	George, Elizabeth	Thomas Lynley & Barbara Havers	Scotland Yard Inspector & Detective Sgt.
London	Giroux, E. X.	Robert Forsythe & Abigail Sanderson	London barrister & his secretary
London	Grant-Adamson, Lesley	Rain Morgan	newspaper reporter
London	Grant-Adamson, Lesley	Laura Flynn	P.I.
London	Grimes, Martha	Richard Jury	Scotland Yard investigator

United Kingdom . . . continued

Setting	Author	Series Character(s)	Occupation

England . . . continued

Setting	Author	Series Character(s)	Occupation
London	James, P. D.	Cordelia Gray	fledgling P.I.
London	James, P. D.	Adam Dalgleish	published poet of Scotland Yard
London	LaPlante, Lynda	Jane Tennison	London Detective Chief Inspector
London	Marsh, Ngaio	Roderick Alleyn	Inspector son of a baronet
London	Meek, M. R. D.	Lennox Kemp	London solicitor detective
London	Mitchell, Gladys	Beatrice Lestrange Bradley	psychiatrist & consultant to Home Office
London	Moyes, Patricia	Henry & Emmy Tibbett	Scotland Yard Inspector & wife
London	Ross, Kate	Julian Kestrel	early 19th century Londoner
London	Sayers, Dorothy L.	Peter Wimsey, Lord	pianist, book collector & criminologist
London	Slovo, Gillian	Kate Baeier	freelance journalist turned detective
London	Tey, Josephine	Alan Grant	Scotland Yard detective
London	Wakefield, Hannah	Dee Street	American attorney
London	Wentworth, Patricia	Maud Silver	retired governess & spinster P.I.
London	Wilson, Barbara	Cassandra Reilly	London-based Spanish translator
Manchester	McDermid, Val	Kate Brannigan	P.I.
Nottingham	Shepherd, Stella	Richard Montgomery	Nottingham CID Inspector
Oxford	Caudwell, Sarah	Hilary Tamar	Oxford professor of medieval law
Oxford	Stallwood, Veronica	Kate Ivory	Oxford novelist
Oxford	Yorke, Margaret	Patrick Grant, Dr.	Oxford don teaching English literature
Shrewsbury	Peters, Ellis	Brother Cadfael	Medieval monk & herbalist
Shropshire	Pargeter, Edith	George, Bunty & Dominic Felse	family of detectives
St. Mary's Mead	Christie, Agatha	Jane Marple	elderly spinster
Suffolk	Radley, Sheila	Douglas Quantrill & Hilary Lloyd	Det. Chief Inspector & Sgt. partner
Sussex	Rendell, Ruth	Reginald Wexford	Chief Inspector
Thames Valley	Curzon, Clare	Mike Yeadings	Detective Superintendent Serious Crimes Squad
West Calleshire	Aird, Catherine	Christopher Dennis "Seedy" Sloan	Berebury CID department head
Yorkshire	Lacey, Sarah	Leah Hunter	Yorkshire tax inspector

Ireland

Setting	Author	Series Character(s)	Occupation
Dublin	Fallon, Ann	James Fleming	Dublin solicitor

Scotland

Setting	Author	Series Character(s)	Occupation
	Beaton, M. C.	Hamish Macbeth	Scottish police constable
Edinburgh	Knight, Alanna	Jeremy Faro	Victorian detective inspector

Wales

Setting	Author	Series Character(s)	Occupation
	McGown, Jill	Chief Inspector Lloyd & Judy Hill	detective inspectors

Other

Setting	Author	Series Character(s)	Occupation

Australia

Setting	Author	Series Character(s)	Occupation
	Day, Marele	Claudia Valentine	Australian P.I.
	Greenwood, Kerry	Phryne Fisher	1920s Australian sleuth
	Rowe, Jennifer	Verity "Birdie" Birdwood	Australian TV researcher
Sydney	Geason, Susan	Syd Fish	Sydney P.I.

Canada

Setting	Author	Series Character(s)	Occupation
Calgary, Alberta	North, Suzanne	Phoebe Fairfax	Calgary TV video photographer
British Columbia	Kelly, Nora	Gillian Adams	University of the Pacific Northwest history chair
British Columbia	Wright, L. R.	Martin Karl Alberg	RCMP Staff Sgt
Vancouver, BC	Bowers, Elisabeth	Meg Lacey	P.I.
Victoria, BC	Douglas, Lauren Wright	Caitlin Reece	lesbian detective
Fredericton, NB	Craig, Alisa	Madoc & Janet Rhys	RCMP Inspector & wife
Lobelia Falls, Ont.	Craig, Alisa	Dittany Henbit Monk & Osbert Monk	garden club member & author of westerns
Toronto, Ontario	Gordon, Alison	Kate Henry	baseball newswriter
Toronto, Ontario	Millar, Margaret	Paul Prye	psychiatrist
Toronto, Ontario	Millar, Margaret	Inspector Sands	police detective
Toronto, Ontario	Sale, Medora	John Sanders & Harriet Jeffries	police detective & architectural photographer

France

Setting	Author	Series Character(s)	Occupation
	Fawcett, Quinn	Victoire Vernet	wife of Napoleonic gendarme
	Newman, Sharan	Catherine LeVendeur	novice & scholar
Paris	Douglas, Carole Nelson	Irene Adler	19th century French sleuth
Paris	Friedman, Mickey	Georgia Lee Maxwell	Paris-based freelance writer

Germany

Setting	Author	Series Character(s)	Occupation
	Peters, Elizabeth	Vicky Bliss	art historian

Italy

Setting	Author	Series Character(s)	Occupation
	Eyre, Elizabeth	Sigismondo	agent of a Renaissance duke
Florence	Nabb, Magdalen	Salvatore Guarnaccia	Italian police marshal
Rome	Davis, Lindsey	Marcus Didius Falco	P.I. in ancient Rome
Venice	Leon, Donna	Guido Brunetti	Venetian policeman

Japan

Setting	Author	Series Character(s)	Occupation
	McFall, Patricia	Nora James	American linguistics grad student working in Japan

Kenya

Setting	Author	Series Character(s)	Occupation
	McQuillan, Karin	Jazz Jasper	American safari guide in Africa

New Zealand

Setting	Author	Series Character(s)	Occupation
	Scott, Rosie	Glory Day	artist & singer

Other . . . continued

Setting	Author	Series Character(s)	Occupation
Spain			
	Oliver, Maria Antonia	Lonia Guiu	Catalan private investigator
World Travelers			
	Arnold, Margot	Penny Spring & Toby Glendower, Sir	Amer. anthropologist & British archeologist
	Crane, Frances	Pat & Jean Abbot	husband & wife detection team

Five

Mystery Chronology

1900s

1909   The Clue (Wells, Carolyn)

1910s

1911   The Gold Bag (Wells, Carolyn)

1912   A Chain of Evidence (Wells, Carolyn)

1913   The Maxwell Mystery (Wells, Carolyn)

1914   Anybody but Anne (Wells, Carolyn)

1915   The Whit Alley (Wells, Carolyn)

1916   The Curved Blades (Wells, Carolyn)

1917   The Mark of Cain (Wells, Carolyn)

1918   Vicky Van (Wells, Carolyn)

1919   The Diamond Pin (Wells, Carolyn)

1920s

1920   The Mysterious Affair at Styles (Christie, Agatha)
1920   Raspberry Jam (Wells, Carolyn)

1921   The Mystery of the Sycamore (Wells, Carolyn)

1922   The Secret Adversary (Christie, Agatha)
1922   The Mystery Girl (Wells, Carolyn)

1923   Murder on the Links (Christie, Agatha)
1923   Whose Body? (Sayers, Dorothy L.)
1923   Feathers Left Around (Wells, Carolyn)
1923   Spooky Hollow (Wells, Carolyn)

1924   Prilligirl (Wells, Carolyn)
1924   The Furthest Fury (Wells, Carolyn)

1925   Anything but the Truth (Wells, Carolyn)
1925   The Daughter of the House (Wells, Carolyn)

1926   The Murder of Roger Ackroyd (Christie, Agatha)
1926   Clouds of Witness (Sayers, Dorothy L.)
1926   The Bronze Hand (Wells, Carolyn)
1926   The Red-Haired Girl (Wells, Carolyn)

1927   The Big Four (Christie, Agatha)
1927   Unnatural Death [U.S.–The Dawson Pedigree]
           (Sayers, Dorothy L.)
1927   All at Sea (Wells, Carolyn)
1927   Where's Emily (Wells, Carolyn)

1928   The Mystery of the Blue Train (Christie, Agatha)
1928   The Unpleasantness at the Bellona Club
           (Sayers, Dorothy L.)
1928   The Crime in the Crypt (Wells, Carolyn)
1928   The Tannahill Tangle (Wells, Carolyn)
1928   Grey Mask (Wentworth, Patricia)

1929   Look to the Lady [U.S.–The Gryth Chalice Mystery]
           (Allingham, Margery)
1929   The Crime at Black Dudley [U.S.–The Black Dudley
           Murder] (Allingham, Margery)
1929   Partners in Crime [short stories] (Christie, Agatha)
1929   The Patient in Room 18 (Eberhart, Mignon Good)
1929   Speedy Death (Mitchell, Gladys)
1929   Lord Peter Views the Body (Sayers, Dorothy L.)
1929   The Man in the Queue (Tey, Josephine)
1929   The Tapestry Room Murder (Wells, Carolyn)
1929   Triple Murder (Wells, Carolyn)

1930s

1930   Mystery Mile (Allingham, Margery)
1930   The Murder at the Vicarage (Christie, Agatha)
1930   The Mystery of Hunting's End
           (Eberhart, Mignon Good)
1930   While the Patient Slept (Eberhart, Mignon Good)
1930   The Diamond Feather (Reilly, Helen)
1930   Strong Poison (Sayers, Dorothy L.)
1930   The Doomed Five (Wells, Carolyn)
1930   The Ghosts' High Noon (Wells, Carolyn)

1930s . . . continued

1931 Police at the Funeral (Allingham, Margery)
1931 Dead Man's Mirror (Christie, Agatha)
1931 Peril at End House (Christie, Agatha)
1931 From This Dark Stairway (Eberhart, Mignon Good)
1931 Murder in the Mews (Reilly, Helen)
1931 Five Red Herrings [U.S.–Suspicious Characters] (Sayers, Dorothy L.)
1931 The Cape Cod Mystery (Taylor, Phoebe Atwood)
1931 Horror House (Wells, Carolyn)
1931 The Umbrella Murder (Wells, Carolyn)

1932 Murder by an Aristocrat (Eberhart, Mignon Good)
1932 The Saltmarsh Murders (Mitchell, Gladys)
1932 Miss Pinkerton (Rinehart, Mary Roberts)
1932 Have His Carcase (Sayers, Dorothy L.)
1932 Death Lights a Candle (Taylor, Phoebe Atwood)
1932 Fuller's Earth (Wells, Carolyn)
1932 The Roll-Top Desk Mystery (Wells, Carolyn)

1933 Sweet Danger [U.S.–Kingdom of Death] (Allingham, Margery)
1933 The Fear Sign (Allingham, Margery)
1933 Lord Edgeware Dies [U.S.–Thirteen at Dinner] (Christie, Agatha)
1933 Hangman's Holiday [short story collection] (Sayers, Dorothy L.)
1933 Murder Must Advertise (Sayers, Dorothy L.)
1933 The Mystery of the Cape Cod Players (Taylor, Phoebe Atwood)
1933 The Broken O (Wells, Carolyn)
1933 The Clue of the Eyelash (Wells, Carolyn)
1933 The Master Murderer (Wells, Carolyn)

1934 Death of a Ghost (Allingham, Margery)
1934 Murder on the Orient Express [U.S.–Murder in the Calais Coach] (Christie, Agatha)
1934 Three-Act Tragedy [U.S.–Murder in Three Acts] (Christie, Agatha)
1934 A Man Lay Dead (Marsh, Ngaio)
1934 Death at the Opera [U.S.–Death in the Wet] (Mitchell, Gladys)
1934 McKee of Centre Street (Reilly, Helen)
1934 The Line-up (Reilly, Helen)
1934 The Nine Tailors (Sayers, Dorothy L.)
1934 Sandbar Sinister (Taylor, Phoebe Atwood)
1934 The Mystery of the Cape Cod Tavern (Taylor, Phoebe Atwood)
1934 Eyes in the Wall (Wells, Carolyn)
1934 In the Tiger's Case (Wells, Carolyn)
1934 The Visiting Villian (Wells, Carolyn)

1935 Death in the Clouds [U.S.–Death in the Air] (Christie, Agatha)
1935 Enter a Murderer (Marsh, Ngaio)
1935 Gaudy Night (Sayers, Dorothy L.)
1935 Deathblow Hill (Taylor, Phoebe Atwood)
1935 The Tinkling Symbol (Taylor, Phoebe Atwood)
1935 For Goodness Sake (Wells, Carolyn)
1935 The Beautiful Derelict (Wells, Carolyn)
1935 The Wooden Indian (Wells, Carolyn)

1936 Flowers for the Judge [U.S.–Legacy in Blood] (Allingham, Margery)
1936 Cards on the Table (Christie, Agatha)
1936 Murder in Mesopotamia (Christie, Agatha)
1936 The ABC Murders [U.S.–The Alphabet Murders] (Christie, Agatha)

1936 Death in Ecstasy (Marsh, Ngaio)
1936 The Nursing Home Murder (Marsh, Ngaio)
1936 Dead Man's Control (Reilly, Helen)
1936 Mr. Smith's Hat (Reilly, Helen)
1936 Out of Order (Taylor, Phoebe Atwood)
1936 The Crimson Patch (Taylor, Phoebe Atwood)
1936 A Shilling for Candles (Tey, Josephine)
1936 Money Musk (Wells, Carolyn)
1936 Murder in the Bookshop (Wells, Carolyn)
1936 The Huddle (Wells, Carolyn)

1937 Dancers in Mourning [U.S.–Who Killed Chloe?] (Allingham, Margery)
1937 The Case of the Late Pig (Allingham, Margery)
1937 Murder in Hospital (Bell, Josephine)
1937 Death on the Nile (Christie, Agatha)
1937 Dumb Witness [U.S.–Poirot Loses a Client] (Christie, Agatha)
1937 Murder in the Mews [U.S.–Dead Man's Mirror] (Christie, Agatha)
1937 Vintage Murder (Marsh, Ngaio)
1937 Busman's Honeymoon (Sayers, Dorothy L.)
1937 Figure Away (Taylor, Phoebe Atwood)
1937 Octagon House (Taylor, Phoebe Atwood)
1937 Beginning with a Bash (Tilton, Alice)
1937 The Mystery of the Tarn (Wells, Carolyn)
1937 The Radio Studio Murder (Wells, Carolyn)
1937 The Case is Closed (Wentworth, Patricia)

1938 The Fashion in Shrouds (Allingham, Margery)
1938 Fall Over Cliff (Bell, Josephine)
1938 A Holiday for Murder (Christie, Agatha)
1938 Appointment with Death (Christie, Agatha)
1938 Hercule Poirot's Christmas [U.S.–Murder for Christmas] (Christie, Agatha)
1938 Artists in Crime (Marsh, Ngaio)
1938 Death in a White Tie (Marsh, Ngaio)
1938 Dance of Death [Britain–Design for Dying] (McCloy, Helen)
1938 St. Peter's Finger (Mitchell, Gladys)
1938 Death Wears a White Gardenia (Popkin, Zelda)
1938 Banbury Bog (Taylor, Phoebe Atwood)
1938 The Annulet of Gilt (Taylor, Phoebe Atwood)
1938 The Cut Direct (Tilton, Alice)
1938 Gilt-Edged Guilt (Wells, Carolyn)
1938 The Killer (Wells, Carolyn)
1938 The Missing Link (Wells, Carolyn)

1939 Death at Half-Term [U.S.–Curtain Call for a Corpse] (Bell, Josephine)
1939 Sad Cypress (Christie, Agatha)
1939 Overture to Death (Marsh, Ngaio)
1939 All Concerned Notified (Reilly, Helen)
1939 Dead for a Ducat (Reilly, Helen)
1939 In the Teeth of the Evidence (Sayers, Dorothy L.)
1939 Spring Harrowing (Taylor, Phoebe Atwood)
1939 Cold Steal (Tilton, Alice)
1939 Calling All Suspects (Wells, Carolyn)
1939 Crime Tears On (Wells, Carolyn)
1939 The Importance of Being Murdered (Wells, Carolyn)
1939 Lonesome Road (Wentworth, Patricia)

1940s

1940 Black Plumes (Allingham, Margery)
1940 Murder Draws a Line (Barber, Willetta A.)
1940 One, Two, Buckle My Shoe [U.S.–The Patriotic Murders] (Christie, Agatha)

1940s . . . continued

1940   Deadly Nightshade (Daly, Elizabeth)
1940   Unexpected Night (Daly, Elizabeth)
1940   The Norths Meet Murder
            (Lockridge, Frances & Richard)
1940   Death at the Bar (Marsh, Ngaio)
1940   Death of a Peer [Britain–Surfeit of Campreys]
            (Marsh, Ngaio)
1940   The Man in the Moonlight (McCloy, Helen)
1940   Murder in the Mist (Popkin, Zelda)
1940   Time Off for Murder (Popkin, Zelda)
1940   Death Demands an Audience (Reilly, Helen)
1940   Murder in Shinbone Alley (Reilly, Helen)
1940   The Dead Can Tell (Reilly, Helen)
1940   The Criminal C.O.D. (Taylor, Phoebe Atwood)
1940   The Deadly Sunshade (Taylor, Phoebe Atwood)
1940   The Left Leg (Tilton, Alice)
1940   Crime Incarnate (Wells, Carolyn)
1940   Devil's Work (Wells, Carolyn)
1940   Murder on Parade (Wells, Carolyn)
1940   Murder Plus (Wells, Carolyn)

1941   Traitor's Purse [U.S.–The Sabotage Murder
            Mystery] (Allingham, Margery)
1941   Pencil Points to Murder (Barber, Willetta A.)
1941   Heads You Lose (Brand, Christianna)
1941   Evil Under the Sun (Christie, Agatha)
1941   Five Little Pigs [U.S.–Murder in Retrospect]
            (Christie, Agatha)
1941   N or M? (Christie, Agatha)
1941   The Turquoise Shop (Crane, Frances)
1941   Murder in Volume 2 (Daly, Elizabeth)
1941   A Pinch of Poison (Lockridge, Frances & Richard)
1941   Murder Out of Turn (Lockridge, Frances & Richard)
1941   Death and the Dancing Footman (Marsh, Ngaio)
1941   The Deadly Truth (McCloy, Helen)
1941   The Invisible Worm (Millar, Margaret)
1941   When Last I Died (Mitchell, Gladys)
1941   Dead Man's Gift (Popkin, Zelda)
1941   Mourned on Sunday (Reilly, Helen)
1941   Three Women in Black (Reilly, Helen)
1941   The Perennial Border (Taylor, Phoebe Atwood)
1941   The Hollow Chest (Tilton, Alice)
1941   Murder at the Casino (Wells, Carolyn)
1941   The Black Night Murders (Wells, Carolyn)
1941   In the Balance [Britain–Danger Point]
            (Wentworth, Patricia)

1942   Lay on, Mac Duff! (Armstrong, Charlotte)
1942   Drawn Conclusion (Barber, Willetta A.)
1942   Murder Enters the Picture (Barber, Willetta A.)
1942   The Body in the Library (Christie, Agatha)
1942   The Moving Finger (Christie, Agatha)
1942   The Golden Box (Crane, Frances)
1942   The House Without the Door (Daly, Elizabeth)
1942   Wolf in Man's Clothing (Eberhart, Mignon Good)
1942   Death on the Aisle (Lockridge, Frances & Richard)
1942   Hanged for a Sheep
            (Lockridge, Frances & Richard)
1942   Cue for Murder (McCloy, Helen)
1942   Who's Calling (McCloy, Helen)
1942   The Devil Loves Me (Millar, Margaret)
1942   The Weak-Eyed Bat (Millar, Margaret)
1942   Laurels are Poison (Mitchell, Gladys)
1942   No Crime for a Lady (Popkin, Zelda)
1942   Name Your Poison (Reilly, Helen)
1942   Haunted Lady (Rinehart, Mary Roberts)

1942   3 Plots for Asey Mayo (Taylor, Phoebe Atwood)
1942   Six Iron Spiders (Taylor, Phoebe Atwood)
1942   Who Killed Caldwell (Wells, Carolyn)

1943   The Case of the Weird Sisters (Armstrong,
            Charlotte)
1943   The Applegreen Cat (Crane, Frances)
1943   The Pink Umbrella (Crane, Frances)
1943   The Yellow Violet (Crane, Frances)
1943   Evidence of Things Seen (Daly, Elizabeth)
1943   Norhing Can Rescue Me (Daly, Elizabeth)
1943   Death Takes a Bow (Lockridge, Frances & Richard)
1943   Color Scheme (Marsh, Ngaio)
1943   The Goblin Market (McCloy, Helen)
1943   Wall of Eyes (Millar, Margaret)
1943   Going, Going, Gone (Taylor, Phoebe Atwood)
1943   File for Record (Tilton, Alice)
1943   The Chinese Shawl (Wentworth, Patricia)

1944   Death at the Medical Board (Bell, Josephine)
1944   Green for Danger (Brand, Christianna)
1944   The Amethyst Spectacles (Crane, Frances)
1944   Arrow Pointing Nowhere (Daly, Elizabeth)
1944   The Book of the Dead (Daly, Elizabeth)
1944   Killing the Goose (Lockridge, Frances & Richard)
1944   The Opening Door (Reilly, Helen)
1944   Dead Earnest (Tilton, Alice)
1944   Miss Silver Deals with Death [Britain–Miss S.
            Intervenes] (Wentworth, Patricia)
1944   The Clock Strikes Twelve (Wentworth, Patricia)
1944   The Key (Wentworth, Patricia)

1945   Coroner's Pidgin [U.S.–Pearls Before Swine]
            (Allingham, Margery)
1945   The Innocent Flower (Armstrong, Charlotte)
1945   The Indigo Necklace (Crane, Frances)
1945   Any Shape or Form (Daly, Elizabeth)
1945   Payoff for the Banker
            (Lockridge, Frances & Richard)
1945   Dyed in the Wool (Marsh, Ngaio)
1945   The One That Got Away (McCloy, Helen)
1945   The Iron Gates (Millar, Margaret)
1945   The Rising of the Moon (Mitchell, Gladys)
1945   Murder on Angler's Island (Reilly, Helen)
1945   Proof of the Pudding (Taylor, Phoebe Atwood)
1945   She Came Back [Britain–The Traveller Returns]
            (Wentworth, Patricia)

1946   Suddenly at his Residence [U.S.–The Crooked
            Wreath] (Brand, Christianna)
1946   The Hollow [U.S.–Murder After Hours]
            (Christie, Agatha)
1946   The Cinnamon Murder (Crane, Frances)
1946   The Shocking Pink Hat (Crane, Frances)
1946   Somewhere in the House (Daly, Elizabeth)
1946   The Wrong Way Down (Daly, Elizabeth)
1946   Dark Road (Disney, Doris Miles)
1946   Death of a Tall Man (Lockridge, Frances & Richard)
1946   Murder within Murder
            (Lockridge, Frances & Richard)
1946   The Silver Leopard (Reilly, Helen)
1946   Punch with Care (Taylor, Phoebe Atwood)
1946   The Asey Mayo Trio (Taylor, Phoebe Atwood)
1946   Pilgrim's Rest (Wentworth, Patricia)

1947   Murder on the Purple Water (Crane, Frances)
1947   Night Walk (Daly, Elizabeth)
1947   Untidy Murder (Lockridge, Frances & Richard)
1947   Final Curtain (Marsh, Ngaio)
1947   The Farmhouse (Reilly, Helen)

1940s . . . continued

1947   The Iron Clew (Britain–The Iron Hand) (Tilton, Alice)
1947   The Latter End (Wentworth, Patricia)
1947   Wicked Uncle [Britain–The Spotlight]
      (Wentworth, Patricia)

1948   Death of a Jezebel (Brand, Christianna)
1948   Taken at the Flood [U.S.–There is a Tide]
      (Christie, Agatha)
1948   Black Cypress (Crane, Frances)
1948   The Book of the Lion (Daly, Elizabeth)
1948   Murder is Served (Lockridge, Frances & Richard)
1948   The Dancing Druids (Mitchell, Gladys)
1948   The Case of William Smith (Wentworth, Patricia)
1948   The Eternity Ring (Wentworth, Patricia)

1949   More Work for the Undertaker (Allingham, Margery)
1949   Death in Clairvoyance (Bell, Josephine)
1949   The Flying Red Horse (Crane, Frances)
1949   And Dangerous to Know (Daly, Elizabeth)
1949   Family Skeleton (Disney, Doris Miles)
1949   The Dishonest Murder
      (Lockridge, Frances & Richard)
1949   Swing, Brother, Swing [U.S.–A Wreath for Rivera]
      (Marsh, Ngaio)
1949   Tom Brown's Body (Mitchell, Gladys)
1949   Staircase 4 (Reilly, Helen)
1949   The Gun in Daniel Webster's Bust
      (Scherf, Margaret)
1949   The Franchise Affair (Tey, Josephine)
1949   Miss Silver Comes to Stay (Wentworth, Patricia)
1949   The Catharine Wheel (Wentworth, Patricia)

1950s

1950   The Summer School Mystery (Bell, Josephine)
1950   A Murder is Announced (Christie, Agatha)
1950   The Daffodil Blonde (Crane, Frances)
1950   Death and Letters (Daly, Elizabeth)
1950   Murder in a Hurry (Lockridge, Frances & Richard)
1950   Through a Glass Darkly (McCloy, Helen)
1950   Murder at Arroways (Reilly, Helen)
1950   To Love and Be Wise (Tey, Josephine)
1950   The Ivory Dagger (Wentworth, Patricia)
1950   Through the Wall (Wentworth, Patricia)

1951   Murder in Blue Street [Britain–Murder in Blue Hour]
      (Crane, Frances)
1951   The Polkadot Murder (Crane, Frances)
1951   The Book of the Crime (Daly, Elizabeth)
1951   Straw Man [Britain–The Case of the Straw Man]
      (Disney, Doris Miles)
1951   Murder Comes First (Lockridge, Frances & Richard)
1951   Opening Night [U.S.–Night at the Vulcan]
      (Marsh, Ngaio)
1951   Alias Basil Willing (McCloy, Helen)
1951   Fallen into the Pit (Pargeter, Edith)
1951   Lament for the Bride (Reilly, Helen)
1951   Diplomatic Corpse (Taylor, Phoebe Atwood)
1951   The Daughter of Time (Tey, Josephine)
1951   Anna, Where Are You? (Wentworth, Patricia)
1951   Watersplash (Wentworth, Patricia)

1952   The Tiger in the Smoke (Allingham, Margery)
1952   Mrs. McGinty's Dead [U.S.–Blood Will Tell]
      (Christie, Agatha)

1952   They Do It with Mirrors [U.S.–Murder With Mirrors]
      (Christie, Agatha)
1952   Dead as a Dinosaur (Lockridge, Frances & Richard)
1952   The Double Man (Reilly, Helen)
1952   The Wandering Knife (Rinehart, Mary Roberts)
1952   The Singing Sands (Tey, Josephine)
1952   Ladies' Bane (Wentworth, Patricia)

1953   Bones in the Barrow (Bell, Josephine)
1953   London Particular [U.S.–Fog of Doubt]
      (Brand, Christianna)
1953   A Pocket Full of Rye (Christie, Agatha)
1953   After the Funeral [U.S.–Funerals are Fatal]
      (Christie, Agatha)
1953   Murder in Bright Red (Crane, Frances)
1953   Thirteen White Tulips (Crane, Frances)
1953   Curtain for a Jester (Lockridge, Frances & Richard)
1953   Death Has a Small Voice
      (Lockridge, Frances & Richard)
1953   Spinsters in Jeopardy (Marsh, Ngaio)
1953   The Velvet Hand (Reilly, Helen)
1953   Out of the Past (Wentworth, Patricia)
1953   The Silent Pool (Wentworth, Patricia)
1953   The Vanishing Point (Wentworth, Patricia)

1954   No Love Lost (Allingham, Margery)
1954   The Coral Princess Murders (Crane, Frances)
1954   Man Missing (Eberhart, Mignon Good)
1954   A Key to Death (Lockridge, Frances & Richard)
1954   Faintly Speaking (Mitchell, Gladys)
1954   Tell Her It's Murder (Reilly, Helen)
1954   The Benevent Treasure (Wentworth, Patricia)

1955   The Beckoning Lady [U.S.–The Estate of the
      Beckoning Lady] (Allingham, Margery)
1955   Tour de Force (Brand, Christianna)
1955   Hickory, Dickory, Dock [U.S.–Hickory, Dickory,
      Death] (Christie, Agatha)
1955   Death in Lilac Time (Crane, Frances)
1955   Trick or Treat [Britain–The Halloween Murder]
      (Disney, Doris Miles)
1955   The Talented Mr. Ripley (Highsmith, Patricia)
1955   Death of an Angel (Lockridge, Frances & Richard)
1955   Scales of Justice (Marsh, Ngaio)
1955   The Long Body (McCloy, Helen)
1955   Watson's Choice (Mitchell, Gladys)
1955   Compartment K [Britain–Murder Rides the Express]
      (Reilly, Helen)
1955   The Gazebo (Wentworth, Patricia)
1955   The Listening Eye (Wentworth, Patricia)

1956   The China Roundabout [U.S.–Murder on the Merry-
      Go-Round] (Bell, Josephine)
1956   Dead Man's Folly (Christie, Agatha)
1956   Horror on the Ruby X (Crane, Frances)
1956   The Ultraviolet Widow (Crane, Frances)
1956   Shroud for a Lady (Daly, Elizabeth)
1956   Voyage into Violence
      (Lockridge, Frances & Richard)
1956   Death of a Fool [Britain–Off With His Head]
      (Marsh, Ngaio)
1956   Two-thirds of a Ghost (McCloy, Helen)
1956   The Canvas Dagger (Reilly, Helen)
1956   The Fingerprint (Wentworth, Patricia)

1957   Dead in a Row (Butler, Gwendoline)
1957   4:50 from Paddington [U.S.–What Mrs.
      McGillicuddy Saw] (Christie, Agatha)
1957   Method in Madness [Britain–Quiet Violence]
      (Disney, Doris Miles)

1950s . . . continued

1957   Poison in the Pen (Wentworth, Patricia)

1958   Ten Were Missing (Allingham, Margery)
1958   The Seeing Eye (Bell, Josephine)
1958   The Dull Dead (Butler, Gwendoline)
1958   The Murdering Kind (Butler, Gwendoline)
1958   The Buttercup Case (Crane, Frances)
1958   The Man in Gray [Britain–The Gray Stranger]
           (Crane, Frances)
1958   The Long Skeleton (Lockridge, Frances & Richard)
1958   Swinging in the Shrouds (Marsh, Ngaio)
1958   Spotted Hemlock (Mitchell, Gladys)
1958   Ding Dong Bell (Reilly, Helen)
1958   The Malignant Heart (Sibley, Celestine)
1958   The Alington Inheritance (Wentworth, Patricia)

1959   Cat Among the Pigeons (Christie, Agatha)
1959   Did She Fall or Was She Pushed?
           (Disney, Doris Miles)
1959   Murder is Suggested
           (Lockridge, Frances & Richard)
1959   False Scent (Marsh, Ngaio)
1959   Dead Men Don't Ski (Moyes, Patricia)
1959   Not Me, Inspector (Reilly, Helen)

1960s

1960   Death Lives Next Door (Butler, Gwendoline)
1960   Death Wish Green (Crane, Frances)
1960   The Judge is Reversed
           (Lockridge, Frances & Richard)
1960   Say It with Flowers (Mitchell, Gladys)
1960   Follow Me (Reilly, Helen)
1960   Case Pending (Shannon, Dell)
1960   The Ace of Spades (Shannon, Dell)

1961   Make Me a Murderer (Butler, Gwendoline)
1961   Banking on Death (Lathen, Emma)
1961   Murder Has its Points
           (Lockridge, Frances & Richard)
1961   Down Among the Dead Men (Moyes, Patricia)
1961   Certain Sleep (Reilly, Helen)
1961   Extra Kill (Shannon, Dell)
1961   The Girl in the Cellar (Wentworth, Patricia)

1962   The China Governess (Allingham, Margery)
1962   Coffin in Oxford (Butler, Gwendoline)
1962   The Mirror Cracked from Side to Side [U.S.–The
           Mirror Cracked] (Christie, Agatha)
1962   The Amber Eyes (Crane, Frances)
1962   Find the Woman (Disney, Doris Miles)
1962   Cover Her Face (James, P. D.)
1962   Hand in Glove (Marsh, Ngaio)
1962   Come Home and Be Killed (Melville, Jennie)
1962   Death on the Agenda (Moyes, Patricia)
1962   Death and the Joyful Woman (Pargeter, Edith)
1962   The Day She Died (Reilly, Helen)
1962   Knave of Hearts (Shannon, Dell)
1962   Bloody Instructions (Woods, Sara)
1962   Malice Domestic (Woods, Sara)

1963   A Coffin for Baby (Butler, Gwendoline)
1963   The Clocks (Christie, Agatha)
1963   A Mind to Murder (James, P. D.)
1963   A Place for Murder (Lathen, Emma)
1963   Murder by the Book (Lockridge, Frances & Richard)

1963   Dead Water (Marsh, Ngaio)
1963   Burning is a Substitute for Loving (Melville, Jennie)
1963   Murder a la Mode (Moyes, Patricia)
1963   The Diplomat and the Gold Piano (Scherf,
           Margaret)
1963   Death of a Busybody (Shannon, Dell)
1963   Double Bluff (Shannon, Dell)
1963   Error of the Moon (Woods, Sara)
1963   The Taste of Fears [U.S.–The Third Encounter]
           (Woods, Sara)

1964   Coffin Waiting (Butler, Gwendoline)
1964   A Caribbean Mystery (Christie, Agatha)
1964   In the Last Analysis (Cross, Amanda)
1964   The Transcendental Murder (Langton, Jane)
1964   Accounting for Murder (Lathen, Emma)
1964   Is There a Traitor in the House (McGerr, Patricia)
1964   Murderer's Houses (Melville, Jennie)
1964   Death of a Delft Blue (Mitchell, Gladys)
1964   Falling Star (Moyes, Patricia)
1964   Flight of a Witch (Pargeter, Edith)
1964   From Doon With Death (Rendell, Ruth)
1964   Mark of Murder (Shannon, Dell)
1964   Root of All Evil (Shannon, Dell)
1964   This Little Measure (Woods, Sara)
1964   Trusted Like the Fox (Woods, Sara)

1965   The Mind Readers (Allingham, Margery)
1965   At Bertram's Hotel (Christie, Agatha)
1965   The Body Beneath a Mandarin Tree (Crane,
           Frances)
1965   There Lies Your Love (Melville, Jennie)
1965   Johnny Underground (Moyes, Patricia)
1965   A Nice Derangement of Epitaphs [U.S.–Who Lies
           Here] (Pargeter, Edith)
1965   Death by Inches (Shannon, Dell)
1965   The Death-Bringers (Shannon, Dell)
1965   The Windy Side of the Law (Woods, Sara)
1965   Though I Know She Lies (Woods, Sara)

1966   The Religious Body (Aird, Catherine)
1966   The Cat Who Could Read Backwards
           (Braun, Lilian Jackson)
1966   A Nameless Coffin (Butler, Gwendoline)
1966   Third Girl (Christie, Agatha)
1966   The Unexpected Mrs. Pollifax (Gilman, Dorothy)
1966   Death Shall Overcome (Lathen, Emma)
1966   Murder Makes the Wheels Go 'Round
           (Lathen, Emma)
1966   Killer Dolphin [Britain–Death at the Dolphin]
           (Marsh, Ngaio)
1966   Nell Alone (Melville, Jennie)
1966   Heavy as Lead (Mitchell, Gladys)
1966   The Piper on the Mountain (Pargeter, Edith)
1966   Chance to Kill (Shannon, Dell)
1966   Coffin Corner (Shannon, Dell)
1966   With a Vengeance (Shannon, Dell)
1966   Enter Certain Murderers (Woods, Sara)
1966   Let's Choose Executors (Woods, Sara)

1967   The Cat Who Ate Danish Modern
           (Braun, Lilian Jackson)
1967   The James Joyce Murder (Cross, Amanda)
1967   Unnatural Causes (James, P. D.)
1967   Murder Against the Grain (Lathen, Emma)
1967   A Different Kind of Summer (Melville, Jennie)
1967   Late and Cold (Mitchell, Gladys)
1967   Murder Fantastical (Moyes, Patricia)
1967   Black is the Colour of My True Love's Heart
           (Pargeter, Edith)

1960s . . . continued

1967 A New Lease on Death (Rendell, Ruth)
1967 A Wolf to Slaughter (Rendell, Ruth)
1967 Rain with Violence (Shannon, Dell)
1967 And Shame the Devil (Woods, Sara)
1967 The Case is Altered (Woods, Sara)

1968 Henrietta Who? (Aird, Catherine)
1968 Cargo of Eagles (Allingham, Margery)
1968 The Cat Who Turned On and Off
         (Braun, Lilian Jackson)
1968 Coffin Following (Butler, Gwendoline)
1968 By the Pricking of My Thumbs (Christie, Agatha)
1968 Murder Sunny Side Up (Dominic, R. B.)
1968 A Stitch in Time (Lathen, Emma)
1968 Come to Dust (Lathen, Emma)
1968 Mr. Splitfoot (McCloy, Helen)
1968 Your Secret Friend (Mitchell, Gladys)
1968 Death and the Dutch Uncle (Moyes, Patricia)
1968 The Grass Widow's Tale (Pargeter, Edith)
1968 The Banker's Bones (Scherf, Margaret)
1968 Kill with Kindness (Shannon, Dell)
1968 The Bait (Uhnak, Dorothy)
1968 Knives Have Edges (Woods, Sara)
1968 Past Praying For (Woods, Sara)

1969 The Complete Steel [U.S.–The Stately Home
         Murder] (Aird, Catherine)
1969 Mr. Campion's Farthing (Allingham, Margery)
1969 Coffin's Dark Number (Butler, Gwendoline)
1969 Halowe'en Party (Christie, Agatha)
1969 Murder to Go (Lathen, Emma)
1969 When in Greece (Lathen, Emma)
1969 Clutch of Constables (Marsh, Ngaio)
1969 Churchyard Salad (Mitchell, Gladys)
1969 Morning Raga (Pargeter, Edith)
1969 The House of Green Turf (Pargeter, Edith)
1969 The Best Man to Die (Rendell, Ruth)
1969 Crime on Their Hands (Shannon, Dell)
1969 Schooled to Kill (Shannon, Dell)
1969 The Witness (Uhnak, Dorothy)
1969 Tarry and Be Hanged (Woods, Sara)

1970s

1970 A Late Phoenix (Aird, Catherine)
1970 Mr. Campion's Falcon [U.S.–Mr. Campion's Quarry]
         (Allingham, Margery)
1970 A Coffin from the Past (Butler, Gwendoline)
1970 Poetic Justice (Cross, Amanda)
1970 Murder in High Place (Dominic, R. B.)
1970 The Amazing Mrs. Pollifax (Gilman, Dorothy)
1970 Ripley Underground (Highsmith, Patricia)
1970 Pick Up Sticks (Lathen, Emma)
1970 Legacy of Danger (McGerr, Patricia)
1970 A New Kind of Killer (Melville, Jennie)
1970 Shades of Darkness (Mitchell, Gladys)
1970 Death in the Grand Manor (Morice, Ann)
1970 Many Deadly Returns (Moyes, Patricia)
1970 The Knocker on Death's Door (Pargeter, Edith)
1970 A Guilty Thing Surprised (Rendell, Ruth)
1970 Unexpected Death (Shannon, Dell)
1970 The Ledger (Uhnak, Dorothy)
1970 An Improbable Fiction (Woods, Sara)
1970 Dead in the Morning (Yorke, Margaret)

1971 Cover-up Story (Babson, Marian)
1971 Nemesis (Christie, Agatha)
1971 The Chandler Policy (Disney, Doris Miles)
1971 To Spite Her Face (Dolson, Hildegarde)
1971 There is No Justice (Dominic, R. B.)
1971 The Elusive Mrs. Pollifax (Gilman, Dorothy)
1971 Shroud for a Nightingale (James, P. D.)
1971 Ashes to Ashes (Lathen, Emma)
1971 The Longer the Thread (Lathen, Emma)
1971 When in Rome (Marsh, Ngaio)
1971 Bismarck Herrings (Mitchell, Gladys)
1971 Murder in Married Life (Morice, Ann)
1971 Season of Snows and Sins (Moyes, Patricia)
1971 No More Dying Then (Rendell, Ruth)
1971 The Ringer (Shannon, Dell)
1971 Whim to Kill (Shannon, Dell)
1971 Not One of Us (Thomson, June)
1971 Serpent's Tooth (Woods, Sara)
1971 The Knavish Crows (Woods, Sara)

1972 Murder on Show [U.S.–Murder at the Cat Show]
         (Babson, Marian)
1972 Elephants Can Remember (Christie, Agatha)
1972 The Theban Mysteries (Cross, Amanda)
1972 An Unsuitable Job for a Woman (James, P. D.)
1972 Murder Without Icing (Lathen, Emma)
1972 Troublecross [U.S.–The Only Security]
         (Mann, Jessica)
1972 Tied up in Tinsel (Marsh, Ngaio)
1972 Death in the Round (Morice, Ann)
1972 The Phone Calls (O'Donnell, Lillian)
1972 Death to the Landlords! (Pargeter, Edith)
1972 The Seventh Sinner (Peters, Elizabeth)
1972 Murder Being Once Done (Rendell, Ruth)
1972 To Cache a Millionaire (Scherf, Margaret)
1972 Murder with Love (Shannon, Dell)
1972 With Intent to Kill (Shannon, Dell)
1972 They Love Not Poison (Woods, Sara)
1972 Silent Witness (Yorke, Margaret)

1973 His Burial Too (Aird, Catherine)
1973 Postern of Fate (Christie, Agatha)
1973 A Dying Fall (Dolson, Hildegarde)
1973 A Palm for Mrs. Pollifax (Gilman, Dorothy)
1973 Lady With a Cool Eye (Moffat, Gwen)
1973 Death of a Dog (Morice, Ann)
1973 Murder on French Leave (Morice, Ann)
1973 The Curious Affair of the Third Dog
         (Moyes, Patricia)
1973 Don't Wear Your Wedding Ring (O'Donnell, Lillian)
1973 City of Gold and Shadows (Pargeter, Edith)
1973 Borrower of the Night (Peters, Elizabeth)
1973 Some Lie and Some Die (Rendell, Ruth)
1973 No Holiday for Crime (Shannon, Dell)
1973 Spring of Violence (Shannon, Dell)
1973 Death Cap (Thomson, June)
1973 Enter the Corpse (Woods, Sara)
1973 Yet She Must Die (Woods, Sara)
1973 Curiosity Didn't Kill the Cat (Wren, M. K.)
1973 Grave Matters (Yorke, Margaret)

1974 A Coffin for the Canary [U.S.–Sarsen Place]
         (Butler, Gwendoline)
1974 Epitaph for a Lobbyist (Dominic, R. B.)
1974 Ripley's Game (Highsmith, Patricia)
1974 Sweet and Low (Lathen, Emma)
1974 Black as He's Painted (Marsh, Ngaio)
1974 Death of a Dutiful Daughter (Morice, Ann)
1974 Death of a Heavenly Twin (Morice, Ann)

1970s . . . continued

1974   Dial 557 R-A-P-E (O'Donnell, Lillian)
1974   The Murders of Richard III (Peters, Elizabeth)
1974   Crime File (Shannon, Dell)
1974   The Long Revenge (Thomson, June)
1974   Done to Death (Woods, Sara)
1974   Mortal Remains (Yorke, Margaret)

1975   Slight Mourning (Aird, Catherine)
1975   The Last Curtain (Christie, Agatha)
1975   Please Omit Funeral (Dolson, Hildegarde)
1975   The Black Tower (James, P. D.)
1975   Dark Nantucket Noon (Langton, Jane)
1975   By Hook or By Crook (Lathen, Emma)
1975   Captive Audience (Mann, Jessica)
1975   Miss Pink at the Edge of the World (Moffat, Gwen)
1975   Killing with Kindness (Morice, Ann)
1975   Nursery Tea and Poison (Morice, Ann)
1975   Black Widower (Moyes, Patricia)
1975   The Baby Merchants (O'Donnell, Lillian)
1975   Crocodile on the Sandbank (Peters, Elizabeth)
1975   Shake Hands Forever (Rendell, Ruth)
1975   Deuces Wild (Shannon, Dell)
1975   A Show of Violence (Woods, Sara)
1975   A Multitude of Sins (Wren, M. K.)

1976   Sleeping Murder (Christie, Agatha)
1976   The Question of Max (Cross, Amanda)
1976   A Death in the Life (Davis, Dorothy Salisbury)
1976   Murder out of Commission (Dominic, R. B.)
1976   Mrs. Pollifax on Safari (Gilman, Dorothy)
1976   The Big Payoff (Law, Janice)
1976   Someone is Killing the Great Chefs of Europe
          (Lyons, Nan & Ivan)
1976   Ask Me for Tomorrow (Millar, Margaret)
1976   Over the Sea to Death (Moffat, Gwen)
1976   Death of a Wedding Guest (Morice, Ann)
1976   Leisure Dying (O'Donnell, Lillian)
1976   Streets of Death (Shannon, Dell)
1976   A Medium for Murder (Warner, Mignon)
1976   My Life is Done (Woods, Sara)
1976   Ogilvie, Tallant and Moon [Bad Medicine in '90]
          (Yarbro, Chelsea Quinn)
1976   Cast for Death (Yorke, Margaret)

1977   Parting Breath (Aird, Catherine)
1977   Beauty Sleep (Dolson, Hildegarde)
1977   Quiet as a Nun (Fraser, Antonia Pakenham)
1977   Death of an Expert Witness (James, P. D.)
1977   Gemini Trip (Law, Janice)
1977   Last Ditch (Marsh, Ngaio)
1977   Murder in Mimicry (Morice, Ann)
1977   Scared to Death (Morice, Ann)
1977   The Coconut Killings (Moyes, Patricia)
1977   Edwin of the Iron Shoes (Muller, Marcia)
1977   Aftershock (O'Donnell, Lillian)
1977   A Morbid Taste for Bones (Peters, Ellis)
1977   Appearances of Death (Shannon, Dell)
1977   A Question of Identity (Thomson, June)
1977   Case Closed (Thomson, June)
1977   The Fourth Stage of Gainsborough Brown
          (Watson, Clarissa)
1977   A Thief or Two (Woods, Sara)
1977   The Law's Delay (Woods, Sara)
1977   Oh Bury Me Not (Wren, M. K.)

1978   In at the Kill (Ferrars, E. X.)
1978   Last Will and Testament (Ferrars, E. X.)
1978   The Wild Island (Fraser, Antonia Pakenham)
1978   Fair Game [Britain–A Running Duck]
          (Gosling, Paula)
1978   The Memorial Hall Murder (Langton, Jane)
1978   Double, Double, Oil and Trouble (Lathen, Emma)
1978   Under Orion (Law, Janice)
1978   Rest You Merry (MacLeod, Charlotte)
1978   Grave Mistake (Marsh, Ngaio)
1978   Persons Unknown (Moffat, Gwen)
1978   Murder by Proxy (Morice, Ann)
1978   Rainbow's End (Pargeter, Edith)
1978   Street of the Five Moons (Peters, Elizabeth)
1978   Death and the Maiden [U.S.–Death in the Morning]
          (Radley, Sheila)
1978   A Sleeping Life (Rendell, Ruth)
1978   The Beaded Banana (Scherf, Margaret)
1978   Death on the Slopes (Schier, Norma)
1978   Cold Trail (Shannon, Dell)
1978   The Tarot Murders (Warner, Mignon)
1978   Exit Murderer (Woods, Sara)
1978   Nothing's Certain But Death (Wren, M. K.)

1979   Some Die Eloquent (Aird, Catherine)
1979   Exit Actors, Dying (Arnold, Margot)
1979   Zadock's Treasure (Arnold, Margot)
1979   A Leaven of Malice (Curzon, Clare)
1979   Introducing C. B. Greenfield (Kallen, Lucille)
1979   The Family Vault (MacLeod, Charlotte)
1979   The Luck Runs Out (MacLeod, Charlotte)
1979   The Murder of Miranda (Millar, Margaret)
1979   Murder in Outline (Morice, Ann)
1979   Who is Simon Warwick? (Moyes, Patricia)
1979   Falling Star (O'Donnell, Lillian)
1979   No Business Being a Cop (O'Donnell, Lillian)
1979   The Cater Street Hangman (Perry, Anne)
1979   One Corpse Too Many (Peters, Ellis)
1979   Death Goes Skiing (Schier, Norma)
1979   Murder by the Book (Schier, Norma)
1979   Felony at Random (Shannon, Dell)
1979   Deadly Relations [U.S.–The Habit of Loving]
          (Thomson, June)
1979   Proceed to Judgement (Woods, Sara)
1979   This Fatal Writ (Woods, Sara)

1980s

1980   Passing Strange (Aird, Catherine)
1980   The Cape Cod Caper (Arnold, Margot)
1980   Dupe (Cody, Liza)
1980   A Pint of Murder (Craig, Alisa)
1980   The Hands of Healing Murder (D'Amato, Barbara)
1980   Scarlet Night (Davis, Dorothy Salisbury)
1980   The Attending Physician (Dominic, R. B.)
1980   Frog in the Throat (Ferrars, E. X.)
1980   Death and the Pregnant Virgin (Haymon, S. T.)
1980   The Boy Who Followed Ripley (Highsmith, Patricia)
1980   The Tanglewood Murder (Kallen, Lucille)
1980   The Shadow of the Palms (Law, Janice)
1980   The Withdrawing Room (MacLeod, Charlotte)
1980   Photo-Finish (Marsh, Ngaio)
1980   Burn This (McCloy, Helen)
1980   Angel Death (Moyes, Patricia)
1980   Death is Forever (O'Callaghan, Maxine)
1980   Wicked Designs (O'Donnell, Lillian)
1980   Sports Freak (OCork, Shannon)
1980   Callander Square (Perry, Anne)

1980s . . . continued

1980 Monk's Hood (Peters, Ellis)
1980 The Chief Inspector's Daughter (Radley, Sheila)
1980 Demon at the Opera (Schier, Norma)
1980 Felony File (Shannon, Dell)
1980 Alibi in Time (Thomson, June)
1980 Death in Time (Warner, Mignon)
1980 The Bishop in the Back Seat (Watson, Clarissa)
1980 They Stay for Death (Woods, Sara)
1980 Weep for Her (Woods, Sara)

1981 Thus Was Adonis Murdered (Caudwell, Sarah)
1981 Murder Goes Mumming (Craig, Alisa)
1981 The Grub-and-Stakers Move a Mountain
      (Craig, Alisa)
1981 Death in a Tenured Position (Cross, Amanda)
1981 Special Occasion (Curzon, Clare)
1981 The Eyes on Utopia Murders (D'Amato, Barbara)
1981 Karma (Dunlap, Susan)
1981 Thinner than Water (Ferrars, E. X.)
1981 A Splash of Red (Fraser, Antonia Pakenham)
1981 The Man with a Load of Mischief (Grimes, Martha)
1981 Going for the Gold (Lathen, Emma)
1981 Death Under Par (Law, Janice)
1981 The Palace Guard (MacLeod, Charlotte)
1981 One Coffee With (Maron, Margaret)
1981 Murder Has a Pretty Face (Melville, Jennie)
1981 The Death-Cap Dancers (Mitchell, Gladys)
1981 Men in Her Death (Morice, Ann)
1981 Death of an Englishman (Nabb, Magdalen)
1981 Run from Nightmare (O'Callaghan, Maxine)
1981 The Children's Zoo (O'Donnell, Lillian)
1981 End of the Line (OCork, Shannon)
1981 Paragon Walk (Perry, Anne)
1981 Resurrection Row (Perry, Anne)
1981 The Curse of the Pharaohs (Peters, Elizabeth)
1981 St. Peter's Fair (Peters, Ellis)
1981 The Leper of St. Giles (Peters, Ellis)
1981 Put on by Cunning [U.S.–Death Notes]
      (Rendell, Ruth)
1981 Murder Most Strange (Shannon, Dell)
1981 The Night She Died (Simpson, Dorothy)
1981 The Cable Car Murder (Taylor, Elizabeth Atwood)
1981 Shadow of a Doubt (Thomson, June)
1981 Cry Guilty (Woods, Sara)
1981 Dearest Enemy (Woods, Sara)
1981 Seasons of Death (Wren, M. K.)

1982 Last Respects (Aird, Catherine)
1982 Death of a Voodoo Doll (Arnold, Margot)
1982 Death on a Dragon's Tongue (Arnold, Margot)
1982 Lament for a Lady Laird (Arnold, Margot)
1982 Blood Will Have Blood (Barnes, Linda)
1982 The Case of the Hook-Billed Kites (Borthwick, J. S.)
1982 Bad Company (Cody, Liza)
1982 Cool Repentance (Fraser, Antonia Pakenham)
1982 "A" is for Alibi (Grafton, Sue)
1982 The Old Fox Deceived (Grimes, Martha)
1982 Ritual Murder (Haymon, S. T.)
1982 The Skull Beneath the Skin (James, P. D.)
1982 Devices and Desires (James, P. D.)
1982 No Lady in the House (Kallen, Lucille)
1982 Natural Enemy (Langton, Jane)
1982 Green Grow the Dollars (Lathen, Emma)
1982 Wrack and Rune (MacLeod, Charlotte)
1982 Funeral Sites (Mann, Jessica)
1982 Light Thickens (Marsh, Ngaio)

1982 Mermaid (Millar, Margaret)
1982 Die Like a Dog (Moffat, Gwen)
1982 Miss Pink's Mistake (Moffat, Gwen)
1982 Hollow Vengeance (Morice, Ann)
1982 Sleep of Death (Morice, Ann)
1982 Ask the Cards a Question (Muller, Marcia)
1982 Murder in Pug's Parlour (Myers, Amy)
1982 Death of a Dutchman (Nabb, Magdalen)
1982 Indemnity Only (Paretsky, Sara)
1982 The Virgin in the Ice (Peters, Ellis)
1982 A Talent for Destruction (Radley, Sheila)
1982 The Cooking School Murders (Rich, Virginia)
1982 The Motive on Record (Shannon, Dell)
1982 Six Feet Under (Simpson, Dorothy)
1982 Death Turns a Trick (Smith, Julie)
1982 To Make a Killing [U.S.–Portrait of Lilith]
      (Thomson, June)
1982 The Girl Who Was Clairvoyant (Warner, Mignon)
1982 Enter a Gentlewoman (Woods, Sara)
1982 Most Grievous Murder (Woods, Sara)
1982 Villains by Necessity (Woods, Sara)

1983 Bitter Finish (Barnes, Linda)
1983 The Terrible Tide (Craig, Alisa)
1983 I Give You Five Days (Curzon, Clare)
1983 Murder on Cue (Dentinger, Jane)
1983 An Equal Opportunity Death (Dunlap, Susan)
1983 Death of a Minor Character (Ferrars, E. X.)
1983 Mrs. Pollifax on the China Station (Gilman, Dorothy)
1983 The Anondyne Necklace (Grimes, Martha)
1983 The Lost Madonna (Holland, Isabelle)
1983 Garden of Malice (Kenney, Susan)
1983 Something the Cat Dragged In
      (MacLeod, Charlotte)
1983 The Bilbao Looking Glass (MacLeod, Charlotte)
1983 No Man's Island (Mann, Jessica)
1983 A Perfect Match (McGown, Jill)
1983 With Flowers that Fell [#1 in Britain]
      (Meek, M. R. D.)
1983 Last Chance Country (Moffat, Gwen)
1983 Murder Post-Dated (Morice, Ann)
1983 A Six-Letter Word for Death (Moyes, Patricia)
1983 The Cheshire Cat's Eye (Muller, Marcia)
1983 The Tree of Death (Muller, Marcia)
1983 Death in Springtime (Nabb, Magdalen)
1983 Cop Without a Shield (O'Donnell, Lillian)
1983 Hell Bent for Heaven (OCork, Shannon)
1983 Rutland Place (Perry, Anne)
1983 Silhouette in Scarlet (Peters, Elizabeth)
1983 The Devil's Novice (Peters, Ellis)
1983 The Sanctuary Sparrow (Peters, Ellis)
1983 Blood on the Happy Highway [U.S.–The Quiet Road
      to Death] (Radley, Sheila)
1983 The Speaker of Mandarin (Rendell, Ruth)
1983 The Baked Bean Supper Murders (Rich, Virginia)
1983 Exploit of Death (Shannon, Dell)
1983 Puppet for a Corpse (Simpson, Dorothy)
1983 Samson's Deal (Singer, Shelley)
1983 Devil's Knell (Warner, Mignon)
1983 Dead Man's Thoughts (Wheat, Carolyn)
1983 Call Back Yesterday (Woods, Sara)
1983 The Lie Direct (Woods, Sara)
1983 Where Should He Die? (Woods, Sara)

1984 Harm's Way (Aird, Catherine)
1984 Striving With Gods (Bannister, Jo)
1984 Dead Heat (Barnes, Linda)
1984 Death in a Deck Chair (Beck, K. K.)

1980s . . . continued

1984   The Thin Woman (Cannell, Dorothy)
1984   Stalker (Cody, Liza)
1984   The Other David (Coker, Carolyn)
1984   Sweet Death, Kind Death (Cross, Amanda)
1984   Masks and Faces (Curzon, Clare)
1984   Lullaby of Murder (Davis, Dorothy Salisbury)
1984   First Hit of the Season (Dentinger, Jane)
1984   Unexpected Developments (Dominic, R. B.)
1984   As a Favor (Dunlap, Susan)
1984   Amateur City (Forrest, Katherine V.)
1984   A Death for Adonis (Giroux, E. X.)
1984   Jerusalem Inn (Grimes, Martha)
1984   The Dirty Duck (Grimes, Martha)
1984   Stately Homicide (Haymon, S. T.)
1984   A Death at St. Anselm's (Holland, Isabelle)
1984   The Piano Bird (Kallen, Lucille)
1984   In the Shadow of King's (Kelly, Nora)
1984   Emily Dickinson is Dead (Langton, Jane)
1984   The Convivial Codfish (MacLeod, Charlotte)
1984   Grave Goods (Mann, Jessica)
1984   Death of a Butterfly (Maron, Margaret)
1984   Too Sane a Murder (Martin, Lee)
1984   Sick of Shadows (McCrumb, Sharyn)
1984   Hang the Consequences (Meek, M. R. D.)
1984   The Sheriff & the Panhandle Murders
       (Meredith, D. R.)
1984   The Crozier Pharaohs (Mitchell, Gladys)
1984   Grizzly Trail (Moffat, Gwen)
1984   Penny Black (Moody, Susan)
1984   Penny Dreadful (Moody, Susan)
1984   Getting Away with Murder (Morice, Ann)
1984   Double (Muller, Marcia)
1984   Games to Keep the Dark Away (Muller, Marcia)
1984   Leave a Message for Willie (Muller, Marcia)
1984   Death in Autumn (Nabb, Magdalen)
1984   Ladykiller (O'Donnell, Lillian)
1984   A Novena for Murder (O'Marie, Sister Carol Anne)
1984   Sweet, Savage Death (Papazoglou, Orania)
1984   Deadlock (Paretsky, Sara)
1984   A Cadenza for Caruso (Paul, Barbara)
1984   The Renewable Virgin (Paul, Barbara)
1984   Bluegate Fields (Perry, Anne)
1984   Die for Love (Peters, Elizabeth)
1984   The Dead Man's Ransom (Peters, Ellis)
1984   The Pilgrim of Hate (Peters, Ellis)
1984   Generous Death (Pickard, Nancy)
1984   Destiny of Death (Shannon, Dell)
1984   Close Her Eyes (Simpson, Dorothy)
1984   Free Draw (Singer, Shelley)
1984   Morbid Symptoms (Slovo, Gillian)
1984   The Sourdough Wars (Smith, Julie)
1984   Only Half a Hoax (Taylor, L. A.)
1984   Sound Evidence (Thomson, June)
1984   Illusion (Warner, Mignon)
1984   Bleeding Hearts (White, Teri)
1984   Murder in the Collective (Wilson, Barbara)
1984   Defy the Devil (Woods, Sara)
1984   Murder's Out of Tune (Woods, Sara)
1984   The Bloody Book of Law (Woods, Sara)
1984   Wake Up, Darlin' Corey (Wren, M. K.)

1985   Death of a Gossip (Beaton, M. C.)
1985   Murder in a Mummy Case (Beck, K. K.)
1985   The Down East Murders (Borthwick, J. S.)
1985   Down the Garden Path: A Pastoral Mystery
       (Cannell, Dorothy)

1985   Audition for Murder (Carlson, P. M.)
1985   Murder is Academic (Carlson, P. M.)
1985   The Shortest Way to Hades (Caudwell, Sarah)
1985   Last Judgment (Clarke, Anna)
1985   Head Case (Cody, Liza)
1985   The Grub-and-Stakers Quilt a Bee (Craig, Alisa)
1985   The Trojan Hearse (Curzon, Clare)
1985   Not Exactly a Brahmin (Dunlap, Susan)
1985   The Bohemian Connection (Dunlap, Susan)
1985   I Met Murder (Ferrars, E. X.)
1985   Oxford Blood (Fraser, Antonia Pakenham)
1985   Mrs. Pollifax and the Hong Kong Buddha
       (Gilman, Dorothy)
1985   A Death for a Darling (Giroux, E. X.)
1985   Monkey Puzzle (Gosling, Paula)
1985   "B" is for Burglar (Grafton, Sue)
1985   Death on Widow's Walk (Grant-Adamson, Lesley)
1985   The Face of Death (Grant-Adamson, Lesley)
1985   Help the Poor Struggler (Grimes, Martha)
1985   The Deer Leap (Grimes, Martha)
1985   Flight of the Archangel (Holland, Isabelle)
1985   Until Proven Guilty (Jance, J. A.)
1985   The Gemini Man (Kelly, Susan)
1985   Graves of Academe (Kenney, Susan)
1985   The Curse of the Giant Hogweed
       (MacLeod, Charlotte)
1985   The Plain Old Man (MacLeod, Charlotte)
1985   Death in Blue Folders (Maron, Margaret)
1985   Just Another Day in Paradise (Maxwell, A. E.)
1985   Lovely in her Bones (McCrumb, Sharyn)
1985   The Split Second (Meek, M. R. D.)
1985   The Sheriff & the Branding Iron Murders
       (Meredith, D. R.)
1985   Penny Post (Moody, Susan)
1985   Dead on Cue (Morice, Ann)
1985   Night Ferry to Death (Moyes, Patricia)
1985   The Legend of the Slain Soldiers (Muller, Marcia)
1985   There's Nothing to be Afraid Of (Muller, Marcia)
1985   Casual Affairs (O'Donnell, Lillian)
1985   Wicked, Loving Murder (Papazoglou, Orania)
1985   Killing Orders (Paretsky, Sara)
1985   Prima Donna at Large (Paul, Barbara)
1985   Death in Devil's Acre (Perry, Anne)
1985   The Mummy Case (Peters, Elizabeth)
1985   An Excellent Mystery (Peters, Ellis)
1985   Say No to Murder (Pickard, Nancy)
1985   Hidden Agenda (Porter, Anna)
1985   Fate Worse Than Death (Radley, Sheila)
1985   An Unkindness of Ravens (Rendell, Ruth)
1985   The Nantucket Diet Murders (Rich, Virginia)
1985   Chaos of Crime (Shannon, Dell)
1985   Last Seen Alive (Simpson, Dorothy)
1985   True-Life Adventure (Smith, Julie)
1985   Deadly Objectives (Taylor, L. A.)
1985   Shed Light on Death (Taylor, L. A.)
1985   A Dying Fall (Thomson, June)
1985   Speak No Evil (Warner, Mignon)
1985   Runaway (Watson, Clarissa)
1985   An Obscure Grave (Woods, Sara)
1985   Away With Them to Prison (Woods, Sara)
1985   Put Out the Light (Woods, Sara)
1985   The Suspect (Wright, L. R.)

1986   Reel Murder (Babson, Marian)
1986   Cities of the Dead (Barnes, Linda)
1986   The Lace Curtain Murders (Belfort, Sophie)
1986   The Student Body (Borthwick, J. S.)
1986   The Cat Who Saw Red (Braun, Lilian Jackson)

1980s . . . continued

1986 Coffin on the Water (Butler, Gwendoline)
1986 Murder is Pathological (Carlson, P. M.)
1986 Cabin 3033 (Clarke, Anna)
1986 The Mystery Lady (Clarke, Anna)
1986 A Bird in the Hand (Cleeves, Ann)
1986 Under Contract (Cody, Liza)
1986 Phoebe's Knee (Comfort, Barbara)
1986 A Dismal Thing to Do (Craig, Alisa)
1986 No Word from Winifred (Cross, Amanda)
1986 The Quest for K (Curzon, Clare)
1986 The Last Annual Slugfest (Dunlap, Susan)
1986 Murder at the Nightwood Bar (Forrest, Katherine V.)
1986 A Necessary End (Fraser, Anthea)
1986 A Shroud for Delilah (Fraser, Anthea)
1986 Jemima Shore's First Case & Other Stories
         (Fraser, Antonia Pakenham)
1986 A Death for a Dancer (Giroux, E. X.)
1986 A Death for a Doctor (Giroux, E. X.)
1986 The Wychford Murders (Gosling, Paula)
1986 "C" is for Corpse (Grafton, Sue)
1986 Guilty Knowledge (Grant-Adamson, Lesley)
1986 Shattered Moon (Green, Kate)
1986 I am the Only Running Footman (Grimes, Martha)
1986 Malice Domestic (Hardwick, Mollie)
1986 Strangled Prose (Hess, Joan)
1986 The Murder at the Murder at the Mimosa Inn
         (Hess, Joan)
1986 A Lover Scorned (Holland, Isabelle)
1986 A Taste for Death (James, P. D.)
1986 Injustice for All (Jance, J. A.)
1986 Trial by Fury (Jance, J. A.)
1986 A Little Madness (Kallen, Lucille)
1986 The Ritual Bath (Kellerman, Faye)
1986 The Summertime Soldiers (Kelly, Susan)
1986 Trace Elements (Knight, Kathryn Lasky)
1986 Good and Dead (Langton, Jane)
1986 Dark Fields (MacGregor, T. J.)
1986 The Corpse in Oozak's Pond (MacLeod, Charlotte)
1986 A Kind of Healthy Grave (Mann, Jessica)
1986 A Conspiracy of Strangers (Martin, Lee)
1986 Where Lawyers Fear to Tread (Matera, Lia)
1986 The Frog and the Scorpion (Maxwell, A. E.)
1986 Highland Laddie Gone (McCrumb, Sharyn)
1986 In Remembrance of Rose (Meek, M. R. D.)
1986 Penny Royal (Moody, Susan)
1986 Publish and Be Killed (Morice, Ann)
1986 Beyond the Grave (Muller, Marcia)
1986 The Cavalier in White (Muller, Marcia)
1986 Advent of Dying (O'Marie, Sister Carol Anne)
1986 Death's Savage Passion (Papazoglou, Orania)
1986 Lion in the Valley (Peters, Elizabeth)
1986 The Raven in the Foregate (Peters, Ellis)
1986 The Rose Rent (Peters, Ellis)
1986 No Body (Pickard, Nancy)
1986 Murder on the Run (Sale, Medora)
1986 Blood Count (Shannon, Dell)
1986 Dead on Arrival (Simpson, Dorothy)
1986 Full House (Singer, Shelley)
1986 Miss Melville Regrets (Smith, Evelyn E.)
1986 Tourist Trap (Smith, Julie)
1986 The Dark Stream (Thomson, June)
1986 A Case of Loyalties (Wallace, Marilyn)
1986 Where Nobody Dies (Wheat, Carolyn)
1986 Tightrope (White, Teri)
1986 Sisters of the Road (Wilson, Barbara)
1986 Most Deadly Hate (Woods, Sara)

1986 Nor Live So Long (Woods, Sara)
1986 Sleep While I Sing (Wright, L. R.)
1987 A February Face (Adamson, M. J.)
1987 Not Till a Hot January (Adamson, M. J.)
1987 A Dead Liberty (Aird, Catherine)
1987 A Trouble of Fools (Barnes, Linda)
1987 Death of a Cad (Beaton, M. C.)
1987 The Letter of the Law (Berry, Carole)
1987 The Cat Who Played Brahms
         (Braun, Lilian Jackson)
1987 The Cat Who Played Post Office
         (Braun, Lilian Jackson)
1987 Coffin in Fashion (Butler, Gwendoline)
1987 Murder Unrenovated (Carlson, P. M.)
1987 Come Death and High Water (Cleeves, Ann)
1987 THe Hand of the Lion (Coker, Carolyn)
1987 Green Mountain Murder (Comfort, Barbara)
1987 Trail of Fire (Curzon, Clare)
1987 The Habit of Fear (Davis, Dorothy Salisbury)
1987 The Always Anonymous Beast
         (Douglas, Lauren Wright)
1987 A Murder of Crows (Duffy, Margaret)
1987 A Dinner to Die For (Dunlap, Susan)
1987 Too Close to the Edge (Dunlap, Susan)
1987 Your Royal Hostage (Fraser, Antonia Pakenham)
1987 A Death for a Dilletante (Giroux, E. X.)
1987 "D" is for Deadbeat (Grafton, Sue)
1987 The Killings at Badger's Drift (Graham, Caroline)
1987 Wild Justice (Grant-Adamson, Lesley)
1987 The Five Bells and Bladebone (Grimes, Martha)
1987 Parson's Pleasure (Hardwick, Mollie)
1987 Death on Demand (Hart, Carolyn G.)
1987 Design for Murder (Hart, Carolyn G.)
1987 Death of a God (Haymon, S. T.)
1987 Dear Miss Demeanor (Hess, Joan)
1987 Malice in Maggody (Hess, Joan)
1987 No Harm (Hornsby, Wendy)
1987 Taking the Fifth (Jance, J. A.)
1987 Sacred and Profane (Kellerman, Faye)
1987 Murder in Mendocino (Kittredge, Mary)
1987 Bullshot (Kraft, Gabrielle)
1987 Unquiet Grave (LaPierre, Janet)
1987 Kill Flash (MacGregor, T. J.)
1987 The Recycled Citizen (MacLeod, Charlotte)
1987 The Silver Ghost (MacLeod, Charlotte)
1987 The Right Jack (Maron, Margaret)
1987 A Radical Departure (Matera, Lia)
1987 Gatsby's Vineyard (Maxwell, A. E.)
1987 A Worm of Doubt (Meek, M. R. D.)
1987 Murder by Impulse (Meredith, D. R.)
1987 The Sheriff & the Folsom Man Murders
         (Meredith, D. R.)
1987 Snare (Moffat, Gwen)
1987 Scavengers (Montgomery, Yvonne E.)
1987 Treble Exposure (Morice, Ann)
1987 Murder in the Limelight (Myers, Amy)
1987 The Marshal and the Murderer (Nabb, Magdalen)
1987 The Other Side of the Door (O'Donnell, Lillian)
1987 A Study in Lilac (Oliver, Maria Antonia)
1987 Bitter Medicine (Paretsky, Sara)
1987 A Chorus of Detectives (Paul, Barbara)
1987 Cardington Crescent (Perry, Anne)
1987 Trojan Gold (Peters, Elizabeth)
1987 The Hermit of Eyton Forest (Peters, Ellis)
1987 Marriage is Murder (Pickard, Nancy)
1987 Mortal Sins (Porter, Anna)
1987 Murder at the War [aka Knight Fall]
         (Pulver, Mary Monica)

1980s . . . continued

1987   Who Saw Him Die? (Radley, Sheila)
1987   Caught Dead in Philadelphia (Roberts, Gillian)
1987   Murder by Tale [short stories] (Shannon, Dell)
1987   Element of Doubt (Simpson, Dorothy)
1987   Murder is Only Skin Deep (Sims, L. V.)
1987   Spit in the Ocean (Singer, Shelley)
1987   Death Comes Staccato (Slovo, Gillian)
1987   Miss Melville Returns (Smith, Evelyn E.)
1987   A Masculine Ending (Smith, Joan)
1987   Huckleberry Fiend (Smith, Julie)
1987   Goodbye Nanny Gray (Stacey, Susannah)
1987   Murder at Vassar (Taylor, Elizabeth Atwood)
1987   No Flowers by Request (Thomson, June)
1987   The Price You Pay (Wakefield, Hannah)
1987   The Hamlet Trap (Wilhelm, Kate)
1987   She Came Too Late (Wings, Mary)
1987   Naked Villainy (Woods, Sara)

1988   Remember March (Adamson, M. J.)
1988   April When They Woo (Adamson, M. J.)
1988   Death of an Outsider (Beaton, M. C.)
1988   The Year of the Monkey (Berry, Carole)
1988   Ladies' Night (Bowers, Elisabeth)
1988   The Cat Who Knew Shakespeare
          (Braun, Lilian Jackson)
1988   The Cat Who Sniffed Glue (Braun, Lilian Jackson)
1988   Coffin Underground (Butler, Gwendoline)
1988   The Widow's Club (Cannell, Dorothy)
1988   Rehearsal for Murder (Carlson, P. M.)
1988   Suddenly in Her Sorbet (Christmas, Joyce)
1988   Murder in Writing (Clarke, Anna)
1988   The Vermont Village Murder (Comfort, Barbara)
1988   The Man in the Green Chevy
          (Cooper, Susan Rogers)
1988   The Grub-and-Stakers Pinch a Poke (Craig, Alisa)
1988   Shot Bolt (Curzon, Clare)
1988   Three-Core Lead (Curzon, Clare)
1988   The Life and Crimes of Harry Lavender
          (Day, Marele)
1988   Death Mask (Dentinger, Jane)
1988   Fevered (Drake, Alison)
1988   Tango Key (Drake, Alison)
1988   Death of a Raven (Duffy, Margaret)
1988   Snowstorms in a Hot Climate (Dunant, Sarah)
1988   Cast a Cold Eye (Eccles, Marjorie)
1988   The Nine Bright Shiners (Fraser, Anthea)
1988   Magic Mirror (Friedman, Mickey)
1988   A Question of Guilt (Fyfield, Frances)
1988   A Great Deliverance (George, Elizabeth)
1988   Mrs. Pollifax and the Golden Triangle
          (Gilman, Dorothy)
1988   A Death for a Dietician (Giroux, E. X.)
1988   "E" is for Evidence (Grafton, Sue)
1988   Random Access Murder (Grant, Linda)
1988   Threatening Eye (Grant-Adamson, Lesley)
1988   Uneaseful Death (Hardwick, Mollie)
1988   Honeymoon with Murder (Hart, Carolyn G.)
1988   Something Wicked (Hart, Carolyn G.)
1988   A Really Cute Corpse (Hess, Joan)
1988   Mischief in Maggody (Hess, Joan)
1988   A More Perfect Union (Jance, J. A.)
1988   Improbable Cause (Jance, J. A.)
1988   Trail of the Dragon (Kelly, Susan)
1988   Katwalk (Kijewski, Karen)
1988   Enter Second Murderer (Knight, Alanna)

1988   Screwdriver (Kraft, Gabrielle)
1988   Murder at the Gardner (Langton, Jane)
1988   Something in the Air (Lathen, Emma)
1988   Death Sweet (MacGregor, T. J.)
1988   Death Beyond the Nile (Mann, Jessica)
1988   Baby Doll Games (Maron, Margaret)
1988   Death Warmed Over (Martin, Lee)
1988   Murder at the Blue Owl (Martin, Lee)
1988   The Smart Money (Matera, Lia)
1988   Just Enough Light to Kill (Maxwell, A. E.)
1988   Bimbos of the Death Sun (McCrumb, Sharyn)
1988   Paying the Piper (McCrumb, Sharyn)
1988   Murder at the Old Vicarage (McGown, Jill)
1988   A Mouthful of Sand (Meek, M. R. D.)
1988   Windsor Red (Melville, Jennie)
1988   Murder by Impulse (Meredith, D. R.)
1988   Penny Wise (Moody, Susan)
1988   Fatal Charm (Morice, Ann)
1988   Eye of the Storm (Muller, Marcia)
1988   There Hangs the Knife (Muller, Marcia)
1988   The Marshal and the Madwoman (Nabb, Magdalen)
1988   Death's Bright Angel (Neel, Janet)
1988   The Missing Madonna (O'Marie, Sister Carol Anne)
1988   Rich, Radiant Slaughter (Papazoglou, Orania)
1988   Blood Shot (Britain–Toxic Shock) (Paretsky, Sara)
1988   Silence in Hanover Close (Perry, Anne)
1988   The Deeds of the Disturber (Peters, Elizabeth)
1988   The Confession of Brother Haluin (Peters, Ellis)
1988   The Nocturne Murder (Peterson, Audrey)
1988   Dead Crazy (Pickard, Nancy)
1988   Ashes to Ashes (Pulver, Mary Monica)
1988   The Unforgiving Minutes (Pulver, Mary Monica)
1988   The Veiled One (Rendell, Ruth)
1988   The J. Alfred Prufrock Murders
          (Sawyer, Corinne Holt)
1988   First Kill All the Lawyers (Shankman, Sarah)
1988   Suspicious Death (Simpson, Dorothy)
1988   To Sleep, Perchance to Kill (Sims, L. V.)
1988   Suicide King (Singer, Shelley)
1988   Death by Analysis (Slovo, Gillian)
1988   Why Aren't They Screaming (Smith, Joan)
1988   Murder at Markham (Sprinkle, Patricia Houck)
1988   A Knife at the Opera (Stacey, Susannah)
1988   Body of Opinion (Stacey, Susannah)
1988   Dead Men Don't Give Seminars (Sucher, Dorothy)
1988   Rosemary for Remembrance (Thomson, June)
1988   North of the Border (Van Gieson, Judith)
1988   Primary Target (Wallace, Marilyn)
1988   Small Favors (Wallace, Patricia)
1988   Last Plane from Nice (Watson, Clarissa)
1988   Somebody Killed the Messenger (Watson, Clarissa)
1988   The Dark Door (Wilhelm, Kate)
1988   Death by Deception (Wingate, Ann)
1988   Murder at the PTA Luncheon (Wolzien, Valerie)
1988   May's Newfangled Mirth (Adamson, M. J.)

1989   The Menehune Murders (Arnold, Margot)
1989   Encore Murder (Babson, Marian)
1989   Tourists are for Trapping (Babson, Marian)
1989   Gilgamesh (Bannister, Jo)
1989   The Snake Tattoo (Barnes, Linda)
1989   Death of a Perfect Wife (Beaton, M. C.)
1989   Peril Under the Palms (Beck, K. K.)
1989   Madison Avenue Murder (Bennett, Liza)
1989   Love Lies Bleeding (Blackmur, L. L.)
1989   Love Lies Slain (Blackmur, L. L.)
1989   Working Murder (Boylan, Eleanor)
1989   The Cat Who Went Underground
          (Braun, Lilian Jackson)

1980s . . . continued

1989 Murder in Store (Brod, D. C.)
1989 Coffin in the Black Museum (Butler, Gwendoline)
1989 Coffin in the Museum of Crime (Butler, Gwendoline)
1989 The Sirens Sang of Murder (Caudwell, Sarah)
1989 Simply to Die For (Christmas, Joyce)
1989 Grime & Punishment (Churchill, Jill)
1989 The Whitelands Affair (Clarke, Anna)
1989 A Prey to Murder (Cleeves, Ann)
1989 Murder in Paradise (Cleeves, Ann)
1989 Grave Consequences (Comfort, Barbara)
1989 A New Leash on Death (Conant, Susan)
1989 Trouble in the Brasses (Craig, Alisa)
1989 A Trap for Fools (Cross, Amanda)
1989 The Face in the Stone (Curzon, Clare)
1989 User Deadly (Danks, Denise)
1989 Silver Pigs (Davis, Lindsey)
1989 Ninth Life (Douglas, Lauren Wright)
1989 Black Moon (Drake, Alison)
1989 Brass Eagle (Duffy, Margaret)
1989 Pious Deception (Dunlap, Susan)
1989 Death of a Good Woman (Eccles, Marjorie)
1989 Hush, Money (Femling, Jean)
1989 The Beverly Malibu (Forrest, Katherine V.)
1989 Six Proud Walkers (Fraser, Anthea)
1989 A Temporary Ghost (Friedman, Mickey)
1989 Shadows on the Mirror (Fyfield, Frances)
1989 Payment in Blood (George, Elizabeth)
1989 A Death for a Dreamer (Giroux, E. X.)
1989 The Dead Pull Hitter (Gordon, Alison)
1989 Backlash (Gosling, Paula)
1989 "F" is for Fugitive (Grafton, Sue)
1989 Death of a Hollow Man (Graham, Caroline)
1989 Deathly Misadventure [aka Cocaine Blues]
        (Greenwood, Kerry)
1989 The Old Silent (Grimes, Martha)
1989 The Grandfather Medicine (Hager, Jean)
1989 Emma Chizzit and the Queen Anne Killer
        (Hall, Mary Bowen)
1989 Perish in July (Hardwick, Mollie)
1989 The Bandersnatch (Hardwick, Mollie)
1989 A Little Class on Murder (Hart, Carolyn G.)
1989 Hallowed Murder (Hart, Ellen)
1989 A Very Particular Murder (Haymon, S. T.)
1989 A Diet to Die For (Hess, Joan)
1989 Much Ado in Maggody (Hess, Joan)
1989 A Fatal Advent (Holland, Isabelle)
1989 Mrs. Malory Investigates [Britain–Gone Away]
        (Holt, Hazel)
1989 The Mother Shadow (Howe, Melodie Johnson)
1989 Dismissed with Prejudice (Jance, J. A.)
1989 The Quality of Mercy (Kellerman, Faye)
1989 Dead and Gone (Kittredge, Mary)
1989 Bloodline (Knight, Alanna)
1989 Deadly Beloved (Knight, Alanna)
1989 Let's Rob Roy (Kraft, Gabrielle)
1989 Children's Games (LaPierre, Janet)
1989 On Ice (MacGregor, T. J.)
1989 The Gladstone Bag (MacLeod, Charlotte)
1989 Vane Pursuit (MacLeod, Charlotte)
1989 Corpus Christmas (Maron, Margaret)
1989 Hal's Own Murder Case (Martin, Lee)
1989 Hidden Agenda (Matera, Lia)
1989 The Art of Survival (Maxwell, A. E.)
1989 Gone to Her Death (McGown, Jill)
1989 A Loose Connection (Meek, M. R. D.)

1989 Making Good Blood (Melville, Jennie)
1989 Murder in the Garden (Melville, Jennie)
1989 Murder by Deception (Meredith, D. R.)
1989 Murder by Deception (Meredith, D. R.)
1989 The Big Killing (Meyers, Annette)
1989 The Stone Hawk (Moffat, Gwen)
1989 Penny Pinching (Moody, Susan)
1989 Black Girl, White Girl (Moyes, Patricia)
1989 Dark Star (Muller, Marcia)
1989 The Shape of Dread (Muller, Marcia)
1989 There's Something in a Sunday (Muller, Marcia)
1989 Death on Site (Neel, Janet)
1989 Hit and Run (O'Callaghan, Maxine)
1989 A Good Night to Kill (O'Donnell, Lillian)
1989 Antipodes (Oliver, Maria Antonia)
1989 A Little Neighborhood Murder (Orde, A. J.)
1989 Naked Once More (Peters, Elizabeth)
1989 The Heretic's Apprentice (Peters, Ellis)
1989 The Potter's Field (Peters, Ellis)
1989 Death in Wessex (Peterson, Audrey)
1989 Murder in Burgundy (Peterson, Audrey)
1989 Bum Steer (Pickard, Nancy)
1989 Unorthodox Practices (Piesman, Marissa)
1989 This Way Out (Radley, Sheila)
1989 Philly Stakes (Roberts, Gillian)
1989 The Spirit Stalker (Romberg, Nina)
1989 A Real Shot in the Arm (Roome, Annette)
1989 Murder by the Book (Rowe, Jennifer)
1989 Murder in the Cotswolds (Rowlands, Betty)
1989 Murder in Focus (Sale, Medora)
1989 Murder in Gray & White (Sawyer, Corinne Holt)
1989 Glory Days (Scott, Rosie)
1989 Then Hang All the Liars (Shankman, Sarah)
1989 Black Justice (Shepherd, Stella)
1989 Dead by Morning (Simpson, Dorothy)
1989 The Mark Twain Murders (Skom, Edith)
1989 Miss Melville's Revenge (Smith, Evelyn E.)
1989 Dead Men Don't Marry (Sucher, Dorothy)
1989 The Spoils of Time (Thomson, June)
1989 Murder at the Kennedy Center (Truman, Margaret)
1989 A Collector of Photographs (Valentine, Deborah)
1989 Unorthodox Methods (Valentine, Deborah)
1989 Deadly Grounds (Wallace, Patricia)
1989 Smart House (Wilhelm, Kate)
1989 The Dog Collar Murders (Wilson, Barbara)
1989 The Eye of Anna (Wingate, Ann)
1989 The Last Billable Hour (Wolfe, Susan)
1989 The Fortieth Birthday Body (Wolzien, Valerie)
1989 Body and Soul (Woods, Sherryl)
1989 Reckless (Woods, Sherryl)

1980s Miss Seeton Draws the Line (Crane, Hamilton)
1980s Miss Seeton Sings (Crane, Hamilton)
1980s Odds on Miss Seeton (Crane, Hamilton)
1980s Picture Miss Seeton (Crane, Hamilton)
1980s Witch Miss Seeton (Crane, Hamilton)
1980s Fetish (Hart, Jeanne)
1980s Some Die Young (Hart, Jeanne)

1990s

1990 A Cat in the Manger (Adamson, Lydia)
1990 A Cat of a Different Color (Adamson, Lydia)
1990 Toby's Folly (Arnold, Margot)
1990 In the Teeth of Adversity (Babson, Marian)
1990 The Going Down of the Sun (Bannister, Jo)
1990 Coyote (Barnes, Linda)

1990s . . . continued

1990   Death of a Hussy (Beaton, M. C.)
1990   Seventh Avenue Murder (Bennett, Liza)
1990   Good Night, Sweet Prince (Berry, Carole)
1990   A Vow of Silence (Black, Veronica)
1990   Bodies of Water (Borthwick, J. S.)
1990   Murder Observed (Boylan, Eleanor)
1990   The Cat Who Lived High (Braun, Lilian Jackson)
1990   The Cat Who Talked to Ghosts
          (Braun, Lilian Jackson)
1990   Error In Judgment (Brod, D. C.)
1990   Wish You Were Here (Brown, Rita Mae)
1990   Screaming Bones (Burden, Pat)
1990   Wreath of Honesty (Burden, Pat)
1990   Mum's the Word (Cannell, Dorothy)
1990   Murder in the Dog Days (Carlson, P. M.)
1990   Murder Misread (Carlson, P. M.)
1990   A Fete Worse than Death (Christmas, Joyce)
1990   A Lesson in Dying (Cleeves, Ann)
1990   The Balmoral Nude (Coker, Carolyn)
1990   Dead and Doggone (Conant, Susan)
1990   A Common Death (Cooper, Natasha)
1990   Houston in the Rear View Mirror
          (Cooper, Susan Rogers)
1990   Other People's Houses (Cooper, Susan Rogers)
1990   Postmortem (Cornwell, Patricia Daniels)
1990   The Grub-and-Stakers Spin a Yarn (Craig, Alisa)
1990   Advantage Miss Seeton (Crane, Hamilton)
1990   Miss Seeton at the Helm (Crane, Hamilton)
1990   Miss Seeton, By Appointment (Crane, Hamilton)
1990   The Players Come Again (Cross, Amanda)
1990   Hardball (D'Amato, Barbara)
1990   Catering to Nobody (Davidson, Diane Mott)
1990   Shadows in Bronze (Davis, Lindsey)
1990   Kindred Crimes (Dawson, Janet)
1990   The Case of the Chinese Boxes (Day, Marele)
1990   Good Morning, Irene (Douglas, Carole Nelson)
1990   Good Night, Mr. Holmes (Douglas, Carole Nelson)
1990   Who Killed Cock Robin? (Duffy, Margaret)
1990   Diamond in the Buff (Dunlap, Susan)
1990   More Deaths than One (Eccles, Marjorie)
1990   Requiem for a Dove (Eccles, Marjorie)
1990   Blood is Thicker (Fallon, Ann)
1990   Not That Kind of Place (Fyfield, Frances)
1990   Well-Schooled in Murder (George, Elizabeth)
1990   Mrs. Pollifax and the Whirling Dervish
          (Gilman, Dorothy)
1990   A Death for a Double (Giroux, E. X.)
1990   "G" is for Gumshoe (Grafton, Sue)
1990   Blind Trust (Grant, Linda)
1990   Curse the Darkness (Grant-Adamson, Lesley)
1990   The Old Contemptibles (Grimes, Martha)
1990   Hot Water (Gunning, Sally)
1990   Not a Creature was Stirring (Haddam, Jane)
1990   Night Walker (Hager, Jean)
1990   Emma Chizzit and the Sacramento Stalker
          (Hall, Mary Bowen)
1990   The Dreaming Damozel (Hardwick, Mollie)
1990   Real Murders (Harris, Charlaine)
1990   Deadly Valentine (Hart, Carolyn G.)
1990   The Long Search (Holland, Isabelle)
1990   Dead Ahead (Horansky, Ruby)
1990   Half a Mind (Hornsby, Wendy)
1990   The American Pearl (Jackson, Marian J. A.)
1990   The Punjat's Ruby (Jackson, Marian J. A.)
1990   Minor in Possession (Jance, J. A.)

1990   Milk and Honey (Kellerman, Faye)
1990   Parklane South, Queens (Kelly, Mary Ann)
1990   Until Proven Innocent (Kelly, Susan)
1990   Hope Against Hope (Kelly, Susan B.)
1990   Time of Hope (Kelly, Susan B.)
1990   One Fell Sloop (Kenney, Susan)
1990   Katapult (Kijewski, Karen)
1990   Fatal Diagnosis (Kittredge, Mary)
1990   Poison Pen (Kittredge, Mary)
1990   Killing Cousins (Knight, Alanna)
1990   Mortal Words (Knight, Kathryn Lasky)
1990   Bloody Mary (Kraft, Gabrielle)
1990   Cruel Mother (LaPierre, Janet)
1990   A Deepe Coffyn (Laurence, Janet)
1990   Ropedancer's Fall (Lorens, M. K.)
1990   Sweet Narcissus (Lorens, M. K.)
1990   Kin Dread (MacGregor, T. J.)
1990   Deficit Ending (Martin, Lee)
1990   The Mensa Murders (Martin, Lee)
1990   The Good Fight (Matera, Lia)
1990   Murder at the Spa (Matteson, Stephanie)
1990   Pet Peeves (McCafferty, Taylor)
1990   If Ever I Return, Pretty Peggy-O
          (McCrumb, Sharyn)
1990   The Windsor Knot (McCrumb, Sharyn)
1990   Report for Murder (McDermid, Val)
1990   Deadly Safari (McQuillan, Karin)
1990   This Blessed Plot (Meek, M. R. D.)
1990   Witching Murder (Melville, Jennie)
1990   Murder by Masquerade (Meredith, D. R.)
1990   Tender Death (Meyers, Annette)
1990   Rage (Moffat, Gwen)
1990   Obstacle Course (Montgomery, Yvonne E.)
1990   A Slay at the Races (Morgan, Kate)
1990   Trophies and Dead Things (Muller, Marcia)
1990   The Marshal's Own Case (Nabb, Magdalen)
1990   Salmon in the Soup (O'Brien, Meg)
1990   The Daphne Decisions (O'Brien, Meg)
1990   A Wreath for the Bride (O'Donnell, Lillian)
1990   Dead in the Scrub (Oliphant, B. J.)
1990   The Unexpected Corpse (Oliphant, B. J.)
1990   Death and the Dogwalker (Orde, A. J.)
1990   The Body in the Belfry (Page, Katherine Hall)
1990   Once and Always Murder (Papazoglou, Orania)
1990   Burn Marks (Paretsky, Sara)
1990   Bethlehem Road (Perry, Anne)
1990   The Face of a Stranger (Perry, Anne)
1990   Deadly Rehearsal (Peterson, Audrey)
1990   Elegy in a Country Graveyard (Peterson, Audrey)
1990   A Second Shot in the Dark (Roome, Annette)
1990   A Little Gentle Sleuthing (Rowlands, Betty)
1990   Murder in a Good Cause (Sale, Medora)
1990   Death Down Home (Sandstrom, Eve K.)
1990   As Crime Goes By (Shah, Diane K.)
1990   Now Let's Talk of Graves (Shankman, Sarah)
1990   Murderous Remedy (Shepherd, Stella)
1990   Larkspur (Simonson, Sheila)
1990   Sea of Troubles (Smith, Janet L.)
1990   Don't Leave Me This Way (Smith, Joan)
1990   New Orleans Mourning (Smith, Julie)
1990   Murder in the Charleston Manner
          (Sprinkle, Patricia Houck)
1990   Grave Responsibility (Stacey, Susannah)
1990   Past Reckoning (Thomson, June)
1990   Murder at the National Cathedral
          (Truman, Margaret)
1990   Raptor (Van Gieson, Judith)
1990   Missing Members (Vlasopolos, Anca)

1990s . . . continued

1990 A Woman's Own Mystery (Wakefield, Hannah)
1990 Murder by the Book (Welch, Pat)
1990 Sweet, Sweet Poison (Wilhelm, Kate)
1990 Gaudi Afternoon (Wilson, Barbara)
1990 She Came in a Flash (Wings, Mary)
1990 Stolen Moments (Woods, Sherryl)
1990 A Chill Rain in January (Wright, L. R.)
1990 False Notes (Yarbro, Chelsea Quinn)

1991 A Cat in Wolf's Clothing (Adamson, Lydia)
1991 The Catacomb Conspiracy (Arnold, Margot)
1991 Bagged (Bailey, Jo)
1991 In the Game (Baker, Nikki)
1991 Steel Guitar (Barnes, Linda)
1991 Death of a Snob (Beaton, M. C.)
1991 The Marvell College Murders (Belfort, Sophie)
1991 Island Girl (Berry, Carole)
1991 No Forwarding Address (Bowers, Elisabeth)
1991 The Cat Who Knew a Cardinal
        (Braun, Lilian Jackson)
1991 Headhunt (Brennan, Carol)
1991 Date With a Dead Doctor (Brill, Toni)
1991 Masquerade in Blue [paperback title–Framed in
        Blue] (Brod, D. C.)
1991 Coffin and the Paper Man (Butler, Gwendoline)
1991 Bad Blood (Carlson, P. M.)
1991 Raw Data (Chapman, Sally)
1991 A Deadly Drink of Wine (Charles, Kate)
1991 A Stunning Way to Die (Christmas, Joyce)
1991 Friend or Faux (Christmas, Joyce)
1991 A Farewell to Yarns (Churchill, Jill)
1991 The Case of the Paranoid Patient (Clarke, Anna)
1991 Murder in My Backyard (Cleeves, Ann)
1991 Sea Fever (Cleeves, Ann)
1991 Backhand (Cody, Liza)
1991 A Bite of Death (Conant, Susan)
1991 Poison Flowers (Cooper, Natasha)
1991 Chasing Away the Devil (Cooper, Susan Rogers)
1991 Body of Evidence (Cornwell, Patricia Daniels)
1991 Miss Seeton Cracks the Case (Crane, Hamilton)
1991 Miss Seeton Paints the Town (Crane, Hamilton)
1991 The Trouble with a Small Raise (Crespi, Trella)
1991 The Trouble with Moonlighting (Crespi, Trella)
1991 The Blue-Eyed Boy (Curzon, Clare)
1991 Hard Tack (D'Amato, Barbara)
1991 Fowl Prey (Daheim, Mary)
1991 Just Desserts (Daheim, Mary)
1991 Venus in Copper (Davis, Lindsey)
1991 The Daughters of Artemis (Douglas, Lauren Wright)
1991 Rook-Shoot (Duffy, Margaret)
1991 Rogue Wave (Dunlap, Susan)
1991 Where Death Lies (Fallon, Ann)
1991 Getting Mine (Femling, Jean)
1991 Murder by Tradition (Forrest, Katherine V.)
1991 A Deadline for Murder (Frankel, Valerie)
1991 The Cavalier Case (Fraser, Antonia Pakenham)
1991 Scalpel's Edge (Fromer, Margot J.)
1991 Deep Sleep (Fyfield, Frances)
1991 A Suitable Vengeance (George, Elizabeth)
1991 Adjusted to Death (Girdner, Jaqueline)
1991 The Last Resort (Girdner, Jaqueline)
1991 A Death for a Dancing Doll (Giroux, E. X.)
1991 Safe at Home (Gordon, Alison)
1991 Death Penalties (Gosling, Paula)
1991 "H" is for Homicide (Grafton, Sue)

1991 Say it with Poison (Granger, Ann)
1991 Love Nor Money (Grant, Linda)
1991 Too Many Questions (Grant-Adamson, Lesley)
1991 Partners in Crime (Gray, Gallagher)
1991 Deadly Errand (Green, Christine)
1991 Clerical Errors (Greenwood, Diane M.)
1991 Flying Too High (Greenwood, Kerry)
1991 Act of Darkness (Haddam, Jane)
1991 Precious Blood (Haddam, Jane)
1991 Quoth the Raven (Haddam, Jane)
1991 Orchestrated Death (Harrod-Eagles, Cynthia)
1991 The Christie Caper (Hart, Carolyn G.)
1991 Vital Lies (Hart, Ellen)
1991 Threnody for Two (Hart, Jeanne)
1991 Death of a Warrior Queen (Haymon, S. T.)
1991 Murder on the Iditarod Trail (Henry, Sue)
1991 Madness in Maggody (Hess, Joan)
1991 Mortal Remains in Maggody (Hess, Joan)
1991 Roll Over and Play Dead (Hess, Joan)
1991 The Cruellest Month (Holt, Hazel)
1991 Crime of Passion (Hooper, Kay)
1991 House of Cards (Hooper, Kay)
1991 Cat's Eye (Jackson, Marian J. A.)
1991 The Turquoise Tattoo (Jacobs, Nancy Baker)
1991 Payment in Kind (Jance, J. A.)
1991 And Soon I'll Come to Kill You (Kelly, Susan)
1991 Kat's Cradle (Kijewski, Karen)
1991 Rigor Mortis (Kittredge, Mary)
1991 Mumbo Jumbo (Knight, Kathryn Lasky)
1991 Dogtown (Lambert, Mercedes)
1991 The Dante Game (Langton, Jane)
1991 Grandmother's House (LaPierre, Janet)
1991 East is East (Lathen, Emma)
1991 A Tasty Way to Die (Laurence, Janet)
1991 Sister Beneath the Sheet (Linscott, Gillian)
1991 Deception Island (Lorens, M. K.)
1991 A Relative Stranger (Lucke, Margaret)
1991 Death Flats (MacGregor, T. J.)
1991 An Owl Too Many (MacLeod, Charlotte)
1991 Faith, Hope and Homicide (Mann, Jessica)
1991 Past Imperfect (Maron, Margaret)
1991 Prior Convictions (Matera, Lia)
1991 Murder at Teatime (Matteson, Stephanie)
1991 Murder on the Cliff (Matteson, Stephanie)
1991 Money Burns (Maxwell, A. E.)
1991 Missing Susan (McCrumb, Sharyn)
1991 Open and Shut (McDermid, Val)
1991 The Murders of Mrs. Austin & Mrs. Beale
        (McGown, Jill)
1991 Murder by Masquerade (Meredith, D. R.)
1991 Murder by Reference (Meredith, D. R.)
1991 The Deadliest Option (Meyers, Annette)
1991 Murder Most Fowl (Morgan, Kate)
1991 Where Echoes Live (Muller, Marcia)
1991 The Marshal Makes His Report (Nabb, Magdalen)
1991 Hare Today, Gone Tomorrow (O'Brien, Meg)
1991 Set-Up (O'Callaghan, Maxine)
1991 A Private Crime (O'Donnell, Lillian)
1991 Murder in Ordinary Time
        (O'Marie, Sister Carol Anne)
1991 The Body in the Bouillon (Page, Katherine Hall)
1991 The Body in the Kelp (Page, Katherine Hall)
1991 Guardian Angel (Paretsky, Sara)
1991 A Dangerous Mourning (Perry, Anne)
1991 Highgate Rise (Perry, Anne)
1991 The Last Camel Died at Noon (Peters, Elizabeth)
1991 Summer of the Danes (Peters, Ellis)

1990s . . . continued

1991   Lament for Christabel (Peterson, Audrey)
1991   I. O. U. (Pickard, Nancy)
1991   Personal Effects (Piesman, Marissa)
1991   Original Sin (Pulver, Mary Monica)
1991   I'd Rather Be in Philadelphia (Roberts, Gillian)
1991   The Bulrush Murders (Rothenberg, Rebecca)
1991   Grim Pickings (Rowe, Jennifer)
1991   Sleep of the Innocent (Sale, Medora)
1991   The Devil Down Home (Sandstrom, Eve K.)
1991   Everything You Have is Mine
            (Scoppettone, Sandra)
1991   She Walks in Beauty (Shankman, Sarah)
1991   Ah, Sweet Mystery (Sibley, Celestine)
1991   Doomed to Die (Simpson, Dorothy)
1991   Miss Melville Rides a Tiger (Smith, Evelyn E.)
1991   Dead in the Water (Smith, Julie)
1991   The Axeman's Jazz (Smith, Julie)
1991   Murder on Peachtree Street
            (Sprinkle, Patricia Houck)
1991   Murder on Her Mind (Steiner, Susan)
1991   Read Sea, Dead Sea (Stevens, Serita)
1991   Bones (Thompson, Joyce)
1991   Foul Play (Thomson, June)
1991   Still Waters (Tucker, Kerry)
1991   Fine Distinctions (Valentine, Deborah)
1991   The Other Side of Death (Van Gieson, Judith)
1991   Zero at the Bone (Walker, Mary Willis)
1991   A Single Stone (Wallace, Marilyn)
1991   Blood Lies (Wallace, Patricia)
1991   Cold Tracks (Wallingford, Lee)
1991   Murder on the Run (White, Gloria)
1991   Death Qualified (Wilhelm, Kate)
1991   The Buzzards Must Also Be Fed (Wingate, Ann)
1991   We Wish You a Merry Murder (Wolzien, Valerie)
1991   Hot Property (Woods, Sherryl)
1991   Ties That Bind (Woods, Sherryl)
1991   Fall From Grace (Wright, L. R.)
1991   Poison Fruit (Yarbro, Chelsea Quinn)
1991   The Hour of the Knife (Zukowski, Sharon)

1992   A Cat by Any Other Name (Adamson, Lydia)
1992   A Cat in the Wings (Adamson, Lydia)
1992   Thyme of Death (Albert, Susan Wittig)
1992   Quaker Silence (Allen, Irene)
1992   Trail of Murder (Andreae, Christine)
1992   Cape Cod Conundrum (Arnold, Margot)
1992   Aunt Dimity's Death (Atherton, Nancy)
1992   A World the Color of Salt (Ayres, Noreen)
1992   The Lavender House Murder (Baker, Nikki)
1992   Agatha Raisin and the Quiche of Death
            (Beaton, M. C.)
1992   Death of a Prankster (Beaton, M. C.)
1992   A Hopeless Case (Beck, K. K.)
1992   Eyewitness to Murder (Belfort, Sophie)
1992   A Vow of Chastity (Black, Veronica)
1992   Dead Time (Bland, Eleanor Taylor)
1992   Dude on Arrival (Borthwick, J. S.)
1992   Murder Machree (Boylan, Eleanor)
1992   The Cat Who Moved a Mountain (Braun, Lilian
            Jackson)
1992   Full Commission (Brennan, Carol)
1992   Rest in Pieces (Brown, Rita Mae)
1992   Contents Under Pressure (Buchanan, Edna)
1992   Bury Him Kindly (Burden, Pat)
1992   Coffin on Murder Street (Butler, Gwendoline)

1992   Femmes Fatal (Cannell, Dorothy)
1992   Gravestone (Carlson, P. M.)
1992   It's Her Funeral (Christmas, Joyce)
1992   Decked (Clark, Carol Higgins)
1992   A Tail of Two Murders (Cleary, Melissa)
1992   A Day in the Death of Dorothea Cassidy
            (Cleeves, Ann)
1992   Bloodlines (Conant, Susan)
1992   Gone to the Dogs (Conant, Susan)
1992   Paws Before Dying (Conant, Susan)
1992   Bloody Roses (Cooper, Natasha)
1992   One, Two, What Did Daddy Do?
            (Cooper, Susan Rogers)
1992   All that Remains (Cornwell, Patricia Daniels)
1992   The Wrong Rite (Craig, Alisa)
1992   Hands Up, Miss Seeton (Crane, Hamilton)
1992   Miss Seeton By Moonlight (Crane, Hamilton)
1992   Miss Seeton Rocks the Cradle (Crane, Hamilton)
1992   The Trouble with Too Much Sun (Crespi, Trella)
1992   Cat's Cradle (Curzon, Clare)
1992   Hard Luck (D'Amato, Barbara)
1992   Holy Terrors (Daheim, Mary)
1992   The Alpine Advocate (Daheim, Mary)
1992   Lay It on the Line (Dain, Catherine)
1992   Frame Grabber (Danks, Denise)
1992   Dying for Chocolate (Davidson, Diane Mott)
1992   Iron Hand of Mars (Davis, Lindsey)
1992   The Last Tango of Delores Delgado (Day, Marele)
1992   Dead Pan (Dentinger, Jane)
1992   Catnap (Douglas, Carole Nelson)
1992   Irene at Large (Douglas, Carole Nelson)
1992   A Tiger's Heart (Douglas, Lauren Wright)
1992   High Strangeness (Drake, Alison)
1992   Birth Marks (Dunant, Sarah)
1992   Death and Taxes (Dunlap, Susan)
1992   Death of the Duchess (Eyre, Elizabeth)
1992   Dead Ends (Fallon, Ann)
1992   Alibi for an Actress (Farrell, Gillian B.)
1992   Beware of the Dog (Ferrars, E. X.)
1992   Born to the Purple (Florian, S.L.)
1992   Murder on Wheels (Frankel, Valerie)
1992   The Novice's Tale (Frazer, Margaret)
1992   For the Sake of Elena (George, Elizabeth)
1992   Murder Most Mellow (Girdner, Jaqueline)
1992   Showcase (Glen, Alison)
1992   The Body in Blackwater Bay (Gosling, Paula)
1992   "I" is for Innocent (Grafton, Sue)
1992   A Season for Murder (Granger, Ann)
1992   A Cast of Killers (Gray, Gallagher)
1992   Deadly Admirer (Green, Christine)
1992   Unholy Ghosts (Greenwood, Diane M.)
1992   Under Water (Gunning, Sally)
1992   Caught in the Shadows (Haddad, Carolyn A.)
1992   A Great Day for the Deadly (Haddam, Jane)
1992   A Stillness in Bethlehem (Haddam, Jane)
1992   Feast of Murder (Haddam, Jane)
1992   Ghostland (Hager, Jean)
1992   Ravenmocker (Hager, Jean)
1992   Emma Chizzit and the Napa Nemesis
            (Hall, Mary Bowen)
1992   A Bone to Pick (Harris, Charlaine)
1992   The Good Friday Murder (Harris, Lee)
1992   The Yom Kippur Murder (Harris, Lee)
1992   Death Watch (Harrod-Eagles, Cynthia)
1992   Southern Ghost (Hart, Carolyn G.)
1992   Stage Fright (Hart, Ellen)
1992   Principal Defense (Hartzmark, Gini)
1992   Death by the Light of the Moon (Hess, Joan)

1990s . . . continued

1992 Maggody in Manhattan (Hess, Joan)
1992 Ripley Under Water (Highsmith, Patricia)
1992 Telling Lies (Hornsby, Wendy)
1992 Diamond Head (Jackson, Marian J. A.)
1992 The Garden Club (Jackson, Muriel Resnick)
1992 A Slash of Scarlett (Jacobs, Nancy Baker)
1992 Without Due Process (Jance, J. A.)
1992 Day of Atonement (Kellerman, Faye)
1992 False Prophet (Kellerman, Faye)
1992 Foxglove (Kelly, Mary Ann)
1992 My Sister's Keeper (Kelly, Nora)
1992 Out of the Darkness (Kelly, Susan)
1992 Copy Kat (Kijewski, Karen)
1992 Cadaver (Kittredge, Mary)
1992 Walking Dead Man (Kittredge, Mary)
1992 Switching the Odds (Knight, Phyllis)
1992 The Holiday Murders (Landreth, Marsha)
1992 God in Concord (Langton, Jane)
1992 Hotel Morgue (Laurence, Janet)
1992 Time Lapse (Law, Janice)
1992 Death a la Fenice (Leon, Donna)
1992 Hanging on the Wire (Linscott, Gillian)
1992 Dreamland (Lorens, M. K.)
1992 Spree (MacGregor, T. J.)
1992 The Resurrection Man (MacLeod, Charlotte)
1992 Body English (Mariz, Linda French)
1992 Snake Dance (Mariz, Linda French)
1992 Bootlegger's Daughter (Maron, Margaret)
1992 Hacker (Martin, Lee)
1992 A Hard Bargain (Matera, Lia)
1992 Murder on the Silk Road (Matteson, Stephanie)
1992 The King of Nothing (Maxwell, A. E.)
1992 Bed Bugs (McCafferty, Taylor)
1992 Ruffled Feathers (McCafferty, Taylor)
1992 MacPherson's Lament (McCrumb, Sharyn)
1992 The Hangman's Beautiful Daughter
           (McCrumb, Sharyn)
1992 Zombies of the Gene Pool (McCrumb, Sharyn)
1992 Dead Beat (McDermid, Val)
1992 Night Butterfly (McFall, Patricia)
1992 Emergency Murder (McGiffin, Janet)
1992 The Other Woman (McGown, Jill)
1992 Blood on the Street (Meyers, Annette)
1992 Murder at Moot Point (Millhiser, Marlys)
1992 Seneca Falls Inheritance (Monfredo, Miriam Grace)
1992 Days of Crime and Roses (Morgan, Kate)
1992 Home Sweet Homicide (Morgan, Kate)
1992 Mystery Loves Company (Morgan, Kate)
1992 Pennies on a Dead Woman's Eyes (Muller, Marcia)
1992 Blanche on the Lamb (Neely, Barbara)
1992 Eagles Die Too (O'Brien, Meg)
1992 Pushover (O'Donnell, Lillian)
1992 Death and the Delinquent (Oliphant, B. J.)
1992 Deservedly Dead (Oliphant, B. J.)
1992 Death For Old Times' Sake (Orde, A. J.)
1992 The Body in the Vestibule (Page, Katherine Hall)
1992 You Have the Right to Remain Silent
           (Paul, Barbara)
1992 Belgrave Square (Perry, Anne)
1992 Defend and Betray (Perry, Anne)
1992 The Snake, The Crocodile and the Dog
           (Peters, Elizabeth)
1992 The Holy Thief (Peters, Ellis)
1992 Dartmoor Burial (Peterson, Audrey)
1992 The Two-Bit Tango (Pincus, Elizabeth)

1992 Show Stopper (Pulver, Mary Monica)
1992 Cross My Heart and Hope to Die (Radley, Sheila)
1992 Jinx (Robitaille, Julie)
1992 Death in Store [short stories with Birdie]
           (Rowe, Jennifer)
1992 Pursued by Shadows (Sale, Medora)
1992 Murder by Owl Light (Sawyer, Corinne Holt)
1992 Death and the Chapman (Sedley, Kate)
1992 Dying Cheek to Cheek (Shah, Diane K.)
1992 The King is Dead (Shankman, Sarah)
1992 Thinner Than Blood (Shepherd, Stella)
1992 Straight as an Arrow (Sibley, Celestine)
1992 Skylark (Simonson, Sheila)
1992 Wake Her Dead (Simpson, Dorothy)
1992 Practice to Deceive (Smith, Janet L.)
1992 Somebody's Dead in Snellville
           (Sprinkle, Patricia Houck)
1992 A Cold Day for Murder (Stabenow, Dana)
1992 The Late Lady (Stacey, Susannah)
1992 The Northwest Murders (Taylor, Elizabeth Atwood)
1992 Every Crooked Nanny (Trocheck, Kathy Hogan)
1992 Murder at the Pentagon (Truman, Margaret)
1992 Cold Feet (Tucker, Kerry)
1992 The Wolf Path (Van Gieson, Judith)
1992 The Winter Widow (Weir, Charlene)
1992 Seven Kinds of Death (Wilhelm, Kate)
1992 Exception to Murder (Wingate, Ann)
1992 All Hallow's Evil (Wolzien, Valerie)
1992 An Old Faithful Murder (Wolzien, Valerie)
1992 Hot Secret (Woods, Sherryl)
1992 Cat's Claw (Yarbro, Chelsea Quinn)
1992 Cancellation by Death (Yeager, Dorian)
1992 Dancing in the Dark (Zukowski, Sharon)

1993 A Cat in a Glass House (Adamson, Lydia)
1993 A Cat with a Fiddle (Adamson, Lydia)
1993 A Going Concern (Aird, Catherine)
1993 Witches' Bane (Albert, Susan Wittig)
1993 Quaker Witness (Allen, Irene)
1993 Shadows in Their Blood (Babson, Marian)
1993 Recycled (Bailey, Jo)
1993 Minerva Cries Murder (Ballard, Mignon)
1993 Death by Dressage (Banks, Carolyn)
1993 A Bleeding of Innocents (Bannister, Jo)
1993 Snapshot (Barnes, Linda)
1993 Track of the Cat (Barr, Nevada)
1993 Agatha Raisin and the Vicious Vet (Beaton, M. C.)
1993 Death of a Travelling Man (Beaton, M. C.)
1993 Death of a Glutton (Beaton, M. C.)
1993 Amateur Night (Beck, K. K.)
1993 A Vow of Obedience (Black, Veronica)
1993 A Vow of Sanctity (Black, Veronica)
1993 Slow Burn (Bland, Eleanor Taylor)
1993 One for the Money (Borton, D. B.)
1993 Two Points for Murder (Borton, D. B.)
1993 Pushing Murder (Boylan, Eleanor)
1993 The Cat Who Wasn't There (Braun, Lilian Jackson)
1993 Mrs. Jeffries Dusts for Clues (Brightwell, Emily)
1993 The Ghost and Mrs. Jeffries (Brightwell, Emily)
1993 The Inspector and Mrs. Jeffries (Brightwell, Emily)
1993 Date With a Plummeting Publisher (Brill, Toni)
1993 Brothers in Blood (Brod, D. C.)
1993 Goodnight, Irene (Burke, Jan)
1993 Cracking Open a Coffin (Butler, Gwendoline)
1993 A Pocketful of Karma (Cannon, Taffy)
1993 The Snares of Death (Charles, Kate)
1993 This Business is Murder (Christmas, Joyce)
1993 A Fridge Too Many (Churchill, Jill)

1990s . . . continued

1993 A Quiche Before Dying (Churchill, Jill)
1993 Snagged (Clark, Carol Higgins)
1993 Deadlier Than Death (Clark, Carolyn Chambers)
1993 Dog Collar Crime (Cleary, Melissa)
1993 Hounded to Death (Cleary, Melissa)
1993 Another Man's Poison (Cleeves, Ann)
1993 Bucket Nut (Cody, Liza)
1993 Appearance of Evil (Coker, Carolyn)
1993 The Cashmere Kid (Comfort, Barbara)
1993 Ruffly Speaking (Conant, Susan)
1993 Bitter Herbs (Cooper, Natasha)
1993 Funny as a Dead Comic (Cooper, Susan Rogers)
1993 Cruel and Unusual (Cornwell, Patricia Daniels)
1993 The Grub-and-Stakers House a Haunt (Craig, Alisa)
1993 Miss Seeton Goes to Bat (Crane, Hamilton)
1993 Miss Seeton Plants Suspicion (Crane, Hamilton)
1993 The Trouble with Thin Ice (Crespi, Trella)
1993 A Share in Death (Crombie, Deborah)
1993 Dead as Dead Can Be (Crowleigh, Ann)
1993 First Wife, Twice Removed (Curzon, Clare)
1993 Hard Women (D'Amato, Barbara)
1993 Bantam of the Opera (Daheim, Mary)
1993 The Alpine Betrayal (Daheim, Mary)
1993 The Alpine Christmas (Daheim, Mary)
1993 Sing a Song of Death (Dain, Catherine)
1993 Cereal Murders (Davidson, Diane Mott)
1993 Take a Number (Dawson, Janet)
1993 Till the Old Men Die (Dawson, Janet)
1993 Throw Darts at a Cheesecake (Dietz, Denise)
1993 Pussyfoot (Douglas, Carole Nelson)
1993 Goblin Market (Douglas, Lauren Wright)
1993 Fat Lands (Dunant, Sarah)
1993 Time Expired (Dunlap, Susan)
1993 Curtains for the Cardinal (Eyre, Elizabeth)
1993 Potter's Field (Fallon, Ann)
1993 Death Wears a Crown (Fawcett, Quinn)
1993 Napoleon Must Die (Fawcett, Quinn)
1993 Dead in the Water (Feddersen, Connie)
1993 Answer Came There None (Ferrars, E. X.)
1993 Jemima Shore at the Sunny Grave [9 stories]
     (Fraser, Antonia Pakenham)
1993 The Servant's Tale (Frazer, Margaret)
1993 Night Shift (Fromer, Margot J.)
1993 Shadow Play (Fyfield, Frances)
1993 Dogfish (Geason, Susan)
1993 Sharkbait (Geason, Susan)
1993 Shaved Fish (Geason, Susan)
1993 Missing Joseph (George, Elizabeth)
1993 Mrs. Pollifax and the Second Thief
     (Gilman, Dorothy)
1993 Final Design (Gilpatrick, Noreen)
1993 Fat-Free and Fatal (Girdner, Jaqueline)
1993 A Death for a Dodo (Giroux, E. X.)
1993 Burning Time (Glass, Leslie)
1993 Night Game (Gordon, Alison)
1993 "J" is for Judgment (Grafton, Sue)
1993 Death in Disguise (Graham, Caroline)
1993 Cold in the Earth (Granger, Ann)
1993 Murder Among Us (Granger, Ann)
1993 Black Dreams (Green, Kate)
1993 Idol Bones (Greenwood, Diane M.)
1993 Murder on the Ballarat Train (Greenwood, Kerry)
1993 The Killing of Ellis Martin (Grindle, Lucretia)
1993 Ice Water (Gunning, Sally)
1993 Troubled Water (Gunning, Sally)

1993 Festival of Deaths (Haddam, Jane)
1993 Murder Superior (Haddam, Jane)
1993 Emma Chizzit and the Mother Lode Marauder
     (Hall, Mary Bowen)
1993 The Poison Pool (Hall, Patricia)
1993 The Christening Day Murder (Harris, Lee)
1993 Dead Man's Island (Hart, Carolyn G.)
1993 A Killing Cure (Hart, Ellen)
1993 With Deadly Intent (Hendrickson, Louise)
1993 O Little Town of Maggody (Hess, Joan)
1993 Poisoned Pins (Hess, Joan)
1993 Satan's Lambs (Hightower, Lynn)
1993 Mrs. Malory and the Festival Murders (Holt, Hazel)
1993 Midnight Baby (Hornsby, Wendy)
1993 The Silver Scalpel (Jacobs, Nancy Baker)
1993 Desert Heat (Jance, J. A.)
1993 Failure to Appear (Jance, J. A.)
1993 Murder in Bandora (Karr, Leona)
1993 Grievous Sin (Kellerman, Faye)
1993 Body Chemistry (Kelly, Nora)
1993 Hope Will Answer (Kelly, Susan B.)
1993 Down Home Murder (Kelner, Toni L. P.)
1993 A Grave Talent (King, Laurie R.)
1993 Room With a Clue (Kingsbury, Kate)
1993 Desperate Remedy (Kittredge, Mary)
1993 Fair Game (Krich, Rochelle Majer)
1993 Murder Once Removed (Kunz, Kathleen)
1993 File Under: Deceased (Lacey, Sarah)
1993 Questionable Behavior (Lamb, J. Dayne)
1993 A Clinic for Murder (Landreth, Marsha)
1993 Divine Inspiration (Langton, Jane)
1993 Old Enemies (LaPierre, Janet)
1993 Prime Suspect (LaPlante, Lynda)
1993 Prime Suspect 2 (LaPlante, Lynda)
1993 Right on the Money (Lathen, Emma)
1993 Recipe for Death (Laurence, Janet)
1993 A Safe Place to Die (Law, Janice)
1993 Death in a Strange Country (Leon, Donna)
1993 Stage Fright (Linscott, Gillian)
1993 Still Explosion (Logue, Mary)
1993 Brotherly Love (Lorden, Randye)
1993 Sorrowheart (Lorens, M. K.)
1993 Someone is Killing the Great Chefs of America
     (Lyons, Nan & Ivan)
1993 Storm Surge (MacGregor, T. J.)
1993 Southern Discomfort (Maron, Margaret)
1993 The Day That Dusty Died (Martin, Lee)
1993 Frozen Stiff (Mason, Sarah Jill)
1993 Murder in the Maze (Mason, Sarah Jill)
1993 Murder at the Falls (Matteson, Stephanie)
1993 Murder Hurts (Maxwell, A. E.)
1993 Kickback (McDermid, Val)
1993 Prescription for Death (McGiffin, Janet)
1993 Murder Now and Then (McGown, Jill)
1993 Until Proven Guilty (McGuire, Christine)
1993 Murder Beach (McKenna, Bridget)
1993 Elephants' Graveyard (McQuillan, Karin)
1993 Touch & Go (Meek, M. R. D.)
1993 Mail-Order Murder (Meier, Leslie)
1993 Dead Set (Melville, Jennie)
1993 Footsteps in the Blood (Melville, Jennie)
1993 Murder by Sacrilege (Meredith, D. R.)
1993 Murder by Sacrilege (Meredith, D. R.)
1993 The Sheriff & the Pheasant Hunt Murders
     (Meredith, D. R.)
1993 Murder: The Musical (Meyers, Annette)
1993 Death of the Office Witch (Millhiser, Marlys)
1993 North Star Conspiracy (Monfredo, Miriam Grace)

1990s . . . continued

1993 Death Takes a Hand [Britain–Takeout Double]
        (Moody, Susan)
1993 Penny Saving (Moody, Susan)
1993 Twice in a Blue Moon (Moyes, Patricia)
1993 Wolf in the Shadows (Muller, Marcia)
1993 Death Comes as Epiphany (Newman, Sharan)
1993 Thin Ice (O'Brien, Meg)
1993 Skins (O'Donnell, Catherine)
1993 Used to Kill (O'Donnell, Lillian)
1993 Murder Makes a Pilgrimmage
        (O'Marie, Sister Carol Anne)
1993 Murder in Mellingham (Oleksiw, Susan)
1993 Looking for the Aardvark [paperback title–Dead on
        Sunday] (Orde, A. J.)
1993 Child of Silence (Padgett, Abigail)
1993 The Body in the Cast (Page, Katherine Hall)
1993 The Apostrophe Thief (Paul, Barbara)
1993 Something's Cooking (Pence, Joanne)
1993 A Sudden, Fearful Death (Perry, Anne)
1993 Farrier's Lane (Perry, Anne)
1993 But I Wouldn't Want to Die There (Pickard, Nancy)
1993 Heading Uptown (Piesman, Marissa)
1993 The Solitary Twist (Pincus, Elizabeth)
1993 By Evil Means (Prowell, Sandra West)
1993 Cold Call (Pugh, Dianne G.)
1993 Murder Most Grizzly (Quinn, Elizabeth)
1993 Kissing the Grocer's Daughter (Rendell, Ruth)
1993 The 27-Ingredient Chili Con Carne Murders
        (Rich, Virginia)
1993 The Apothecary Rose (Robb, Candace M.)
1993 Pray God to Die (Roberts, Carey)
1993 With Friends Like These (Roberts, Gillian)
1993 Shadow Walkers (Romberg, Nina)
1993 Cut to the Quick (Ross, Kate)
1993 The Makeover Murders (Rowe, Jennifer)
1993 Finishing Touch (Rowlands, Betty)
1993 Over the Edge (Rowlands, Betty)
1993 The Down Home Heifer Heist (Sandstrom, Eve K.)
1993 The Peanut Butter Murders (Sawyer, Corinne Holt)
1993 I'll Be Leaving You Always (Scoppettone, Sandra)
1993 Everywhere That Mary Went (Scottoline, Lisa)
1993 The Plymouth Cloak (Sedley, Kate)
1993 The Weaver's Tale (Sedley, Kate)
1993 He Was Her Man (Shankman, Sarah)
1993 Dire Happenings at Scratch Ankle
        (Sibley, Celestine)
1993 Mudlark (Simonson, Sheila)
1993 No Laughing Matter (Simpson, Dorothy)
1993 Following Jane (Singer, Shelley)
1993 Picture of David (Singer, Shelley)
1993 Jazz Funeral (Smith, Julie)
1993 Other People's Skeletons (Smith, Julie)
1993 Death of a Dunwoody Matron
        (Sprinkle, Patricia Houck)
1993 A Fatal Thaw (Stabenow, Dana)
1993 Dead in the Water (Stabenow, Dana)
1993 Death and the Oxford Box (Stallwood, Veronica)
1993 Murder at the Class Reunion (Stein, Triss)
1993 Library: No Murder Aloud (Steiner, Susan)
1993 Bagels for Tea (Stevens, Serita)
1993 A Sudden Death at the Norfolk Cafe
        (Sullivan, Winona)
1993 To Live and Die in Dixie (Trocheck, Kathy Hogan)
1993 Death Echo (Tucker, Kerry)
1993 The Lies that Bind (Van Gieson, Judith)

1993 Clear Cut Murder (Wallingford, Lee)
1993 The Wyndham Case (Walsh, Jill Paton)
1993 Consider the Crows (Weir, Charlene)
1993 Money to Burn (White, Gloria)
1993 Justice for Some (Wilhelm, Kate)
1993 Trouble in Transylvania (Wilson, Barbara)
1993 Yakuza, Go Home! (Wingate, Ann)
1993 A Star-Spangled Murder (Wolzien, Valerie)
1993 Bank on It (Woods, Sherryl)
1993 Hide and Seek (Woods, Sherryl)
1993 Hot Money (Woods, Sherryl)
1993 Dead Matter (Wren, M. K.)
1993 Prized Possessions (Wright, L. R.)
1993 Eviction by Death (Yeager, Dorian)

1994 A Cat on the Cutting Edge (Adamson, Lydia)
1994 A Cat with No Regrets (Adamson, Lydia)
1994 Dr. Nightingale Comes Home (Adamson, Lydia)
1994 Dr. Nightingale Rides the Elephant
        (Adamson, Lydia)
1994 Hangman's Root (Albert, Susan Wittig)
1994 Grizzly, A Murder (Andreae, Christine)
1994 Tensleep (Andrews, Sarah)
1994 Dirge for a Dorset Druid (Arnold, Margot)
1994 Aunt Dimity and the Duke (Atherton, Nancy)
1994 Carcass Trade (Ayres, Noreen)
1994 Charisma (Bannister, Jo)
1994 A Superior Death (Barr, Nevada)
1994 Agatha Raisin and the Potted Gardener
        (Beaton, M. C.)
1994 Death of a Charming Man (Beaton, M. C.)
1994 Electric City (Beck, K. K.)
1994 Deep Cover (Berenson, Laurien)
1994 The Death of a Difficult Woman (Berry, Carole)
1994 A Taste for Murder (Bishop, Claudia)
1994 A Vow of Penance (Black, Veronica)
1994 Gone Quiet (Bland, Eleanor Taylor)
1994 Chutes and Adders (Block, Barbara)
1994 The Bridled Groom (Borthwick, J. S.)
1994 Three is a Crowd (Borton, D. B.)
1994 Stand-in for Murder (Bradley, Lynn)
1994 The Cat Who Came to Breakfast
        (Braun, Lilian Jackson)
1994 The Cat Who Went into the Closet
        (Braun, Lilian Jackson)
1994 Mrs. Jeffries on the Ball (Brightwell, Emily)
1994 Mrs. Jeffries Takes Stock (Brightwell, Emily)
1994 Murder at Monticello (Brown, Rita Mae)
1994 Miami, It's Murder (Buchanan, Edna)
1994 Sweet Dreams, Irene (Burke, Jan)
1994 A Coffin for Charley (Butler, Gwendoline)
1994 How to Murder Your Mother-in-law
        (Cannell, Dorothy)
1994 Love Bytes (Chapman, Sally)
1994 A Knife to Remember (Churchill, Jill)
1994 Iced (Clark, Carol Higgins)
1994 Dangerous Alibis (Clark, Carolyn Chambers)
1994 The Case of the Ludicrous Letters (Clarke, Anna)
1994 First Pedigree Murder (Cleary, Melissa)
1994 Skull and Dog Bones (Cleary, Melissa)
1994 The Mill on the Shore (Cleeves, Ann)
1994 Monkey Wrench (Cody, Liza)
1994 Deadly Resolutions (Collins, Anna Ashwood)
1994 Dead Moon on the Rise (Cooper, Susan Rogers)
1994 Funny as a Dead Relative (Cooper, Susan Rogers)
1994 The Body Farm (Cornwell, Patricia Daniels)
1994 Miss Seeton Rules (Crane, Hamilton)
1994 Miss Seeton Undercover (Crane, Hamilton)

1990s . . . continued

1994 Starring Miss Seeton (Crane, Hamilton)
1994 All Shall Be Well (Crombie, Deborah)
1994 Cutter (Crum, Laura)
1994 Death Prone (Curzon, Clare)
1994 Hard Case (D'Amato, Barbara)
1994 Fit of Tempera (Daheim, Mary)
1994 The Alpine Decoy (Daheim, Mary)
1994 Lament for a Dead Cowboy (Dain, Catherine)
1994 Walk a Crooked Mile (Dain, Catherine)
1994 Wink a Hopeful Eye (Danks, Denise)
1994 The Last Suppers (Davidson, Diane Mott)
1994 Incident at Palmyra (Davis, Lindsey)
1994 Poseiden's Gold (Davis, Lindsey)
1994 Don't Turn Your Back on the Ocean
        (Dawson, Janet)
1994 The Queen is Dead (Dentinger, Jane)
1994 Miss Zukas and the Library Murders (Dereske, Jo)
1994 Beat Up a Cookie (Dietz, Denise)
1994 Cat on a Blue Monday (Douglas, Carole Nelson)
1994 Irene's Last Waltz (Douglas, Carole Nelson)
1994 A Rage of Maidens (Douglas, Lauren Wright)
1994 High Fall (Dunlap, Susan)
1994 Late of this Parish (Eccles, Marjorie)
1994 Speak Daggers to Her (Edghill, Rosemary)
1994 One for the Money (Evanovich, Janet)
1994 Poison for the Prince (Eyre, Elizabeth)
1994 Murder and a Muse (Farrell, Gillian B.)
1994 Dead in the Cellar (Feddersen, Connie)
1994 Fool's Puzzle (Fowler, Earlene)
1994 Prime Time for Murder (Frankel, Valerie)
1994 The Bishop's Tale (Frazer, Margaret)
1994 The Outlaw's Tale (Frazer, Margaret)
1994 Perfectly Pure and Good (Fyfield, Frances)
1994 Playing for the Ashes (George, Elizabeth)
1994 Tea-Totally Dead (Girdner, Jaqueline)
1994 Hanging Time (Glass, Leslie)
1994 A Few Dying Words (Gosling, Paula)
1994 "K" is for Killer (Grafton, Sue)
1994 Where Old Bones Lie (Granger, Ann)
1994 A Woman's Place (Grant, Linda)
1994 The Dangerous Edge (Grant-Adamson, Lesley)
1994 Death in the Country (Green, Christine)
1994 So Little to Die For (Grindle, Lucretia)
1994 Rough Water (Gunning, Sally)
1994 Bleeding Hearts (Haddam, Jane)
1994 Edited Out (Haddock, Lisa)
1994 Blooming Murder (Hager, Jean)
1994 The Redbird's Cry (Hager, Jean)
1994 Three Bedrooms, One Corpse (Harris, Charlaine)
1994 The Christmas Night Murder (Harris, Lee)
1994 The St. Patrick's Day Murder (Harris, Lee)
1994 Death To Go (Harrod-Eagles, Cynthia)
1994 Scandal in Fair Haven (Hart, Carolyn G.)
1994 A Small Sacrifice (Hart, Ellen)
1994 This Little Piggy Went to Murder (Hart, Ellen)
1994 Final Option (Hartzmark, Gini)
1994 A Beautiful Death (Haymon, S. T.)
1994 What's a Girl Gotta Do (Hayter, Sparkle)
1994 Grave Secrets (Hendrickson, Louise)
1994 Martians in Maggody (Hess, Joan)
1994 Tickled to Death (Hess, Joan)
1994 Murder at St. Adelaide's (Hollingsworth, Gerelyn)
1994 Mrs. Malory Detective in Residence (Holt, Hazel)
1994 The Shortest Journey (Holt, Hazel)
1994 Something to Kill For (Holtzer, Susan)

1994 Dead Center (Horansky, Ruby)
1994 Bad Intent (Hornsby, Wendy)
1994 Beauty Dies (Howe, Melodie Johnson)
1994 The Sunken Treasure (Jackson, Marian J. A.)
1994 Murder Among Neighbors (Jacobs, Jonnie)
1994 Lying in Wait (Jance, J. A.)
1994 Tombstone Courage (Jance, J. A.)
1994 Sanctuary (Kellerman, Faye)
1994 Kid's Stuff (Kelly, Susan B.)
1994 Dead Ringer (Kelner, Toni L. P.)
1994 Wild Kat (Kijewski, Karen)
1994 Do Not Disturb (Kingsbury, Kate)
1994 Eat, Drink, and Be Buried (Kingsbury, Kate)
1994 Service for Two (Kingsbury, Kate)
1994 Dark Swain (Knight, Kathryn Lasky)
1994 Shattered Rhythms (Knight, Phyllis)
1994 Angel of Death (Krich, Rochelle Majer)
1994 File Under: Missing (Lacey, Sarah)
1994 A Question of Preference (Lamb, J. Dayne)
1994 Prime Suspect 3 (LaPlante, Lynda)
1994 Death and the Epicure (Laurence, Janet)
1994 Backfire (Law, Janice)
1994 Sister's Keeper (Lorden, Randye)
1994 Blue Pearl (MacGregor, T. J.)
1994 Something in the Water (MacLeod, Charlotte)
1994 Death Pays the Rose Rent (Malmont, Valerie S.)
1994 Shooting at Loons (Maron, Margaret)
1994 Inherited Murder (Martin, Lee)
1994 Corpse in the Kitchen (Mason, Sarah Jill)
1994 Dying Breath (Mason, Sarah Jill)
1994 Face Value (Matera, Lia)
1994 Blood of an Aries (Mather, Linda)
1994 Murder on High (Matteson, Stephanie)
1994 Death in the Off Season (Matthews, Francine)
1994 The Lessons (McAllester, Melanie)
1994 Thin Skins (McCafferty, Taylor)
1994 The Bluejay Shaman (McClendon, Lise)
1994 She Walks These Hills (McCrumb, Sharyn)
1994 Crack Down (McDermid, Val)
1994 Dead Ahead (McKenna, Bridget)
1994 The Cheetah Chase (McQuillan, Karin)
1994 Tippy-Toe Murder (Meier, Leslie)
1994 These Bones Were Made for Dancing
        (Meyers, Annette)
1994 Grand Slam (Moody, Susan)
1994 Wanted Dude or Alive (Morgan, Kate)
1994 Till the Butchers Cut Him Down (Muller, Marcia)
1994 Too Many Crooks Spoil the Broth (Myers, Tamar)
1994 The Marshal at the Villa Torrini (Nabb, Magdalen)
1994 Death Among the Dons (Neel, Janet)
1994 Death of a Partner (Neel, Janet)
1994 Blanche Among the Talented Tenth (Neely, Barbara)
1994 The Devil's Door (Newman, Sharan)
1994 Healthy, Wealthy & Dead (North, Suzanne)
1994 Trade-Off (O'Callaghan, Maxine)
1994 Mallory's Oracle (O'Connell, Carol)
1994 Lockout (O'Donnell, Lillian)
1994 Double Take (Oleksiw, Susan)
1994 Death Served Up Cold (Oliphant, B. J.)
1994 Dead on Sunday (Orde, A. J.)
1994 Murder Offscreen (Osborne, Denise)
1994 Strawgirl (Padgett, Abigail)
1994 The Body in the Basement (Page, Katherine Hall)
1994 Death at Bishop's Keep (Paige, Robin)
1994 Tunnel Vision (Paretsky, Sara)
1994 Suspicion of Innocence (Parker, Barbara)
1994 Too Many Cooks (Pence, Joanne)
1994 Sins of the Wolf (Perry, Anne)

1990s . . . continued

1994 The Hyde Park Headsman (Perry, Anne)
1994 Night Train to Memphis (Peters, Elizabeth)
1994 Brother Cadfael's Penance (Peters, Ellis)
1994 Death Too Soon (Peterson, Audrey)
1994 Confession (Pickard, Nancy)
1994 Close Quarters (Piesman, Marissa)
1994 The Killing of Monday Brown
        (Prowell, Sandra West)
1994 Slow Squeeze (Pugh, Dianne G.)
1994 Simisola (Rendell, Ruth)
1994 The Lady Chapel (Robb, Candace M.)
1994 How I Spent My Summer Vacation (Roberts, Gillian)
1994 Murder in a Nice Neighborhood (Roberts, Lora)
1994 Iced (Robitaille, Julie)
1994 A Broken Vessel (Ross, Kate)
1994 The Dandelion Murders (Rothenberg, Rebecca)
1994 Stranglehold (Rowe, Jennifer)
1994 Exhaustive Inquiries (Rowlands, Betty)
1994 Short Cut to Santa Fe (Sale, Medora)
1994 Murder Has No Calories (Sawyer, Corinne Holt)
1994 In Blacker Moments (Schenkel, S. E.)
1994 My Sweet Untraceable You (Scoppettone, Sandra)
1994 Final Appeal (Scottoline, Lisa)
1994 Angel's Bidding (Short, Sharon Gwyn)
1994 Past Pretense (Short, Sharon Gwyn)
1994 Searching for Sara (Singer, Shelley)
1994 Writers of the Purple Sage (Smith, Barbara Burnett)
1994 Miss Melville Runs for Cover (Smith, Evelyn E.)
1994 A Vintage Murder (Smith, Janet L.)
1994 What Men Say (Smith, Joan)
1994 New Orleans Beat (Smith, Julie)
1994 Every Breath You Take (Spring, Michelle)
1994 A Mystery Bred in Buckhead
        (Sprinkle, Patricia Houck)
1994 Remember the Alibi (Squire, Elizabeth Daniels)
1994 Who Killed What's-Her-Name?
        (Squire, Elizabeth Daniels)
1994 A Cold-Blooded Business (Stabenow, Dana)
1994 Homemade Sin (Trocheck, Kathy Hogan)
1994 Murder on the Potomac (Truman, Margaret)
1994 Drift Away (Tucker, Kerry)
1994 Strangers in the Night (Tyre, Peg)
1994 The Red Scream (Walker, Mary Willis)
1994 Deadly Devotion (Wallace, Patricia)
1994 When Death Comes Stealing
        (Wesley, Valerie Wilson)
1994 The Best Defense (Wilhelm, Kate)
1994 A Good Year for a Corpse (Wolzien, Valerie)
1994 Tis the Season to be Murdered (Wolzien, Valerie)
1994 Hot Schemes (Woods, Sherryl)
1994 Wages of Sin (Woods, Sherryl)
1994 A Touch of Panic (Wright, L. R.)
1994 Leap of Faith (Zukowski, Sharon)

1995 Rosemary Remembered (Albert, Susan Wittig)
1995 A Fall in Denver (Andrews, Sarah)
1995 Aunt Dimity's Good Deed (Atherton, Nancy)
1995 Hardware (Barnes, Linda)
1995 A Dash of Death (Bishop, Claudia)
1995 Four Years Buried (Borton, D. B.)
1995 The Cat Who Blew the Whistle
        (Braun, Lilian Jackson)
1995 Suitable for Framing (Buchanan, Edna)
1995 Dear Irene (Burke, Jan)
1995 Tangled Roots (Cannon, Taffy)

1995 Bloodstream (Carlson, P. M.)
1995 The Maltese Puppy (Cleary, Melissa)
1995 Killjoy (Cleeves, Ann)
1995 Black Ribbon (Conant, Susan)
1995 An Imperfect Spy (Cross, Amanda)
1995 The Alpine Escape (Daheim, Mary)
1995 Bet Against the House (Dain, Catherine)
1995 Cat in a Crimson Haze (Douglas, Carole Nelson)
1995 Book of Moons (Edghill, Rosemary)
1995 Dead in the Melons (Feddersen, Connie)
1995 Irish Chain (Fowler, Earlene)
1995 Mrs. Pollifax Pursued (Gilman, Dorothy)
1995 A Stiff Critique (Girdner, Jaqueline)
1995 Trunk Show (Glen, Alison)
1995 The Julius House (Harris, Charlaine)
1995 The Mint Julep Murder (Hart, Carolyn G.)
1995 Termination Dust (Henry, Sue)
1995 Flashpoint (Hightower, Lynn)
1995 Curly Smoke (Holtzer, Susan)
1995 Trouble Looking for a Place to Happen
        (Kelner, Toni L. P.)
1995 Alley Cat Blues (Kijewski, Karen)
1995 Check-out Time (Kingsbury, Kate)
1995 Speak No Evil (Krich, Rochelle Majer)
1995 Death in a Private Place (Kunz, Kathleen)
1995 File Under: Arson (Lacey, Sarah)
1995 Inquestioned Loyalty (Lamb, J. Dayne)
1995 Vial Murders (Landreth, Marsha)
1995 The Odd Job (MacLeod, Charlotte)
1995 Fugitive Colors (Maron, Margaret)
1995 Caught Dead (McKenna, Bridget)
1995 Murder in a Hot Flash (Millhiser, Marlys)
1995 Blackwater Spirits (Monfredo, Miriam Grace)
1995 Cut to: Murder (Osborne, Denise)
1995 Turtle Baby (Padgett, Abigail)
1995 Death at Gallows Green (Paige, Robin)
1995 Fare Play (Paul, Barbara)
1995 The Hangdog Hustle (Pincus, Elizabeth)
1995 The Nun's Tale (Robb, Candace M.)
1995 Murder in the Marketplace (Roberts, Lora)
1995 Death Days (Schenkel, S. E.)
1995 Interview with Mattie (Singer, Shelley)
1995 Memory Can Be Murder (Squire, Elizabeth Daniels)
1995 Play With Fire (Stabenow, Dana)
1995 Oxford Exit (Stallwood, Veronica)
1995 Happy Never After (Trocheck, Kathy Hogan)
1995 Parrot Blues (Van Gieson, Judith)
1995 August Nights (Wallace, Patricia)
1995 Family Medicine (Weir, Charlene)
1995 Fresh Kills (Wheat, Carolyn)
1995 Charged with Guilt (White, Gloria)
1995 Deadly Obsession (Woods, Sherryl)
1995 Hot Ticket (Woods, Sherryl)
1995 King of the Mountain (Wren, M. K.)

Six

Pseudonyms

Pseudonym	Author Identity	Series Characters(s)
Adamson, Lydia	noted mystery writer	Alice Nestleton; Deidre Quinn Nightingale
Aird, Catherine	Kinn Hamilton McIntosh	C. D. Sloan
Allen, Irene	Harvard- and Princeton-educated geologist	Elizabeth Elliott
Arnold, Margot	Petronelle Cook	Penny Spring & Toby Glendower
Beaton, M. C.	Marion Chesney	Hamish Macbeth
Beck, K. K.	Katherine Marris	Iris Cooper; Jane da Silva
Belfort, Sophie	Massachusetts historian	Molly Rafferty
Bell, Josephine	Doris Bell Collier Ball	Dr. David Wintringham
Bishop, Claudia	Mary Stanton	Sarah & Meg Quilliam
Borton, D. B.	Lynette Carpenter	Cat Caliban
Brand, Christianna	Mary Christianna Lewis	Inspector Cockrill
Brill, Toni	husband & wife writing team	Midge Cohen
Caudwell, Sarah	Sarah Cockburn	Hilary Tamar
Churchill, Jill	Janice Young Brooks	Jane Jeffry
Cooper, Natasha	British author	Willow King & Cressida Woodruffe
Craig, Alisa	Charlotte MacLeod	Madoc & Janet Rhys; Grub-and-Stakers
Crane, Hamilton	Sarah J. Mason	Miss Seeton
Cross, Amanda	Carolyn G. Heilbrun	Kate Fansler
Curzon, Claire	Eileen-Marie Duell	Mike Yeadings
Dain, Catherine	Judith Garwood	Freddie O'Neal
Dominic, R. B.	Mary Latsis & Martha Henissart	Ben Safford
Drake, Alison	T. J. MacGregor	Aline Scott
Early, Jack	Sandra Scoppettone	Lauren Laurano
Eyre, Elizabeth	Jill Staynes & Margaret Storey	Sigismondo
Fawcett, Quinn	unknown	Victoire Vernet

Pseudonym	Author Identity	Series Characters(s)
Ferrars, E. X.	Morna Doris MacTaggart Brown	Virginia & Felix Freer; Sara Marriott
Frazer, Margaret	Mary Pulver Kuhfeld & Gail Bacon	Sister Frevisse
Fyfield, Frances	Frances Hegarty	Helen West; Sarah Fortune
Giroux, E. X.	Doris Shannon	Robert Forsythe & Abigail Sanderson
Glen, Alison	Cheryl Meredith Lowry & Louise Vetter	Charlotte Sams
Gray, Gallagher	Katy Munger	T. S. Hubbert & Auntie Lil
Haddam, Jane	Orania Papazoglou	Gregor Demarkian
Hadley, Joan	Joan Hess	Theo Bloomer
Harris, Lee	unknown	Christine Bennett
Kingsbury, Kate	Doreen Roberts	Cecily Sinclair
Lathen, Emma	Mary Latsis & Martha Hennisart	John Putnam Thatcher
Lockridge, Frances & Richard	Frances Louise Davis & Richard Orsen	Pam & Jerry North
Martin, Lee	Anne Wingate	Deb Ralston
Maxwell, A. E.	Ann & Evan Maxwell	Fiddler & Fiora Flynn
Melville, Jennie	Gwendoline Butler	Charmian Daniels
Morgan, Kate	Ann Hamilton Whitman	Dewey James
Morice, Ann	Felicity Shaw	Tessa Crichton
Oliphant, B. J.	Sheri S. Tepper	Shirley McClintock
Orde, A. J.	Sheri S. Tepper	Jason Lynx
Paige, Robin	Susan Wittig Albert & Bill Albert	Kathryn Ardleigh
Peters, Elizabeth	Barbara Mertz	Amelia Peabody; Jacqueline Kirby; Vicky Bliss
Peters, Ellis	Edith Mary Pargeter	Brother Cadfael
Radley, Sheila	Sheila Robinson	Douglas Quantrill
Rendell, Ruth	Barbara Graseman	Reginald Wexford
Roberts, Gillian	Judith Greber	Amanda Pepper
Shannon, Dell	Elizabeth Linnington	Luis Mendoza
Stacey, Sussanah	Jill Staynes & Margaret Storey	Inspector Robert Bone
Tey, Josephine	Elizabeth Mackintosh	Inspector Alan Grant
Tilton, Alice	Phoebe Atwood Taylor	Leonidas Witherall
Torrie, Malcolm	Gladys Mitchell	Timothy Herring
Wakefield, Hannah	two American-born women in London	Dee Street
Wentworth, Patricia	Dora Amy Elles	Miss Silver
Woods, Sara	Sara Bowen-Judd	Anthony Maitland
Wren, M. K.	Martha Kay Renfroe	Conan Flagg
Yorke, Margaret	Margaret Beda Larminie Nicholson	Dr. Patrick Grant

Seven

✒ Short Stories

Once upon a time, the short story was the predominant form of crime fiction. In fact, the origin of the genre is often traced to the stories of Edgar Allen Poe ("Murders in the Rue Morgue," "The Mystery of Marie Roget" and "The Purloined Letter"). And everyone knows the stories of Sherlock Holmes. But short stories were more than art or entertainment—they were an economic necessity for writers of the time. Actually, until well into the 20th century, book publishing continued to be a luxury most writers could not afford. As a result, some of the best-known sleuths of the Golden Age of Detection (perhaps now better-known for their appearances in full-length novels) were also featured in numerous short stories. Among them are Albert Campion created by Margery Allingham, Hercule Poirot from the pen of Agatha Christie and Lord Peter Wimsey, the fantasy detective of Dorothy L. Sayers.

Short stories, particularly those featured in anthologies, are regaining popularity in detective fiction. The bonus for readers, of course, is finding detectives who also appear in longer works of fiction. Reading the stories selected for a particular collection can lead you to authors whose work you'd like to know more about. To that end, we've selected ten anthologies with a total of 184 short stories written by women. Using the story-grid shown on pages 220 and 221, you can locate stories by authors you are already familiar with, as well as those who might be new to you. Seventy-seven of the 99 writers featured in these anthologies have series detectives identified in the Master List of Chapter 1. And some of them are well-known for their series novels. If you thought you'd run out of Kinsey, Sharon and V. I. stories, you'll be happy to find a baker's dozen that can help you avoid some of the withdrawal symptoms experienced while waiting for the next installment of our favorite detectives. So, find your favorite author in the story-grid and wherever you see a black square, you'll know there's a story by that author in the anthology identified at the top of the column. A longer description of each anthology can be found in the short story bibliography on page 222, along with a list of awards won by some of these stories.

Author	Sisters In Crime					Wom Eye	Wom Myst	Malice Domestic		
	1	2	3	4	5	Eye	Myst	1	2	3
Adams, Deborah										Mal 3
Adamson, Mary Jo			SinC 3							
Albert, Susan and Bill										Mal 3
Anders, K. T.					SinC 5					
Barnes, Linda	SinC 1									
Beck, K. K.					SinC 5				Mal 2	
Biederman, Marcia			SinC 3							
Braun, Lilian Jackson			SinC 3							
Cannell, Dorothy	SinC 1		SinC 3							Mal 3
Carlson, P. M.		SinC 2			SinC 5			Mal 1		
Chehak, Susan Taylor					SinC 5					
Clark, Mary Higgins		SinC 2					Myst		Mal 2	
Cody, Liza						Eye				
Craig, May Shura	SinC 1									
Crespi, Camilla T.										Mal 3
Cross, Amanda						Eye	Myst		Mal 2	
Dalton, Elizabeth A.							Myst			
D'Amato, Barbara				SinC 4						
Davidson, Diane Mott					SinC 5			Mal 1		
Davis, Dorothy Salisbury	SinC 1		SinC 3			Eye	Myst			
Dawson, Janet				SinC 4						
Douglas, Carole Nelson									Mal 2	
Dunlap, Sue	SinC 1	SinC 2			SinC 5	Eye			Mal 2	
Elkins, Charlotte & Aaron								Mal 1		
Fiedler, Jean		SinC 2		SinC 4						
Frankel, Valerie								Mal 1		
Fraser, Antonia						Eye	Myst			
Fremlin, Celia							Myst			
Friedman, Mickey	SinC 1	SinC 2								
Fyfield, Frances									Mal 2	
George, Elizabeth		SinC 2								
Girdner, Jaqueline					SinC 5					
Grafton, Sue	SinC 1	SinC 2		SinC 4		Eye				
Grant, Linda			SinC 3	SinC 4						
Grape, Jan									Mal 2	
Greenwood, L. B.								Mal 1		Mal 3
Grindle, Lucretia									Mal 2	
Gunning, Sally									Mal 2	
Haddam, Jane				SinC 4						
Hager, Jean					SinC 5					
Hall, Mary Bowen				SinC 4						
Harrington, Joyce		SinC 2			SinC 5					
Hart, Carolyn G.		SinC 2				Eye		Mal 1		
Hart, Jeanne		SinC 2								
Hess, Joan		SinC 2		SinC 4			Myst	Mal 1		Mal 3
Hornsby, Wendy				SinC 4						Mal 3
Howe, Melodie Johnson				SinC 4						
Hughes, Dorothy B.						Eye				
Kellerman, Faye	SinC 1		SinC 3			Eye	Myst			
Kelly, Susan	SinC 1		SinC 3							

Author	Sisters In Crime					Wom Eye	Wom Myst	Malice Domestic		
	1	2	3	4	5	Eye	Myst	1	2	3
Kelman, Judith				SinC 4						
Kijewski, Karen			SinC 3		SinC 5					
Kraft, Gabrielle			SinC 3		SinC 5					
Krich, Rochelle Majer					SinC 5					
Laiken, Deidre		SinC 2								
LaPierre, Janet			SinC 3		SinC 5			Mal 1		
MacGregor, T. J.		SinC 2			SinC 5					
MacLeod, Charlotte								Mal 1		
Maron, Margaret		SinC 2		SinC 4		Eye			Mal 2	
Matera, Lia	SinC 1	SinC 2								
McCafferty, Taylor									Mal 2	Mal 3
McCrumb, Sharyn		SinC 2		SinC 4				Mal 1		Mal 3
McGerr, Patricia							Myst			
McQuillan, Karin				SinC 4						
Meredith, D. R.								Mal 1		Mal 3
Michaels, Barbara	SinC 1									
Millhiser, Marlys										Mal 3
Muller, Marcia	SinC 1	SinC 2		SinC 4		Eye				
Neville, Katherine				SinC 4						
Oates, Joyce Carol					SinC 5					
O'Brien, Meg			SinC 3							
O'Callaghan, Maxine				SinC 4						
Oliver, Maria Antonia						Eye				
O'Marie, Sr. Carol Anne					SinC 5					
Paretsky, Sara	SinC 1		SinC 3		SinC 5	Eye	Myst			
Paul, Barbara			SinC 3	SinC 4				Mal 1		
Perry, Anne							Myst			
Peters, Elizabeth	SinC 1							Mal 1		
Peterson, Audrey								Mal 1		
Pickard, Nancy	SinC 1	SinC 2		SinC 4		Eye				
Rendell, Ruth							Myst			
Roberts, Gillian	SinC 1		SinC 3		SinC 5				Mal 2	
Scoppettone, Sandra	SinC 1									
Shankman, Sarah			SinC 3	SinC 4					Mal 2	
Singer, Shelley	SinC 1		SinC 3			Eye				
Slovo, Gillian						Eye				
Smith, Julie	SinC 1	SinC 2				Eye				
Stevens, B. K.							Myst			
Stockey, Janet							Myst			
Sucher, Dorothy					SinC 5					
Trott, Susan			SinC 3							
Valentine, Deborah		SinC 2								
Wallace, Marilyn	SinC 1	SinC 2	SinC 3	SinC 4	SinC 5	Eye				Mal 3
Watts, Carolyn Jensen							Myst			
Wheat, Carolyn	SinC 1	SinC 2		SinC 4		Eye				
White, Teri	SinC 1		SinC 3							
Wilson, Barbara						Eye				
Wings, Mary						Eye				
Yarbro, Chelsea Quinn			SinC 3							

Short Story Bibliography

Malice Domestic 1, presented by Elizabeth Peters. *Malice Domestic 2*, presented by Mary Higgins Clark. *Malice Domestic 3*, presented by Nancy Pickard. Martin Greenburg, ed. New York: Pocket Books, 1992–1994. 240–275 pages, $4.99, softcover.

Manson, Cynthia, ed. *Women of Mystery*. 15 stories previously published in Ellery Queen's Mystery Magazine. New York: Berkley Books, 1993 [Carroll & Graf edition published 1992]. 317 pages, $5.50, softcover.

Paretsky, Sara, ed. *A Woman's Eye*. 21 short stories by women writers with women sleuths. New York: Dell Publishing, 1991. 448 pages, $4.99, softcover. [includes a brief description of each author and her work along with an introduction by Sara Paretsky]. *Anthony winner* ★

Wallace, Marilyn, ed. *Sisters in Crime*, Volumes 1-5. New York: The Berkley Publishing Group, 1989-1992. 278-352 pages, $4.25 each, softcover. [includes a photo of each author and a brief description of her work] *Anthony nominee* ☆

Short Story Awards

from Sisters in Crime (1989)
    Barnes, Linda. "Lucky Penny." *Anthony winner* ★
    Pickard, Nancy. "Afraid All the Time." *Anthony, Macavity & American Mystery Award winner* ★ *Agatha & Edgar nominee* ☆
    Singer, Shelly. "A Terrible Thing." *Anthony nominee* ☆

from Sisters in Crime 2 (1990) Anthony nominee for best anthology ☆
    Dunlap, Sue. "The Celestial Buffet." *Anthony winner* ★
    Grafton, Sue. "A Poison That Leaves No Trace." *Shamus winner* ★ *Edgar nominee* ☆
    Hess, Joan. "Too Much to Bare." *Agatha & Macavity winner* ★
    McCrumb, Sharyn. "The Luncheon." *Anthony nominee* ☆

from Sisters in Crime 3 (1990)
    Cannell, Dorothy. "The High Cost of Living." *Agatha nominee* ☆
    Shankman, Sarah. "Say You're Sorry." *Anthony nominee* ☆
    Wallace, Marilyn. "A Tale of Two Pretties." *Anthony nominee* ☆

from Sisters in Crime 4 (1991)
    Hornsby, Wendy. "Nine Sons." *Edgar winner* ★

from A Woman's Eye (1991) Anthony winner for best anthology ★
    Cody, Liza. "Lucky Dip." *Anthony winner* ★

Eight

✒ Periodicals

The magazines and newsletters listed here are excellent sources for author interviews, book reviews and news about future releases and upcoming events in the mystery field. Single copies are often available at mystery bookstores and national bookstore chains. Try one each month or the whole lot of them and you'll be sure to find the one(s) that please you.

Subscriptions to **The Armchair Detective** are $26 per year in the U.S., $30 elsewhere. Published **quarterly** by The Armchair Detective Inc. (typical length 130 pages). Individual issues are $7.50 on the newsstand. Telephone 212-765-0902 or fax 212-265-5478. Publisher: Otto Penzler. Editor-in-Chief: Kate Stine.

> The Armchair Detective
> 129 West 56th Street
> New York NY 10019

Subscriptions to **The Drood Review of Mystery** are $14 per year or $25 for two years in the U.S.; $18 per year or $34 for two years in Canada and Mexico; $24 per year and $44 for two years overseas. Published **six times per year** by The Drood Review (typical length 24 pages). Telephone 616-349-3006. Editor & Publisher: Jim Huang.

> The Drood Review of Mystery
> Box 50267
> Kalamazoo MI 49005

Subscriptions to **Mostly Murder** are $10 for one year and $18 for two years. Also available free at selected bookstores and public libraries throughout the U.S. Published **quarterly** by Mostly Book Reviews Inc. (typical length 18 pages tabloid style). Telephone 214-821-9493. Editor & Publisher: Jay W. Setliff.

> Mostly Murder
> P.O. Box 191207
> Dallas TX 75219

Subscriptions to **Murder & Mayhem, The Mystery Reader's Guide** are $15 per year. Published **six times per year**. Individual issues are $2.95 on the newsstand. They promise to send your first issue with the reply envelope for your payment. Telephone 816-753-5035:

> Murder & Mayhem
> P.O. Box 415024
> Kansas City MO 64141

Subscriptions to **Mystery News** are $15 per year. Washington residents add 7.9% sales tax. Additional postage for Canada and overseas. Published **six times per year** by Mystery News (typical length 36 pages tabloid style). Publisher: Laurence Stay. Editor: Harriet Stay.

> Mystery News
> P.O. Box 1201
> Port Townsend WA 98368-0901

Subscriptions to **Mystery Readers Journal** are $24 per year ($36 overseas air mail) including membership in Mystery Readers International which allows each member to vote for the annual Macavity awards. Published **quarterly** as a thematic journal (typical length 52 pages). 1995 issues will focus on Suburban Mysteries (spring), San Francisco (summer), Regional British Mysteries (fall) and Technological Mysteries (winter). 1994 themes were Literary Mysteries, Old Crimes, Senior Sleuths and Detectives in Pairs. Editor: Janet A. Rudolph. Fax to 510-339-8309.

> Mystery Readers Journal
> P.O. Box 8116
> Berkeley CA 94707-8116

Subscriptions to **The Mystery Review, A Quarterly Publication for Mystery Readers** are $21.50 per year in Canada, $20 U.S. in the United States and $25 U.S. elsewhere. Individual issues are $5.95 on the newsstand. Published **quarterly** by C. von Hessert & Associates Ltd. (typical length 64 pages). Telephone 613-475-4440 or fax 613-475-3400. Publisher: Christian von Hessert. Editor: Barbara Davey.

> C. von Hessert & Associates Ltd.
> P.O. Box 233
> Colborne, Ontario K0K 1S0 Canada

Subscriptions to **Mystery Scene** magazine are $35 per year in the U.S. and $63.50 elsewhere. Foreign subscriptions are sent surface mail. Published **six times per year** by Mystery Enterprises (typical length 88 pages). Telephone 414-728-0793. Publisher: Martin H. Greenburg. Editor: Joe Gorman.

> Mystery Scene
> P.O. Box 669
> Cedar Rapids IA 52406-0669

Nine

Awards & Organizations

The **American Crime Writers League** (ACWL), founded in 1987, is a professional organization for published authors only. The group does not confer awards but has taken strong stands on a number of controversial issues such as unsigned reviews, which ACWL members find particularly distasteful. Not only is the reviewer deprived of much-deserved recognition, but the unsigned review invites malicious attacks on certain books when the reviewer's identity can be hidden.

Bouchercon, the popular name for the World Mystery Convention, is mystery fiction's largest fan and author convention. 1500 writers and fans convened in Seattle October 6-9, 1994 for Bouchercon 25. In 1995 the group will move to Nottingham, England and then St. Paul, Minnesota for the 1996 convention. The **Anthony Awards**, voted each year by the membership, are presented at Bouchercon for work published during the prior year.

The Anthony Awards are named for famed mystery critic **Anthony Boucher** whose real name was William Anthony Parker White. For 17 years Boucher wrote a weekly column *Criminals at Large* for *The New York Times Review of Books*. He also wrote eight novels and dozens of short stories, edited a science fiction magazine and reviewed plays, opera and science fiction.

The Anthony Awards include:

> Best Novel
> Best First Novel
> Best True Crime
> Best Individual Short Story
> Best Short Story Collection/Anthology
> Best Critical Work

The British **Crime Writers Association** (CWA), formed in 1953, was patterned after its counterpart, the Mystery Writers of America. In 1955 CWA began awarding special honors to the best crime fiction novel of the year. Originally named the Crossed Red Herrings Award, the prize later became known as the **Gold Dagger**. A **Silver Dagger** is awarded to the runner-up. Beginning in 1978 CWA also gave an award for best true crime book. Starting in 1986, Cartier and the CWA confer the **Diamond Dagger Award** based on a writer's lifetime achievement.

CWA also awards annually the **John Creasey Memorial Award** for best first novel, in honor of the famous British mystery writer (1908-1973) who produced almost 600 titles of mystery, crime, romance, western and suspense under 28 pseudonyms. He sometimes wrote two full-length books a month and often consoled aspiring writers with tales of the 743 rejection slips he received before his first sale.

The **Arthur Ellis Awards**, given by the **Crime Writers of Canada**, were established in 1984 and named after the nom de travail of Canada's official hangman. The Ellis Awards include:

Best Novel	Best True Crime
Best First Novel	Best Juvenile
Best Short Story	Best Play

The **International Association of Crime Writers** (North American Branch) was established in 1987 to provide information about crime-writing worldwide and publishing opportunities around the world. Membership is open to published authors and professionals (agents, editors, booksellers) in the mystery field. This association presents the North American **Hammett Prize** annually for the best work (fiction or nonfiction) of literary excellence in crime-writing.

Malice Domestic is an annual fan convention held in suburban Washington, DC in late April or early May. The conference is dedicated to cozy and traditional mysteries and their creators and bestows the **Agatha Award** in honor of Dame Agatha Christie. The actual award is in the form of a teapot. Malice Domestic and St. Martin's Press also sponsor a Best First Novel contest for cozy mysteries.

Mystery Readers of America present the **Macavity Awards** in a variety of categories each year. The awards are voted by the readership of the Mystery Readers Journal of Mystery Readers International.

Mystery Writers of America (MWA) was formed in 1945 with the purpose of offering membership to all writers of good repute in the mystery field, including fiction, fact, books, magazines, film and radio. Associate membership was also available to interested editors, critics, publishers, actors, directors and accredited fans. The organization now has nine regional chapters.

Each year, usually in April or May, MWA awards the **Edgar Awards** (named for Edgar Allen Poe) in a variety of categories, including:

Best Novel
Best First Novel
Best Original Paperback
Best Fact Crime
Best Critical/Biographical
Best Young Adult
Ellery Queen Award

Best Juvenile
Best Short Story
Best Episode in a TV series
Best TV Feature
Best Motion Picture
Robert L. Fish Award for best short story
from the MWA training program

Beginning with its selection of Agatha Christie in 1954, MWA began naming **Grand Masters** which now include 35 best-of-the-best:

1992	Donald Westlake	1975	Eric Ambler
1991	Elmore Leonard	1974	no award given
1990	Tony Hillerman	1973	Ross Macdonald
1989	**Helen McCloy**	1972	Judson Philips
1988	Hillary Waugh	1971	John D. MacDonald
1987	**Phyllis A. Whitney**	**1970**	**Mignon G. Eberhart**
1986	Michael Gilbert	1969	James M. Cain
1985	Ed McBain	1968	John Creasey
1984	**Dorothy Salisbury Davis**	1967	no award given
1983	John le Carre	1966	Baynard Kendrick
1982	**Margaret Millar**	1965	Georges Simenon
1981	Julian Symons	1964	no award given
1980	Stanley Ellin	1963	George Harmon Coxe
1979	W. R. Burnett	1962	John Dickson Carr
1978	Aaron Marc Stein	1961	Erle Stanley Gardner
1977	**Daphne du Marier**	1960	Ellery Queen
	Dorothy B. Hughes	1958	Rex Stout
	Ngaio Marsh	1957	Vincent Starrett
1976	Graham Greene	**1954**	**Agatha Christie**

The **Private Eye Writers of America** (PWA), formed in early 1982, gave its first **Shamus Awards** (for works published in 1981) at Bouchercon XIII in San Francisco. In recent years the category of P.I. has been expanded to include investigators who are paid for services rendered as part of their investigative work, such as news reporters and attorneys who do their own investigating.

Shamus Awards, honoring the private eye in mystery fiction, include:

Best Private Eye Novel
Best Private Eye Paperback Original
Best Private Eye Short Story (beginning in 1983)
Best First Private Eye Novel (beginning in 1984)
The Eye Life Achievement Award

In 1986 PWA and St. Martin's Press launched a contest for First Private Eye Novel which has become an annual event. The award-winning P.I. novel is published simultaneously in the U.S. by St. Martin's Press and in England by Macmillan.

Shamus Awards for works published in 1994, including the PWA/SMP Award, will be presented at **EyeCon '95**—the first PWA Conference, scheduled for June 15-18, 1995 in Milwaukee, Wisconsin with Sue Grafton as Guest of Honor and Les Roberts as Toastmaster. For additional information and registration forms, write to EyeCon '95, P. O. Box 341218, Milwaukee WI 53234.

Sisters in Crime was founded in 1986 "to combat discrimination against women in the mystery field, educate publishers and the general public as to inequalities in the treatment of female authors, and raise the level of awareness of their contribution to the mystery field." Sisters in Crime, with chapters in 20-some states, has more than 2500 members worldwide including writers, editors, agents, librarians, booksellers and fans. Chicago mystery writer Sara Paretsky was the founding president. For membership information, write to M. Beth Wasson, Executive Secretary, **Sisters in Crime**, P.O. Box 442124, Lawrence KS 66044-8933.

The **World Mystery Convention**, also known as **Bouchercon**, is the site of Anthony Award presentations and mystery fiction's largest fan and author convention. Fifteen hundred writers, editors, publishers, reviewers and fans convened in Seattle October 6-9, 1994 for **Bouchercon 25** with Marcia Muller as Guest of Honor and George C. Chesbro as Toastmaster. Tony Hillerman was the convention's honoree for lifetime achievement. More than 20 hours of double- and triple-track author panels were spread over four days, along with readings and book signings, films, meetings, the awards banquet and other special events.

In 1995 the World Mystery Convention moves to Nottingham, England—the mystery capital of Britain and home of **Shots in the Dark** mystery and thriller festival and **Shots on the Page** crime writing convention. Since 1990 Shots in the Dark celebrations have included all aspects of mysteries and thrillers in film, literature, theatre, music and visual arts, attracting guests from all over Britain and around the world. The slightly earlier date for **Bouchercon 26** (September 28 to October 1, 1995) is set to coincide with Shots in the Dark which will run September 21 through October 1,1995. Bouchercon 26 Guests of Honor will be James Ellroy and Colin Dexter. For more information about **Bouchercon 26** write to Conference Nottingham, The Business Information Centre, 309 Haydn Road, Nottingham NG5 1DG. Phone international 44-(0115) 985 6545 or fax 44-(0115) 985 6612.

The following year, St. Paul, Minnesota will host **Bouchercon 27** with Mary Higgins Clark as Guest of Honor and Jeremiah Healy as Toastmaster. For more information about the St. Paul Bouchercon (October 9-13, 1996) write to **Bouchercon 27**, P. O. Box 8296, Minneapolis MN 55408-0296. Bouchercon 28 is scheduled to return to San Francisco in 1997, site of the original World Mystery Convention in 1970. For early information about **Bouchercon 28** in San Francisco write to **Bouchercon 28**, P. O. Box 6202, Hayward CA 94540.

Ten

Search Logs

10

The search logs reprinted in this chapter are ones I created for my own personal use after several embarrassing reminders from librarians and booksellers that I had asked them to search for the very same book not six months earlier. In the interest of keeping their good will, I decided to start a record of my book searches along with my inter-library loan and library reserve requests. It can sometimes take months to find an out-of-print title and even those of us with good memories can sometimes forget what we're looking for. Keeping track of subscription orders seemed like a good idea too. So I present all four of these log sheets for your use and enjoyment.

Inter-library loan is a wonderful way to find books that have long since been retired from the shelves of your local library. Each library has its own system for handling inter-library loan requests, but your librarian will be happy to acquaint you with the rules. My library allows two requests per month, so I try to keep a running list of titles that I'm looking for so that I'm always ready to submit another request when the new month rolls around. **Library reserve requests** are also easy to forget. Our library installed a new computer system this year and soon patrons will be able to type in their own reserve requests. Until that happy day, we have to bother a reference librarian every time we want to make a reserve request. I feel guilty taking up their time this way—especially when one of them cheerfully informs me that I placed a reserve request for the very same book two weeks ago! So now I keep track.

As an amateur genealogist, I recognized the similarities between book hunting and ancestor hunting very early in my **book searching** efforts. Keeping track of where you've looked for a certain title can be important. When you find a new source for old titles, you ask yourself, "where was the last place I looked for that book?" You'd be surprised how soon you can forget where it is you've already searched. And if you read as many periodicals, journals and newsletters as I do, keeping track of current **subscriptions** is no small task. Even the best-organized among us can remember paying twice for the same subscription or failing to send the renewal check before the expiration date. And how about those gift subscriptions that seemed like such a wonderful idea at the time. Who's keeping track of those?

Inter-Library Loan Request Log

Request Date	Receipt Date	Library	Book Title	Author	©	Series Character(s)	Series #

Inter-Library Loan Request Log ✍

Request Date	Receipt Date	Library	Book Title	Author	©	Series Character(s)	Series #

Library Reserve Request Log

Request Date	Receipt Date	Library	Book Title	Author	©	Series Character(s)	Series #

Library Reserve Request Log 🎀

Request Date	Receipt Date	Library	Book Title	Author	©	Series Character(s)	Series #

Book Search Log

Search Date	Find Date	Book Title	Author	©	Series Character(s)	Dealer	Contact
							☐ phone ☐ fax ☐ mail
							☐ phone ☐ fax ☐ mail
							☐ phone ☐ fax ☐ mail
							☐ phone ☐ fax ☐ mail
							☐ phone ☐ fax ☐ mail
							☐ phone ☐ fax ☐ mail
							☐ phone ☐ fax ☐ mail
							☐ phone ☐ fax ☐ mail
							☐ phone ☐ fax ☐ mail
							☐ phone ☐ fax ☐ mail
							☐ phone ☐ fax ☐ mail
							☐ phone ☐ fax ☐ mail
							☐ phone ☐ fax ☐ mail
							☐ phone ☐ fax ☐ mail
							☐ phone ☐ fax ☐ mail
							☐ phone ☐ fax ☐ mail
							☐ phone ☐ fax ☐ mail
							☐ phone ☐ fax ☐ mail
							☐ phone ☐ fax ☐ mail

Book Search Log

Search Date	Find Date	Book Title	Author	©	Series Character(s)	Dealer	Contact
							☐ phone ☐ fax ☐ mail
							☐ phone ☐ fax ☐ mail
							☐ phone ☐ fax ☐ mail
							☐ phone ☐ fax ☐ mail
							☐ phone ☐ fax ☐ mail
							☐ phone ☐ fax ☐ mail
							☐ phone ☐ fax ☐ mail
							☐ phone ☐ fax ☐ mail
							☐ phone ☐ fax ☐ mail
							☐ phone ☐ fax ☐ mail
							☐ phone ☐ fax ☐ mail
							☐ phone ☐ fax ☐ mail
							☐ phone ☐ fax ☐ mail
							☐ phone ☐ fax ☐ mail
							☐ phone ☐ fax ☐ mail
							☐ phone ☐ fax ☐ mail
							☐ phone ☐ fax ☐ mail
							☐ phone ☐ fax ☐ mail
							☐ phone ☐ fax ☐ mail

Subscriptions & Memberships Log

Periodical or Organization	Term	Frequency	# Issues	Start Date	Expire Date	Cost	Payment
	☐ one year ☐ six months ☐	☐ quarterly ☐ bimonthly ☐ monthly					☐ check # ___ ☐ VISA/MC ☐
	☐ one year ☐ six months ☐	☐ quarterly ☐ bimonthly ☐ monthly					☐ check # ___ ☐ VISA/MC ☐
	☐ one year ☐ six months ☐	☐ quarterly ☐ bimonthly ☐ monthly					☐ check # ___ ☐ VISA/MC ☐
	☐ one year ☐ six months ☐	☐ quarterly ☐ bimonthly ☐ monthly					☐ check # ___ ☐ VISA/MC ☐
	☐ one year ☐ six months ☐	☐ quarterly ☐ bimonthly ☐ monthly					☐ check # ___ ☐ VISA/MC ☐
	☐ one year ☐ six months ☐	☐ quarterly ☐ bimonthly ☐ monthly					☐ check # ___ ☐ VISA/MC ☐
	☐ one year ☐ six months ☐	☐ quarterly ☐ bimonthly ☐ monthly					☐ check # ___ ☐ VISA/MC ☐
	☐ one year ☐ six months ☐	☐ quarterly ☐ bimonthly ☐ monthly					☐ check # ___ ☐ VISA/MC ☐
	☐ one year ☐ six months ☐	☐ quarterly ☐ bimonthly ☐ monthly					☐ check # ___ ☐ VISA/MC ☐
	☐ one year ☐ six months ☐	☐ quarterly ☐ bimonthly ☐ monthly					☐ check # ___ ☐ VISA/MC ☐
	☐ one year ☐ six months ☐	☐ quarterly ☐ bimonthly ☐ monthly					☐ check # ___ ☐ VISA/MC ☐
	☐ one year ☐ six months ☐	☐ quarterly ☐ bimonthly ☐ monthly					☐ check # ___ ☐ VISA/MC ☐
	☐ one year ☐ six months ☐	☐ quarterly ☐ bimonthly ☐ monthly					☐ check # ___ ☐ VISA/MC ☐
	☐ one year ☐ six months ☐	☐ quarterly ☐ bimonthly ☐ monthly					☐ check # ___ ☐ VISA/MC ☐
	☐ one year ☐ six months ☐	☐ quarterly ☐ bimonthly ☐ monthly					☐ check # ___ ☐ VISA/MC ☐

Eleven

✒ Preview of Next Edition

11

We plan to introduce a new and updated edition of *Detecting Women* each year in early October. To do that, we're going to need your help keeping up with new authors, titles and series characters, as well as newsletters and other publications, conventions and organizations. To encourage the widest participation possible, we have included a fax back form for your comments, suggestions, corrections and revisions. Feel free to mail us your form or send it via e-mail. And send us more than one form. In fact, we've printed the form twice (pages 239-240) so you can keep a copy of the suggestions you send us.

Seventy-nine authors with 74 series and 310 titles have already been identified for future editions of *Detecting Women*. Among the authors you will find in next year's Master List are:

Adams, Deborah	Ford, Leslie	Linnington, Elizabeth
Baker, Abby Penn	Froetschel, Susan	Maney, Mabel
Bedford, Jean	Frommer, Sara	McCafferty, Jeanne
Bookluck, Adelaide	Granger, Ann	Nielsen, Helen
Bowen, Gail	Grey, Jillian	Porter, Joyce
Callahan, Sheila	Hall, Patricia	Quest, Erica
Dank, Gloria	Heberden, Mary Violet	Redman, J. M.
Dengler, Sandy	Heyer, Georgette	Rosen, S. J.
Donald, Anabel	Hill, Susan	Shaffer, Louise
Dunbar, Sophie	Hitchcock, Jane	Smith, April
Dunnett, Dorothy	Hite, Molly	Tell, Dorothy
Eagan, Lesley	Kelly, Mary	Travis, Elizabeth
Edwards, Ruth	Kershaw, Valerie	West, Chassie
Eichler, Selma	Kreuter, Katherine	Wilson, Karen
Evans, Geraldine	Kruger, Mary	Wiltz, Chris
Fennelly, Tony	Lee, Wendi	Winslow, Pauline
Flora, Kate	Lemarchand, Elizabeth	Zachary, Fay

In the next edition, you will also find:

- more award citations
- expanded author profiles
- large print titles
- books on tape
- on-line services
- more newsletters and periodicals
- expanded short story lists
- more authors from outside the US
- titles by men writing women series characters

How you can help

Every effort has been made to identify all the women who are currently writing and have written mystery series characters, to identify their detectives and arrange the corresponding titles in proper order, all the while spelling everyone's name correctly. No small task indeed. Somewhere out there are experts on authors whose work I haven't yet had the pleasure of reading. So let me hear from you—about my sins of omission and unintentional blunders, large and small.

If you're an author or an expert on something I've overlooked, or worse yet, something I've botched, please let me know. We want to get it exactly right next time. If you are the editor or publisher of a newsletter or other publication, please send the particulars that you would like included or perhaps removed. The second edition of *Detecting Women* is scheduled to go to press in early August 1995 for a late September delivery (in time for Bouchercon 26).

If you have suggestions, comments or ideas for improvement, I'd enjoy hearing from you. To be sure we have your information in time for the next edition, please make sure it arrives at Purple Moon Press before June 15, 1995. If you think we might need to follow up with you, please provide an address or fax number where you can be reached. We look forward to hearing from you. And thanks for your help!

Feedback Form

Detecting Women at Purple Moon Press

Fax: 313-593-4087

Mail: 3319 Greenfield Rd., Suite 317
                Dearborn, MI 48120-1212

E-mail: nrgx40a@prodigy.com

☐ Additions & Suggestions
for New Information

☐ Corrections, Revisions, Errors
(please note page numbers)

Name (optional): _____

Contact me at: _____

Best time: _____

Feedback Form

Detecting Women at Purple Moon Press

Fax: 313-593-4087

Mail: 3319 Greenfield Rd., Suite 317
              Dearborn, MI 48120-1212

E-mail: nrgx40a@prodigy.com

☐ Additions & Suggestions
  for New Information

☐ Corrections, Revisions, Errors
  (please note page numbers)

Name (optional): _____

Contact me at: _____

Best time: _____

Twelve

ᴏᴄ Glossary

The **Agatha Awards**, in honor of Dame Agatha Christie, are presented annually in various categories by the Malice Domestic Mystery Convention which is devoted to the traditional or cozy mystery. The actual award is in the form of a teapot. See *Chapter 9, Awards and Organizations*, for more information.

An **amateur detective**, unlike a private investigator or police officer, is not paid for the work of investigating and is likely to be a volunteer, working for nothing. The amateur detective is often a working professional in another field, such as journalism, academia, law or medicine. In some cases, the amateur detective is independently wealthy or retired.

The **American Crime Writers League** (ACWL), founded in 1987, is a professional organization for published authors only. Applicants must have published a novel, three short stories or a work of non-fiction.

The **American Mystery Awards**, given annually in various categories, are voted by the readership of *Mystery Scene* magazine.

The **Anthony Awards**, named in honor of Anthony Boucher, are voted annually in various categories by members of the World Mystery Convention. See the Glossary entry for World Mystery Convention and also *Chapter 9, Awards and Organizations*, for more information.

Bouchercon is the name given to the World Mystery Convention held in early October each year since 1970 to honor the work of **Anthony Boucher** (1911-1968), a prolific mystery writer. From 1951 until his death he wrote the weekly column *Criminals at Large* for the *New York Times Review of Books*. He also wrote eight novels and dozens of short stories, edited a science fiction magazine and reviewed plays, opera and science fiction. His real name was William Anthony Parker White. See the Glossary entry for World Mystery Convention and also *Chapter 9, Awards and Organizations*, for more information about World Mystery Conventions for 1995, 1996 and 1997.

Chief Superintendent or Detective Chief Superintendent is the officer rank above Superintendent in the County or Metropolitan Police Force in Great Britain.

Constable or Detective Constable is the lowest officer rank in the County or Metropolitan Police Force in Great Britain.

Cozy or traditional mysteries are classically English and most often feature an inspired amateur detective who restores order to the town or village by solving an elaborate puzzle. Violence is most likely off stage and the murderer, often devilishly clever, uses ingenious methods for murder and mayhem. Agatha Christie is the quintessential creator of the cozy mystery.

John **Creasey Memorial Award** is conferred annually by the British Crime Writers Association (CWA) for best first novel, in honor of the British mystery writer who was a significant force in the founding of CWA. John Creasey (1908-1973) was a prolific writer of romance, crime, suspense, mystery and western novels—close to 600 titles under 28 pseudonyms. He sometimes wrote two full-length books a month and often consoled aspiring writers with tales of the 743 rejections he received before his first sale.

The British **Crime Writers Association** (CWA), formed in 1953, was patterned after its counterpart, the Mystery Writers of America. Since 1955 the Crime Writers Association has conferred awards (Gold and Silver Daggers) for best novel and best true crime book. Beginning in 1986, Cartier and CWA have sponsored the Diamond Dagger Award, given in honor of lifetime achievement in crime writing.

Beginning in 1986, the British Crime Writers Association and Cartier have sponsored the **Diamond Dagger Award**, given in honor of lifetime achievement in crime writing.

Dime novels were a distinctly American phenomenon dating from 1860 to 1901, when a change in postal laws eliminated their second-class mailing privileges. Immensely popular during the Civil War era, these ten-cent paperbacks were reportedly shipped by the train car load to soldiers in the field.

Edgar Allen Poe (1809-1849) is widely recognized as the inventor of the detective story with his 1841 entry "The Murders in the Rue Morgue." Some think he would also be credited with the first novel of detection were it not for his early and untimely death.

The **Edgar Awards**, in honor of Edgar Allen Poe, are awarded annually by the Mystery Writers of America in various categories. See *Chapter 9, Awards and Organizations*, for more information.

The **Ellis Awards** are given annually by the Crime Writers of Canada in various categories. The award takes its name from Arthur Ellis, the nom de travail of Canada's official hangman. See *Chapter 9, Awards and Organizations*, for more information.

The **Gold Dagger**, which was originally called the Crossed Red Herrings, is the top award given annually in various categories by the British Crime Writers Association.

Runners up are awarded the Silver Dagger. See *Chapter 9, Awards and Organizations,* for more information.

Golden Age of Mystery, sometimes called the Golden Age of Detection, was ushered in by Agatha Christie's 1920 debut novel, *The Mysterious Affair at Styles,* followed shortly by Lord Peter Wimsey's arrival in Dorothy Sayers' 1923 novel *Whose Body?*

The **Grand Master Award** is given by the Mystery Writers of America (elected by its board of directors) in recognition of a lifetime of excellence in crime fiction. The first to be named to this mystery hall of fame was Agatha Christie in 1954. See *Chapter 9, Awards and Organizations,* for a complete list of Grand Masters.

The **Hammett Prize**, awarded by the International Association of Crime Writers, is given for excellence in crime writing, either fiction or non-fiction. Nominations are made by members of the publishing and reading committees and a trophy is presented at the Edgar ceremonies in New York City. See *Chapter 9, Awards and Organizations,* for more information.

Hard-boiled mysteries, typically narrated by a cynical private investigator walking the mean streets of anytown, are generally thought of as an American invention.

Inspector or Detective Inspector is the officer rank above Sergeant but below Chief Inspector in the County or Metropolitan Police Force in Great Britain.

Macavity Award winners in various categories are selected by the readers of the Mystery Readers Journal of Mystery Readers International. See *Chapter 8, Periodicals,* for subscription information.

A **pen name** (from the French nom de plume) is another term for pseudonym or alias used by an author to conceal identity.

A **penny dreadful** (chiefly a British term circa 1870-1875) is a sensational novel of adventure, crime or violence, typically cheaply produced. The writers of these novels were often paid only a penny per line and later a penny per word.

A **police procedural** is a mystery novel, film or television drama that deals realistically with police work.

The **Private Eye Writers of America** (PWA), founded in 1982 to promote and recognize private-eye writers, confers the annual Shamus Awards in a variety of categories. See *Chapter 9, Awards and Organizations,* for more information.

The **protagonist** is the leading character or hero of a literary work, from the Greek term for the first actor and main character in a drama.

Pulp fiction got its name originally from the rough and low-quality paper (manufactured from wood pulp) on which it was printed. The term is often synonymous with fiction involving lurid and sensational subjects.

A **red herring** was once an actual smoked herring (more brown than red) that was dragged across a hunting trail for the purpose of confusing the tracking dogs. The term in crime fiction is used to describe any false clue planted for the purpose of confusing the reader.

Scotland Yard is the popular name for England's Metropolitan Police Force which is responsible for Greater London.

Sergeant or Detective Sergeant is the officer rank above Constable but below Inspector in the County or Metropolitan Police Force in Great Britain.

Shamus Awards are given annually by the Private Eye Writers of America (PWA) in various categories pertaining to the P.I. story and novel. Nominations, which are made by publishers and voted by PWA members, are open to novels or short stories featuring any investigator not employed by or paid by a unit of government. See *Chapter 9, Awards and Organizations*, for more information on Private Eye Writers and EyeCon '95—site of the 1995 Shamus Awards for works produced in 1994.

The **Silver Dagger** is awarded annually by the British Crime Writers Association in various categories. See *Chapter 9, Awards and Organizations*, for more information.

Sisters in Crime was founded in 1986 to combat discrimination against women in the mystery field and to raise the level of awareness regarding the contribution of women to the field. The organization now has more than 2500 members worldwide including writers, editors, agents, librarians, booksellers and fans. Chicago mystery writer Sara Paretsky was the founding president. See also *Chapter 9, Awards and Organizations*, for more information.

The **World Mystery Convention** (also known as Bouchercon), is held each year in early October to honor the work of Anthony Boucher (1911-1968), a prolific mystery writer. From 1951 until his death he wrote a weekly column (*Criminals at Large*) for the *New York Times Review of Books*. He also wrote eight novels and dozens of short stories, edited a science fiction magazine and reviewed plays, opera and science fiction. His real name was William Anthony Parker White. See also *Chapter 9, Awards and Organizations*, for more information about World Mystery Conventions for 1995, 1996 and 1997.

Thirteen

Bibliography

The Armchair Detective, Vol. 27, No. 1-3 (1994). New York: The Armchair Detective, Inc., 1994. 130 pages, $7.50, magazine.

Collingwood, Donna, ed. *Mystery Writers Market Place and Sourcebook.* Cincinnati: Writer's Digest Books, 1993. 312 pages, $17.95, hardcover.

DeAndrea, William L. *Encyclopedia Mysteriosa, A Comprehensive Guide to the Art of Detection in Print, Film, Radio, and Television.* New York: Prentice Hall General Reference, 1994. 405 pages, $29.95, hardcover.

The Drood Review of Mystery, selected issues, 1994. Kalamazoo, Michigan: The Drood Review.

Genreflecting, A Guide to Reading Interests in Genre Fiction. Betty Rosenberg and Diana Tixier Herald, eds. Third Edition, 1991. Englewood, Colorado: Libraries Unlimited, Inc.

Gorman, Ed, Martin H. Greenburg, Larry Segriff, editors with Jon L. Breen. *The Fine Art of Murder, The Mystery Reader's Indispensable Companion.* New York: Carroll & Graf, 1993. 390 pages, $17.95, softcover. Anthony winner for best critical work ★

Klein, Kathleen Gregory. *The Woman Detective, Gender & Genre.* Urbana and Chicago: University of Illinois Press, 1988. 261 pages, $27.95, hardcover.

Lachman, Marvin. *A Reader's Guide to The American Novel of Detection.* New York: G. K. Hall & Co., 1993. 435 pages, $45.00, hardcover. Anthony nominee for best critical work ☆

Malice Domestic 1, presented by Elizabeth Peters. Martin Greenburg, ed. An anthology of original traditional mystery stores. New York: Pocket Books, 1992. 275 pages, $4.99, softcover.

Malice Domestic 2, presented by Mary Higgins Clark. Martin Greenburg, ed. An anthology of original traditional mystery stores. New York: Pocket Books, 1993. 255 pages, $4.99, softcover.

Malice Domestic 3, presented by Nancy Pickard. Martin Greenburg, ed. An anthology of original traditional mystery stores. New York: Pocket Books, 1994. 240 pages, $4.99, softcover.

Manson, Cynthia, ed. *Women of Mystery*. 15 stories previously published in Ellery Queen's Mystery Magazine. New York: Berkley Books, 1993 [Carroll & Graf edition published 1992]. 317 pages, $5.50, softcover.

Mostly Murder, Your Guide to Reading Mysteries. Vol. 3, No. 1 (Jan/Feb/Mar 1992) through Vol. 5, No. 3 (Jul/Aug/Sep 1994). Dallas, Texas: Mostly Book Reviews Inc.

Mystery News, Vol. 12, No. 2 (Feb/Mar 1993) through Vol. 13, No. 5 (Aug/Sep 1994). Port Townsend, Washington.

The Mystery Review, A Quarterly Publication for Mystery Readers. Vol. 2, No. 3-4, 1994. Colborne, Ontario, Canada.

Mystery Scene magazine, Numbers 41-44. Cedar Rapids, Iowa: Mystery Enterprises.

Neibuhr, Gary Warren. *A Reader's Guide to The Private Eye Novel*. New York: G. K. Hall & Co., 1993. 323 pages, $45.00, hardcover. Anthony nominee for best critical work ☆

Oleksiw, Susan. *A Reader's Guide to the Classic British Mystery*. New York: Mysterious Press, 1989. 585 pages, $19.95, softcover. Originally published by G. K. Hall & Co., Boston, 1988.

Paretsky, Sara, ed. *A Woman's Eye*. New York: Dell Publishing, 1991. 448 pages, $4.99, softcover. Anthony winner for best anthology ★

Sisters in Crime Books-in-Print, Spring 1994. Compiled by Sue Henry. Available from Rowan Mountain Literary Associates, Blacksburg, Virginia.

Swanson, Jean and Dean James. *By a Woman's Hand, A Guide to Mystery Fiction by Women*. New York: Berkley Books, 1994. 254 pages, $10.00, softcover.

Wallace, Marilyn, ed. *Sisters in Crime*, Volumes 1-5. New York: The Berkley Publishing Group, 1989-1992. 278-352 pages, $4.25 each, softcover. Anthony nominee ☆

What Do I Read Next? A Reader's Guide to Current Genre Fiction, 1990-1993. (four volumes) Detroit and London: Gale Research Inc., 1991-1994. Available in most public libraries.

Fourteen

Index

14

A

Abigail Doyle . . . 40, 161, 169, 188
Abigail Patience Danforth . . . 75, 158, 163, 169, 191
Abigail Sanderson . . . 61, 165, 179, 193
Adam Dalgleish . . . 76-77, 156, 169, 194
Adams, Deborah . . . 220
➡ Adamson, Lydia . . . 19, 159-160, 167, 169, 172, 188, 208, 210-212, 214, 217
➡ Adamson, M. J. . . . 19, 155, 170, 191, 206-207, 220
Addie Devore . . . 78, 164, 169, 185
Agatha Award . . . 226, 241
Agatha Raisin . . . 26, 161, 169, 193
➡ Aird, Catherine . . . 20, 155, 171, 194, 201-204, 206, 212, 217
Alan Grant . . . 138, 157, 169, 194
Alan Stewart . . . 80, 160, 179, 187
Albenia "Benni" Harper . . . 57, 160, 169, 184
Albert Campion . . . 21, 155, 169, 193
Albert, Susan & Bill . . . 218, 220
➡ Albert, Susan Wittig . . . 20, 161, 171, 190, 211-212, 214, 216, 218
Alex Jensen . . . 72, 159, 162, 175, 183
Alex McKenzie, Dr. . . . 29, 159, 179, 186
Alex Sinclair . . . 68, 156, 169, 192
Alex Winter . . . 136, 158, 169, 183
Alice Nestleton . . . 19, 159, 167, 169, 188
Aline Scott . . . 52, 155, 169, 185
Alison Hope . . . 79, 162, 167, 169, 193
Alix Thorssen . . . 94, 160, 169, 187
➡ Allen, Irene . . . 20, 167, 172, 189, 211-212, 217
➡ Allingham, Margery . . . 21, 155, 169, 193, 197-202
Alonzo Hawkin . . . 80, 156, 175, 184
Amanda Hazard . . . 56, 161, 169, 189
Amanda Knight . . . 58, 166, 169, 191
Amanda Pepper . . . 123, 159, 169, 189
Amanda Roberts . . . 151, 164, 169, 185
Amelia Peabody . . . 115, 159, 163, 169, 192
American Crime Writers League . . . 225, 241
American Mystery Awards . . . 241

Amy Prescott . . . 71, 166, 169, 190
Anders, K. T. . . . 220
Andrea Perkins . . . 40, 160, 170, 186
➡ Andreae, Christine . . . 22, 166, 176, 191, 211, 214
➡ Andrews, Sarah . . . 22, 162, 172, 191, 214, 216
Angela Benbow . . . 126, 168, 170, 183
Angelina Amalfi . . . 114, 163, 170, 184
Anna Lee . . . 40, 157, 170, 193
Anna Peters . . . 86, 162, 170, 191
Anna Pigeon . . . 26, 162, 170, 191
Annabel Reed . . . 140, 165, 177, 191
Anne Fitzhugh . . . 123, 157, 170, 191
Anneke Haagen . . . 74, 162, 167, 170, 187
Annie Laurance . . . 69, 161, 170, 190
Annie MacPherson . . . 133, 165, 170, 190
Annie McGrogan . . . 55, 157, 170, 188
Anthony Award . . . 225, 228, 241
Anthony Maitland . . . 150-151, 165, 170, 193
April Woo . . . 61, 155, 170, 188
Arly Hanks . . . 72, 156, 170, 183
Armchair Detective . . . 223
➡ Armstrong, Charlotte . . . 22, 159, 177, 191, 199
➡ Arnold, Margot . . . 22, 159, 178, 196, 203-204, 208, 210-211, 214, 217
Asey Mayo . . . 137-138, 166, 170, 186
Ashley Johnson . . . 94, 156, 172, 191
➡ Atherton, Nancy . . . 23, 166, 170, 186, 211, 214, 216
Auguste Didier . . . 106, 163, 170, 192
Aunt Dimity . . . 23, 166, 170, 186
Auntie Lil . . . 64, 161, 180, 188
Aurora Teagarden . . . 68, 161, 170, 185
➡ Ayres, Noreen . . . 23, 155, 179, 184, 211, 214

B

➡ Babson, Marian . . . 23-24, 161, 167, 172, 193, 202, 205, 207-208, 212
Bacon, Gail . . . 218

➡ Bailey, Jo . . . 24, 166, 174, 187, 210, 212
➡ Baker, Nikki . . . 24, 161, 165, 181, 191, 210-211
Ball, Doris Bell Collier . . . 217
➡ Ballard, Mignon . . . 24, 166, 172, 191, 212
Balthazar Marten . . . 19, 155, 170, 191
➡ Banks, Carolyn . . . 24, 159, 179, 190, 212
➡ Bannister, Jo . . . 25, 155, 160, 171, 176, 192, 193, 204, 207-208, 212, 214
Barbara Havers . . . 59, 155, 180, 193
Barbara Holloway . . . 148, 165, 170, 189
Barbara Joan "Bo" Bradley . . . 111, 158, 170, 184
➡ Barber, Willetta A. . . . 25, 155, 171, 188, 198-199
➡ Barnes, Linda . . . 25-26, 157, 171, 177, 186, 204-208, 210, 212, 216, 220, 222
➡ Barr, Nevada . . . 26, 162, 170, 191, 212, 214
Barrett Lake . . . 132, 159, 170, 183
Basil Willing, Dr. . . . 95, 166, 170, 188
➡ Beaton, M. C. . . . 26, 155, 161, 169, 173, 193-194, 205-207, 209-212, 214, 217
Beatrice Lestrange Bradley . . . 101, 166, 170, 194
➡ Beck, K. K. . . . 27, 163, 167, 174, 184, 190, 204-205, 207, 211-212, 214, 217, 220
Becky Belski . . . 66, 161, 167, 170, 186
➡ Belfort, Sophie . . . 27, 159, 178, 186, 205, 210-211, 217
➡ Bell, Josephine . . . 27, 166, 172, 193, 198-201, 217
Ben Haskell . . . 34, 166, 172, 193
Ben Safford . . . 51, 165, 170, 191
Benjamin Jurnet . . . 71, 156, 170, 192
➡ Bennett, Liza . . . 28, 161, 178, 188, 207, 209
➡ Berenson, Laurien . . . 28, 167, 178, 191, 214
➡ Berry, Carole . . . 28, 161, 170, 188, 206-207, 209-210, 214

➡ denotes authors in Master List

B . . . continued

Betty Trenka . . . 38, 161, 170, 185
Biederman, Marcia . . . 220
Bill Slider . . . 69, 156, 170, 192
❖ Bishop, Claudia . . . 28, 161, 179, 188, 214, 216-217
❖ Black, Veronica . . . 28, 162, 175, 192, 209, 211-212, 214
❖ Blackmur, L. L. . . . 29, 160, 173, 191, 207
Blackwater Bay Mystery . . . 62, 155, 170, 191
Blaine Stewart . . . 153, 158, 170, 189
Blanche White . . . 107, 161, 162, 170, 191
❖ Bland, Eleanor Taylor . . . 29, 155, 161, 177, 186, 211-212, 214
❖ Block, Barbara . . . 29, 160, 179, 189, 214
Blue Maguire . . . 147, 157, 180, 184
Bonnie Indermill . . . 28, 161, 170, 188
❖ Borthwick, J. S. . . . 29, 159, 179, 186, 204-205, 209, 211, 214
❖ Borton, D. B. . . . 30, 157, 167, 171, 189, 212, 214, 216-217
Boucher, Anthony . . . 225, 241, 244
Bouchercon . . . 225, 228, 241, 244
Bowen-Judd, Sara . . . 218
❖ Bowers, Elisabeth . . . 30, 157, 177, 195, 207, 210
❖ Boylan, Eleanor . . . 30, 167, 171, 188, 207, 209, 211-212
❖ Bradley, Lynn . . . 30, 157, 171, 190, 214
❖ Brand, Christianna . . . 31, 155, 171, 193, 199-200, 217
❖ Braun, Lilian Jackson . . . 31, 159, 164, 175, 191, 201-202, 205, 207, 209-212, 214, 216, 220
❖ Brennan, Carol . . . 32, 161, 176, 188, 210, 211
❖ Brightwell, Emily . . . 32, 163, 174, 193, 212, 214
❖ Brill, Toni . . . 32, 160, 177, 188, 210, 212, 217
Britt Montero . . . 33, 164, 170, 185
❖ Brod, D. C. . . . 32, 157, 179, 186, 208-210, 212
Brooks, Janice Young . . . 217
Brown, Morna Doris MacTaggart . . . 218
❖ Brown, Rita Mae . . . 32-33, 159, 177, 190, 209, 211, 214
❖ Buchanan, Edna . . . 33, 164, 170, 185, 211, 214, 216
Bunty Felse . . . 113, 156, 173, 194
❖ Burden, Pat . . . 33, 155, 174, 193, 209, 211
❖ Burke, Jan . . . 33, 164, 174, 183, 212, 214, 216
❖ Butler, Gwendoline . . . 34, 155, 175, 193, 200-202, 206-208, 210-212, 214, 218

C

C. B. Greenfield . . . 77, 164, 177, 185
Cadfael, Brother . . . 116-117, 161, 162, 163, 170, 194
Caitlin Reece . . . 52, 157, 165, 170, 195
Cal Donovan . . . 25, 155, 176, 193
Caledonia Wingate . . . 126, 168, 170, 183
Caley Burke . . . 97, 158, 171, 184
Calista Jacobs . . . 81, 161, 171, 186

❖ Cannell, Dorothy . . . 34, 166, 172, 193, 205, 207, 209, 211, 214, 220, 222
❖ Cannon, Taffy . . . 35, 165, 178, 184, 212, 216
Carl Pedersen . . . 70, 156, 171, 183
Carlos Cruz . . . 142, 157, 174, 184
Carlotta Carlyle . . . 25, 157, 171, 186
❖ Carlson, P. M. . . . 35, 155, 159, 177, 186, 188, 205-207, 209-211, 216, 220
Carmen Ramirez . . . 67, 164, 171, 191
Carpenter, Lynette . . . 217
Cass Jameson . . . 147, 165, 171, 189
Cassandra Reilly . . . 148, 162, 171, 194
Cassandra Swann . . . 103, 166, 171, 192
Cat Caliban . . . 30, 157, 167, 171, 189
Cat Marsala . . . 46, 164, 171, 186
Catherine LeVendeur . . . 107, 163, 171, 195
Catherine Sayler . . . 63, 158, 171, 184
❖ Caudwell, Sarah . . . 35, 159, 165, 174, 194, 204-205, 208, 217
Cecile Buddenbrooks, Sister . . . 137, 158, 171, 186
Cecily Sinclair . . . 80, 163, 171, 192
❖ Chapman, Sally . . . 36, 157, 175, 185, 210, 214
Charles Spotted Moon . . . 152, 163, 165, 171, 185
❖ Charles, Kate . . . 36, 162, 165, 176, 192, 210, 212
Charlie Greene . . . 101, 167, 171, 184
Charlie Meiklejohn . . . 148, 158, 171, 189
Charlotte Graham . . . 93, 167, 171, 188
Charlotte Kent . . . 81, 160, 171, 185
Charlotte Pitt . . . 115, 156, 180, 192
Charlotte Sams . . . 61, 160, 171, 189
Charmian Daniels . . . 99, 156, 171, 193
Chehak, Susan Taylor . . . 220
Chesney, Marion . . . 217
China Bayles . . . 20, 161, 171, 190
❖ Christie, Agatha . . . 36-37, 157, 166-167, 174, 181, 192-194, 197-203
Christine Bennett . . . 69, 162, 171, 188
Christine Martin . . . 124, 164, 171, 193
Christine Opara . . . 141, 157, 171, 189
❖ Christmas, Joyce . . . 38, 161, 166, 170, 177, 185, 188, 207-212
Christopher "Kit" Storm . . . 25, 155, 171, 188
Christopher Dennis "Seedy" Sloan . . . 20, 155, 171, 194
Christopher McKee . . . 120-121, 156, 171, 189
❖ Churchill, Jill . . . 38, 167, 174, 186, 208, 210, 212-214, 217
Claire Aldington, Rev. . . . 73, 162, 171, 188
Claire Breslinsky . . . 78, 164, 171, 188
Claire Camden . . . 117, 159, 171, 192
Claire Conrad . . . 75, 158, 171, 183
Claire Malloy . . . 72, 161, 171, 183
Claire Sharples . . . 124, 161, 171, 183
Clara Gamadge . . . 30, 167, 171, 188
Clare Clively . . . 45, 163, 178, 193
❖ Clark, Carol Higgins . . . 38, 157, 179, 184, 211, 213-214
❖ Clark, Carolyn Chambers . . . 38, 157, 166, 177, 180, 185, 213-214
Clark, Mary Higgins . . . 220
❖ Clarke, Anna . . . 39, 159, 178, 193, 205-208, 210, 214
Claudia Valentine . . . 49, 157, 171, 195

❖ Cleary, Melissa . . . 39, 159, 174, 191, 211, 213-214, 216
❖ Cleeves, Ann . . . 39-40, 155, 162, 173, 180, 192-193, 206, 208-211, 213-214, 216
Clio Rees, Dr. 25, 160, 171, 192
Cockburn, Sarah . . . 217
Cockrill, Inspector . . . 31, 155, 171, 193
❖ Cody, Liza . . . 40, 157, 167, 170, 172, 193, 203-206, 210, 213-214, 220, 222
❖ Coker, Carolyn . . . 40, 160, 170, 186, 205-206, 209, 213
Cole January . . . 30, 157, 171, 190
❖ Collins, Anna Ashwood . . . 40, 161, 169, 188, 214
❖ Comfort, Barbara . . . 41, 160, 181, 190, 206-208, 213
Conan Flagg . . . 152, 161, 171, 189
❖ Conant, Susan . . . 41, 159, 174, 186, 208-211, 213, 216
Constance Leidl . . . 148, 158, 171, 189
Cook, Petronelle . . . 217
❖ Cooper, Natasha . . . 41, 160, 181, 193, 209-211, 213, 217
❖ Cooper, Susan Rogers . . . 42, 155, 160, 167, 172, 176, 178, 186, 189-190, 207, 209-211, 213-214
Cordelia Gray . . . 77, 158, 171, 194
❖ Cornwell, Patricia Daniels . . . 42, 166, 176, 190, 209-211, 213-214
❖ Craig, Alisa . . . 42-43, 155, 161, 172, 177, 195, 203-209, 211, 213, 217
Craig, May Shura . . . 220
❖ Crane, Frances . . . 43, 169, 178, 196, 199-201
❖ Crane, Hamilton . . . 44, 159, 172, 192, 208-211, 213-215, 217
Creasey Memorial Award . . . 226, 242, 242
Crespi, Trella . . . 163, 180, 188, 210-211, 213 [see Crespi, Camilla T.]
❖ Crespi, Camilla T. 44, 220
Cressida Woodruffe . . . 41, 160, 181, 193
Crime Writers Association . . . 226, 242, 242
Crime Writers of Canada . . . 226
❖ Crombie, Deborah . . . 45, 155, 172, 193, 213, 215
❖ Cross, Amanda . . . 45, 159, 175, 188, 201-206, 208-209, 216-217, 220
❖ Crowleigh, Ann . . . 45, 163, 178, 193, 213
❖ Crum, Laura . . . 45, 159, 173, 184, 215
❖ Curzon, Clare . . . 46, 155, 178, 194, 203-208, 210-211, 213, 215, 217
CWA . . . 226, 242

D

❖ D'Amato, Barbara . . . 46, 164, 166, 171, 173, 186, 191, 203-204, 209-211, 213, 215, 220
D. S. Trewley . . . 92, 156, 172, 192
❖ Daheim, Mary . . . 47, 161, 164, 172, 175, 190, 210-211, 213, 215-216
❖ Dain, Catherine . . . 47, 157, 173, 188, 211, 213, 215-217
Dalton, Elizabeth A. . . . 220
❖ Daly, Elizabeth . . . 47-48, 160, 161, 174, 188
❖ Danks, Denise . . . 48, 164, 167, 173, 193, 208, 211, 215
Darina Lisle . . . 85, 163, 172, 192

❖ denotes authors in Master List

D . . . continued

David Middleton-Brown . . . 36, 162, 165, 176, 192

David Webb . . . 57, 155, 172, 192

David Wintringham . . . 27, 166, 172, 193

➥ Davidson, Diane Mott . . . 48, 163, 173, 185, 209, 211, 213, 215, 220

➥ Davis, Dorothy Salisbury . . . 48-49, 164, 167, 175, 188, 203-204, 206, 220

Davis, Frances Louise . . . 218

➥ Davis, Lindsey . . . 49, 157, 177, 195, 208-211, 215

➥ Dawson, Janet . . . 49, 157, 174, 184, 209, 213, 215, 220

➥ Day, Marele . . . 49, 157, 171, 195, 207, 209, 211

Deb Ralston . . . 92, 156, 172, 190

Deborah Knott . . . 90, 165, 172, 187

Dee Street . . . 142, 165, 172, 194

Deidre Quinn Nightingale . . . 19, 160, 172, 188

Delia Ross-Merlani, Viscountess . . . 57, 166, 172, 188

Delilah West . . . 108, 158, 172, 184

➥ Dentinger, Jane . . . 50, 167, 175, 188, 204-205, 207, 211, 215

➥ Dereske, Jo . . . 50, 161, 173, 190, 215

Devon MacDonald . . . 76, 158, 172, 187

Dewey James . . . 103, 161, 172, 188

Diamond Dagger . . . 226, 242

➥ Dietz, Denise . . . 50, 163, 172, 191, 213, 215

➥ Disney, Doris Miles . . . 50, 157, 174, 186, 199-202

Dittany Henbit Monk . . . 43, 161, 172, 195

Dixie T. Struthers . . . 131, 157, 172, 185

➥ Dolson, Hildegarde . . . 51, 167, 177, 185, 202-203

Dominic Felse . . . 113, 156, 173, 194

➥ Dominic, R. B. . . . 51, 165, 170, 191, 202-204, 217

Doran Fairweather . . . 68, 160, 172, 192

Douglas Perkins . . . 23, 161, 172, 193

Douglas Quantrill . . . 120, 156, 172, 194

➥ Douglas, Carole Nelson . . . 51-52, 159, 161-162, 174, 180, 188, 195, 209, 211, 213, 215-216, 220

➥ Douglas, Lauren Wright . . . 52, 157, 165, 170, 195, 206, 208, 210-211, 213, 215

➥ Drake, Alison . . . 52, 155, 169, 185, 207-208, 211, 217

Drood Review of Mystery . . . 223

Duell, Eileen-Marie . . . 217

➥ Duffy, Margaret . . . 52, 160, 166, 174, 192, 206-210

➥ Dunant, Sarah . . . 53, 157, 159, 173, 177, 192-193, 207, 211, 213

Duncan Kincaid . . . 45, 155, 172, 193

➥ Dunlap, Susan . . . 53, 155, 157, 162, 175-176, 181, 183-184, 204-206, 208-211, 213, 215, 220, 222

E

E. J. Pugh . . . 42, 160, 172, 190

Early, Jack . . . 217

➥ Eberhart, Mignon Good . . . 54, 155, 180, 188, 197-200

➥ Eccles, Marjorie . . . 54, 155, 173, 192, 207-209, 215

Edgar Awards . . . 226, 242

➥ Edghill, Rosemary . . . 54, 166, 175, 188, 215-216

Edwina Charles . . . 143, 166, 172, 193

Edwina Crusoe . . . 81, 166, 172, 185

Elena Oliverez . . . 105, 160, 172, 185

Eliza Figg . . . 24, 166, 172, 191

Elizabeth Austin . . . 132, 159, 172, 191

Elizabeth Elliot . . . 20, 167, 172, 189

Elizabeth MacPherson . . . 95, 159, 172, 191

Elizabeth Mendoza . . . 94, 156, 172, 191

Elkins, Charlotte & Aaron . . . 220

Ellery Queen Award . . . 227

Elles, Dora Amy . . . 218

Ellie Bernstein . . . 50, 163, 172, 191

Ellie Haskell . . . 34, 166, 172, 193

Ellis Award . . . 226, 242

Em Hansen . . . 22, 162, 172, 191

Emily Bryce . . . 127, 160, 172, 189

Emily D. Seeton . . . 44, 159, 172, 192

Emily Pollifax . . . 60, 166-167, 172, 187

Emma Chizzit . . . 68, 167, 172, 184

Emma Lord . . . 47, 164, 172, 190

Emma Victor . . . 149, 165, 172, 186

Emmy Tibbett . . . 104-105, 156, 174, 194

Enrico Caruso . . . 114, 167, 172, 189

Eugenia Potter . . . 122, 163, 172, 187

Eva Wylie . . . 40, 167, 172, 193

➥ Evanovich, Janet . . . 54, 157, 180, 187, 215

Eve Sinclair . . . 24, 167, 172, 193

EyeCon . . . 228

➥ Eyre, Elizabeth . . . 55, 163, 180, 195, 211, 213, 215, 217

F

Faith Sibley Fairchild . . . 112, 162, 163, 173, 186

➥ Fallon, Ann . . . 55, 165, 174, 194, 209-211, 213

Fanny Zindel . . . 136, 168, 173, 191

➥ Farrell, Gillian B. . . . 55, 157, 170, 188, 211, 215

➥ Fawcett, Quinn . . . 55, 163, 181, 195, 213, 217

➥ Feddersen, Connie . . . 56, 161, 169, 189, 213, 215-216

Felix Freer . . . 56, 161, 166, 181, 192

➥ Femling, Jean . . . 56, 157, 177, 185, 208, 210

➥ Ferrars, E. X. . . . 56, 161, 164, 166, 179, 181, 192, 203-205, 211, 213, 218

Fiddler . . . 94, 162, 173, 183

Fiedler, Jean . . . 220

Finch, Inspector . . . 139, 157, 174, 193

Finny Aletter . . . 102, 162, 173, 185

Fiora Flynn . . . 94, 162, 173, 183

Fleming Stone . . . 144-146, 158, 173, 189

➥ Florian, S.L. . . . 56-57, 166, 172, 188, 211

➥ Forrest, Katherine V. . . . 57, 155, 175, 184, 205-206, 208, 210

➥ Fowler, Earlene . . . 57, 160, 169, 184, 215-216

Frances Finn . . . 73, 158, 173, 186

Francesca Wilson . . . 107, 156, 175, 192

Frank Carver . . . 143, 162, 173, 189

➥ Frankel, Valerie . . . 57, 157, 181, 188, 210-211, 215, 220

➥ Fraser, Anthea . . . 57, 155, 172, 192, 206-208, 220

➥ Fraser, Antonia Pakenham . . . 58, 164, 174, 193, 203-206, 210, 213

➥ Frazer, Margaret . . . 58, 162-163, 180, 192, 211, 213, 215, 218

Freda Pedersen . . . 70, 156, 171, 183

Freddie O'Neal . . . 47, 157, 173, 188

Frederika Bascomb . . . 139, 166, 173, 190

Fremlin, Celia . . . 220

Frevisse, Sister . . . 58, 162-163, 180, 192

➥ Friedman, Mickey . . . 58, 160, 173, 195, 207-208, 220

➥ Fromer, Margot J. . . . 58, 166, 169, 191, 210, 213

➥ Fyfield, Frances . . . 59, 165, 173, 180, 192-193, 207-210, 213, 215, 218, 220

G

Gail Connor . . . 114, 165, 173, 191

Gail McCarthy . . . 45, 159, 173, 184

Galen Shaw . . . 29, 160, 173, 191

Garwood, Judith . . . 217

➥ Geason, Susan . . . 59, 157, 180, 195, 213

Gemma James . . . 45, 155, 172, 193

George Felse . . . 113, 156, 173, 194

George Palmer-Jones . . . 39, 162, 173, 193

➥ George, Elizabeth . . . 59, 155, 180, 193, 207-211, 213, 215, 220

Georgia Lee Maxwell . . . 58, 160, 173, 195

Georgina Powers . . . 48, 164, 167, 173, 193

Geraldine Farrar . . . 114, 167, 172, 189

Gerritt De Graaf . . . 46, 166, 173, 191

Gil Mayo . . . 54, 155, 173, 192

Gillian Adams . . . 78, 159, 173, 195

➥ Gilman, Dorothy . . . 60, 166-167, 172, 187, 201-205, 207, 209, 213, 216

➥ Gilpatrick, Noreen . . . 60, 155, 175, 190, 213

Ginny Trask . . . 143, 162, 173, 189

➥ Girdner, Jaqueline . . . 60, 161, 175, 184, 210-211, 213, 215-216, 220

➥ Giroux, E. X. . . . 61, 165, 179, 193, 205-210, 213, 218

➥ Glass, Leslie . . . 61, 155, 170, 188, 213, 215

➥ Glen, Alison . . . 61, 160, 171, 189, 211, 216, 218

Glory Day . . . 128, 167, 173, 195

Glynis Tryon . . . 102, 163, 173, 189

Gold Dagger . . . 226, 243, 243

Golden Age of Detection . . . 243

Golden Age of Mystery . . . 243

Goldy Bear . . . 48, 163, 173, 185

➥ Gordon, Alison . . . 61, 164, 167, 175, 195, 208, 210, 213

➥ Gosling, Paula . . . 62, 155, 170, 174, 177, 189, 191-192, 203, 205-206, 208, 210-211, 215

Grace Severance, Dr. . . . 127, 166, 173, 183

➥ Grafton, Sue . . . 62-63, 157, 176, 185, 204-211, 213, 215, 220, 222

➥ Graham, Caroline . . . 63, 155, 181, 192, 206, 208, 213

Grand Master . . . 227, 243

➥ denotes authors in Master List

G . . . continued

➥ Granger, Ann . . . 63, 156, 177, 192, 210-211, 213, 215
➥ Grant, Linda . . . 63, 158, 171, 184, 207, 209-210, 215, 220
➥ Grant-Adamson, Lesley . . . 64, 158, 164, 176, 179, 193, 205-207, 209-210, 215
Grape, Jan . . . 220
➥ Gray, Gallagher . . . 64, 161, 180, 188, 210-211, 218
Greber, Judith . . . 218
➥ Green, Christine . . . 64, 156, 166, 175, 192, 210-211, 215
➥ Green, Kate . . . 65, 156, 180, 184, 206, 213
➥ Greenwood, Diane M. . . . 65, 162, 180, 192, 210-211, 213
➥ Greenwood, Kerry . . . 65, 163, 179, 195, 208, 210, 213
Greenwood, L. B. . . . 220
Gregor Demarkian . . . 67, 158, 173, 189
➥ Grimes, Martha . . . 65-66, 156, 179, 193, 204-206, 208-209
➥ Grindle, Lucretia . . . 66, 156, 173, 192, 213, 215, 220
Guido Brunetti . . . 86, 156, 173, 195
➥ Gunning, Sally . . . 66, 161, 179, 186, 209, 211, 213, 215, 220
Gwenn Ramadge . . . 109, 158, 173, 188

H

H. W. Ross . . . 66, 156, 173, 192
➥ Haddad, Carolyn A. . . . 66, 161, 167, 170, 186, 211
➥ Haddam, Jane . . . 66-67, 158, 173, 189, 209-211, 213, 215, 218, 220
➥ Haddock, Lisa . . . 67, 164, 171, 191, 215
Hadley, Joan . . . 218
➥ Hager, Jean . . . 67, 156, 161, 163, 178, 180, 187, 189, 208-209, 211, 215, 220
➥ Hall, Mary Bowen . . . 68, 167, 172, 184, 208-209, 211, 213, 220
➥ Hall, Patricia . . . 68, 156, 169, 192, 213
Hamish Macbeth . . . 26, 155, 173, 194
Hammett Prize . . . 226, 243
Hannah Wolfe . . . 53, 157, 173, 193
➥ Hardwick, Mollie . . . 68, 160, 172, 192, 206-209
Harriet Jeffries . . . 125, 157, 175, 195
Harrington, Joyce . . . 220
➥ Harris, Charlaine . . . 68, 161, 170, 185, 209, 211, 215-216
➥ Harris, Lee . . . 69, 162, 171, 188, 211, 213, 215, 218
➥ Harrod-Eagles, Cynthia . . . 69, 156, 170, 192, 210-211, 215
Harry Marsh . . . 25, 160, 171, 192
➥ Hart, Carolyn G. . . . 69-70, 161, 164, 167, 170, 174, 190, 206-211, 213, 215-216, 220
➥ Hart, Ellen . . . 70, 163-165, 174, 180, 187, 208, 210-211, 213, 215
➥ Hart, Jeanne . . . 70, 156, 171, 183, 208, 210, 220
➥ Hartzmark, Gini . . . 71, 165, 176, 186, 211, 215
Haskell Blevins . . . 94, 158, 173, 186

➥ Haymon, S. T. . . . 71, 156, 170, 192, 203-206, 208, 210, 215
➥ Hayter, Sparkle . . . 71, 164, 179, 188, 215
Hegarty, Frances . . . 218
Heilbrun, Carolyn G. . . . 217
Helen Black . . . 144, 158, 165, 173, 185
Helen Marsh Shandy . . . 89, 159, 179, 187
Helen West . . . 59, 165, 173, 193
Helma Zukas . . . 50, 161, 173, 190
➥ Hendrickson, Louise . . . 71, 166, 169, 190, 213, 215
Henissart, Martha . . . 217, 218
Henrietta O'Dwyer Collins . . . 70, 164, 167, 174, 190
Henry Bassett . . . 33, 155, 174, 193
Henry Bryce . . . 127, 160, 172, 189
Henry Gamadge . . . 47-48, 160, 161, 174, 188
Henry Tibbett . . . 104-105, 156, 174, 194
➥ Henry, Sue . . . 72, 159, 162, 175, 183, 210, 216
Hercule Poirot . . . 36-37, 157, 174, 193
➥ Hess, Joan . . . 72, 156, 161, 170-171, 183, 206-208, 210-213, 215, 218, 220, 222
➥ Highsmith, Patricia . . . 72-73, 162, 181, 192, 200, 202-203, 212
➥ Hightower, Lynn . . . 73, 156, 158, 176, 180, 186, 189, 213, 216
Hilary Lloyd . . . 120, 156, 172, 194
Hilary Tamar . . . 35, 159, 165, 174, 194
Hilda Adams . . . 122, 166, 174, 193
➥ Holland, Isabelle . . . 73, 162, 171, 188, 204-206, 208-209
➥ Hollingsworth, Gerelyn . . . 73, 158, 173, 186, 215
Holly Winter . . . 41, 159, 174, 186
➥ Holt, Hazel . . . 74, 164, 180, 192, 208, 210, 213, 215
➥ Holtzer, Susan . . . 74, 162, 167, 170, 187, 215-216
Homer Kelly . . . 84, 156, 174, 186
➥ Hooper, Kay . . . 74, 158, 176, 185, 210
➥ Horansky, Ruby . . . 74, 156, 178, 188, 209, 215
➥ Hornsby, Wendy . . . 75, 156, 164, 176-177, 183, 206, 209, 212-213, 215, 220, 222
➥ Howe, Melodie Johnson . . . 75, 158, 171, 183, 208, 215, 220
Hughes, Dorothy B. . . . 220

I

Imogen Quy . . . 143, 166, 174, 193
Ingrid Langley . . . 52, 160, 166, 174, 192
International Association of Crime Writers . . . 226
Irene Adler . . . 51, 163, 174, 195
Irene Kelly . . . 33, 164, 174, 183
Iris Cooper . . . 27, 163, 174, 184
Iris Thorne . . . 119, 162, 174, 184

J

J. J. Jamison . . . 137, 162, 167, 174, 187
J. P. Beaumont . . . 77, 156, 174, 190
Jack Stryker . . . 62, 155, 174, 189
Jackie Walsh . . . 39, 159, 174, 191

➥ Jackson, Marian J. A. . . . 75, 158, 163, 169, 191, 209-210, 212, 215
➥ Jackson, Muriel Resnick . . . 76, 166, 177, 187, 212
➥ Jacobs, Jonnie . . . 76, 167, 175, 185, 215
➥ Jacobs, Nancy Baker . . . 76, 158, 172, 187, 210, 212-213
Jacqueline Kirby . . . 116, 160, 174, 189
Jake . . . 39, 159, 174, 191
Jake Samson . . . 132, 158, 174, 183
James Fleming . . . 55, 165, 174, 194
James McDougal . . . 51, 167, 177, 185
James Owen Mega . . . 96, 159, 174, 191
➥ James, P. D. . . . 76-77, 156, 158, 169, 171, 194, 201-204, 206
Jan Gallagher . . . 24, 166, 174, 187
➥ Jance, J. A. . . . 77, 156, 174-175, 183, 190, 205-210, 212-213, 215
Jane da Silva . . . 27, 167, 174, 190
Jane Jeffry . . . 38, 167, 174, 186
Jane Lawless . . . 70, 163, 165, 174, 187
Jane Marple . . . 37, 167, 174, 194
Jane Tennison . . . 84, 156, 174, 194
Jane Winfield . . . 117, 164, 174, 193
Janet Rhys . . . 42-43, 155, 177, 195
Jason Lynx . . . 111, 160, 174, 185
Jay Goldstein . . . 142, 157, 174, 184
Jazz Jasper . . . 98, 162, 174, 195
Jean Abbot . . . 43, 169, 178, 196
Jeff Di Marco . . . 50, 157, 174, 186
Jeffries, Mrs. . . . 32, 163, 174, 193
Jemima Shore . . . 58, 164, 174, 193
Jenny Cain . . . 117, 162, 174, 187
Jeremy Faro . . . 81, 156, 174, 194
Jeri Howard . . . 49, 157, 174, 184
Jerry North . . . 87, 161, 178, 188
Jerry Zalman . . . 82, 162, 175, 184
Jessica James . . . 108, 164, 175, 189
Jessica Randolph . . . 88, 158, 175, 184
Jessie Arnold . . . 72, 159, 162, 175, 183
Jessie Drake . . . 82, 156, 175, 184
Jill Smith . . . 53, 155, 175, 183
Jim Qwilleran . . . 31, 159, 164, 175, 191
Jo Hughes . . . 93, 166, 175, 191
Joan, Sister . . . 28, 162, 175, 192
Joanna Bradley . . . 77, 156, 175, 183
Joanna Stark . . . 105, 158, 175, 184
Jocelyn O'Roarke . . . 50, 167, 175, 188
Joe Silva . . . 110, 156, 175, 190
John Coffin . . . 34, 155, 175, 193
John Lloyd Branson . . . 99, 165, 175, 190
John McLeish . . . 107, 156, 175, 192
John Putnam Thatcher . . . 85, 162, 175, 188
John Sanders . . . 125, 157, 175, 195
Jolie Wyatt . . . 133, 160, 175, 190
Judith Hayes . . . 118, 164, 175, 191
Judith McMonigle . . . 47, 161, 175, 190
Judy Hill . . . 97, 156, 171, 194
Julia Callahan Garrity . . . 140, 162, 171, 185
Julian Baugh . . . 29, 160, 173, 191
Julian Kestrel . . . 124, 163, 175, 194
Julie Hayes . . . 49, 164, 167, 175, 188
Juliet Blake . . . 36, 157, 175, 185

K

➥ Kallen, Lucille . . . 77, 164, 177, 185, 203-206
Karen Hightower . . . 54, 166, 175, 188
Karen Levinson . . . 108, 156, 175, 188

➥ denotes authors in Master List

K . . . continued

➬ Karr, Leona . . . 78, 164, 169, 185, 213
Kat Colorado . . . 80, 158, 175, 184
Kate Austen . . . 76, 167, 175, 185
Kate Baeier . . . 132, 158, 175, 194
Kate Brannigan . . . 96, 158, 175, 194
Kate Delafield . . . 57, 155, 175, 184
Kate Driscoll . . . 142, 159, 175, 190
Kate Fansler . . . 45, 159, 175, 188
Kate Frederick . . . 127, 157, 179, 187
Kate Henry . . . 62, 164, 167, 175, 195
Kate Ivory . . . 135, 160, 175, 194
Kate Jasper . . . 60, 161, 175, 184
Kate Kincaid Mulcay . . . 130, 164, 175, 185
Kate Kinsella . . . 64, 166, 175, 192
Kate Martinelli . . . 80, 156, 175, 184
Kate McLean . . . 60, 155, 175, 190
Kate Murray . . . 141, 164, 175, 188
Kate Shugak . . . 135, 158, 175, 183
Kate Teague . . . 75, 156, 176, 183
Kate Trevorne . . . 62, 155, 174, 189
Kate Weston . . . 68, 156, 169, 192
Katharine Craig . . . 141, 160, 176, 183
Katherine Prescott Milholland . . . 71, 165, 176, 186
Kathleen Mallory . . . 108, 156, 176, 188
Kathryn Ardleigh . . . 112, 160, 163, 176, 193
Kathryn Mackay . . . 97, 165, 176, 184
Kay Barth . . . 127, 165, 176, 185
Kay Engles . . . 136, 164, 176, 191
Kay Scarpetta . . . 42, 166, 176, 190
➬ Kellerman, Faye . . . 78, 156, 179, 184, 206, 208-209, 212-213, 215, 220
➬ Kelly, Mary Ann . . . 78, 164, 171, 188, 209, 212
➬ Kelly, Nora . . . 78, 159, 173, 195, 205, 212-213
➬ Kelly, Susan . . . 79, 164, 176, 186, 205-207, 209-210, 212, 220
➬ Kelly, Susan B. . . . 79, 162, 167, 169, 193, 209, 213, 215
Kelman, Judith . . . 221
➬ Kelner, Toni L. P. . . . 79, 158, 176, 187, 213, 215-216
➬ Kenney, Susan . . . 80, 160, 179, 187, 204-205, 209
Kevin Bryce . . . 141, 160, 176, 183
Kiernan O'Shaughnessy . . . 53, 157, 176, 184
➬ Kijewski, Karen . . . 80, 158, 175, 184, 207, 209-210, 212, 215-216, 221
Kimmey Kruse . . . 42, 167, 176, 186
➬ King, Laurie R. . . . 80, 156, 175, 184, 213
➬ Kingsbury, Kate . . . 80, 163, 171, 192, 213, 215-216, 218
Kinsey Millhone . . . 62-63, 157, 176, 185
Kit Powell . . . 123, 164, 167, 176, 184
➬ Kittredge, Mary . . . 81, 160, 166, 171-172, 185, 206, 208-210, 212-213
➬ Knight, Alanna . . . 81, 156, 174, 194, 207-209
➬ Knight, Kathryn Lasky . . . 81, 161, 171, 186, 206, 209-210, 215
➬ Knight, Phyllis . . . 82, 158, 165, 176, 187, 212, 215
Koko . . . 31, 159, 164, 175, 191
Kori Price Brichter . . . 119, 156, 179, 186
➬ Kraft, Gabrielle . . . 82, 162, 175, 184, 206-209, 221

➬ Krich, Rochelle Majer . . . 82, 156, 175, 184, 213, 215-216, 221
Kuhfeld, Mary Pulver . . . 218
➬ Kunz, Kathleen . . . 82, 162, 180, 187, 213, 216

L

➬ Lacey, Sarah . . . 83, 162, 176, 194, 213, 215-216
Laiken, Deidre . . . 221
➬ Lamb, J. Dayne . . . 83, 162, 180, 186, 213, 215-216
➬ Lambert, Mercedes . . . 83, 165, 181, 184, 210
Lance O'Leary . . . 54, 155, 180, 188
➬ Landreth, Marsha . . . 83, 166, 179, 191, 212, 213-216
Lane Montana . . . 74, 158, 176, 185
➬ Langton, Jane . . . 84, 156, 174, 186, 203-207, 210, 212-213
➬ LaPierre, Janet . . . 84, 156, 181, 190, 206, 208-210, 213, 221
➬ LaPlante, Lynda . . . 84, 156, 174, 194, 213, 215
Lark Dailey Dodge . . . 131, 161, 176, 184
➬ Lathen, Emma . . . 85, 162, 175, 188, 201-204, 207, 210, 213, 218
Latsis, Mary . . . 217-218
Laura Di Palma . . . 93, 165, 176, 184
Laura Fleming . . . 79, 158, 176, 187
Laura Flynn . . . 64, 158, 176, 193
Laura Ireland . . . 90, 159, 167, 176, 190
Laura Malloy . . . 87, 164, 176, 187
Laura Principal . . . 134, 158, 176, 193
Lauren Laurano . . . 127, 158, 165, 176, 189
Lauren Maxwell . . . 119, 162, 176, 183
➬ Laurence, Janet . . . 85, 163, 172, 192, 209-210, 212-213, 215
➬ Law, Janice . . . 86, 162, 170, 191, 203-204, 212-213, 215
Leah Hunter . . . 83, 162, 176, 194
Lee Squires . . . 22, 166, 176, 191
Lena Padget . . . 73, 158, 176, 186
Lennox Kemp . . . 98, 165, 176, 194
➬ Leon, Donna . . . 86, 156, 173, 195, 212-213
Leonidas Witherall . . . 139, 161, 176, 186
Leslie Wetzon . . . 100, 162, 181, 188
Lewis, Mary Christianna . . . 217
Libby Kincaid . . . 140, 164, 176, 189
Lil Ritchie . . . 82, 158, 165, 176, 187
Lindsay Gordon . . . 96, 164, 165, 176, 192
Linnington, Elizabeth . . . 218
➬ Linscott, Gillian . . . 86, 163, 178, 192, 210, 212-213
Liz Connors . . . 79, 164, 176, 186
Liz Graham . . . 25, 155, 176, 193
Liz Sullivan . . . 123, 160, 176, 184
Liz Wareham . . . 32, 161, 176, 188
Lloyd, Chief Inspector . . . 97, 156, 171, 194
➬ Lockridge, Frances & Richard . . . 86-87, 161, 178, 188, 199-201, 218
➬ Logue, Mary . . . 87, 164, 176, 187, 213
Lonia Guiu . . . 110, 158, 176, 196
➬ Lorden, Randye . . . 87, 158, 180, 188, 213, 215
➬ Lorens, M. K. . . . 88, 159, 160, 181, 191, 209-210, 212-213

Loretta Lawson . . . 133, 159, 176, 193
Lowry, Cheryl Meredith . . . 218
➬ Lucke, Margaret . . . 88, 158, 175, 184, 210
Lucy Kingsley . . . 36, 162, 165, 176, 192
Lucy Ramsdale . . . 51, 167, 177, 185
Lucy Stone . . . 98, 167, 177, 187
Luis Mendoza . . . 129-130, 157, 177, 184
Luke Abbott . . . 62, 155, 177, 192
Luke Thanet . . . 131, 157, 177, 193
Lydia Fairchild . . . 99, 165, 175, 190
➬ Lyons, Nan & Ivan . . . 88, 163, 178, 191, 203, 213

M

Macavity Award . . . 226, 243
MacDougal Duff . . . 22, 159, 177, 191
➬ MacGregor, T. J. . . . 88-89, 158, 179, 185, 206-210, 212-213, 215, 217, 221
Mackenzie Smith . . . 140, 165, 177, 191
Mackintosh, Elizabeth . . . 218
➬ MacLeod, Charlotte . . . 89, 158-159, 179-180, 186-187, 203-206, 208, 210, 212, 215-217, 221
Madoc Rhys . . . 42-43, 155, 177, 195
Magdalena Yoder . . . 106, 161, 177, 189
Maggie Elliott . . . 137, 158, 177, 185
Maggie Hill . . . 75, 158, 171, 183
Maggie MacGowen . . . 75, 164, 177, 183
Maggie Rome . . . 77, 164, 177, 185
Maggie Ryan . . . 35, 159, 177, 188
Malice Domestic . . . 226
➬ Malmont, Valerie S. . . . 89, 160, 181, 189, 215
➬ Mann, Jessica . . . 90, 159, 166, 180, 192, 202-207, 210
Marcus Didius Falco . . . 49, 157, 177, 195
Margaret Priam, Lady . . . 38, 166, 177, 188
Margit Falk . . . 140, 165, 177, 191
Marian Larch . . . 114, 156, 177, 189
Marian Winchester . . . 123, 163, 177, 190
➬ Mariz, Linda French . . . 90, 159, 167, 176, 190, 212
Mark Shigata . . . 149, 157, 177, 190
Marla Masterson . . . 53, 159, 177, 192
➬ Maron, Margaret . . . 90-91, 156, 165, 172, 180, 187-188, 204-208, 210, 212-213, 215-216, 221
Marris, Katherine . . . 217
➬ Marsh, Ngaio . . . 91-92, 156, 179, 195, 198-204
Martha "Moz" Brant . . . 56, 157, 177, 185
Marti MacAlister . . . 29, 155, 161, 177, 186
Martin Karl Alberg . . . 152, 157, 177, 195
➬ Martin, Lee . . . 92, 156, 172, 190, 205-209, 212-213, 215, 218
Martine LaForte Hopkins . . . 35, 155, 177, 186
Mary Carner . . . 118, 158, 177, 191
Mary DiNunzio . . . 128, 165, 177, 189
Mary Helen, Sister . . . 109, 162, 167, 177, 184
Mary Minor Haristeen . . . 33, 159, 177, 190
➬ Mason, Sarah J. . . . 92, 156, 172, 192, 213, 215, 217
➬ Matera, Lia . . . 92-93, 165, 176, 181, 184, 206-210, 212, 215, 221
➬ Mather, Linda . . . 93, 166, 175, 191, 215

➬ denotes authors in Master List

M . . . continued

❖ Matteson, Stephanie . . . 93, 167, 171, 188, 209-210, 212-213, 215
❖ Matthews, Francine . . . 93, 158, 177, 186, 215
Maud Silver . . . 146, 158, 177, 194
Max Bittersohn . . . 89, 158, 180, 186
Max Darling . . . 69, 161, 170, 190
Maxene St. Clair, Dr. . . . 97, 166, 177, 191
❖ Maxwell, A. E. . . . 94, 162, 173, 183, 205-208, 210, 212-213, 218
Maxwell, Ann . . . 218
Maxwell, Evan . . . 218
❖ McAllester, Melanie . . . 94, 156, 172, 191, 215
❖ McCafferty, Taylor . . . 94, 158, 173, 186, 209, 212, 215, 221
❖ McClendon, Lise . . . 94, 160, 169, 187, 215
❖ McCloy, Helen . . . 95, 166, 170, 188, 198-200, 202-203
❖ McCrumb, Sharyn . . . 95-96, 156, 159, 172, 174, 180, 187, 191, 205-207, 209-210, 212, 215, 221-222
❖ McDermid, Val . . . 96, 158, 164, 165, 175-176, 192, 194, 209-210, 212-213, 215
❖ McFall, Patricia . . . 96, 159, 178, 195, 212
❖ McGerr, Patricia . . . 96, 166, 180, 192, 201-202, 221
❖ McGiffin, Janet . . . 97, 166, 177, 191, 212-213
❖ McGown, Jill . . . 97, 156, 171, 194, 204, 207-208, 210, 212-213
❖ McGuire, Christine . . . 97, 165, 176, 184, 213
McIntosh, Kinn Hamilton . . . 217
❖ McKenna, Bridget . . . 97, 158, 171, 184, 213, 215-216
❖ McQuillan, Karin . . . 98, 162, 174, 195, 209, 213, 215, 221
❖ Meek, M. R. D. . . . 98, 165, 176, 194, 204-209, 213
Meg Halloran . . . 84, 156, 181, 190
Meg Lacey . . . 30, 157, 177, 195
Megan Baldwin . . . 38, 166, 177, 185
❖ Meier, Leslie . . . 98, 167, 177, 187, 213, 215
Melinda Pink . . . 102, 160, 162, 177, 190
Melissa Craig . . . 125, 160, 177, 193
❖ Melville, Jennie . . . 99, 156, 171, 193, 201-202, 204, 207-209, 213, 218
Meredith "Merry" Folger . . . 93, 158, 177, 186
Meredith Mitchell . . . 63, 156, 177, 192
❖ Meredith, D. R. . . . 99, 165, 175, 190, 205-210, 213, 221
Merrie Lee Spencer . . . 76, 166, 177, 187
Mertz, Barbara . . . 218
❖ Meyers, Annette . . . 100, 162, 181, 188, 208-210, 212-213, 218
Michael Spraggue III . . . 26, 157, 177, 186
Michaels, Barbara . . . 221
Mici Anhalt . . . 109, 156, 177, 188
Midge Cohen . . . 32, 160, 177, 188
Midnight Louie . . . 52, 159, 161, 180, 188
Mike McCleary . . . 88-89, 158, 179, 185
Mike Yeadings . . . 46, 155, 178, 194
❖ Millar, Margaret . . . 100, 156, 165-166, 174, 178, 181, 183, 195, 199, 203, 204

❖ Millhiser, Marlys . . . 101, 167, 171, 184, 212-213, 216, 221
Millie Ogden . . . 88, 163, 178, 191
Milton Kovak . . . 42, 155, 178, 189
Miranda Clively . . . 45, 163, 178, 193
Mitch Bushyhead . . . 67, 156, 178, 189
❖ Mitchell, Gladys . . . 101, 160, 166, 170, 181, 192, 194, 197-202, 204-205
❖ Moffat, Gwen . . . 102, 160, 162, 177, 190, 202-206, 208-209
Mollie Cates . . . 142, 164, 178, 190
Molly Bearpaw . . . 67, 163, 178, 189
Molly DeWitt . . . 151, 167, 178, 185
Molly Palmer-Jones . . . 39, 162, 173, 193
Molly Rafferty . . . 27, 159, 178, 186
❖ Monfredo, Miriam Grace . . . 102, 163, 173, 189, 212-213, 216
❖ Montgomery, Yvonne E. . . . 102, 162, 173, 185, 206, 209
❖ Moody, Susan . . . 103, 164, 166, 171, 178, 192, 205-208, 214-215
❖ Morgan, Kate . . . 103, 161, 172, 188, 209-210, 212, 215, 218
❖ Morice, Ann . . . 104, 167, 180, 192, 202-207, 218
Mostly Murder . . . 223
❖ Moyes, Patricia . . . 104-105, 156, 174, 194, 201-205, 208, 214
❖ Muller, Marcia . . . 105-106, 158, 160, 172, 175, 180, 184-185, 203-210, 212, 214-215
Munger, Katy . . . 218
Murder & Mayhem . . . 224
MWA . . . 226
❖ Myers, Amy . . . 106, 163, 170, 192, 204, 206
❖ Myers, Tamar . . . 106, 161, 177, 189, 215
Mystery News . . . 224
Mystery Readers Journal . . . 224
Mystery Readers of America . . . 226
Mystery Review . . . 224
Mystery Scene . . . 224
Mystery Writers of America . . . 226

N

❖ Nabb, Magdalen . . . 106, 156, 179, 195, 204-207, 209-210, 215
Nan Robinson . . . 35, 165, 178, 184
Natasha O'Brien . . . 88, 163, 178, 191
❖ Neel, Janet . . . 107, 156, 175, 192, 207-208, 215
❖ Neely, Barbara . . . 107, 161-162, 170, 191, 212, 215
Neil Hamel . . . 141, 162, 165, 178, 187
Nell Bray . . . 86, 163, 178, 192
Nell Fury . . . 118, 158, 165, 178, 184
Neville, Katherine . . . 221
❖ Newman, Sharan . . . 107, 163, 171, 195, 214-215
Nicholson, Margaret Beda Larminie . . . 218
Nick Trevellyan . . . 79, 162, 167, 169, 193
Nicky Titus . . . 125, 157, 179, 189
Nikki Trakos . . . 74, 156, 178, 188
Nina Fischman . . . 118, 165, 178, 189
Nora James . . . 96, 159, 178, 195
Norah Mulcahaney . . . 109, 156, 178, 188
❖ North, Suzanne . . . 107, 164, 179, 195, 215

O

❖ O'Brien, Meg . . . 108, 164, 175, 189, 209-210, 212, 214
❖ O'Callaghan, Maxine . . . 108, 158, 172, 184, 203-204, 208, 210, 215
❖ O'Connell, Carol . . . 108, 156, 176, 188, 215
❖ O'Donnell, Catherine . . . 108, 156, 175, 188, 214
❖ O'Donnell, Lillian . . . 109, 156, 158, 173, 177-178, 188, 202-206, 208-210, 212, 214-215
❖ O'Marie, Sister Carol Anne . . . 109, 162, 167, 177, 184, 205-207, 210, 214
Oates, Joyce Carol . . . 221
❖ OCork, Shannon . . . 110, 164, 167, 180, 188, 203-204
❖ Oleksiw, Susan . . . 110, 156, 175, 190, 214-215
❖ Oliphant, B. J. . . . 110, 162, 167, 180, 185, 209, 212, 215, 218
Oliver Jardino . . . 65, 156, 180, 184
❖ Oliver, Maria Antonia . . . 110, 158, 176, 206, 208
❖ Orde, A. J. . . . 111, 160, 174, 185, 208-209, 212, 214-215, 218
Orsen, Richard . . . 218
Osbert Monk . . . 43, 161, 172, 195
❖ Osborne, Denise . . . 111, 167, 179, 184, 215-216
Owen Archer . . . 122, 162, 163, 178, 193

P

❖ Padgett, Abigail . . . 111, 158, 170, 184, 214-216
❖ Page, Katherine Hall . . . 112, 162, 163, 173, 186, 209-210, 212, 214-215
❖ Paige, Robin . . . 112, 160, 163, 176, 193, 215-216, 218
Pam Nilsen . . . 148, 165, 178, 190
Pam North . . . 87, 161, 178, 188
❖ Papazoglou, Orania . . . 112, 160, 178, 189, 205-207, 209, 218
❖ Paretsky, Sara . . . 113, 158, 181, 186, 204-207, 209-210, 215, 221-222, 228
❖ Pargeter, Edith . . . 113, 156, 173, 194, 200-203, 218
Paris Chandler . . . 128, 158, 178, 184
❖ Parker, Barbara . . . 114, 165, 173, 191, 215
Pat Abbot . . . 43, 169, 178, 196
Patience Campbell McKenna . . . 112, 160, 178, 189
Patricia Delaney . . . 130, 158, 178, 189
Patrick Gillard . . . 52, 160, 166, 174, 192
Patrick Grant, Dr. . . . 153, 159, 178, 194
Paul MacDonald . . . 134, 160, 178, 184
Paul Prye . . . 100, 166, 178, 195
❖ Paul, Barbara . . . 114, 156, 167, 172, 177, 189, 205-206, 212, 214, 216, 221
Paula Glenning . . . 39, 159, 178, 193
Peaches Dann . . . 135, 168, 178, 187
Peg Goodenough . . . 28, 161, 178, 188
❖ Pence, Joanne . . . 114, 163, 170, 184, 214-215
Penny Spring . . . 23, 159, 178, 196
Penny Wanawake . . . 103, 164, 178, 192

❖ denotes authors in Master List

P .. continued

➡ Perry, Anne . . . 114-115, 156, 180-181, 192, 203-207, 209-210, 212, 214-216, 221
Persis Willum . . . 144, 160, 179, 188
Peter Bartholomew . . . 66, 161, 179, 186
Peter Brichter . . . 119, 156, 179, 186
Peter Decker . . . 78, 156, 179, 184
Peter Shandy . . . 89, 159, 179, 187
Peter Wimsey, Lord . . . 126, 166, 179, 194
➡ Peters, Elizabeth . . . 115-116, 159, 160, 163, 169, 174, 181, 189, 192, 195, 202-208, 210, 212, 216, 218, 221
➡ Peters, Ellis . . . 116-117, 161, 162, 163, 170, 194, 203-208, 210, 212, 216, 218
➡ Peterson, Audrey . . . 117, 159, 164, 171, 174, 192, 207-209, 211-212, 216, 221
Phoebe Fairfax . . . 107, 164, 179, 195
Phoebe Siegel . . . 119, 158, 179, 187
Phryne Fisher . . . 65, 163, 179, 195
➡ Pickard, Nancy . . . 117, 162, 174, 187, 205-208, 211, 214, 216, 221-222
➡ Piesman, Marissa . . . 118, 165, 178, 189, 208, 211, 214, 216
➡ Pincus, Elizabeth . . . 118, 158, 165, 178, 184, 212, 214, 216
Poe, Edgar Allen . . . 242
➡ Popkin, Zelda . . . 118, 158, 177, 191, 198-199
➡ Porter, Anna . . . 118, 164, 175, 191, 205-206
Private Eye Writers of America . . . 227, 243
➡ Prowell, Sandra West . . . 119, 158, 179, 187, 214, 216
➡ Pugh, Dianne G. . . . 119, 162, 174, 184, 214, 216
➡ Pulver, Mary Monica . . . 119, 156, 179, 186, 206, 211-212
PWA . . . 227, 243

Q

Queenie Davilow . . . 111, 167, 179, 184
Quin St. James . . . 88-89, 158, 179, 185
➡ Quinn, Elizabeth . . . 119, 162, 176, 183, 214
Quint McCauley . . . 32, 157, 179, 186

R

➡ Radley, Sheila . . . 120, 156, 172, 194, 203-205, 207-208, 212
Rain Morgan . . . 64, 164, 179, 193
Ray Frederick . . . 127, 157, 179, 187
Rebecca Schwartz . . . 134, 165, 179, 184
Regan Reilly . . . 38, 157, 179, 184
Reginald Wexford . . . 121, 156, 179, 194
➡ Reilly, Helen . . . 120-21, 156, 171, 189, 197-201
➡ Rendell, Ruth . . . 121, 156, 179, 194, 202-205, 207, 214, 216, 221
Renfroe, Martha Kay . . . 218
➡ Rich, Virginia . . . 122, 163, 172, 187, 204-205, 214
Richard Jury . . . 65-66, 156, 179, 193
Richard Montgomery . . . 130, 157, 179, 194
Rina Lazarus . . . 78, 156, 179, 184
➡ Rinehart, Mary Roberts . . . 122, 166, 174, 193, 198-200

➡ Robb, Candace M. . . . 122, 162, 163, 178, 193, 214, 216
Robert Bone . . . 135, 157, 179, 193
Robert Forsythe . . . 61, 165, 179, 193
Robert L. Fish Award . . . 227
➡ Roberts, Carey . . . 123, 157, 170, 191, 214
Roberts, Doreen . . . 218
➡ Roberts, Gillian . . . 123, 159, 169, 189, 207-208, 211, 214, 216, 218, 221
➡ Roberts, Lora . . . 123, 160, 176, 184, 216
Robin Hudson . . . 71, 164, 179, 188
Robin Light . . . 29, 160, 179, 189
Robin Vaughn . . . 24, 159, 179, 190
➡ Robitaille, Julie . . . 123, 164, 167, 176, 184, 212, 216
Roderick Alleyn . . . 91-92, 156, 179, 195
Roger Tejeda . . . 75, 156, 176, 183
Roger the Chapman . . . 128, 163, 179, 193
➡ Romberg, Nina . . . 123, 163, 177, 190, 208, 214
Ronnie Ventana . . . 147, 158, 179, 185
➡ Roome, Annette . . . 124, 164, 171, 193, 208-209
Rosie Vicente . . . 132, 158, 174, 183
➡ Ross, Kate . . . 124, 163, 175, 194, 214, 216
➡ Rothenberg, Rebecca . . . 124, 161, 171, 183, 211, 216
➡ Rowe, Jennifer . . . 124, 164, 181, 195, 208, 211-212, 214, 216
➡ Rowlands, Betty . . . 125, 160, 177, 193, 208-209, 214, 216
Roz Howard . . . 80, 160, 179, 187

S

Sabina Swift . . . 136, 158, 179, 191
➡ Sale, Medora . . . 125, 157, 175, 195, 206, 208-209, 211-212, 216
Salvatore Guarnaccia . . . 106, 156, 179, 195
Sam Titus . . . 125, 157, 179, 189
Samantha "Smokey" Brandon . . . 23, 155, 179, 184
Samantha Adams . . . 129, 164, 179, 185
Samantha Turner, Dr. . . . 83, 166, 179, 191
Sands, Inspector . . . 100, 156, 174, 195
➡ Sandstrom, Eve K. . . . 125, 157, 179, 189, 209, 211, 214
Sara Marriott . . . 56, 164, 179, 192
Sarah & Meg Quilliam . . . 28, 161, 179, 188
Sarah Deane . . . 29, 159, 179, 186
Sarah Drexler . . . 148, 165, 180, 189
Sarah Fortune . . . 59, 165, 180, 192
Sarah Keate . . . 54, 155, 180, 188
Sarah Kelling . . . 89, 158, 180, 186
Sarah Nelson . . . 149, 157, 180, 185
➡ Sawyer, Corinne Holt . . . 126, 168, 170, 183, 207-208, 212, 214, 216
➡ Sayers, Dorothy L. . . . 126, 166, 179, 194, 197-198
➡ Schenkel, S. E. . . . 127, 157, 179, 187, 216
➡ Scherf, Margaret . . . 127, 160, 166, 172-173, 183, 189, 200-203
➡ Schier, Norma . . . 127, 165, 176, 185, 203-204
➡ Scoppettone, Sandra . . . 127, 158, 165, 176, 189, 211, 214, 216-217, 221

➡ Scott, Rosie . . . 128, 167, 173, 195, 208
➡ Scottoline, Lisa . . . 128, 165, 177, 189, 214, 216
➡ Sedley, Kate . . . 128, 163, 179, 193, 212, 214
Selena Mead . . . 96, 166, 180, 192
➡ Shah, Diane K. . . . 128, 158, 178, 184, 209, 212
Shamus Award . . . 227, 244
➡ Shankman, Sarah . . . 128-129, 164, 179, 185, 207-209, 211-212, 214, 221-222
➡ Shannon, Dell . . . 129-130, 157, 177, 184, 201-207, 218
Shannon, Doris . . . 218
Sharon Dair . . . 142, 157, 180, 187
Sharon McCone . . . 105-106, 158, 180, 184
Shaw, Felicity . . . 218
Sheila Malory . . . 74, 164, 180, 192
Sheila Travers . . . 134, 162, 180, 185
➡ Shepherd, Stella . . . 130, 157, 179, 194, 208-209, 212
Shirley McClintock . . . 110, 162, 167, 180, 185
➡ Short, Sharon Gwyn . . . 130, 158, 178, 189, 216
Shots in the Dark . . . 228
Shots on the Page . . . 228
➡ Sibley, Celestine . . . 130, 164, 175, 185, 201, 211-212, 214
Sigismondo . . . 55, 163, 180, 195
Sigrid Harald . . . 91, 156, 180, 188
Silver Dagger . . . 226, 244
Simona Griffo . . . 44, 163, 180, 188
➡ Simonson, Sheila . . . 131, 161, 176, 184, 209, 212, 214
➡ Simpson, Dorothy . . . 131, 157, 177, 193, 204-208, 211-212, 214
➡ Sims, L. V. . . . 131, 157, 172, 185, 207
➡ Singer, Shelley . . . 132, 158-159, 170, 174, 183, 204-207, 214, 216, 221-222
Sisters in Crime . . . 228, 244
Sixto Cardenas . . . 19, 155, 170, 191
Skip Langdon . . . 134, 157, 180, 186
➡ Skom, Edith . . . 132, 159, 172, 191, 208
➡ Slovo, Gillian . . . 132, 158, 175, 194, 205, 207, 221
➡ Smith, Barbara Burnett . . . 133, 160, 175, 190, 216
➡ Smith, Evelyn E. . . . 133, 160, 180, 189, 206-208, 211, 216
➡ Smith, Janet L. . . . 133, 165, 170, 190, 209, 212, 216
➡ Smith, Joan . . . 133, 159, 176, 193, 207, 209, 216
➡ Smith, Julie . . . 134, 157, 160, 165, 178-180, 184, 186, 204-207, 209, 211, 214, 216, 221
Sonora Blair . . . 73, 156, 180, 189
Sophie Greenway . . . 70, 163, 164, 180, 187
Spaceman Kowalski . . . 147, 157, 180, 184
Spencer Arrowood . . . 95, 156, 180, 187
➡ Spring, Michelle . . . 134, 158, 176, 193, 216
➡ Sprinkle, Patricia Houck . . . 134, 162, 180, 185, 207, 209, 211-212, 214, 216
➡ Squire, Elizabeth Daniels . . . 135, 168, 178, 187, 216
➡ Stabenow, Dana . . . 135, 158, 175, 183, 212, 214, 216

➡ denotes authors in Master List

S . . . continued

❖ Stacey, Susannah . . . 135, 157, 179, 193, 207, 209, 212, 218
❖ Stallwood, Veronica . . . 135, 160, 175, 194, 214, 216
Stanton, Mary . . . 217
Staynes, Jill . . . 217-218
❖ Stein, Triss . . . 136, 164, 176, 191, 214
❖ Steiner, Susan . . . 136, 158, 169, 183, 211, 214
Stephanie Plum . . . 54, 157, 180, 187
Stephen Ramsey . . . 40, 155, 180, 192
Stevens, B. K. . . . 221
❖ Stevens, Serita . . . 136, 168, 173, 191, 211, 214
Stockey, Janet . . . 221
Stone, Sgt. . . . 92, 156, 172, 192
Storey, Margaret . . . 217-218
❖ Sucher, Dorothy . . . 136, 158, 179, 191, 207-208, 221
❖ Sullivan, Winona . . . 136-137, 158, 171, 186, 214
Susan Henshaw . . . 149, 167, 180, 185
Susan Melville . . . 133, 160, 180, 189
Susan Wren . . . 144, 157, 180, 186
Syd Fish . . . 59, 157, 180, 195
Sydney Bryant . . . 143, 158, 180, 184
Sydney Sloane . . . 87, 158, 180, 188

T

Tamara Hayle . . . 147, 158, 161, 180, 187
Tamara Hoyland . . . 90, 159, 166, 180, 192
❖ Taylor, Elizabeth Atwood . . . 137, 158, 177, 185, 204, 207, 212
❖ Taylor, L. A. . . . 137, 162, 167, 174, 187, 205
❖ Taylor, Phoebe Atwood . . . 137-138, 166, 170, 186, 198-200, 218
Teal Stewart . . . 83, 162, 180, 186
Tepper, Sheri S. . . . 218
Terry Girard . . . 82, 162, 180, 187
Tess Darcy . . . 67, 161, 180, 187
Tessa Crichton . . . 104, 167, 180, 192
❖ Tey, Josephine . . . 138, 157, 169, 194, 197-198, 200, 218
Thea Crawford . . . 90, 159, 180, 192
Theodora Braithwaite, Rev. . . . 65, 162, 180, 192
Theodore S. Hubbert . . . 64, 161, 180, 188
Theresa Fortunato . . . 65, 156, 180, 184
Theresa Franco . . . 39, 157, 180, 185
Theresa Tracy Baldwin . . . 110, 164, 167, 180, 188
Thomas Lynley . . . 59, 155, 180, 193
Thomas Pitt . . . 115, 156, 180, 192
❖ Thompson, Joyce . . . 138-139, 166, 173, 190, 211
❖ Thomson, June . . . 139, 157, 174, 193, 202-209, 211
❖ Tilton, Alice . . . 139, 161, 176, 186, 198-200, 218
Timothy Herring . . . 101, 160, 181, 192
Tish McWhinney . . . 41, 160, 181, 190
Toby Glendower, Sir . . . 23, 159, 178, 196
Tom Aragon . . . 100, 165, 181, 183
Tom Barnaby . . . 63, 155, 181, 192
Tom Ripley . . . 73, 162, 181, 192

Tommy Beresford . . . 37, 166, 181, 192
Tori Miracle . . . 89, 160, 181, 189
Trey Fortier . . . 74, 158, 176, 185
Trixie Dolan . . . 24, 167, 172, 193
❖ Trocheck, Kathy Hogan . . . 140, 162, 171, 185, 212, 214, 216
Trott, Susan . . . 221
❖ Truman, Margaret . . . 140, 165, 177, 191, 208-209, 212, 216
❖ Tucker, Kerry . . . 140, 164, 176, 189, 211-212, 214, 216
Tuppence Beresford . . . 37, 166, 181, 192
❖ Tyre, Peg . . . 141, 164, 175, 188, 216

U

❖ Uhnak, Dorothy . . . 141, 157, 171, 189, 202

V

V. I. Warshawski . . . 113, 158, 181, 186
❖ Valentine, Deborah . . . 141, 160, 176, 183, 208, 211, 221
❖ Van Gieson, Judith . . . 141, 162, 165, 178, 187, 207-209, 211-212, 214, 216
Vejay Haskell . . . 53, 162, 181, 184
Verity "Birdie" Birdwood . . . 124, 164, 181, 195
Vetter, Louise . . . 218
Vicky Bliss . . . 116, 160, 181, 195
Victoire Vernet . . . 55, 163, 181, 195
Victoria Bowering . . . 153, 160, 167, 181, 189
Vince Gutierrez . . . 84, 156, 181, 190
Virginia Freer . . . 56, 161, 166, 181, 192
Virginia Kelly . . . 24, 161, 165, 181, 191
❖ Vlasopolos, Anca . . . 142, 157, 180, 187, 209

W

❖ Wakefield, Hannah . . . 142, 165, 172, 194, 207, 210, 218
❖ Walker, Mary Willis . . . 142, 159, 164, 175, 178, 190, 211, 216
❖ Wallace, Marilyn . . . 142, 157, 174, 184, 206-207, 211, 221-222
❖ Wallace, Patricia . . . 143, 158, 180, 184, 207-208, 211, 216
❖ Wallingford, Lee . . . 143, 162, 173, 189, 211, 214
❖ Walsh, Jill Paton . . . 143, 166, 174, 193, 214
Wanda Mallory . . . 57, 157, 181, 188
❖ Warner, Mignon . . . 143, 166, 172, 193, 203-205
❖ Watson, Clarissa . . . 144, 160, 179, 188, 203-205, 207
Watts, Carolyn Jensen . . . 221
❖ Weir, Charlene . . . 144, 157, 180, 186, 212, 214, 216
❖ Welch, Pat . . . 144, 158, 165, 173, 185, 210
❖ Wells, Carolyn . . . 144-146, 158, 173, 189, 197-199
❖ Wentworth, Patricia . . . 146, 158, 177, 194, 197-199, 201, 218
❖ Wesley, Valerie Wilson . . . 147, 158, 161, 180, 187, 216

❖ Wheat, Carolyn . . . 147, 165, 171, 189, 204, 206, 216, 221
❖ White, Gloria . . . 147, 158, 179, 185, 211, 214, 216
❖ White, Teri . . . 147, 157, 180, 184, 205-206, 221
Whitman, Ann Hamilton . . . 218
Whitney Logan . . . 83, 165, 181, 184
❖ Wilhelm, Kate . . . 148, 158, 165, 170-171, 180, 189, 207-208, 210-212, 214, 216
Willa Jansson . . . 93, 165, 181, 184
William Anthony Parker White . . . 225
William Monk . . . 115, 156, 181, 192
Willow King . . . 41, 160, 181, 193
❖ Wilson, Barbara . . . 148, 162, 165, 171, 178, 190, 194, 205-206, 208, 210, 214, 221
❖ Wingate, Ann . . . 148-149, 157, 177, 190, 207-208, 211-212, 214, 218
❖ Wings, Mary . . . 149, 165, 172, 186, 207, 210, 221
Winston Marlowe Sherman . . . 88, 159, 160, 181, 191
Witherspoon, Inspector . . . 32, 163, 174, 193
❖ Wolfe, Susan . . . 149, 157, 180, 185, 208
❖ Wolzien, Valerie . . . 149, 167, 180, 185, 207-208, 211-212, 214, 216
❖ Woods, Sara . . . 150-151, 165, 170, 193, 201-207, 218
❖ Woods, Sherryl . . . 151, 164, 167, 169, 178, 185, 208, 210-212, 214, 216
World Mystery Convention . . . 225, 228, 241, 244
❖ Wren, M. K. . . . 152, 161, 171, 189, 202-205, 214, 216, 218
❖ Wright, L. R. . . . 152, 157, 177, 195, 205-206, 210-211, 214, 216

X

Xenia Smith . . . 100, 162, 181, 188

Y

❖ Yarbro, Chelsea Quinn . . . 152, 163, 165, 171, 185, 203, 210-212, 221
❖ Yeager, Dorian . . . 153, 160, 167, 181, 189, 212, 214
❖ Yorke, Margaret . . . 153, 159, 178, 194, 202-203, 218
Yum Yum . . . 31, 159, 164, 175, 191

Z

❖ Zukowski, Sharon . . . 153, 158, 170, 189, 211-212, 216

❖ denotes authors in Master List

Fifteen

About the author

15

Willetta L. Heising, born in Coronado, California, lives in the Detroit area where she owns and operates The Writing Company, a marketing communications firm. She is a Certified Financial Planner and spent 18 years with a large commercial bank where she held positions in facilities planning, market planning and research, product management and private banking. She has also worked as a city planner, a site location analyst and an instructor in economic geography at Wayne State University. She developed her newswriting style as a reporter and campus news editor for the Valparaiso University *Torch* during the late 1960s while earning a BA in geography and sociology.

She is a member of Sisters in Crime, Mystery Readers International, the Institute of Certified Financial Planners and the International Association of Business Communicators. A collector of cast iron building banks, she is also an amateur genealogist and reads four or five mysteries a week.

You can reach her at:

Purple Moon Press

Purple Moon Press
3319 Greenfield Road, Suite 317
Dearborn, Michigan 48120-1212
fax   313-593-4087
e-mail   nrgx40a@prodigy.com

Colophon

The original database used to compile the Master List was designed and developed by the author on her 486-33i PC using Microsoft Excel for Windows (version 4.0). Text for the Master List and other chapters was composed by the author using Microsoft Word for Windows (version 6.0). The author's files were later transferred on disk to Publitech where they were consolidated, sorted, edited and massaged using the Macintosh applications for Excel and Word.

All text was later imported into PageMaker (version 5.0) on a Mac IIcx for page composition. PostScript files were delivered on disk to BookCrafters for final output to film by a Linotronic 530.

The cover was designed by Wendy L. Everett in FreeHand (version 3.1) on the Mac. Trapping was performed by BookCrafters before final output.

The fonts used on the cover are Gill Sans Ultra, Gill Sans Condensed, Mistral, Helvetica, Biffo and Zapf Dingbats.

The fonts used in the book are Bookman (body text), Helvetica (page headers and tables), Mistral (page numbers and chapter cover page) and Gill Sans Ultra (chapter cover page). Our trademark pen nib is a Zapf Dingbat.